Dementia

A NICE–SCIE Guideline on supporting people with dementia and their carers in health and social care

National Clinical Practice Guideline Number 42

National Collaborating Centre for Mental Health

commissioned by the

Social Care Institute for Excellence
National Institute for Health and
Clinical Excellence

published by
The British Psychological Society and Gaskell

British Library Cataloguing-in-Publication Data

A catalogue record for this book is available from
the British Library.

ISBN: 978-1-85433-451-0

Printed in Great Britain by Alden Press.

developed by	National Collaborating Centre for Mental Health
	Royal College of Psychiatrists' Research and Training Unit
	4th Floor, Standon House
	21 Mansell Street
	London
	E1 8AA

commissioned by	National Institute for Health and Clinical Excellence
	MidCity Place, 71 High Holborn
	London
	WCIV 6NA
	www.nice.org.uk

published by

The British Psychological
Society
St Andrews House
48 Princess Road East
Leicester
LE1 7DR
www.bps.org.uk

and

The Royal College of
Psychiatrists
17 Belgrave Square
London
SW1X 8PG
www.rcpsych.ac.uk

CONTENTS

Contents

GUIDELINE DEVELOPMENT GROUP MEMBERSHIP

Dr Andrew Fairbairn (Guideline Chair)
Consultant in Old Age Psychiatry, Newcastle General Hospital, Northumberland, Tyne and Wear NHS Trust

Professor Nick Gould (Guideline Deputy Chair)
Professor of Social Work, University of Bath, representing the Social Care Institute for Excellence

Dr Tim Kendall (Lead Director and Guideline Facilitator)
Joint Director, National Collaborating Centre for Mental Health; Deputy Director, Royal College of Psychiatrists Research and Training Unit; Consultant Psychiatrist and Medical Director, Sheffield Care Trust

Mr Peter Ashley
Service user, Alzheimer's Society; former non-executive director, Warrington Primary Care Trust

Mr Ian Bainbridge
Deputy Director, Commission for Social Care Inspection, London

Ms Lizzy Bower
Health Economist (2004–2006), The National Collaborating Centre for Mental Health

Professor Stephen Brown
Consultant Psychiatrist in Learning Disability, Cornwall Partnership NHS Trust and Honorary Professor of Developmental Neuropsychiatry, Peninsula Medical School Developmental Disabilities Research and Education Group

Mr Alan Duncan
Systematic Reviewer, The National Collaborating Centre for Mental Health

Ms Gillian Garner
Lead Occupational Therapist, Mental Health for Older Adults, South London and Maudsley NHS Trust

Professor Jane Gilliard
Change Agent, Care Services Improvement Partnership, London

Ms Karen Harrison
Senior Nurse, Mental Health Services for Older People, Leicestershire Partnership NHS Trust

Ms Sarah Hopkins
Research Assistant, The National Collaborating Centre for Mental Health

Dr Steve Iliffe
Reader in General Practice, University College London

Professor Roy Jones
Director, The Research Institute for the Care of the Elderly, Bath; Professor of Clinical Gerontology, School for Health, University of Bath; Honorary Consultant Geriatrician, Avon and Wiltshire Mental Health Partnership NHS Trust/ Bath and North East Somerset Primary Care Trust

Professor Jill Manthorpe
Professor of Social Work, Social Care Workforce Research Unit, King's College London

Dr Nick Meader
Systematic Reviewer, The National Collaborating Centre for Mental Health

Dr Ifigeneia Mavranezouli
Health Economist (2006), The National Collaborating Centre for Mental Health

Ms Mary Murrell
Carer representative, Alzheimer's Society volunteer, Lewisham and Greenwich

Professor John O'Brien
Professor of Old Age Psychiatry, Newcastle University, Wolfson Research Centre, Institute for Ageing and Health

Dr Catherine Pettinari
Centre Manager, The National Collaborating Centre for Mental Health

Ms Sarah Stockton
Information Scientist, The National Collaborating Centre for Mental Health

Dr Clare Taylor
Editor, The National Collaborating Centre for Mental Health

Ms Sophie Weithaler
Service Development Manager, Hillingdon Primary Care Trust

Dr Craig Whittington
Senior Systematic Reviewer, The National Collaborating Centre for Mental Health

Ms Jacqui Wood
Carer Representative, Alzheimer's Society volunteer, Enfield

Professor Bob Woods
Professor of Clinical Psychology of Older People, University of Wales, Bangor

Dr Claire Young
Consultant in Old Age Psychiatry, Older Adult Mental Health Care Group, Sheffield

Special appreciation for advice and contributions on palliative care and medical ethics

Dr Julian Hughes
North Tyneside General Hospital, Northumbria Healthcare NHS Trust

ACKNOWLEDGEMENTS

The dementia Guideline Development Group (GDG) and the review team at the National Collaborating Centre for Mental Health (NCCMH) would like to thank the following people:

Advice on palliative care and medical ethics
Dr Julian Hughes

Advice on social care
Ms Enid Levin

Participation in the Expert Practitioners Panel
Mr Andrew Archibald
Ms Julie Ayres
Ms Helen Brown
Ms Rosalind Macbeth
Dr Niall Moore
Ms Susie Newton
Mr Charlie Sheldrick
Mr Nick Webber
Ms Anabel Westall
Mr Stephen Whitfield

Editorial assistance
Ms Emma Brown

THE STRUCTURE OF THIS GUIDELINE

The guideline is divided into chapters, each covering a set of related topics. The first chapter is an executive summary listing the key priorities for implementation and all of the guideline recommendations (a separate version of this chapter is published by NICE and SCIE and can be downloaded from their websites: www.nice.org.uk / www.scie.org.uk). Chapters 2 and 3 provide a general introduction to guidelines and the methods used to develop this guideline. The fourth chapter provides an introduction to dementia, including three care examples, which indicate how clinical and social perspectives interact. Also in Chapter 4, there are sections covering issues related to risk, disclosure/stigma, legal matters, ethics, palliative care and the economic cost of dementia. Chapters 5 to 9 detail the evidence upon which this guideline is based. At the end of each of these chapters, the associated recommendations are provided along with a reference to the relevant chapter section where the evidence that underpins each recommendation can be found.

Each evidence chapter begins with a general introduction to the topic that sets the recommendations in context. Depending on the nature of the evidence, narrative reviews or meta-analyses were conducted. Therefore, the structure of the chapters varies. Where meta-analyses were conducted, information is given about both the interventions included and the studies considered for review. This is followed by tables summarising the important outcomes (complete evidence profiles and forest plots can be found in Appendix 16 and Appendix 20, respectively). Where available, health economic evidence is presented in a separate section, as is qualitative evidence relating to experience of care. A narrative evidence summary is then used to summarise the evidence presented.

On the CD-ROM, further methodological information and details about the included studies and evidence can be found (see Text Box 1 for details). In addition, there is a tutorial about how to use forest plots, which can be accessed via the menu.

Text box 1: Appendices on CD-ROM

Appendix	Content
8	Data extraction form for clinical studies
9	Quality checklists for clinical studies and reviews
10	Quality checklists for economic studies
11	Data extraction form for economic studies
12	Data extraction forms for qualitative studies
13a	Review protocols
13b	Question specific search filters for psychosocial/behavioural interventions for the management of behaviour that challenges
14	Search strategies for the identification of health and social care and economic studies
15	Included/excluded study information tables for quantitative reviews
16	Evidence profile tables for quantitative reviews
17	Economic analysis of the use of acetylcholinesterase inhibitors for the treatment of non-cognitive symptoms of dementia with Lewy bodies
18	Health economics evidence tables
19	Search strategies for the identification of qualitative studies
20	Forest plots from the quantitative reviews

1.   EXECUTIVE SUMMARY

KEY PRIORITIES FOR IMPLEMENTATION

Non-discrimination

● People with dementia should not be excluded from any services because of their diagnosis, age (whether designated too young or too old) or coexisting learning disabilities.

Valid consent

● Health and social care professionals should always seek valid consent from people with dementia. This should entail informing the person of options, and checking that he or she understands, that there is no coercion and that he or she continues to consent over time. If the person lacks the capacity to make a decision, the provisions of the Mental Capacity Act 2005 must be followed.

Carers

● Health and social care managers should ensure that the rights of carers to receive an assessment of needs, as set out in the Carers and Disabled Children Act 2000 and the Carers (Equal Opportunities) Act 2004, are upheld.
● Carers of people with dementia who experience psychological distress and negative psychological impact should be offered psychological therapy, including cognitive behavioural therapy, conducted by a specialist practitioner.

Coordination and integration of health and social care

● Health and social care managers should coordinate and integrate working across all agencies involved in the treatment and care of people with dementia and their carers, including jointly agreeing written policies and procedures. Joint planning should include local service users and carers in order to highlight and address problems specific to each locality.
● Care managers and care coordinators should ensure the coordinated delivery of health and social care services for people with dementia. This should involve:
  – a combined care plan agreed by health and social services that takes into account the changing needs of the person with dementia and his or her carers
  – assignment of named health and/or social care staff to operate the care plan

  – endorsement of the care plan by the person with dementia and/or carers
  – formal reviews of the care plan, at a frequency agreed between professionals involved and the person with dementia and/or carers and recorded in the notes.[1]

Memory services

● Memory assessment services (which may be provided by a memory assessment clinic or by community mental health teams) should be the single point of referral for all people with a possible diagnosis of dementia.

Structural imaging for diagnosis

● Structural imaging should be used in the assessment of people with suspected dementia to exclude other cerebral pathologies and to help establish the subtype diagnosis. Magnetic resonance imaging (MRI) is the preferred modality to assist with early diagnosis and detect subcortical vascular changes, although computed tomography (CT) scanning could be used. Specialist advice should be taken when interpreting scans in people with learning disabilities.

Behaviour that challenges

● People with dementia who develop non-cognitive symptoms that cause them significant distress or who develop behaviour that challenges should be offered an assessment at an early opportunity to establish the likely factors that may generate, aggravate or improve such behaviour. The assessment should be comprehensive and include:
  – the person's physical health
  – depression
  – possible undetected pain or discomfort
  – side effects of medication
  – individual biography, including religious beliefs and spiritual and cultural identity
  – psychosocial factors
  – physical environmental factors
  – behavioural and functional analysis conducted by professionals with specific skills, in conjunction with carers and care workers.
Individually tailored care plans that help carers and staff address the behaviour that challenges should be developed, recorded in the notes and reviewed regularly. The frequency of the review should be agreed by the carers and staff involved and written in the notes.

---

[1]Time periods for review of care plans are stipulated by Care Programme Approach guidance and the Department of Health (2003).

Training

● Health and social care managers should ensure that all staff working with older people in the health, social care and voluntary sectors have access to dementia-care training (skill development) that is consistent with their roles and responsibilities.

Mental health needs in acute hospitals

● Acute and general hospital trusts should plan and provide services that address the specific personal and social care needs and the mental and physical health of people with dementia who use acute hospital facilities for any reason.

1.1   PRINCIPLES OF CARE FOR PEOPLE WITH DEMENTIA

1.1.1   Diversity, equality and language

1.1.1.1   People with dementia should not be excluded from any services because of their diagnosis, age (whether designated too young or too old) or coexisting learning disabilities.

1.1.1.2   Health and social care staff should treat people with dementia and their carers with respect at all times.

1.1.1.3   Heath and social care staff should identify the specific needs of people with dementia and their carers arising from diversity, including gender, ethnicity, age (younger or older), religion and personal care. Care plans should record and address these needs.

1.1.1.4   Health and social care staff should identify the specific needs of people with dementia and their carers arising from ill health, physical disability, sensory impairment, communication difficulties, problems with nutrition, poor oral health and learning disabilities. Care plans should record and address these needs.

1.1.1.5   Health and social care staff, especially in residential settings, should identify and, wherever possible, accommodate the preferences of people with dementia and their carers, including diet, sexuality and religion. Care plans should record and address these preferences.

1.1.1.6   People who are suspected of having dementia because of evidence of functional and cognitive deterioration, but who do not have sufficient memory impairment to be diagnosed with the condition, should not be denied access to support services.

1.1.1.7   If language or acquired language impairment is a barrier to accessing or understanding services, treatment and care, health and social care professionals should provide the person with dementia and/or their carer with:

- information in the preferred language and/or in an accessible format
- independent interpreters
- psychological interventions in the preferred language.

1.1.2   Younger people with dementia

1.1.2.1   Younger people with dementia have special requirements, and specialist multidisciplinary services should be developed, allied to existing dementia services, to meet their needs for assessment, diagnosis and care.

1.1.3   People with a learning disability

1.1.3.1   Health and social care staff working in care environments where younger people are at risk of developing dementia, such as those catering for people with learning disabilities, should be trained in dementia awareness.

1.1.3.2   People with learning disabilities and those supporting them should have access to specialist advice and support regarding dementia.

1.1.4   Ethics, consent and advance decision making

1.1.4.1   Health and social care professionals should always seek valid consent from people with dementia. This should entail informing the person of options, and checking that he or she understands, that there is no coercion and that he or she continues to consent over time. If the person lacks the capacity to make a decision, the provisions of the Mental Capacity Act 2005 must be followed.

1.1.4.2   Health and social care professionals should inform people with dementia and their carers about advocacy services and voluntary support, and should encourage their use. If required, such services should be available for both people with dementia and their carers independently of each other.

1.1.4.3   People with dementia should be given the opportunity to convey information to health and social care professionals involved in their care in a confidential manner. Professionals should discuss with the person any need for information to be shared with colleagues and/or other agencies. Only in exceptional circumstances should confidential information be disclosed to others without the person's consent. However, as dementia worsens and the person becomes more dependent on family or other carers, decisions about sharing information should be made in the context of the Mental Capacity Act 2005 and its Code of Practice. If information is to be shared with others, this should be done only if it is in the best interests of the person with dementia.

1.1.4.4   Health and social care professionals should discuss with the person with dementia, while he or she still has capacity, and his or her carer the use of:
- advance statements (which allow people to state what is to be done if they should subsequently lose the capacity to decide or to communicate)
- advance decisions to refuse treatment[2]
- Lasting Power of Attorney (a legal document that allows people to state in writing who they want to make certain decisions for them if they cannot make them for themselves, including decisions about personal health and welfare)[3]
- a Preferred Place of Care Plan (which allows people to record decisions about future care choices and the place where the person would like to die).[4]

1.1.5   Impact of dementia on personal relationships

1.1.5.1   At the time of diagnosis and when indicated subsequently, the impact of dementia on relationships, including sexual relationships, should be assessed in a sensitive manner. When indicated, people with dementia and/or their partner and/or carers should be given information about local support services.

1.1.6   Risk of abuse and neglect

1.1.6.1   Because people with dementia are vulnerable to abuse and neglect, all health and social care staff supporting them should receive information and training about, and abide by the local multi-agency policy on, adult protection.

1.1.7   Management and coordination of care

1.1.7.1   Health and social care staff should ensure that care of people with dementia and support for their carers is planned and provided within the framework of care management/coordination.[5]

1.1.7.2   Care managers and care coordinators should ensure that care plans are based on an assessment of the person with dementia's life history, social and family circumstance, and preferences, as well as their physical and mental health needs and current level of functioning and abilities.

---

[2]Under the provisions of the Mental Capacity Act 2005.
[3]Under the provisions of the Mental Capacity Act 2005.
[4]See www.cancerlancashire.org.uk/ppc.html.
[5]Care management/care coordination involves four elements: the coordination of a full assessment, agreeing a care plan, arranging action to deliver services, and reviewing changing needs within the framework of the single assessment process.

1.1.7.3   Care managers and care coordinators should ensure the coordinated delivery of health and social care services for people with dementia. This should involve:
- a combined care plan agreed by health and social services that takes into account the changing needs of the person with dementia and his or her carers
- assignment of named health and/or social care staff to operate the care plan
- endorsement of the care plan by the person with dementia and/or carers
- formal reviews of the care plan, at a frequency agreed between professionals involved and the person with dementia and/or carers and recorded in the notes.[6]

1.1.8   Funding arrangements for health and social care

1.1.8.1   Care managers/care coordinators should explain to people with dementia and their carers that they have the right to receive direct payments and individual budgets (where available). If necessary, people with dementia and their carers should be offered additional support to obtain and manage these.

1.1.8.2   People with dementia and their carers should be informed about the statutory difference between NHS care and care provided by local authority social services (adult services) so that they can make informed decisions about their eligibility for NHS Continuing Care.

1.1.9   Training and development of health and social care staff

1.1.9.1   Health and social care managers should ensure that all staff working with older people in the health, social care and voluntary sectors have access to dementia-care training (skill development) that is consistent with their roles and responsibilities.

1.1.9.2   When developing educational programmes for different health and social care staff, trainers should consider the following elements, combined according to the needs of the staff being trained (if staff care for people with learning disabilities, the training package should be adjusted accordingly).
- Early signs and symptoms suggestive of dementia and its major subtypes.

---

[6]Time periods for review of care plans are stipulated by Care Programme Approach guidance and the Department of Health (2003).

- The natural history of the different types of dementia, the main signs and symptoms, the progression and prognosis, and the consequences for the person with dementia and his or her carers, family and social network.
- The assessment and pharmacological treatment of dementia including the administration of medication and monitoring of side effects.
- Applying the principles of person-centred care when working with people with dementia and their carers; particular attention should be paid to respect, dignity, learning about each person's life story, individualising activities, being sensitive to individuals' religious beliefs and spiritual and cultural identity, and understanding behaviour that challenges as a communication of unmet need.
- The importance of and use of communication skills for working with people with dementia and their carers; particular attention should be paid to pacing of communication, non-verbal communication and the use of language that is non-discriminatory, positive, and tailored to an individual's ability.
- Assertive outreach techniques to support people who may not be engaged with services.
- A clear description of the roles of the different health and social care professionals, staff and agencies involved in the delivery of care to people with dementia and basic advice on how they should work together in order to provide a comprehensive service.
- Basic introduction to local adult protection policy and procedures, including the reporting of concerns or malpractice and, in particular, who to contact.
- The palliative care approach.

1.1.9.3 Managers of local mental health and learning disability services should set up consultation and communication channels for care homes and other services for people with dementia and their carers.

1.1.9.4 Liaison teams from local mental health and learning disability services should offer regular consultation and training for healthcare professionals in acute hospitals who provide care for people with dementia. This should be planned by the acute hospital trust in conjunction with mental health, social care and learning disability services.

1.1.9.5 Evidence-based educational interventions, such as decision-support software and practice-based workshops,[7] to improve the diagnosis and management of dementia should be made widely available and implemented in primary care.

1.1.10 Environmental design for people with dementia

1.1.10.1 When organising and/or purchasing living arrangements or care home placements for people with dementia, health and social care managers

---

[7]See, for example, Downs *et al.*, 2006.

should ensure that the design of built environments meets the needs of people with dementia[8] and complies with the Disability Discrimination Acts 1995 and 2005, because dementia is defined as a disability within the meaning of the Acts.

1.1.10.2 When organising and/or purchasing living arrangements and/or care home placements for people with dementia, health and social care managers should ensure that built environments are enabling and aid orientation. Specific, but not exclusive, attention should be paid to: lighting, colour schemes, floor coverings, assistive technology, signage, garden design, and the access to and safety of the external environment.

1.1.10.3 When organising and/or purchasing living arrangements and/or care home placements for people with dementia, health and social care managers should pay careful consideration to the size of units, the mix of residents, and the skill mix of staff to ensure that the environment is supportive and therapeutic.

1.1.11 Care for people with dementia in an acute hospital facility

1.1.11.1 Acute and general hospital trusts should plan and provide services that address the specific personal and social care needs and the mental and physical health of people with dementia who use acute hospital facilities for any reason.

1.1.11.2 Acute trusts should ensure that all people with suspected or known dementia using inpatient services are assessed by a liaison service that specialises in the treatment of dementia. Care for such people in acute trusts should be planned jointly by the trust's hospital staff, liaison teams, relevant social care professionals and the person with suspected or known dementia and his or her carers.

1.2 INTEGRATED HEALTH AND SOCIAL CARE

1.2.1.1 Health and social care staff should use the Department of Health's publication *Everybody's Business. Integrated Mental Health Services for Older Adults: a Service Development Guide* (www.everybodysbusiness.org.uk) in conjunction with this guideline as a framework for the planning, implementation and delivery of:
- primary care
- home care
- mainstream and specialist day services
- sheltered and extra-care housing
- assistive technology and telecare

---

[8]See, for example, Judd et al., 1997.

- mainstream and specialist residential care
- intermediate care and rehabilitation
- care in general hospitals
- specialist mental health services, including community mental health teams, memory assessment services, psychological therapies and inpatient care.

1.2.1.2 Health and social care managers should coordinate and integrate working across all agencies involved in the treatment and care of people with dementia and their carers, including jointly agreeing written policies and procedures. Joint planning should include local service users and carers in order to highlight and address problems specific to each locality.

1.2.1.3 Health and social care professionals should ensure that people with dementia and their carers are given up-to-date information on local arrangements (including inter-agency working) for health and social care, including the independent and voluntary sectors, and on how to access such services.

1.3 RISK FACTORS, PREVENTION AND EARLY IDENTIFICATION

1.3.1 Risk factors, screening and genetic counselling

1.3.1.1 General population screening for dementia should not be undertaken.

1.3.1.2 In middle-aged and older people, vascular and other modifiable risk factors for dementia (for example, smoking, excessive alcohol consumption, obesity, diabetes, hypertension and raised cholesterol) should be reviewed and, if appropriate, treated.

1.3.1.3 Healthcare professionals working with people likely to have a genetic cause for their dementia (for example, familial autosomal dominant Alzheimer's disease or frontotemporal dementia, cerebral autosomal dominant arteriopathy with subcortical infarcts and leukoencephalopathy [CADASIL], or Huntington's disease) should offer to refer them and their unaffected relatives for genetic counselling.

1.3.1.4 Regional genetic services should provide genetic counselling to people who are likely to have a genetic cause for their dementia and their unaffected relatives.

1.3.1.5 If a genetic cause for dementia is not suspected, including late-onset dementia, genotyping should not be undertaken for clinical purposes.

1.3.2 Preventive measures

1.3.2.1 The following interventions should not be prescribed as specific treatments for the primary prevention of dementia:
- statins
- hormone replacement therapy

- vitamin E
- non-steroidal anti-inflammatory drugs.

1.3.2.2 For the secondary prevention of dementia, vascular and other modifiable risk factors (for example, smoking, excessive alcohol consumption, obesity, diabetes, hypertension and raised cholesterol) should be reviewed in people with dementia, and if appropriate, treated.

1.3.3   Early identification of dementia

1.3.3.1 Primary healthcare staff should consider referring people who show signs of mild cognitive impairment (MCI)[9] for assessment by memory assessment services to aid early identification of dementia, because more than 50% of people with MCI later develop dementia.

1.3.3.2 Those undertaking health checks as part of health facilitation for people with learning disabilities should be aware of the increased risk of dementia in this group. Those undertaking health checks for other high-risk groups, for example those who have had a stroke and those with neurological conditions such as Parkinson's disease, should also be aware of the possibility of dementia.

1.3.3.3 Memory assessment services that identify people with MCI (including those without memory impairment, which may be absent in the earlier stages of non-Alzheimer's dementias) should offer follow-up to monitor cognitive decline and other signs of possible dementia in order to plan care at an early stage.

1.4   DIAGNOSIS AND ASSESSMENT OF DEMENTIA

1.4.1   Recognition

1.4.1.1 A diagnosis of dementia should be made only after a comprehensive assessment, which should include:
- history taking
- cognitive and mental state examination
- physical examination and other appropriate investigations
- a review of medication in order to identify and minimise use of drugs, including over-the-counter products, that may adversely affect cognitive functioning.

1.4.1.2 People who are assessed for the possibility of dementia should be asked if they wish to know the diagnosis and with whom this should be shared.

---

[9]Mild cognitive impairment is a syndrome defined as cognitive decline greater than expected for an individual's age and education level, which does not interfere notably with activities of daily living. It is not a diagnosis of dementia of any type, although it may lead to dementia in some cases.

1.4.1.3   Clinical cognitive assessment in those with suspected dementia should include examination of attention and concentration, orientation, short and long-term memory, praxis, language and executive function. As part of this assessment, formal cognitive testing should be undertaken using a standardised instrument. The Mini Mental State Examination (MMSE) has been frequently used for this purpose, but a number of alternatives are now available, such as the 6-item Cognitive Impairment Test (6-CIT), the General Practitioner Assessment of Cognition (GPCOG) and the 7-Minute Screen. Those interpreting the scores of such tests should take full account of other factors known to affect performance, including educational level, skills, prior level of functioning and attainment, language, and any sensory impairments, psychiatric illness or physical/neurological problems.

1.4.1.4   Formal neuropsychological testing should form part of the assessment in cases of mild or questionable dementia.

1.4.1.5   At the time of diagnosis of dementia, and at regular intervals subsequently, assessment should be made for medical comorbidities and key psychiatric features associated with dementia, including depression and psychosis, to ensure optimal management of coexisting conditions.

1.4.2   Investigation

1.4.2.1   A basic dementia screen should be performed at the time of presentation, usually within primary care. It should include:
  ● routine haematology
  ● biochemistry tests (including electrolytes, calcium, glucose, and renal and liver function)
  ● thyroid function tests
  ● serum vitamin B_{12} and folate levels.

1.4.2.2   Testing for syphilis serology or HIV should not be routinely undertaken in the investigation of people with suspected dementia. These tests should be considered only in those with histories suggesting they are at risk or if the clinical picture dictates.

1.4.2.3   A midstream urine test should always be carried out if delirium is a possibility.

1.4.2.4   Clinical presentation should determine whether investigations such as chest X-ray or electrocardiogram are needed.

1.4.2.5   Cerebrospinal fluid examination should not be performed as a routine investigation for dementia.

1.4.3   Diagnosis of subtypes

1.4.3.1   A diagnosis of subtype of dementia should be made by healthcare professionals with expertise in differential diagnosis using international standardised criteria (see Table 1).

Table 1: Diagnostic criteria for dementia

Type of dementia	Diagnostic criteria
Alzheimer's disease	Preferred criteria: NINCDS/ADRDA. Alternatives include ICD-10 and DSM-IV
Vascular dementia	Preferred criteria: NINDS-AIREN. Alternatives include ICD-10 and DSM-IV
Dementia with Lewy bodies	International Consensus criteria for dementia with Lewy bodies
Frontotemporal dementia	Lund-Manchester criteria, NINDS criteria for frontotemporal dementia

DSM-IV, Diagnostic and Statistical Manual of Mental Disorders, fourth edition; ICD-10, International Classification of Diseases, 10th revision; NINCDS/ADRDA, National Institute of Neurological and Communicative Diseases and Stroke/Alzheimer's Disease and Related Disorders Association; NINDS–AIREN, Neuroepidemiology Branch of the National Institute of Neurological Disorders and Stroke–Association Internationale pour la Recherche et l'Enseignement en Neurosciences.

1.4.3.2   Structural imaging should be used in the assessment of people with suspected dementia to exclude other cerebral pathologies and to help establish the subtype diagnosis. Magnetic resonance imaging (MRI) is the preferred modality to assist with early diagnosis and detect subcortical vascular changes, although computed tomography (CT) scanning could be used. Specialist advice should be taken when interpreting scans in people with learning disabilities.

1.4.3.3   Perfusion hexamethylpropyleneamine oxime (HMPAO) single-photon emission computed tomography (SPECT) should be used to help differentiate Alzheimer's disease, vascular dementia and frontotemporal dementia if the diagnosis is in doubt. People with Down's syndrome may show SPECT abnormalities throughout life that resemble those in Alzheimer's disease, so this test is not helpful in this group.

1.4.3.4   If HMPAO SPECT is unavailable, 2-[^{18}F]fluoro-2-deoxy-D-glucose positron emission tomography (FDG PET) should be considered to help differentiate between Alzheimer's disease, vascular dementia and frontotemporal dementia if the diagnosis is in doubt.

1.4.3.5   Dopaminergic iodine-123-radiolabelled 2β-carbomethoxy-3β-(4-iodophenyl)-N-(3-fluoropropyl) nortropane (FP-CIT) SPECT should be used to help establish the diagnosis in those with suspected dementia with Lewy bodies (DLB) if the diagnosis is in doubt.

1.4.3.6   Cerebrospinal fluid examination should be used if Creutzfeldt–Jakob disease or other forms of rapidly progressive dementia are suspected.

1.4.3.7 Electroencephalography should not be used as a routine investigation in people with dementia.

1.4.3.8 Electroencephalography should be considered if a diagnosis of delirium, frontotemporal dementia or Creutzfeldt–Jakob disease is suspected, or in the assessment of associated seizure disorder in those with dementia.

1.4.3.9 Brain biopsy for diagnostic purposes should be considered only in highly selected people whose dementia is thought to be due to a potentially reversible condition that cannot be diagnosed in any other way.

1.4.4 Mixed dementias

1.4.4.1 Many cases of dementia may have mixed pathology (for example, Alzheimer's disease and vascular dementia or Alzheimer's disease and DLB). Unless otherwise stated in this guideline, such cases should be managed according to the condition that is thought to be the predominant cause of dementia.

1.4.5 Specialist services for dementia assessment

1.4.5.1 Memory assessment services (which may be provided by a memory assessment clinic or by community mental health teams) should be the single point of referral for all people with a possible diagnosis of dementia.

1.4.5.2 Memory assessment services should offer a responsive service to aid early identification and should include a full range of assessment, diagnostic, therapeutic, and rehabilitation services to accommodate the needs of people with different types and all severities of dementia and the needs of their carers and family.

1.4.5.3 Memory assessment services should ensure an integrated approach to the care of people with dementia and the support of their carers, in partnership with local health, social care, and voluntary organisations.

1.4.6 Addressing needs that arise from the diagnosis of dementia

1.4.6.1 The experience of the diagnosis of dementia is challenging both for people with dementia and family members and for healthcare professionals, so healthcare professionals should make time available to discuss the diagnosis and its implications with the person with dementia and also with family members (usually only with the consent of the person with dementia). Healthcare professionals should be aware that people with dementia and family members may need ongoing support to cope with the difficulties presented by the diagnosis.

1.4.6.2 Following a diagnosis of dementia, health and social care professionals should, unless the person with dementia clearly indicates to the contrary, provide them and their family with written information about:
- the signs and symptoms of dementia
- the course and prognosis of the condition
- treatments
- local care and support services
- support groups
- sources of financial and legal advice, and advocacy
- medico-legal issues, including driving
- local information sources, including libraries and voluntary organisations.

Any advice and information given should be recorded in the notes.

1.4.6.3 Healthcare professionals who regularly diagnose dementia and discuss this with people with the condition and carers should consider mentoring or providing clinical supervision to less experienced colleagues.

1.5 PROMOTING AND MAINTAINING INDEPENDENCE OF PEOPLE WITH DEMENTIA

1.5.1.1 Health and social care staff should aim to promote and maintain the independence, including mobility, of people with dementia. Care plans should address activities of daily living (ADLs) that maximise independent activity, enhance function, adapt and develop skills, and minimise the need for support. When writing care plans, the varying needs of people with different types of dementia should be addressed. Care plans should always include:
- consistent and stable staffing
- retaining a familiar environment
- minimising relocations
- flexibility to accommodate fluctuating abilities
- assessment and care-planning advice regarding ADLs, and ADL skill training from an occupational therapist
- assessment and care-planning advice about independent toileting skills; if incontinence occurs all possible causes should be assessed and relevant treatments tried before concluding that it is permanent
- environmental modifications to aid independent functioning, including assistive technology, with advice from an occupational therapist and/or clinical psychologist
- physical exercise, with assessment and advice from a physiotherapist when needed
- support for people to go at their own pace and participate in activities they enjoy.

1.5.1.2   When developing a care plan for a person with a learning disability newly
           diagnosed with dementia, an assessment using the Assessment of Motor
           and Process Skills (AMPS)[10] should be considered. The Dementia
           Questionnaire for Mentally Retarded Persons (DMR)[11] and Dalton's Brief
           Praxis Test (BPT)[12] should be considered for monitoring change in
           function over time.

**1.6   INTERVENTIONS FOR COGNITIVE SYMPTOMS AND
           MAINTENANCE OF FUNCTION FOR PEOPLE WITH
           DEMENTIA**

**1.6.1   Non-pharmacological interventions for cognitive symptoms and
           maintaining function**

1.6.1.1   People with mild-to-moderate dementia of all types should be given the
           opportunity to participate in a structured group cognitive stimulation
           programme. This should be commissioned and provided by a range of
           health and social care staff with appropriate training and supervision, and
           offered irrespective of any drug prescribed for the treatment of cognitive
           symptoms of dementia.

**1.6.2   Pharmacological interventions for the cognitive symptoms of
           Alzheimer's disease[13]**

1.6.2.1   The three acetylcholinesterase inhibitors donepezil, galantamine and
           rivastigmine[14] are recommended as options in the management of people
           with Alzheimer's disease of moderate severity only (that is, those with an
           MMSE score of between 10 and 20 points), and under the following
           conditions. [NICE TA 2006]
           ● Only specialists in the care of people with dementia (that is, psychia-
             trists including those specialising in learning disability, neurologists,

---

[10]The AMPS should be carried out by someone with formal training in its use.
[11]Evenhuis *et al.*,1990.
[12]Dalton & Fedor, 1998.
[13]This section includes recommendations from the NICE technology appraisal on the clinical and cost
effectiveness of donepezil, galantamine and rivastigmine for mild-to-moderate Alzheimer's disease and
memantine for moderate-to-severe Alzheimer's disease (see www.nice.org.uk/TA111). Following NICE
protocol, the recommendations have been incorporated verbatim into this guideline (where one of these
recommendations appears, it is indicated as NICE TA 2006).
[14]The guidance applies to the marketing authorisation held for each drug at the time of the appraisal.

and physicians specialising in the care of the elderly) should initiate treatment. Carers' views on the patient's condition at baseline should be sought.

- Patients who continue on the drug should be reviewed every 6 months by MMSE score and global, functional and behavioural assessment. Carers' views on the patient's condition at follow-up should be sought. The drug should only be continued while the patient's MMSE score remains at or above 10 points and their global, functional and behavioural condition remains at a level where the drug is considered to be having a worthwhile effect. Any review involving MMSE assessment should be undertaken by an appropriate specialist team, unless there are locally agreed protocols for shared care.

1.6.2.2   Although it is recommended that acetylcholinesterase inhibitors should be prescribed only to people with Alzheimer's disease of moderate severity, healthcare professionals should not rely on the MMSE score in certain circumstances. These are:

- in those with an MMSE score greater than 20, who have moderate dementia as judged by significant impairments in functional ability and personal and social function compared with premorbid ability
- in those with an MMSE score less than 10 because of a low premorbid attainment or ability or linguistic difficulties, who have moderate dementia as judged by an assessment tool sensitive to their level of competence
- in people with learning disabilities
- in people who are not fluent in spoken English or in the language in which the MMSE is applied.

1.6.2.3   For people with learning disabilities, tools used to assess the severity of dementia should be sensitive to their level of competence. Options include:

- Cambridge Cognitive Examination (CAMCOG)[15]
- Modified Cambridge Examination for Mental Disorders of the Elderly (CAMDEX)[16]
- DMR
- Dementia Scale for Down Syndrome (DSDS)[17], which can be useful in diagnosis of dementia in people with learning disabilities who do not have Down's syndrome.

1.6.2.4   When the decision has been made to prescribe an acetylcholinesterase inhibitor, it is recommended that therapy should be initiated with a drug with the lowest acquisition cost (taking into account required daily dose and the price per dose once shared care has started). However, an alternative acetylcholinesterase inhibitor could be prescribed where it is consid-

---

[15]Hon *et al.*, 1999.
[16]Ball *et al.*, 2004.
[17]Gedye, 1995.

ered appropriate having regard to adverse event profile, expectations around concordance, medical comorbidity, possibility of drug interactions, and dosing profiles. [NICE TA 2006]

1.6.2.5 Memantine is not recommended as a treatment option for people with moderately severe to severe Alzheimer's disease except as part of well-designed clinical studies. [NICE TA 2006]

1.6.2.6 People with mild Alzheimer's disease who are currently receiving donepezil, galantamine or rivastigmine, and people with moderately severe to severe Alzheimer's disease currently receiving memantine, whether as routine therapy or as part of a clinical trial, may be continued on therapy (including after the conclusion of a clinical trial) until they, their carers and/or specialist consider it appropriate to stop. [NICE TA 2006]

1.6.3 Pharmacological interventions for the cognitive symptoms of non-Alzheimer dementias and MCI

1.6.3.1 For people with vascular dementia, acetylcholinesterase inhibitors and memantine should not be prescribed for the treatment of cognitive decline, except as part of properly constructed clinical studies.

1.6.3.2 For people with MCI, acetylcholinesterase inhibitors should not be prescribed, except as part of properly constructed clinical studies.

1.7 INTERVENTIONS FOR NON-COGNITIVE SYMPTOMS AND BEHAVIOUR THAT CHALLENGES IN PEOPLE WITH DEMENTIA

1.7.1 Non-pharmacological interventions for non-cognitive symptoms and behaviour that challenges

1.7.1.1 People with dementia who develop non-cognitive symptoms that cause them significant distress or who develop behaviour that challenges should be offered an assessment at an early opportunity to establish likely factors that may generate, aggravate or improve such behaviour. The assessment should be comprehensive and include:
- the person's physical health
- depression
- possible undetected pain or discomfort
- side effects of medication
- individual biography, including religious beliefs and spiritual and cultural identity

- psychosocial factors
- physical environmental factors
- behavioural and functional analysis conducted by professionals with specific skills, in conjunction with carers and care workers.

Individually tailored care plans that help carers and staff address the behaviour that challenges should be developed, recorded in the notes and reviewed regularly. The frequency of the review should be agreed by the carers and staff involved and written in the notes.

1.7.1.2   For people with all types and severities of dementia who have comorbid agitation, consideration should be given to providing access to interventions tailored to the person's preferences, skills and abilities. Because people may respond better to one treatment than another, the response to each modality should be monitored and the care plan adapted accordingly. Approaches that may be considered, depending on availability, include:

- aromatherapy
- multi-sensory stimulation
- therapeutic use of music and/or dancing
- animal-assisted therapy
- massage.

These interventions may be delivered by a range of health and social care staff and volunteers, with appropriate training and supervision. The voluntary sector has a particular role to play in delivering these approaches. Health and social care staff in the NHS and social care, including care homes, should work together to ensure that some of these options are available, because there is some evidence of their clinical effectiveness. More research is needed into their cost effectiveness.

1.7.2   Pharmacological interventions for non-cognitive symptoms and behaviour that challenges

1.7.2.1   People with dementia who develop non-cognitive symptoms or behaviour that challenges should be offered a pharmacological intervention in the first instance only if they are severely distressed or there is an immediate risk of harm to the person or others. The assessment and care-planning approach, which includes behavioural management, should be followed as soon as possible (see recommendation 1.7.1.1). If distress and/or agitation are less severe, the interventions described in recommendations 1.7.1.2, 1.8.1.2 and 1.8.1.3 should be followed before a pharmacological intervention is considered.

1.7.2.2   People with Alzheimer's disease, vascular dementia or mixed dementias with mild-to-moderate non-cognitive symptoms should not be prescribed antipsychotic drugs because of the possible increased risk of cerebrovascular adverse events and death.[18]

1.7.2.3 People with DLB with mild-to-moderate non-cognitive symptoms, should not be prescribed antipsychotic drugs, because those with DLB are at particular risk of severe adverse reactions.

1.7.2.4 People with Alzheimer's disease, vascular dementia, mixed dementias or DLB with severe non-cognitive symptoms (psychosis and/or agitated behaviour causing significant distress) may be offered treatment with an antipsychotic drug after the following conditions have been met.

- There should be a full discussion with the person with dementia and/or carers about the possible benefits and risks of treatment. In particular, cerebrovascular risk factors should be assessed and the possible increased risk of stroke/transient ischaemic attack and possible adverse effects on cognition discussed.

- Changes in cognition should be assessed and recorded at regular intervals. Alternative medication should be considered if necessary.

- Target symptoms should be identified, quantified and documented.

- Changes in target symptoms should be assessed and recorded at regular intervals.

- The effect of comorbid conditions, such as depression, should be considered.

- The choice of antipsychotic should be made after an individual risk–benefit analysis.

- The dose should be low initially and then titrated upwards.

- Treatment should be time limited and regularly reviewed (every 3 months or according to clinical need).

For people with DLB, healthcare professionals should monitor carefully for the emergence of severe untoward reactions, particularly neuroleptic sensitivity reactions (which manifest as the development or worsening of severe extrapyramidal features after treatment in the accepted dose range or acute and severe physical deterioration following prescription of antipsychotic drugs for which there is no other apparent cause).

1.7.2.5 People with mild, moderate, or severe Alzheimer's disease who have non-cognitive symptoms and/or behaviour that challenges, causing significant distress or potential harm to the individual, may be offered an acetyl-cholinesterase inhibitor if:

- a non-pharmacological approach is inappropriate or has been ineffective, and

- antipsychotic drugs are inappropriate or have been ineffective.

---

[18]In March 2004, the Medicines and Healthcare products Regulatory Agency's Committee on Safety of Medicines issued a safety warning about the atypical antipsychotic drugs risperidone and olanzapine, advising that these drugs should not be used for the treatment of behavioural symptoms of dementia. Further information is available from www.mhra.gov.uk.

1.7.2.6 People with DLB who have non-cognitive symptoms causing significant distress to the individual, or leading to behaviour that challenges, should be offered an acetylcholinesterase inhibitor.

1.7.2.7 People with vascular dementia who develop non-cognitive symptoms or behaviour that challenges should not be prescribed acetylcholinesterase inhibitors, except as part of properly constructed clinical studies.

1.7.3 Behaviour that challenges requiring urgent treatment

Managing risk

1.7.3.1 Health and social care staff who care for people with dementia should identify, monitor and address environmental, physical health and psychosocial factors that may increase the likelihood of behaviour that challenges, especially violence and aggression, and the risk of harm to self or others. These factors include:
- overcrowding
- lack of privacy
- lack of activities
- inadequate staff attention
- poor communication between the person with dementia and staff
- conflicts between staff and carers
- weak clinical leadership.

1.7.3.2 Health and social care staff should be trained to anticipate behaviour that challenges and how to manage violence, aggression and extreme agitation, including de-escalation techniques and methods of physical restraint.

1.7.3.3 Healthcare professionals who use medication in the management of violence, aggression and extreme agitation in people with dementia should:
- be trained in the correct use of drugs for behavioural control, specifically benzodiazepines and antipsychotics
- be able to assess the risks associated with pharmacological control of violence, aggression and extreme agitation, particularly in people who may be dehydrated or physically ill
- understand the cardiorespiratory effects of the acute administration of benzodiazepines and antipsychotics and the need to titrate dosage to effect
- recognise the importance of nursing people who have received these drugs in the recovery position and of monitoring pulse, blood pressure and respiration
- be familiar with and trained in the use of resuscitation equipment
- undertake annual retraining in resuscitation techniques
- understand the importance of maintaining an unobstructed airway.

Principles of pharmacological control of violence, aggression and extreme agitation

1.7.3.4   For people with dementia who are at significant risk to themselves or others because of violence, aggression and extreme agitation, immediate management should take place in a safe, low-stimulation environment, separate from other service users.

1.7.3.5   Drug treatments for the control of violence, aggression and extreme agitation should be used to calm the person with dementia and reduce the risk of violence and harm, rather than treat any underlying psychiatric condition. Healthcare professionals should aim for an optimal response in which agitation or aggression is reduced without sedation.

1.7.3.6   Violent behaviour should be managed without the prescription of high doses or combinations of drugs, especially if the person with dementia is elderly or frail. The lowest effective dose should be used.

1.7.3.7   Drugs for behavioural control should be used with caution, particularly if the person with dementia has been restrained, because of the following risks:

- loss of consciousness instead of sedation
- over-sedation with loss of alertness
- damage to the relationship between the person with dementia, their carers and the health and social care team
- specific issues related to age and physical and mental health.

1.7.3.8   People with dementia who have received involuntary sedation and their carers should be offered the opportunity to discuss their experiences and be provided with a clear explanation of the decision to use urgent sedation. This should be documented in their notes.

Route of drug administration

1.7.3.9   If drugs are necessary for the control of violence, aggression and extreme agitation, oral medication should be offered before parenteral medication.

1.7.3.10   If parenteral treatment is necessary for the control of violence, aggression and extreme agitation, the intramuscular (IM) route should be preferred because it is safer than intravenous administration. Intravenous administration should be used only in exceptional circumstances.

1.7.3.11   Vital signs should be monitored after parenteral treatment for the control of violence, aggression and extreme agitation. Blood pressure, pulse, temperature and respiratory rate should be recorded at regular intervals agreed by the multidisciplinary team until the person with dementia becomes active again. If the person appears to be or is asleep, more intensive monitoring is required.

Intramuscular agents for behavioural control

1.7.3.12 If IM preparations are needed for behavioural control, lorazepam, haloperidol or olanzapine should be used. Wherever possible, a single agent should be used in preference to a combination.

1.7.3.13 If rapid tranquillisation is needed, a combination of IM haloperidol and IM lorazepam should be considered.

1.7.3.14 IM diazepam and IM chlorpromazine are not recommended for the management of behaviour that challenges in people with dementia.

1.7.3.15 If using IM haloperidol (or any other IM conventional antipsychotic) for behavioural control, healthcare professionals should monitor closely for dystonia and other extrapyramidal side effects. If side effects become distressing, especially in acute dystonic reactions, the use of anticholinergic agents should be considered. If using anticholinergic agents, healthcare professionals should monitor for deteriorating cognitive function.

1.8 INTERVENTIONS FOR COMORBID EMOTIONAL DISORDERS IN PEOPLE WITH DEMENTIA

1.8.1 Psychological interventions for people with dementia with depression and/or anxiety

1.8.1.1 Care packages for people with dementia should include assessment and monitoring for depression and/or anxiety.

1.8.1.2 For people with dementia who have depression and/or anxiety, cognitive behavioural therapy, which may involve the active participation of their carers, may be considered as part of treatment.

1.8.1.3 A range of tailored interventions, such as reminiscence therapy, multi-sensory stimulation, animal-assisted therapy and exercise, should be available for people with dementia who have depression and/or anxiety.

1.8.2 Pharmacological interventions for people with dementia with depression

1.8.2.1 People with dementia who also have major depressive disorder should be offered antidepressant medication. Treatment should be started by staff with specialist training, who should follow the NICE clinical guideline 'Depression: management of depression in primary and secondary care'[19] after a careful risk–benefit assessment. Antidepressant drugs with anticholinergic effects should be avoided because they may adversely affect

---

[19]Available from www.nice.org.uk/CG023.

cognition. The need for adherence, time to onset of action and risk of withdrawal effects should be explained at the start of treatment.

1.9　INPATIENT DEMENTIA SERVICES

1.9.1.1　As far as possible, dementia care services should be community-based, but psychiatric inpatient admission may be considered in certain circumstances, including if:

● the person with dementia is severely disturbed and needs to be contained for his or her own health and safety and/or the safety of others (in some cases, this might include those liable to be detained under the Mental Health Act 1983)

● assessment in a community setting is not possible, for example if a person with dementia has complex physical and psychiatric problems.

1.10　PALLIATIVE CARE, PAIN RELIEF AND CARE AT THE END OF LIFE FOR PEOPLE WITH DEMENTIA

1.10.1　Palliative care and end of life issues

1.10.1.1　Health and social care professionals working with people with dementia and their carers should adopt a palliative care approach. They should consider physical, psychological, social and spiritual needs to maximise the quality of life of the person with dementia and their family.

1.10.1.2　Palliative care professionals, other health and social care professionals, and commissioners should ensure that people with dementia who are dying have the same access to palliative care services as those without dementia.

1.10.1.3　Primary care teams should ensure that the palliative care needs of people with dementia who are close to death are assessed and that the resulting information is communicated within the team and with other health and social care staff.

1.10.1.4　Health and social care staff should encourage people with dementia to eat and drink by mouth for as long as possible. Specialist assessment and advice concerning swallowing and feeding in dementia should be available. Dietary advice may also be beneficial. Nutritional support, including artificial (tube) feeding, should be considered if dysphagia is thought to be a transient phenomenon, but artificial feeding should not generally be used in people with severe dementia for whom dysphagia or disinclination to eat is a manifestation of disease severity. Ethical[20] and legal[21] principles

---

[20]See General Medical Council, 2002.
[21]See the Mental Capacity Act 2005.

33

should be applied when making decisions about withholding or withdraw-ing nutritional support.

1.10.1.5 If a person with severe dementia has a fever, especially in the terminal stages, a clinical assessment should be undertaken. Simple analgesics, antipyretics and mechanical means of cooling the person may suffice. Antibiotics may be considered as a palliative measure in the terminal stages of dementia, but this needs an individual assessment.

1.10.1.6 Policies in hospitals and long-stay residential, nursing or continuing care units should reflect the fact that cardiopulmonary resuscitation is unlikely to succeed in cases of cardiopulmonary arrest in people with severe dementia.

1.10.1.7 In the absence of a valid and applicable advance decision to refuse resus-citation, the decision to resuscitate should take account of any expressed wishes or beliefs of the person with dementia, together with the views of the carers and the multidisciplinary team. The decision should be made in accordance with the guidance developed by the Resuscitation Council UK[22] and, if the person lacks capacity, the provisions of the Mental Capacity Act 2005. It should be recorded in the medical notes and care plans.

1.10.2 Pain relief

1.10.2.1 If a person with dementia has unexplained changes in behaviour and/or shows signs of distress, health and social care professionals should assess whether the person is in pain, using an observational pain assessment tool if helpful. However, the possibility of other causes should be considered.

1.10.2.2 The treatment of pain in people with severe dementia should involve both pharmacological and non-pharmacological measures. Non-pharmacologi-cal therapies should be used with the person's history and preferences in mind.

1.11 SUPPORT AND INTERVENTIONS FOR THE CARERS OF PEOPLE WITH DEMENTIA

1.11.1 Assessment of carers' needs

1.11.1.1 Health and social care managers should ensure that the rights of carers to receive an assessment of needs, as set out in the Carers and Disabled Children Act 2000 and the Carers (Equal Opportunities) Act 2004,[23] are upheld.

---

[22]See Resuscitation Council, 2001.
[23]See Social Care Institute for Excellence, 2005.

1.11.2 Interventions

1.11.2.1 Those carrying out carers' assessment should seek to identify any psychological distress and the psychosocial impact on the carer. This should be an ongoing process and should include any period after the person with dementia has entered residential care.

1.11.2.2 Care plans for carers of people with dementia should involve a range of tailored interventions. These may consist of multiple components including:

- individual or group psychoeducation
- peer-support groups with other carers, tailored to the needs of individuals depending on the stage of dementia of the person being cared for and other characteristics
- support and information by telephone and through the internet
- training courses about dementia, services and benefits, and communication and problem solving in the care of people with dementia
- involvement of other family members as well as the primary carer in family meetings.

1.11.2.3 Consideration should be given to involving people with dementia in psychoeducation, support, and other meetings for carers.

1.11.2.4 Health and social care professionals should ensure that support, such as transport or short-break services, is provided for carers to enable them to participate in interventions.

1.11.2.5 Carers of people with dementia who experience psychological distress and negative psychological impact should be offered psychological therapy, including cognitive behavioural therapy, conducted by a specialist practitioner.

1.11.3 Practical support and services

1.11.3.1 Health and social care managers should ensure that carers of people with dementia have access to a comprehensive range of respite/short-break services. These should meet the needs of both the carer (in terms of location, flexibility and timeliness) and the person with dementia and should include, for example, day care, day- and night-sitting, adult placement and short-term and/or overnight residential care. Transport should be offered to enable access to these services if they are not provided in the person's own home.

1.11.3.2 Respite/short-break care of any sort should be characterised by meaningful and therapeutic activity tailored to the person with dementia and provided in an environment that meets their needs. Providing this in the person's own home should be considered whenever possible.

1.12   RESEARCH RECOMMENDATIONS

The Guideline Development Group has made the following recommendations for research, on the basis of its review of the evidence, to improve NICE and SCIE guidance and the care of people with dementia in the future. The effective care of people with dementia (included in standard 7 of the National Service Framework for older people) is of great importance, especially because the proportion of people with dementia will rise in line with the aging population. Therefore, further research is urgently needed to generate a better evidence base for the update of this guideline.

1.12.1   Acetylcholinesterase inhibitors and memantine for the treatment of psychotic symptoms in dementia

For people with dementia who develop severe non-cognitive symptoms (psychosis and/or agitated behaviour causing significant distress), is an acetylcholinesterase inhibitor (donepezil, galantamine or rivastigmine) and/or memantine effective in improving quality of life and reducing non-cognitive symptoms/behaviour that challenges when compared with placebo over 6 months, and is treatment cost effective in dementia and/or its subtypes?

Why this is important

Up to 75% of people with dementia may be affected by non-cognitive symptoms/behaviour that challenges. They are a leading cause of distress to carers and often lead to the institutionalisation of the person with dementia. Several studies have shown that acetylcholinesterase inhibitors may improve non-cognitive symptoms of dementia; however, the cost-effectiveness of these drugs in the treatment of people with dementia with severe non-cognitive symptoms has not been established.

1.12.2   Cognitive stimulation and/or acetylcholinesterase inhibitors in Alzheimer's disease

For people with Alzheimer's disease, are cognitive stimulation (activities involving cognitive processing; usually in a social context and often group-based, with an emphasis on enjoyment of activities), acetylcholinesterase inhibitors (donepezil, galantamine or rivastigmine) or combined treatment clinically and cost effective in terms of cognition, global functioning, ADLs and quality of life when compared with placebo over 6 months?

Why this is important

No randomised studies have directly compared cognitive stimulation with an acetyl-cholinesterase inhibitor, and few randomised studies have compared the combination with an acetylcholinesterase inhibitor alone in people with mild-to-moderate Alzheimer's disease. Evidence suggests that cognitive stimulation is effective in people with dementia, but it is difficult to compare the magnitude of the effect with that of acetylcholinesterase inhibitors.

1.12.3   Psychological interventions for carers of people with dementia

For carers of people with dementia, is a psychological intervention cost effective when compared with usual care?

Why this is important

Those providing care for people with dementia are one of the most vulnerable groups of carers and often have high levels of stress, feelings of guilt, depression and other psychological problems. They often ignore their own health needs in favour of those of the person for whom they care. They may become exhausted, have poor physical health and feel isolated. Current research suggests that psychological interventions may be effective, but there is insufficient evidence to establish cost effectiveness. The promotion of good mental health in older people (many carers are the spouses of people with dementia) – included in standard 7 of the National Service Framework for older people – is vital, especially because the proportion of people with dementia will rise in line with our aging population. Support for carers in general has been given priority in England and Wales through Carers' Strategy documents. Further research is urgently needed to generate a better evidence base for the update of this guideline.

1.12.4   The effect of staff training on behaviour that challenges

Does training of care staff in dementia-specific person-centred care lead to improvement in behaviour that challenges and reduced prescription of medication to control such behaviour in people with dementia requiring 24-hour care when compared with current practice?

Executive summary

Why this is important

According to prescribing advice published by the Royal College of Psychiatrists, there is a history of inappropriate use of antipsychotic drugs in people with dementia. The proportion of people with dementia with behaviour that challenges tends to rise as the dementia progresses; therefore this issue is of particular importance for people requiring 24-hour care.

2.   INTRODUCTION

This guideline has been developed to advise on supporting people with dementia and their carers in health and social care. The guideline recommendations have been developed by a multidisciplinary team of health and social care professionals, a person with dementia, carers and guideline methodologists after careful consideration of the best available evidence. It is intended that the guideline will be useful to practitioners and service commissioners in providing and planning high-quality care for those with dementia while also emphasising the importance of the experience of care for people with dementia and carers.

2.1   NATIONAL GUIDELINES

2.1.1   What are practice guidelines?

Practice guidelines are 'systematically developed statements that assist clinicians and patients in making decisions about appropriate treatment for specific conditions' (Mann, 1996). In the context of social work, they have been defined as 'a set of systematically compiled and organised statements of empirically tested knowledge and procedures to help practitioners select and implement interventions that are most effective and appropriate for attaining the desired outcomes' (Rosen & Proctor, 2003). They are derived from the best available experimental and qualitative research evidence and they use predetermined and systematic methods to identify and evaluate all the evidence relating to the specific condition in question. Where evidence is lacking, the guidelines incorporate statements and recommendations based upon consensus statements developed by the Guideline Development Group (GDG).

Practice guidelines are intended to improve the process and outcomes of health and social care in a number of different ways. They can:
- provide up-to-date evidence-based recommendations for the management of conditions and disorders by health and social care professionals
- be used as the basis to set standards to assess the practice of health and social care professionals
- form the basis for education and training of health and social care professionals
- assist service users and carers in making informed decisions about their treatment and care
- improve communication between health and social care professionals, service users and carers
- help identify priority areas for further research.

2.1.2 Uses and limitations of practice guidelines

Guidelines are not a substitute for professional knowledge and clinical judgement. They can be limited in their usefulness and applicability by a number of different factors: the availability of high-quality research evidence, the quality of the methodology used in the development of the guideline, the generalisability of research findings and the uniqueness of individual people with dementia.

Although the quality of research in dementia is variable, the methodology used here reflects current international understanding on the appropriate practice for guideline development (AGREE: Appraisal of Guidelines for Research and Evaluation Instrument; www.agreecollaboration.org), ensuring the collection and selection of the best research evidence available, and the systematic generation of care recommendations applicable to the majority of people with dementia and situations. However, there will always be some people with dementia and their carers for whom practice guideline recommendations are not appropriate and situations in which the recommendations are not readily applicable. This guideline does not, therefore, override the individual responsibility of professionals to make appropriate decisions in the circumstances of the individual, in consultation with the person with dementia and/or his or her carer.

In addition to the clinical evidence, cost-effectiveness information, where available, is taken into account in the generation of statements and recommendations of the guidelines. While national guidelines are concerned with clinical and cost effectiveness, issues of affordability and implementation costs are to be determined by the NHS and those commissioning social care services.

In using guidelines, it is important to remember that the absence of empirical evidence for the effectiveness of a particular intervention is not the same as evidence for ineffectiveness. In addition, of particular relevance in mental health, evidence-based treatments are often delivered within the context of an overall care programme including a range of activities, the purpose of which may be to help engage the person with dementia or carer, and provide an appropriate context for the delivery of specific interventions. It is important to maintain and enhance the service context in which these interventions are delivered; otherwise the specific benefits of effective interventions will be lost. Indeed, the importance of organising care, so as to support and encourage a good therapeutic relationship, is at times as important as the specific treatments offered.

2.1.3 Why develop national guidelines?

The National Institute for Health and Clinical Excellence (NICE) was established as a Special Health Authority for England and Wales in 1999, with a remit to provide a single source of authoritative and reliable guidance for patients, professionals and the public. NICE guidance aims to improve standards of care, to diminish unacceptable variations in the provision and quality of care across the NHS and to ensure that the health service is patient-centred. All guidance is developed in a transparent and collaborative manner using the best available evidence and involving all relevant stakeholders.

NICE generates guidance in a number of different ways, two of which are relevant here. First, national guidance is produced by the Technology Appraisal Committee to give robust advice about a particular treatment, intervention, procedure or other health technology. Second, NICE commissions the production of national clinical practice guidelines focused upon the overall treatment and management of a specific condition. To enable this latter development, NICE established seven National Collaborating Centres in conjunction with a range of professional organisations involved in healthcare.

The Social Care Institute for Excellence (SCIE) was launched in October 2001 as part of the government's drive to improve social care. It is an independent registered charity, governed by a board of trustees, whose role is to develop and promote knowledge about good practice in social care. SCIE works with people and organisations throughout the social care sector to identify useful information, research and examples of good practice. Using this information, SCIE produces resources that evaluate practice in a particular area of social care, draws out key messages for good practice and identifies areas where more research is needed to inform good practice.

2.1.4 The National Collaborating Centre for Mental Health

This guideline has been commissioned by NICE and developed within the National Collaborating Centre for Mental Health (NCCMH) in collaboration with the Social Care Institute for Excellence (SCIE). The NCCMH is led by a partnership between the Royal College of Psychiatrists' research and training unit (College Research and Training Unit – CRTU) and the British Psychological Society's equivalent unit (Centre for Outcomes Research and Effectiveness – CORE).

2.1.5 From national guidelines to local implementation

Once a national guideline has been published and disseminated, local health and social care groups will be expected to produce a plan and identify resources for implementation, along with appropriate timetables. Subsequently, a multidisciplinary group involving commissioners of health and social care, primary care and specialist mental health professionals, people with dementia and carers should undertake the translation of the implementation plan into local protocols. The nature and pace of the local plan will reflect local healthcare needs and the nature of existing services; full implementation may take a considerable time, especially where substantial training needs are identified

2.1.6 Auditing the implementation of guidelines

This guideline identifies key areas of practice and service delivery for local and national audit. Although generating audit standards is an important and necessary step in implementing this guidance, a more broadly based implementation strategy should be developed. Nevertheless, it should be noted that the Healthcare Commission will monitor the extent to which Primary Care Trusts (PCTs), trusts responsible for mental health and social care and Health Authorities have implemented these guidelines. In addition, the Commission for Social Care Inspection will use practice guidelines to underpin and develop inspection standards.

2.2   THE NATIONAL DEMENTIA GUIDELINE

2.2.1   Who has developed this guideline?

The Guideline Development Group (GDG) was convened by the NCCMH and SCIE, and supported by funding from NICE and SCIE. The GDG consisted of people with dementia, carers and professionals from psychiatry, clinical psychology, social work, general practice, nursing and occupational therapy.

Staff from the NCCMH provided leadership and support throughout the process of guideline development, undertaking systematic searches, information retrieval, appraisal and systematic review of the evidence. Members of the GDG received training in the process of guideline development. The National Guidelines Support and Research Unit, also established by NICE, provided advice and assistance regarding aspects of the guideline development process.

All members of the group made formal declarations of interest at the outset, updated at every GDG meeting. GDG members met a total of 18 times throughout the process of guideline development. For ease of evidence identification and analysis, some members of the GDG became topic leads, covering identifiable treatment approaches. The NCCMH technical team supported group members, with additional expert advice from special advisers where necessary. All statements and recommendations in this guideline have been generated and agreed by the whole GDG.

2.2.2   For whom is this guideline intended?

This guideline will be of relevance to people of all ages who suffer from dementia and their carers.

The care and treatment of dementia is a cross-cutting issue for mainstream health and social care services, very few of which are not in contact with people with dementia. The guideline covers the care provided by social care practitioners and primary, secondary and other healthcare professionals who have direct contact with, and make decisions concerning, the care of people with dementia.

In sum, this guideline is intended for use by:
- professional groups who share in the treatment and care for people with a diagnosis of dementia, including psychiatrists, clinical psychologists, general practitioners, mental health nurses, community psychiatric nurses, other community nurses, geriatricians, neurologists, social workers and other social care practitioners, counsellors, practice

nurses, occupational therapists, pharmacists, optometrists and dispensing opticians and others
- professionals in other health and non-health sectors who may have direct contact with or are involved in the provision of health, social care and other public services for those diagnosed with dementia. These may include accident and emergency staff, paramedical staff, prison doctors, the police and professionals who work in the criminal justice and education sectors
- those with responsibility for planning services for people with a diagnosis of dementia, and their carers, including directors of public health, NHS trust managers, managers in PCTs, and councils with social services responsibilities.

2.2.3   Specific aims of this guideline

The guideline makes recommendations for pharmacological treatments and the use of psychological, psychosocial and service-level interventions. Specifically it aims to:
- evaluate the role of specific pharmacological agents, psychological and psychosocial interventions in the treatment and management of dementia
- evaluate the role of specific services and systems for providing those services in the treatment and management of dementia
- integrate the above to provide best practice advice on the care of individuals with a diagnosis of dementia through the different phases of illness, including the initiation of treatment, the treatment of acute episodes and the promotion of well-being.
- consider economic aspects of various interventions for dementia.
    The guideline does not cover treatments that are not normally available on the NHS or provided by social care services.

2.2.4   Other versions of this guideline

There are other versions of *Dementia: Supporting People with Dementia and their Carers in Health and Social Care*, including:
- the NICE-SCIE guideline, which is a shorter version of this guideline, containing the key recommendations and all other recommendations
- the Quick Reference Guide, which is a summary of the main recommendations in the NICE-SCIE guideline
- Understanding NICE Guidance, which describes the guidance using non-technical language. It is written chiefly for people with dementia but may also be useful for family members, advocates or those who care for people with dementia.

3. METHODS USED TO DEVELOP THIS GUIDELINE

3.1 OVERVIEW

The development of this guideline drew upon methods outlined by NICE (*Guideline Development Methods: Information for National Collaborating Centres and Guideline Developers*[24]). A team of health and social care professionals, lay representatives and technical experts known as the Guideline Development Group (GDG), with support from the NCCMH staff, undertook the development of an evidence-based guideline focusing on people with dementia and their carers. There are six basic steps in the process of developing a guideline:

- define the scope, which sets the parameters of the guideline and provides a focus and steer for the development work
- define key questions considered important for health and social care professionals and service users
- develop criteria for evidence searching and search for evidence
- design validated protocols for systematic review and apply to evidence recovered by the search
- synthesise and (meta-) analyse data retrieved, guided by the key questions, and produce evidence profiles
- answer key questions with evidence-based recommendations for health and social care.

The recommendations made by the GDG are therefore derived from the most up-to-date and robust evidence base for the treatment and care of people with dementia. In addition, to ensure a service user and carer focus, the concerns of service users and carers regarding health and social care have been highlighted and addressed by recommendations agreed by the whole GDG.

3.2 THE SCOPE

Guideline topics are selected by the Department of Health and the Welsh Assembly Government, which identify the main areas to be covered by the guideline in a specific remit (see *The Guideline Development Process – An Overview for Stakeholders, the Public and the NHS*[25]). The remit for this guideline was translated into a scope document by staff at the NCCMH.

---

[24] Available from www.nice.org.uk.
[25] Available from www.nice.org.uk.

The purpose of the scope was to:
- provide an overview of what the guideline will include and exclude
- identify the key aspects of care that must be included
- set the boundaries of the development work and provide a clear framework to enable work to stay within the priorities agreed by NICE and the NCCMH and the remit from the Department of Health/Welsh Assembly Government
- inform the development of the key questions and search strategy
- inform professionals and the public about the expected content of the guideline
- keep the guideline to a reasonable size to ensure that its development can be carried out within the allocated time period.

The draft scope was subject to consultation with stakeholders over a 4-week period. During the consultation period, the scope was posted on the NICE website (www.nice.org.uk). Comments were invited from stakeholder organisations and the Guideline Review Panel (GRP). Further information about the GRP can also be found on the NICE website. The NCCMH and NICE reviewed the scope in light of comments received, and the revised scope was signed off by the GRP.

3.3   THE GUIDELINE DEVELOPMENT GROUP

The GDG consisted of clinical and academic experts in old age psychiatry and geriatric medicine, clinical psychology, nursing, social work, occupational therapy and general practice, a person with dementia and representatives from a service-user organisation. The perspectives of people with dementia and their carers were provided through the full participation of a person with dementia and two carers in the guideline development process and a qualitative review of user experience. The guideline development process was supported by staff from the NCCMH, who undertook the literature searches, reviewed and presented the evidence to the GDG, managed the process and contributed to drafting the guideline.

3.3.1   Guideline development group meetings

Twenty GDG meetings were held between 8 September 2004 and 6 October 2006. During day-long GDG meetings, in a plenary session, key questions and health/social care and economic evidence were reviewed and assessed, and recommendations formulated. At each meeting, all GDG members declared any potential conflict of interest, and the concerns of the person with dementia and the carers were routinely discussed as part of a standing agenda

3.3.2   Topic groups

The GDG divided its workload along health and social care relevant lines to simplify the guideline development process, and GDG members formed smaller topic groups to undertake guideline work in that area of health and social care. Topic Group 1 covered questions relating to considerations relevant to the care of all people with dementia and considerations relevant to carers, Topic Group 2 covered prevention/ early identification/assessment/diagnosis, Topic Group 3 covered pharmacological treatment and Topic Group 4 covered non-pharmacological interventions. These groups were designed to efficiently manage the large volume of evidence appraisal prior to presenting it to the GDG as a whole. Each topic group was chaired by a GDG member with expert knowledge of the topic area. Topic groups refined the key questions, refined the definitions of treatment interventions and social care, reviewed and prepared the evidence with the systematic reviewer before presenting it to the GDG as a whole, and helped the GDG to identify further expertise in the topic. Topic-group leaders reported the status of the group's work as part of the standing agenda. They also introduced and led the GDG discussion of the evidence review for that topic and assisted the GDG Chair in drafting that section of the guideline relevant to the work of each topic group.

3.3.3   People with dementia and their carers

Individuals with direct experience of services gave an integral service-user focus to the GDG and the guideline. The GDG included a person with dementia and two carers. They contributed as full GDG members to writing the key questions, helping to ensure that the evidence addressed their views and preferences, highlighting sensitive issues and terminology relevant to the guideline, and bringing service-user and carer research to the attention of the GDG. In drafting the guideline, they identified areas of good practice from the perspective of people with dementia and their carers and contributed to writing the guideline's introduction and the Understanding NICE Guidance version of the guideline.

3.3.4   Special advisors

Special advisors, who had specific expertise in one or more aspects of treatment and management relevant to the guideline, assisted the GDG, commenting on specific aspects of the developing guideline and making presentations to the GDG. Appendix 2 lists those who agreed to act as special advisors.

3.3.5   National and international experts

National and international experts in the area under review were identified through the literature search and through the experience of the GDG members. These experts were contacted to recommend unpublished or soon-to-be published studies in order to ensure up-to-date evidence was included in the development of the guideline. They informed the group about completed trials at the pre-publication stage, systematic reviews in the process of being published, studies relating to the cost-effectiveness of treatment, and study data if the GDG could be provided with full access to the complete report. Appendix 5 lists researchers who were contacted.

3.4 KEY QUESTIONS

Key questions were used to guide the identification and interrogation of the evidence base relevant to the topic of the guideline. Before the first GDG meeting, draft questions were prepared by NCCMH staff based on the scope and an overview of existing guidelines, and modified during a meeting with the guideline chair. They were then discussed by the GDG at the first few meetings and amended to draw up a final list. The PICO (patient, intervention, comparison and outcome) framework was used to help formulate questions where they related to the effectiveness of interventions. This structured approach divides each question into four components: the patients or service users (the population under study), the interventions (what is being done or test/risk factor), the comparisons (other main treatment options) and the outcomes (the measures of how effective the interventions have been or what is being predicted/prevented). Other question formats were employed where this was appropriate. Appendix 6 lists the key questions.

To help facilitate the literature review, a note was made of the best study design type to answer each question. There are four main types of key questions of relevance to NICE guidelines. These are listed in Text Box 2. For each type of question, the best primary study design varies, where 'best' is interpreted as 'least likely to give misleading answers to the question'.

However, in all cases, a well-conducted systematic review of the appropriate type of study is likely to always yield a better answer than a single study.

Deciding on the best design type to answer a specific key question does not mean that studies of different design types addressing the same question were discarded.

Text box 2: Best study design to answer each type of question

Type of question	Best primary study design
Effectiveness or other impact of an intervention	Randomised controlled trial; other studies that may be considered in the absence of an RCT are the following: internally/externally controlled before and after trial, interrupted time series
Accuracy of information (for example, risk factor, test, prediction rule)	Comparing the information against a valid gold standard in a randomised trial or inception cohort study
Rates (of disease, patient experience, rare side effects)	Cohort, registry, cross-sectional study
Costs	Naturalistic prospective cost study

3.5   SYSTEMATIC LITERATURE REVIEW

The aim of the literature review was to systematically identify and synthesise relevant evidence from the literature in order to answer the specific key questions developed by the GDG. Thus, recommendations are evidence based, where possible, and if evidence was not available, consensus of the GDG (see Section 3.5.6) was used, and the need for future research was specified.

For questions that could best be addressed by qualitative evidence (in particular, experiences of people with dementia and their carers of the support he/she receives from health and social care services), a separate review process was developed that ran in parallel to the review of other types of evidence (see Section 3.6).

3.5.1   Methodology

A stepwise, hierarchical approach was taken to locating and presenting evidence to the GDG. The NCCMH developed this process based on methods set out in *Guideline Development Methods: Information for National Collaborating Centres and Guideline Developers*[26] and after considering recommendations from a range of other sources. These included:

● Clinical Policy and Practice Program of the New South Wales Department of Health (Australia)
● Clinical Evidence online
● The Cochrane Collaboration
● Health Development Agency
● New Zealand Guidelines Group
● NHS Centre for Reviews and Dissemination
● Oxford Centre for Evidence-Based Medicine
● Scottish Intercollegiate Guidelines Network (SIGN)
● Social Care Institute of Excellence
● United States Agency for Healthcare Research and Quality
● Oxford Systematic Review Development Programme
● Grading of Recommendations: Assessment, Development and Evaluation (GRADE) Working Group.

3.5.2   The review process

After the scope was finalised, a more extensive search for systematic reviews and published guidelines was undertaken. Existing NICE guidelines were updated where necessary and other relevant guidelines were assessed for quality using the AGREE instrument (AGREE Collaboration, 2003). The evidence base underlying existing high-quality guidelines was utilised and updated as appropriate.

---

[26]Available from www.nice.org.uk.

At this point, the review team, in conjunction with the GDG, developed a review protocol that detailed all the information necessary to construct an appropriate search strategy to answer the key questions (see Appendix 6). The initial approach taken to locating primary-level studies depended on the type of question and availability of evidence.

The GDG decided which questions were best addressed by good practice based on expert opinion, which questions were likely to have a good evidence base and which questions were likely to have little or no directly relevant evidence. Recommendations based on good practice were developed by informal consensus of the GDG. For questions with a good evidence base, the review process depended on the type of key question (see below). For questions that were unlikely to have a good evidence base, a brief descriptive review was initially undertaken by a member of the GDG.

Searches for evidence were updated between 6 and 8 weeks before the stakeholder consultation. After this point, studies were included only if they were judged by the GDG to be exceptional (for example, the evidence was likely to change a recommendation).

Standard electronic databases searched
The following standard health-related bibliographic databases were searched for relevant evidence:
- CINAHL
- EMBASE
- MEDLINE
- PsycINFO
- Cochrane.

The search strategy for questions concerning interventions
For questions related to interventions, the initial evidence base was formed from well-conducted randomised controlled trials (RCTs) that addressed at least one of the key questions. Although there are a number of difficulties with the use of RCTs in the evaluation of interventions in health and social care, the RCT remains the most important method for establishing treatment efficacy. For harm-related outcomes and for questions not directly related to interventions, searches were conducted for the appropriate study design (see Text Box 2).

Where appropriate, the following databases were searched in addition to the standard databases listed above: Age Info, Age Line, ASSIA, Care Data, Social Services Abstracts, Social Work Abstracts, SSCI, AMED, BNI, CENTRAL, HMIC.

Where the evidence base was large, recent high-quality English-language systematic reviews were used primarily as a source of RCTs (see Appendix 9 for quality criteria used to assess systematic reviews). However, in some circumstances existing data sets were utilised. Where this was the case, data were cross-checked for accuracy before use. New RCTs meeting inclusion criteria set by the GDG were incorporated into the existing reviews and fresh analyses performed.

After the initial search results were scanned liberally to exclude irrelevant papers, the review team used a purpose-built 'study information' database to manage both the included and the excluded studies (eligibility criteria were developed after consultation with the GDG). For questions without good quality evidence (after the initial search), a decision was made by the GDG about whether to conduct a new search for lower levels of evidence or adopt a consensus process (see Section 3.5.6). Future guidelines will be able to update and extend the usable evidence base starting from the evidence collected, synthesised and analysed for this guideline.

In addition, searches were made of the reference lists of all eligible systematic reviews and included studies, as well as the list of evidence submitted by stakeholders. Known experts in the field (see Appendix 5), based both on the references identified in early steps and on advice from GDG members, were sent letters requesting relevant studies that were in the process of being published[27]. In addition, the tables of contents of appropriate journals were periodically checked for relevant studies.

The search strategy for questions of diagnosis and prognosis
For questions related to diagnosis and prognosis, the search strategy was the same as described above, except that the initial evidence base was formed from systematic reviews of studies with the most appropriate and reliable design to answer the particular question. That is, for questions about diagnosis, cross-sectional studies are most appropriate; for questions about prognosis, cohort studies of representative patients are most appropriate. In situations where it was not possible to identify systematic reviews that directly addressed each key question, a consensus process was adopted (see Section 3.5.6).

Search filters
Search filters developed by the review team consisted of a combination of subject heading and free-text phrases. Specific filters were developed for the guideline topic and, where necessary, for each key question. In addition, the review team used filters developed for systematic reviews, RCTs and other appropriate research designs (see Appendix 14).

Study selection
All primary-level studies included after the first scan of citations were acquired in full and re-evaluated for eligibility at the time they were being entered into the study information database. Specific eligibility criteria were developed for each key question and are described in the relevant review protocol (see Appendix 13a). Eligible systematic reviews and primary-level studies were critically appraised for methodological quality (see Appendix 9). The eligibility of each study was confirmed by at least one member of the appropriate topic group.

For some key questions, it was necessary to prioritise the evidence with respect to the UK context (that is, external validity). To make this process explicit, the topic groups took into account the following factors when assessing the evidence:

---

[27]Unpublished full trial reports were also accepted where sufficient information was available to judge eligibility and quality (see section on unpublished evidence).

- participant factors (for example, gender, age, ethnicity)
- provider factors (for example, model fidelity, the conditions under which the intervention was performed, the availability of experienced staff to undertake the procedure)
- cultural factors (for example, differences in standard care, differences in the welfare system).

It was the responsibility of each topic group to decide which prioritisation factors were relevant to each key question in light of the UK context and then decide how they should modify their recommendations.

Unpublished evidence

The GDG used a number of criteria when deciding whether or not to accept unpublished data. First, the evidence must be accompanied by a trial report containing sufficient detail to properly assess the quality of the data. Second, the evidence must be submitted with the understanding that data from the study and a summary of the study's characteristics will be published in the full guideline. However, the GDG recognised that unpublished evidence submitted by investigators might later be retracted by those investigators if the inclusion of such data would jeopardise publication of their research.

3.5.3 Synthesising the evidence

Where possible, meta-analysis was used to synthesise the evidence using Review Manager (Review Manager 4.2.8, The Cochrane Collaboration, Copenhagen) or Comprehensive Meta-Analysis (Comprehensive Meta Analysis 2.2.023, BioStat). If necessary, reanalyses of the data or sub-analyses were used to answer key questions not addressed in the original studies or reviews.

For a given outcome (continuous and dichotomous), where more than 50% of the number randomised to any group were not accounted for[28] by trial authors, the data were excluded from the review because of the risk of bias. However, where possible, dichotomous efficacy outcomes were calculated on an intention-to-treat basis (that is, a 'once-randomised-always-analyse' basis). This assumes that those participants who ceased to engage in the study – from whatever group – had an unfavourable outcome. This meant that the 50% rule was not applied to dichotomous outcomes where there was good evidence that those participants who ceased to engage in the study were likely to have an unfavourable outcome (in this case, early withdrawals were included in both the numerator and denominator). Adverse effects were entered into Review Manager as reported by the study authors because it was usually not possible to determine if early withdrawals had an unfavourable outcome. For the outcome 'leaving the study early for any reason', the denominator was the number randomised.

---

[28]'Accounted for' in this context means using an appropriate method for dealing with missing data (for example, last observation carried forward (LOCF) or a regression technique).

The number needed to treat for benefit (NNTB) or the number needed to treat for harm (NNTH) was reported for each outcome where the baseline risk (that is, control group event rate) was similar across studies. In addition, NNTs calculated at follow-up were only reported where the length of follow-up was similar across studies. When the length of follow-up or baseline risk varies (especially with low risk), the NNT is a poor summary of the treatment effect (Deeks, 2002). Further information about how to interpret the confidence intervals associated with NNTB/H can be found in Altman (1998).

Included/excluded studies tables, generated automatically from the study information database, were used to summarise general information about each study (see Appendix 15). Where meta-analysis was not appropriate and/or possible, the reported results from each primary-level study were also presented in the included studies table (and included, where appropriate, in a narrative review).

Consultation was used to overcome difficulties with coding. Data from studies included in existing systematic reviews were extracted independently by one reviewer and cross-checked with the existing data set. Where possible, two independent reviewers extracted data from new studies. Where double data extraction was not possible, data extracted by one reviewer was checked by the second reviewer. Disagreements were resolved with discussion. Where consensus could not be reached, a third reviewer resolved the disagreement. Masked assessment (that is, blind to the journal from which the article comes, the authors, the institution, and the magnitude of the effect) was not used since it is unclear that doing so reduces bias (Jadad *et al.*, 1996; Berlin, 2001).

3.5.4 Presenting the data to the GDG

Summary characteristics tables and, where appropriate, forest plots generated with Review Manager, were presented to the GDG in order to prepare an evidence profile for each review and to develop recommendations.

Evidence profile tables
An evidence profile table was used to summarise both the quality of the evidence and the results of the evidence synthesis (see Appendix 16). Each table included a list of studies used in the analysis; a quality assessment of the included studies, which was categorised by the level of evidence (see Appendix 9 for the quality checklists and Section 3.5.5 for further information about levels of evidence); information about the consistency of the evidence (see below for how consistency was measured); and the directness of the evidence (directness refers to how closely the outcome measures, interventions and participants match those of interest). The four components (study design/quality, consistency and directness) were used to produce an overall quality of evidence grade. The following definitions were used:

- High = Further research is very unlikely to change our confidence in the estimate of the effect.
- Moderate = Further research is likely to have an important impact on our confidence in the estimate of the effect and may change the estimate.
- Low = Further research is very likely to have an important impact on our confidence in the estimate of the effect and is likely to change the estimate.

● Very low = Any estimate of effect is very uncertain.

For further information about the rationale of producing an evidence profile table, see GRADE (2004). Also included in the evidence profile table was a summary of the findings. Once the evidence profile tables relating to a particular key question were completed, the topic-group lead produced a narrative evidence summary. For the purpose of presenting the evidence in the body of the full guideline, evidence summary tables were produced, which provided summary statistics from only the key outcomes.

Forest plots
Forest plots were used to present the results of the meta-analyses to the GDG (see Appendix 20). Each forest plot displayed the effect size and confidence interval (CI) for each study as well as the overall summary statistic. The graphs were generally organised so that the display of data in the area to the left of the 'line of no effect' indicated a favourable outcome for the treatment in question. Dichotomous outcomes were presented as relative risks (RR) with the associated 95% CI (for an example, see Figure 1). A relative risk (or risk ratio) is the ratio of the treatment event rate to the control event rate. An RR of 1 indicates no difference between treatment and control. In Figure 1, the overall RR of 0.73 indicates that the event rate (that is, non-remission rate) associated with intervention A is about three quarters of that with the control intervention, or in other words, the relative risk reduction is 27%.

The CI shows with 95% certainty the range within which the true treatment effect should lie and can be used to determine statistical significance. If the CI does not cross the 'line of no effect', the effect is statistically significant.

Continuous outcomes were analysed as weighted mean differences (WMD), or as standardised mean differences (SMD) when different measures were used in different studies to estimate the same underlying effect (for an example, see Figure 2). If provided, intention-to-treat data, using a method such as last observation carried forward (LOCF), were preferred over data from completers[29].

To check for consistency between studies, both the I^2 test of heterogeneity and a visual inspection of the forest plots were used. The I^2 statistic describes the proportion of total variation in study estimates that is due to statistical heterogeneity (Higgins & Thompson, 2002). Unlike Cochran's chi-squared test, which is often used to indicate the extent of heterogeneity, the I^2 statistic is independent of the number of studies and the treatment-effect metric. An I^2 of less than 30% was taken to indicate mild heterogeneity and a fixed effects model was used to synthesise the results. An I^2 of more than 50% was taken as notable heterogeneity. In this case, an attempt was made to explain the variation (for example, outliers were removed from the analysis, or sub-analyses were conducted to examine the possibility of moderators). If studies with heterogeneous results were found to be comparable, a random effects model was used to summarise the results (DerSimonian & Laird, 1986). In the random-effects analysis, heterogeneity is accounted for both in the width of confidence intervals and in the estimate of the treatment effect.

---

[29]Although we acknowledge that there are problems interpreting LOCF data from trials involving people with a progressive disease, the potential for bias is high if the evidence is based solely on people who complete the trial, especially when there is differential attrition from the study groups.

Figure 1: Example of a forest plot displaying dichotomous data

Review: NCCMH clinical guideline review (Example)
Comparison: 01 Intervention A compared to a control group
Outcome: 01 Number of people who did not show remission

Study or sub-category	Intervention A n/N	Control n/N	RR (fixed) 95% CI	Weight %	RR (fixed) 95% CI
01 Intervention A vs. control					
Griffiths1994	13/23	27/28		38.79	0.59 [0.41, 0.84]
Lee1986	11/15	14/15		22.30	0.79 [0.56, 1.10]
Treasure1994	21/28	24/27		38.92	0.84 [0.66, 1.09]
Subtotal (95% CI)	45/66	65/70		100.00	0.73 [0.61, 0.88]

Test for heterogeneity: Chi² = 2.83, df = 2 (P = 0.24), I² = 29.3%
Test for overall effect: Z = 3.37 (P = 0.0007)

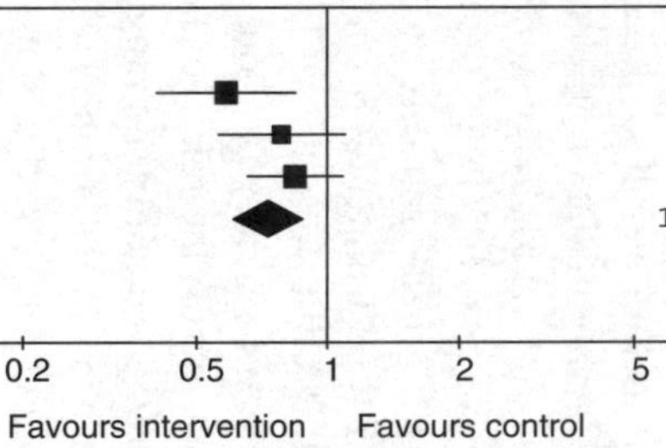

0.2   0.5   1   2   5

Favours intervention   Favours control

Figure 2: Example of a forest plot displaying continuous data

Review: NCCMI- clinical guideline review (Example)
Comparison: 01 Intervention A compared to a control group
Outcome: 03 Mean frequency (endpoint)

Study or sub-category	Intervention A N	Mean (SD)	Control N	Mean (SD)	SMD (fixed) 95% CI	Weight %	SMD (fixed) 95% CI
01 Intervention A vs. control							
Freeman1988	32	1.30 (3.40)	20	3.70 (3.60)		25.91	-0.68 [-1.25, -0.10]
Griffiths1994	20	1.25 (1.45)	22	4.14 (2.21)		17.83	-1.50 [-2.20, -0.81]
Lee1986	14	3.70 (4.00)	14	10.10 (17.50)		15.08	-0.49 [-1.24, 0.26]
Treasure1994	28	44.23 (27.04)	24	61.40 (24.97)		27.28	-0.65 [-1.21, -0.09]
Wolf1992	15	5.30 (5.10)	11	7.10 (4.60)		13.90	-0.36 [-1.14, 0.43]
Subtotal (95% CI)	109		91			100.00	-0.74 [-1.04, -0.45]

Test for heterogeneity: Chi² = 6.13, df = 4 (P = 0.19), I² = 34.8%
Test for overall effect: Z = 4.98 (P < 0.00001)

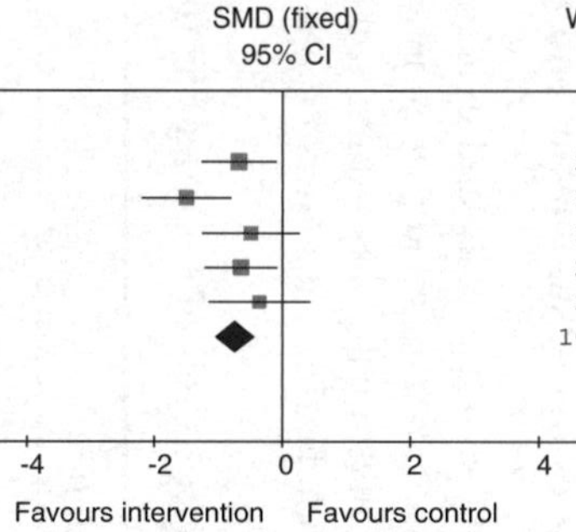

-4   -2   0   2   4
Favours intervention   Favours control

With decreasing heterogeneity, the random effects approach moves asymptotically towards a fixed-effects model. An I^2 of 30 to 50% was taken to indicate moderate heterogeneity. In this case, both the chi-squared test of heterogeneity and a visual inspection of the forest plot were used to decide between a fixed and random-effects model.

To explore the possibility that the results entered into each meta-analysis suffered from publication bias, data from included studies were entered; where there was sufficient data, into a funnel plot. Asymmetry of the plot was taken to indicate possible publication bias and investigated further.

3.5.5 Forming the evidence summaries and recommendations

The included study tables, forest plots and evidence profiles formed the basis for developing the evidence summaries and recommendations.

For intervention studies, quality assessment was conducted using SIGN methodology (SIGN, 2001) and classified according to a hierarchy (Text Box 3).

Text box 3: Levels of evidence for intervention studies

Level	Type of evidence
1^{++}	High-quality meta-analyses, systematic reviews of RCTs, or RCTs with a very low risk of bias
1^{+}	Well-conducted meta-analyses, systematic reviews of RCTs, or RCTs with a low risk of bias
1^{-}	Meta-analyses, systematic reviews of RCTs, or RCTs with a high risk of bias*
2^{++}	High-quality case-control or cohort studies with a very low risk of confounding, bias or chance and a high probability that the relationship is causal
2^{+}	Well-conducted case-control or cohort studies with a low risk of confounding, bias or chance and a moderate probability that the relationship is causal
2^{-}	Case-control or cohort studies with a high risk of confounding bias or chance and a significant risk that the relationship is not causal*
3	Non-analytic studies (for example, case reports, case series)
4	Expert opinion, consensus methods
*Studies with a level of evidence '–' should not be used as a basis for making a recommendation. Reproduced with permission from the Scottish Intercollegiate Guidelines Network	

For studies reporting diagnostic tests of accuracy, the review team used a hierarchy developed by NICE that takes into account the various factors likely to affect the validity of these studies (Text Box 4).

Once the evidence profile tables and evidence summaries were finalised and agreed by the GDG, recommendations were developed, taking into account factors from the evidence including trade-offs between the benefits and risks of treatment. Other important factors that were considered in developing recommendations included economic considerations, values of the development group and society, and the group's awareness of practical issues (Eccles *et al.*, 1998).

Text box 4: Hierarchy of evidence and recommendation grading scheme for studies of the accuracy of diagnostic tests

Level	Type of evidence
Ia	Systematic review (with homogeneity)[†] of level I studies[‡]
Ib	Level I studies[‡]
II	Level II studies[§] Systematic reviews of level II studies
III	Level III studies[§§] Systematic reviews of level III studies
IV	Evidence obtained from expert committee reports or opinions and/or clinical experiences without critical experience, based on physiology, bench research or 'first principles'

[†]Homogeneity means there are no, or minor, variations in the directions and degrees of results between individual studies that are included in the systematic review.
[‡]Level I studies:
- that use a blind comparison of the test with a validated reference standard (gold standard) **and**
- in a sample of patients that reflects the population to whom the test would apply.

[§]Level II studies are studies that have **only one** of the following:
- narrow population (the sample does not reflect the population to whom the test would apply)
- a poor reference standard (defined as that where the 'test' is included in the 'reference', or where the 'testing' affects the 'reference')
- non-blind comparison between the test and reference standard
- case-control studies

[§§]Level III studies are studies that have **at least two or three** of the features listed above[§]
Adapted from *The Guidelines Manual*. Available from: www.nice.org.uk

3.5.6 Method used to answer a key question in the absence of appropriately designed, high-quality research

In the absence of level I evidence (or a level that is appropriate to the question), or where the GDG were of the opinion (on the basis of previous searches or their knowledge of the literature) that there was unlikely to be such evidence, a consensus process was adopted. This process focused on those questions that the GDG considered a priority.

Consensus of the GDG

The starting point for the process of consensus was that a member of the topic group identified, with help from the systematic reviewer, a narrative review that most directly addressed the key question. Where this was not possible, a brief review of the recent literature was initiated.

This existing narrative review or new review was used as a basis for beginning an iterative process to identify lower levels of evidence relevant to the key question and to lead to written statements for the guideline. The process involved a number of steps:

1. A description of what is known about the issues concerning the key question was written by one of the topic group members.
2. Evidence from the existing review or new review was then presented in narrative form to the GDG and further comments were sought about the evidence and its perceived relevance to the key question.
3. Based on the feedback from the GDG, additional information was sought and added to the information collected. This may include studies that did not directly address the key question but were thought to contain relevant data.
4. If, during the course of preparing the report, a significant body of primary-level studies (of appropriate design to answer the question) were identified, a full systematic review was done.
5. At this time, subject possibly to further reviews of the evidence, a series of statements that directly addressed the key question was developed.
6. Following this, on occasions and as deemed appropriate by the development group, the report was then sent to appointed experts outside of the GDG for peer review and comment. The information from this process was then fed back to the GDG for further discussion of the statements.
7. Recommendations were then developed and could also be sent for further external peer review.
8. After this final stage of comment, the statements and recommendations were again reviewed and agreed upon by the GDG.

3.6 QUALITATIVE EVIDENCE REVIEW

3.6.1 The review process

The following databases were searched: ASSIA, AMED, CINAHL, EMBASE, PsycINFO, AgeInfo, Medline, AgeLine, SSCI, CareData, Sociological Abstracts,

Social Work Abstracts, Gerolit and IBSS. Databases maintained by the Centre for Reviews and Dissemination (DARE, NHS EED and the HTA) were also searched. Organisations maintaining relevant libraries such as the King's Fund and the Dementia Services Development Centre in Stirling were consulted. Internet searches were made, in particular, for materials originating in the voluntary sector, professional and governmental organisations, using the websites of the Modernisation Agency, Care Services Improvement Partnership, National Council for Voluntary Organisations, age-specific charities, carers' organisations and Alzheimer's societies. These were also used to identify the plethora of websites reporting personal experiences by people with dementia and carers/caregivers (for example, Dementia Advocacy and Support Network International), with a focus on the UK. Newsletters, such as those produced by the Alzheimer's Society, were examined as these may contain personal accounts of the experience of using services. An agreed list of key journals (those that produce a significant number of retrieved items), such as the *Journal of Dementia Care*, were hand searched. Citation tracking was used to identify any items that had not been retrieved through the electronic databases. Finally, personal bibliographies maintained by the GDG and stakeholders were used to see whether all the key texts had been identified.

It is widely acknowledged that social science electronic databases tend to index less precisely than medical databases. Furthermore, the use of structured abstracts in social science journals is less common. In social care literature, the terminology relating to dementia is often imprecise and other terms may appear, such as memory problems, mental confusion, mental infirmity, senile dementia and so on. This has implications for the precision of the search strategies and makes it more likely that the searches will produce comparatively large numbers of non-relevant items. For example, it is unlikely that a search strategy can be developed that will be precise enough to extract references about people's experiences of services without also including those that relate to the experience of having dementia.

A record of each search strategy can be found in Appendix 14. Each search was re-run 4 weeks before the review was completed in order to identify any newly published pieces of work.

The items identified through the methods listed above were screened for their relevance to the guideline by reading the abstracts of each document (if available). If the document discussed material relevant to social care or to a particular experience, then it was marked for further assessment of its relevance.

All data sources were read and data extracted using a framework method. A minimum of two reviewers categorised all documents and used a data extraction form for recording (see Appendix 12). Material was recorded using a bibliographic software package and an Excel database was used to produce an analytical matrix.

Individual sources of evidence were categorised as either:
1. Evidence from empirical research and other professional literature:
   - A1 (systematic review that includes at least one RCT)
   - A2 (other systematic and high-quality reviews that synthesise studies)
   - B1 (individual RCTs)
   - B2 (individual experimental/intervention non-randomised studies)

- B3 (individual non-experimental studies, controlled statistically if appropriate; includes studies using case control, longitudinal, cohort, matched pairs or cross-sectional random sample methodologies and sound qualitative studies)
- C1 (descriptive and other research or evaluation not in B), or

2. Evidence from expert opinion (in the absence of empirical research evidence):

- C2 (case studies and examples of good practice)
- D (summary review articles and discussions of relevant literature and conference proceedings, not otherwise classified)
- E (professional opinion-based practice or reports of committees)
- U (user opinion from carers or carer organisations, or people with dementia).

In addition, a small series of analytical charts was created, each focusing on a particular theme. These included:

Chart 1 – General information
Chart 2 – Antecedents
Chart 3 – Context/structure
Chart 4 – Process
Chart 5 – Population
Chart 6 – Outcomes
Chart 7 – Staff
Chart 8 – Evidence

The theme of each chart was broken down into a number of relevant sub-themes and data from documents were entered into the charts where appropriate. This method enables a clear view of the range of data emergent from the literature and also facilitates comparison between published documents and other types of knowledge.

Salient and recurrent themes were drawn out of the charts when data extraction was complete and these were analysed in response to the guideline key questions. While it would have been possible to undertake a narrative synthesis of the material at this point, as a wide-ranging area, this approach was not followed.

3.6.2 Inclusion and exclusion criteria

The review focused on recent material. Although there was no time exclusion, it was expected that most material would be from the last 20 years. Since the aim of the review was to identify material relevant to a UK audience, searches were restricted to English-language publications.

As noted above, since some of the terms to be included and much of the language used in the research was expected to be imprecise, the stakeholder group that consulted on qualitative review was asked for guidance on other terms to be included. It is also important to note that, for the purposes of the guideline, the definition of 'experience' covers people's subjective experiences as well as qualitative descriptions and accounts. Therefore, the review did not attempt to confirm people's experiences, receipt of care and treatment, and/or health status. Thus, any type of study design or report was considered, including meta-analyses. In many of the personal accounts, it was not possible to know if people had received a diagnosis or medication and, if so, what it may have been. That said, the review aimed to synthesise and include many people's experiences and their thoughts to inform the GDG.

3.6.3   Specific information collection strategies

In addition to the literature search strategies outlined above, this review was based upon the recognition that a considerable amount of information on the experiences of people with dementia is contained within the 'grey' literature. An attempt was made to maximise the potential of personal experiences to inform the GDG. Thus, organisations of people with dementia, carers' organisations and dementia care groups were contacted to request views, experiences or evidence. The Dementia Services Development Centre was a key source, as were reports of studies from readers of the Journal of Dementia Care through the placing of a 'call for help' editorial.

The second extension to the literature review involved communicating with research networks. These included the early detection and timely intervention in dementia (INTERDEM) network (http://interdem.alzheimer-europe.org/), a European network of researchers and practitioners interested in psychosocial interventions in dementia.

3.6.4   Quality assurance

There is a growing literature on the methods for appraising the quality of primarily qualitative studies (Spencer *et al.*, 2003). We used a similar framework to that developed as a SCIE framework to scrutinise assessment of mental health in later life (undertaken by Jo Moriarty). Jill Manthorpe and colleagues (Manthorpe *et al.*, 2004; Pinkney *et al.*, 2005) have recent experience of using this framework for a review of the evidence from research on elder abuse for the Department of Health.

The challenges of assessing personal experience were acknowledged from the outset and a quality-assurance process was designed to alert to the difficulty of making judgements on the basis of subjective and likely incomplete information.

'Quality' is a concept that applies more to research methodology than the evaluation of personal experience. Advice was sought from the stakeholder group about the framework for categorising and assessing experiential data. The stakeholder group was given anonymous (where possible) examples of experiences and the suggested means of classifying these in order to consider the feasibility of grading the strength of different types of user, carer and practitioner evidence, as is done for primary research or systematic reviews.

3.7 HEALTH ECONOMICS REVIEW

3.7.1 Health economics review strategies

The aim of the health economics review was to provide evidence on the economic cost of dementia and the cost-effectiveness of different diagnosis, care and treatment options included in the guideline to assist with the decision-making process.

The process was based on a preliminary analysis of the clinical evidence and had three stages:

- identification of the areas with likely major cost impacts within the scope of the guideline
- systematic review of the existing data on the economic cost of dementia and cost-effectiveness evidence of the different diagnosis, care and treatment options for dementia
- primary economic analysis was undertaken alongside the guideline development process, in areas with likely major resource implications where the relevant data did not already exist.

3.7.2 Key economic issues

The economic issues identified by the GDG in collaboration with the health economist to be key issues considered in the guideline were:

- the economic cost of dementia, with particular reference to the UK
- comparative cost-effectiveness of pharmacological, psychosocial and diagnostic interventions, and the provision of care for the treatment of people with dementia.

3.7.3 Systematic literature review

A systematic review of the health economic evidence was conducted. The aim of the review was threefold:

- to identify publications providing information on the economic cost of dementia, relevant to the UK context
- to identify the existing economic evaluations of pharmacological, psychosocial and diagnostic interventions, as well as the provision of care, for the management of people with dementia that could be transferable to the UK population and health and social care settings
- to identify studies reporting health state utility data generalisable to the UK setting to facilitate a possible cost-utility modelling process.

Although no attempt was made to systematically review studies with only resource use or cost data, relevant UK-based information was extracted for future modelling exercises if it was considered appropriate.

3.7.4 Search strategy

For the systematic review of the economic evidence on dementia, the standard mental-health-related bibliographic databases (EMBASE, MEDLINE, CINAHL,

PsychINFO, HTA) were searched. For these databases, a health economics search filter adapted from the Centre for Reviews and Dissemination (CRD) at the University of York was used in combination with the general filter for dementia. The subject filter employed a combination of free-text terms and medical subject headings, with the subject headings having been exploded. Additional searches were performed in specific health economic databases (NHS EED, OHE HEED). HTA and NHS EED databases were accessed via the Cochrane Library, using the general filter for dementia. OHE HEED was searched using a shorter, database-specific strategy. Initial searches were carried out between December 2004 and March 2005. The searches were updated regularly, with the final search 6 weeks before the consultation period. Search strategies used for the health economics systematic review are provided in Appendix 14.

In parallel to searches of electronic databases, reference lists of eligible studies and relevant reviews were searched by hand, and experts in the field of dementia and mental health economics were contacted in order to identify additional published and unpublished work relevant to the guideline. Studies included in the clinical review were also assessed for economic evidence.

3.7.5   Review process

The database searches for general health-economic evidence for dementia resulted in 45 potentially eligible references. Full texts of all potentially eligible studies (including those for which the relevance or eligibility was not clear from the abstract) were obtained. These publications were then assessed against a set of standard inclusion criteria by the health economist, and the papers eligible for inclusion as economic evaluations were subsequently assessed for internal validity. The quality assessment was based on the 35-point checklist used by the *British Medical Journal* to assist referees in appraising full economic analyses (Drummond & Jefferson, 1996) (see Appendix 10).

3.7.6   Selection criteria

The following inclusion criteria were applied to selected studies identified by the economic searches for further analysis:
- No restriction was placed on the language or publication status of the papers.
- Studies published between 1990 and 2006 were included. This date restriction was imposed in order to obtain data relevant to the current health and social care settings.
- Only studies from Organisation for Economic Co-operation and Development (OECD) countries were included, as the aim of the review was to identify economic evidence transferable to the UK setting.
- Selection criteria based on types of clinical conditions and people were identical to the clinical literature review.

- Studies were included provided that sufficient details regarding methods and results were available to enable the methodological quality of the study to be assessed, and provided that the study data and results were extractable.
Additional selection criteria were applied in the case of economic evaluations:
- Only full economic evaluations that compared two or more options and considered both costs and consequences (that is, cost-minimisation analysis, cost-consequences analysis, cost-effectiveness analysis, cost-utility analysis or cost-benefit analysis) were included in the review.
- Economic studies were considered if the clinical evidence utilised was derived from a meta-analysis, a well-conducted literature review, an RCT, a quasi-experimental trial or a cohort study.

3.7.7   Data extraction

Data were extracted by the health economist using an economic data extraction form (see Appendix 11). Masked assessment, whereby data extractors are blind to the details of the journal, authors, and so on, was not undertaken.

3.7.8   Presentation of the results

The economic evidence identified by the health economics systematic review is summarised in the respective chapters of the guideline, following presentation of the clinical and qualitative evidence. The characteristics and results of all economic studies included in the review are provided in the form of evidence tables in Appendix 18. Additional economic modelling undertaken alongside the guideline development process is also presented in the relevant chapters.

3.8   STAKEHOLDER CONTRIBUTIONS

Professionals, service users and companies have contributed to and commented on the guideline at key stages in its development. Stakeholders for this guideline include:
- service user/carer stakeholders: the national service user and carer organisations that represent people whose care is described in this guideline
- professional stakeholders: the national organisations that represent healthcare professionals who are providing services to people with dementia
- commercial stakeholders: the companies that manufacture medicines used in the treatment of dementia
- Primary Care Trusts
- Department of Health and Welsh Assembly Government.

Stakeholders have been involved in the guideline's development at the following points:
- commenting on the initial scope of the guideline and attending a briefing meeting held by NICE
- contributing lists of evidence to the GDG
- commenting on the first and second drafts of the guideline.

3.9 VALIDATION OF THIS GUIDELINE

Registered stakeholders had an opportunity to comment on the draft guideline, which was posted on the NICE website during the consultation period. The GRP also reviewed the guideline and checked that stakeholders' comments had been addressed.

Following the consultation period, the GDG finalised the recommendations and the NCCMH produced the final documents. These were then submitted to NICE and SCIE. NICE and SCIE then formally approved the guideline and issued its guidance to the NHS in England and Wales.

4.   DEMENTIA

4.1   INTRODUCTION

This guideline is concerned with the identification and treatment of, and care for, dementia as defined in the 10th edition of the *International Classification of Diseases* (ICD-10) (World Health Organization, 1992). Care for people with dementia is provided by both health and social care organisations, each bringing its own particular perspectives on both the nature of the dementia and, more particularly, our response to people with dementia. As a result, this guideline has been jointly developed for the Social Care Institute for Excellence (SCIE) and the National Institute for Health and Clinical Excellence (NICE), and we have drawn on the combined knowledge and evidence base of both social and clinical perspectives within the area of dementia care. This has presented challenges for guideline development in analysing and synthesising the two different approaches to 'evidence' and the sheer volume of literature needing appraisal, and the need to produce 'joined up' practice guidelines to address the sometimes contrasting perspectives in health and social care approaches to dementia care.

For example, from a clinical perspective, dementia can be described as a group of usually progressive neurodegenerative brain disorders characterised by intellectual deterioration and more or less gradual erosion of mental and later physical function, leading to disability and death. This approach has allowed the development and deployment of pharmacological interventions for people with dementia and holds the hope that one day some dementia may be preventable or curable.

Alternatively, from a social perspective, dementia can viewed as one of the ways in which an individual's personal and social capacities may change for a variety of reasons, and changes in such capacities are only experienced as disabilities when environmental supports (which we all depend upon to varying degrees) are not adaptable to suit them. Moreover, dementia thought of from a clinical perspective (that is, disease and disability leading to death) may also prefigure our collective social and professional approach to people with dementia as people irretrievably ill and fundamentally different from able-bodied healthy young people. This view may well underpin many of the problems faced by people with dementia and their carers when seeking help and in their experience of care in different settings.

We have found that these two perspectives – the medical and the social – are often not mutually exclusive; good practice that serves the needs of people with dementia and their carers is respectful of both. Thus, we hope that this guideline has gone some way to integrate evidence of the best approaches to dementia care in the medical and social traditions.

4.1.1   Medical model of dementia

Dementia as a clinical syndrome is characterised by global cognitive impairment, which represents a decline from previous level of functioning, and is associated with impairment in functional abilities and, in many cases, behavioural and psychiatric disturbances. Several formal definitions exist, such as that of the ICD-10:

> *'a syndrome due to disease of the brain, usually of a chronic or progressive nature, in which there is disturbance of multiple higher cortical functions, including memory, thinking, orientation, comprehension, calculation, learning capability, language, and judgement. Consciousness is not impaired. Impairments of cognitive function are commonly accompanied, occasionally preceded, by deterioration in emotional control, social behaviour, or motivation. The syndrome occurs in Alzheimer's disease, in cerebrovascular disease, and in other conditions primarily or secondarily affecting the brain'.*

By convention, young-onset dementia refers to those who develop dementia before the age of 65 (previously called 'pre-senile' dementia); late-onset dementia refers to those who develop the illness after the age of 65 (previously 'senile' dementia). The distinction between young- and late-onset illness still has clinical utility because aetiology and characteristics of people with dementia differ between young- and late-onset cases, and people with dementia are thought to require and benefit from a different approach, leading to the widespread, but not yet universal, establishment of local specialist young-onset dementia services (Harvey *et al.*, 2003).

There are a number of conditions that cause the symptoms of dementia. Alzheimer's disease (AD) accounts for around 60% of all cases; other common causes in older people include cerebrovascular disease (vascular dementia [VaD]) and dementia with Lewy bodies (DLB) (accounting for 15–20% of cases each). In cases of young onset, frontotemporal dementia (FTD) is also a common cause, second only to AD. Numerous other causes exist, including other degenerative diseases (for example, Huntington's disease), prion diseases (Creutzfeldt-Jakob Disease [CJD]), HIV dementia and several toxic and metabolic disorders (for example, alcohol-related dementia). Dementia also develops in between 30–70% of people with Parkinson's disease, depending on duration and age (Aarsland *et al.*, 2003). The distinction between Parkinson's disease dementia (PDD) and DLB lies in the relationship between motor and cognitive impairment. If dementia precedes, or occurs within 12 months of, motor disorder, DLB is diagnosed (McKeith *et al.*, 1996); otherwise the convention is to use the term PDD.

Some conditions have been described that can cause a 'reversible' dementia; in other words, a global cognitive decline for which there is some potentially reversible cause. These include psychiatric disorders (particularly the 'pseudodementia' of depression), space-occupying lesions, toxic states and metabolic and endocrine abnormalities (for example, vitamin B_{12}, folate deficiency and hypothyroidism). The differentiation between depression and dementia can be challenging and has important implications for treatment. The other conditions listed are not common causes of dementia (less than 5%) in the UK, since such physical problems would often be detected at an earlier stage, before giving rise to cognitive impairment. However, their importance lies in the fact that, when such conditions are detected, appropriate interventions offer a real chance of stabilisation, improvement or even (in rare cases) recovery.

Increasingly it is recognised that mixed cases of dementia (for example, AD and VaD, and AD and DLB) are commonly encountered, especially in older people. It has been shown that different pathologies can each contribute to the clinical expression of dementia (Snowdon *et al.*, 1997); a large UK-based neuropathological study showed that mixed pathology was the most common finding at autopsy in the brains of older people (MRC/CFAS, 2001).

Dementia can be distinguished from the mild and variable cognitive decline associated with normal ageing by the severity and global nature of cognitive impairment and the accompanying functional disability that results. More challenging is its distinction from more subtle patterns of cognitive impairment which fall short of the standard definitions of dementia but which may represent a 'pre-clinical' dementia state. For example, the syndrome of 'mild cognitive impairment' (MCI) has been defined as an isolated cognitive impairment (or impairments) identified as abnormal by a statistical rule (usually 1½ standard deviations below that expected on the basis of age and education) and representing a decline from previous level of function (Petersen *et al.*, 1999). Verification of cognitive difficulties by an informant and/or the individual concerned is required and the cognitive impairment should not be so severe as to affect social or occupational functioning (at which point the diagnosis of dementia would be more appropriate).

Several different types of MCI have now been proposed, including 'amnestic' when memory is affected and 'non-amnestic' reflecting impairments in a non-memory domain. Single-domain and multiple-domain types of MCI have been proposed, depending on the number of cognitive functions affected, though their nosological status is unclear. However, several authors have shown that those with amnestic MCI are at an increased risk of subsequently developing frank dementia, most usually of the Alzheimer type (10–15% per annum) (Bischkopf *et al.*, 2002). Those with MCI due to cerebrovascular disease also appear to be at an increased risk of subsequently developing dementia (Wentzel *et al.*, 2001). The usefulness of the concept is, firstly, that it provides a means to characterise patients with early cognitive impairments who are increasingly presenting to both primary and secondary care and, secondly, such individuals also represent a group who might also be appropriately targeted for putative disease-modifying therapies (Petersen *et al.*, 2005).

4.1.2   Symptoms, presentation and patterns of illness

AD usually presents with loss of memory, especially for learning new information, reflecting the disturbances of function of the anatomical sites (medial temporal lobe and the hippocampus), which are the primary focus of pathological change. Later in the illness other higher cortical functions (for example language, praxis and executive function) become affected and behavioural and psychiatric disturbances are seen. These have been referred to in the literature in a number of ways, including behavioural and psychological symptoms of dementia (BPSD), challenging behaviour, neuropsychiatric symptoms and, more recently, behaviour that challenges. Such symptoms commonly include depression, apathy, agitation, disinhibition, psychosis (delusions and hallucinations), wandering, aggression, incontinence and altered eating habits. They are important because they are frequent symptoms, which are often difficult to manage and cause great distress to individuals and carers. They are stronger predictors than cognitive impairment of both carer stress (Donaldson *et al.*, 1997) and entry to institutional care (Bianchetti *et al.*, 1995). Sometimes AD can present initially as behavioural disturbance, language disturbance or praxis but these may also be manifestations of other causes of dementia.

Frontotemporal dementia usually presents with language disturbance and/or behavioural difficulties (either disinhibition or apathy), whilst DLB is characterised by recurrent visual hallucinations, fluctuating cognitive disturbance and motor features of parkinsonism. Associated features in DLB are falls, disturbances of consciousness, autonomic dysfunction and rapid eye movement (REM) sleep behaviour disorder (McKeith *et al.*, 2005).

VaD can present after an acute vascular event (for example, a stroke) or subacutely and insidiously with progressive attentional and executive/planning problems, gait disturbance and apraxia, reflecting 'subcortical' frontostriatal dysfunction due to vascular pathology. Focal neurological signs are common (and their presence is required by some diagnostic criteria) as are changes on brain imaging, including cortical infarcts, multiple lacunae and extensive white matter change. Behaviours that challenge are also common in VaD, with depression and apathy seen most frequently (O'Brien *et al.*, 2003).

4.1.3   Course and prognosis

AD is characterised by a progressive decline in cognition and ability to function. Behavioural disturbances can occur early but tend to become more frequent as the severity of dementia increases. As independence is lost, people become unable to care for themselves, dress, wash, eat and toilet. There may be brief plateaus during the illness but decline is fairly consistent, tending to increase or accelerate.

Similarly, DLB and FTD are associated with progressive decline, although often superimposed on the progressive course of DLB is a pattern of fluctuating confusion whereby cognitive function can vary over minutes, hours, days or weeks. Parkinsonism also progresses over time in DLB, although about 25% of people will not develop parkinsonism during the illness. The combination of cognitive impairment and motor disorder in DLB and FTD causes considerably greater impairment in ability of function than that predicted by the degree of cognitive dysfunction present.

The course of VaD is less predictable, since in some cases relative stability may be seen for a period, if underlying VaD can be stabilised. Alternatively, a subsequent vascular event can cause a sudden and 'stepwise' deterioration in cognitive function.

Overall, decline is usual in VaD, and in naturalistic studies the rate of overall cognitive change is surprisingly similar across all three main types of dementia (AD, DLB and VaD) at 3–4 points per year on the Mini Mental State Examination (MMSE). In clinical trials, people with VaD show a more stable course, possibly because of better management of vascular risk factors (Black *et al.*, 2003). Due to comorbid conditions, people with VaD in particular have increased risk of mortality due to cardiovascular and cerebrovascular disease.

4.1.4   Physical and social consequences of dementia

People with dementia are at increased risk of physical health problems, and dementia is a major risk factor for delirium due to physical illness or medication. There are many reasons for this association. Dementias such as VaD and DLB frequently occur in those with other severe illnesses (such as stroke and Parkinson's disease). Progressive dementia during the course of AD itself can be associated with marked changes in autonomic function, appetite and eating habits, sleep and neurological signs. Decreased mobility and attention to personal care and diet, together with lack of compliance with medical treatments, renders people with dementia more susceptible to other illnesses and causes particular challenges for their treatment. Nutritional problems and weight loss are common problems in dementia, especially as the severity of illness increases. The Alzheimer's Society 'Food for Thought' practice guides and advice sheets were produced specifically to help health and social care staff and carers deal with the challenges experienced by people with dementia concerning food, eating and drinking (www.alzheimers.org.uk). These guides are based on research conducted for the Society (Alzheimer's Society, 2000; Watson *et al.*, 2002).

The multiple difficulties and increased risk of physical health problems mean that people with dementia may have multiple contacts with different NHS and social care professionals. By definition, dementia has an impact on activities of daily living (ADL), which in mild cases may consist of difficulties in shopping, maintaining a home and personal care but in more advanced cases may lead to difficulties in mobility, toileting and language skills.

People with dementia, therefore, become increasingly reliant on family, friends and neighbours, and health and social care services. Carers (usually relatives but sometimes friends and neighbours) provide the majority of such care. Carer stress is common, with approximately 30% of carers having significant psychiatric morbidity (Donaldson *et al.*, 1997). Despite much public education over the last 2 decades, dementia remains a stigmatising illness, causing difficulties for both people with dementia and carers.

4.2   SOCIAL MODEL OF DEMENTIA

While the clinical model of dementia presented above describes the changes occurring within the brain, the way that dementia affects a person in day-to-day life will vary from one individual to the next. For many years, people with dementia were written off as incapable, regarded as little more than 'vegetables' and often hidden from society at large. During the 1980s and 1990s, there was a move away from regarding people with dementia as incapable and excluding them from society, and towards a 'new culture of dementia care', which encouraged looking for the person behind the dementia (Gilleard, 1984; Kitwood & Benson, 1995; Kitwood,1997). People with dementia could now be treated as individuals with a unique identity and biography and cared for with greater understanding.

Building on this work, others (notably Marshall, 2004) have advocated that dementia should be regarded as a disability and framed within a social model. The social model, as developed in relation to disability, understands disability not as an intrinsic characteristic of the individual, but as an outcome produced by social processes of exclusion. Thus, disability is not something that exists purely at the level of individual psychology, but is a condition created by a combination of social and material factors including income and financial support, employment, housing, transport and the built environment (Barnes *et al.*, 1999). From the perspective of the social model, people with dementia may have an *impairment* (perhaps of cognitive function) but their *disability* results from the way they are treated by, or excluded from, society. For people with dementia, this model carries important implications, for example:

- the condition is not the 'fault' of the individual
- the focus is on the skills and capacities the person retains rather than loses
- the individual can be fully understood (his or her history, likes/dislikes, and so on)
- the influence is recognised of an enabling or supportive environment
- the key value is endorsed of appropriate communication
- opportunities should be taken for rehabilitation or re-enablement
- the responsibility to reach out to people with dementia lies with people who do not (yet) have dementia (Gilliard *et al.*, 2005).

The social model of care seeks to understand the emotions and behaviours of the person with dementia by placing him or her within the context of his or her social circumstances and biography. By learning about each person with dementia as an individual, with his or her own history and background, care and support can be designed to be more appropriate to individual needs. If, for example, it is known that a man with dementia was once a prisoner of war, it can be understood why he becomes very distressed when admitted to a locked ward. If care providers have learned that a person with dementia has a strong dislike for a certain food, it can be understood why the person might spit it out. Without this background knowledge and understanding, the man who rattles the door may be labelled a 'wanderer' because he tries to escape and cowers when approached, or the person who spits out food is labelled as 'antisocial'.

Moreover, a variety of aspects of care may affect a person as the dementia progresses. Some extrinsic factors in the care environment can be modified, for instance noise levels can be highly irritating but are controllable. Other intrinsic factors, such as the cultural or ethnic identity of the person with dementia, may also have a bearing on how needs are assessed and care is delivered. Some aspects will be more important or relevant to one person than to another. The social model of care asserts that dementia is more than, but inclusive of, the clinical damage to the brain.

4.3   EXAMPLES OF EXPERIENCES OF CARE

Dementia by its nature does not lend itself to a clear, sequential care pathway, as it affects people in very individual ways. However, using particular scenarios as examples (Care Examples 1, 2 and 3 below), some key elements and issues can be illustrated, which indicate how clinical and social perspectives interact. The care examples are given to illustrate significant issues; they do not imply that negative experiences are universal.

The diagrams in each care example illustrate the interconnection between the needs of a person with dementia, his or her carer and other relevant services or sources of information. The circles vary in size according to the significance of likely need at that given time. Need is a dynamic concept; in other words, needs will change over time, with consequent changes in their relative level of significance. It should be noted that the scenarios below are independent of one another and do not imply any progression of severity.

4.4   INCIDENCE AND PREVALENCE

There have been several epidemiological studies of dementia. The Eurodem Consortium found prevalence rose from 1% for 60–65 year olds to 13% for 80–85 year olds and 32% for 90–95 year olds (Hofman *et al.*, 1991). Dementia therefore affects around 5% of the over 65s, rising to 20% of the over 80s. The best prevalence data for England and Wales came from the Medical Research Council (MRC)-funded Cognitive Function and Ageing Study (CFAS), which found very similar prevalence rates in six different geographically diverse sites (MRC/CFAS, 1998). This study estimated that there were then 550,000 people in England and Wales with dementia, a figure that has now been revised to nearly 700,000 cases (Alzheimer's Society, 2006, www.alzheimers.org.uk). Prevalence is higher in women than men, partly reflecting their greater longevity. Table 2 gives estimates of the number of people over 65 years of age with dementia in England and Wales for 5-year age bands according to prevalence estimates for England and Wales from the MRC CFAS study (MRC/CFAS, 1998) and population data for 2005 (the most recent actual population data available from the Office for National Statistics). Table 3 gives estimates of the number of people over 65 years of age with AD in England and Wales for 5-year age bands according to prevalence estimates calculated from European population-based studies of people aged 65 and older (Lobo *et al.*, 2000) and population data for 2005. Incidence studies have shown rates of 1–3 per 1000 for those aged 65–70, rising to 14–30 per 1000 for those aged 80–85 (Fratiglioni *et al.*, 2000; Jorm & Jolley, 1998). In most studies, women also seem to have an increased incidence rate, suggesting their higher prevalence figures are not entirely due to greater life span. Possible explanations include confounding effects of education and possible hormonal influences.

Prevalence rates for VaD are generally lower than for AD (Lobo *et al.*, 2000), with prevalence calculated to double every 5.3 years as opposed to every 4.5 years for AD (Jorm *et al.*, 1987). Table 4 gives estimates of the number of people over 65 years of age with VaD in England and Wales for 5-year age bands according to prevalence estimates calculated from European population-based studies of people aged 65 and

CARE EXAMPLE 1

Mr R is 54 years old and married, with two daughters aged 20 and 14. He lives with his wife and youngest daughter; his eldest daughter lives locally. Mr R has his own textile company, which he has managed successfully with a business partner and close friend for many years.

There is a familial history of young-onset AD; his mother developed the condition in her late 50s, which eventually resulted in her requiring nursing-home care, and died in her mid 60s.

In the months prior to referral, Mrs R had noticed increasing incidents of forgetfulness in her husband; he would forget conversations and repeat questions. She also noted that he would be searching the house for things he had misplaced and, on occasion, accuse her of hiding or losing items. He had forgotten instructions and planned tasks. This resulted in him forgetting to collect the youngest daughter following a school trip and not arriving at pre-arranged meeting places. He had taken his wife into town and, after visiting a shop on his own, had driven home without her.

His business partner had also, on an increasing number of occasions, contacted Mr R's wife to enquire as to his whereabouts, as he had not turned up to an arranged appointment. This was having a detrimental effect on business, and customers were expressing their annoyance. Despite prompting and careful and supportive organising of his workload by his partner and secretary, the situation was deteriorating rapidly.

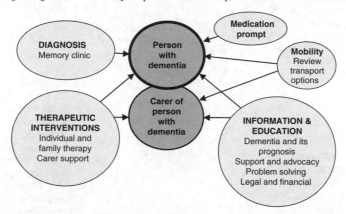

Mr R did not appear to be aware of these difficulties at the time and felt it was 'just his age'. He did however mention that people were concerned about his memory when visiting his GP regarding an unrelated health matter, resulting in a referral to the local memory clinic. Mr R was diagnosed with AD and offered acetylcholinesterase inhibitor medication.

Their daughters were also extremely distressed; the oldest was able to talk over some of her concerns with her mother, but the younger daughter found this very difficult and became quite withdrawn and declined the option of talking to a member of the clinical team.

On commencing treatment, there were issues regarding concordance with Mr R's medication. He had a good rapport with the nurse specialist and during discussion stated, 'If I accept that I need the medication I have to accept that I have the condition'. There seemed to be resolution following this discussion and to date Mr R is fully concordant with the treatment.

Mr R decided to sell his company in order to 'do the things we always wanted to do while I'm still able'.

Each member of the family said they would like to talk to someone in a similar situation.

Unfortunately, Mr R quickly developed visuospatial problems and was told he should stop driving. He saw this as a 'devastating blow' and angrily challenged this directive. He underwent a driving assessment at the DVLA centre, the outcome of which supported clinical opinion, and his licence was withdrawn. This had a far-ranging and major effect on the family. Mrs R did not drive, and there were no local shops. They used to spend the family holidays touring in their caravan.

Mrs R had a part-time job and was understandably worried that her husband would become more isolated and housebound.

CARE EXAMPLE 2

Mrs H is 79 years old, with a diagnosis of multi-infarct dementia, and lives alone in a 19th century mid-terraced house in an isolated rural village. She moved to this country from Bangladesh with her husband and has never learned to speak English. She was widowed 2 years ago, when her husband died of lung cancer. She has two daughters; J lives 15 miles away in the same county and N lives 140 miles away in North Yorkshire. Both work full time and have teenage children.

Mrs H was first diagnosed with dementia 5 years ago and, as is characteristic, experienced several small strokes over these years, causing further impact on her ability to care for herself independently. She often failed to remember to take prescribed medication and was unable to effectively manage her personal care.

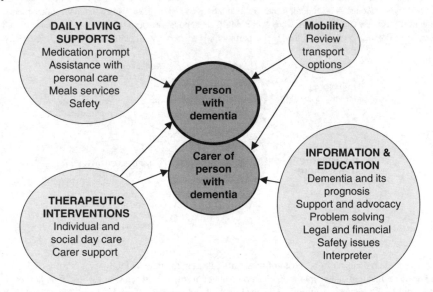

Mrs H was referred by her GP to social services, who have undertaken the first contact assessment within the Single Assessment Process. The Social Services Access team is trying to encourage Mrs H to accept a care package of day care for 2 days a week and meals services for the remaining days, a medicine prompt and a safety check in the evening by a home carer. Communication difficulties and family concerns about whether the food preparation meets Mrs H's cultural needs, together with Mrs H's sense of independence and lack of insight, have led to her refusal of all offers of help.

J is frequently called by neighbours when her mother wanders from her home at inappropriate times and is often not dressed appropriately for the weather conditions. She tends to leave home with the door open, which means her home is unsafe.

J is becoming very stressed and expresses concerns that she knows little about the diagnosis her mother has received and its likely progression. She also fears the stigma of the condition within her culture. Without any knowledge of the care possibilities, and with pressure from family members to continue caring for Mrs H, J feels that there is no alternative but to care for her mother herself and is considering working part-time to do this. However, this will create a lot of financial stress and difficulty for her own family; having been made redundant, her husband is currently not working and J is the main earner of the household.

CARE EXAMPLE 3

Mr J was diagnosed with AD 8 years ago. He and his wife lived together in their detached suburban house with minimal support for at least 6 of these years. Mrs J was a very able and committed carer who provided for almost all of her husbands needs.

During the course of the AD, Mr J was also diagnosed with bowel cancer, which resulted in a colostomy. Mrs J continued to care for her husband and fulfilled the additional needs of colostomy care. Mr J can become extremely distressed during the daily care of his colostomy and it is believed that he suffers a high degree of associated pain since the surgical procedure.

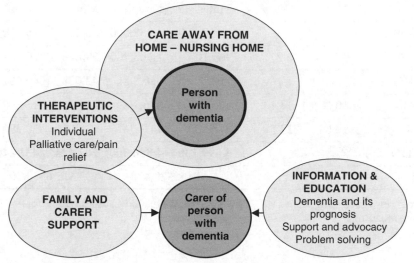

During the Christmas period, Mrs J suffered a significant stroke; Mr J was admitted to a local private nursing home for emergency respite care. Mrs J made a good recovery over a period of months and returned home. Due to the effects of the stroke, Mrs J now required home help twice daily to support her with personal care, which meant that she was no longer physically able to care for her husband at home. Mr J's placement in the nursing home was made permanent.

Mrs J has found it very difficult to 'let go' of the direct caring role she had with her husband and feels guilty that she is unable to care for him. She visits Mr J every day for several hours and often complains to the home manager that the standard of care is not adequate.

older (Lobo *et al.*, 2000) and population data for 2005. Incidence rates are higher in males (1.2 per 1000 for males aged 65–70; 0.3 per 1000 for females aged 65–70) but females catch up at older ages (prevalence 6 per 1000 for both males and females aged 85–90). There have been too few studies on DLB to determine incidence and prevalence; the one population-based UK study published to date found DLB was the cause of 11% of dementia cases in a sample taken from north London (Stevens *et al.*, 2002). A study of young-onset dementia revealed a prevalence of 54 per 100,000 people aged 30–64 (Harvey *et al.*, 2003), suggesting that there would currently be around 14,000 people with young-onset dementia in England and Wales[30]. Table 5 gives estimates of the number of people under 65 years of age with dementia in

---

[30] Based on mid-2005 population estimates (available at: www.statistics.gov.uk).

**Table 2: Number of people with dementia in England
and Wales aged over 65**

Age group	Prevalence of dementia (rate/100 people)		Population in England & Wales (2005)		Estimated number of people with dementia (England & Wales)	
	Males	Females	Males	Females	Males	Females
65–69	1.4	1.5	1,158,600	1,238,000	16,220	18,570
70–74	3.1	2.2	963,100	1,103,700	29,856	24,281
75–79	5.6	7.1	750,500	980,800	42,028	69,637
80–84	10.2	14.1	508,000	816,700	51,816	115,155
≥85	19.6	27.5	318,900	741,100	62,504	20,3803
Total (≥65)			3,699,100	4,880,300	202,424	431,446
			All: 8,579,400		All: 633,870	

Source: prevalence of dementia (MRC/CFAS, 1998), population statistics (Office for National Statistics).

**Table 3: Number of people with AD in England
and Wales aged over 65**

Age group	Prevalence of AD (rate/100 people)		Population in England & Wales (2005)		Estimated number of people with dementia (England & Wales)	
	Males	Females	Males	Females	Males	Females
65–69	0.6	0.7	1,158,600	1,238,000	6,952	8,666
70–74	1.5	2.3	963,100	1,103,700	14,447	25,385
75–79	1.8	4.3	750,500	980,800	13,509	42,174
80–84	6.3	8.4	508,000	816,700	32,004	68,603
85–89	8.8	14.2	Data not available		–	–
≥90	17.6	23.6	Data not available		–	–

Source: prevalence of AD (Lobo *et al.*, 2000), population statistics (Office for National Statistics).

Table 4: Number of people with VaD in England and Wales aged over 65

Age group	Prevalence of VaD (rate/100 people)		Population in England & Wales (2005)		Estimated number of people with VaD (England & Wales)	
	Males	Females	Males	Females	Males	Females
65–69	0.5	0.1	1,158,600	1,238,000	5,793	1,238
70–74	0.8	0.6	963,100	1,103,700	7,705	6,622
75–79	1.9	0.9	750,500	980,800	14,260	8,827
80–84	2.4	2.3	508,000	816,700	12,192	18,784
85–89	2.4	3.5	Data not available		–	–
≥90	3.6	5.8	Data not available		–	–

Source: prevalence of VaD (Lobo *et al.*, 2000), population statistics (Office for National Statistics).

Table 5: Number of people with young-onset dementia (aged under 65) in England and Wales

Age group	Prevalence of young-onset dementia (rate/100 people)		Population in England & Wales (2005)		Estimated number of people with young-onset dementia (England & Wales)	
	Males	Females	Males	Females	Males	Females
30–34	0.0126	0.0128	1,847,800	1,864,400	233	239
35–39	0.0054	0.0105	2,054,300	2,070,600	111	217
40–44	0.0053	0.0255	2,016,100	2,053,500	107	524
45–49	0.0363	0.0298	1,764,900	1,792,800	641	534
50–54	0.0659	0.0591	1,602,100	1,637,200	1,056	968
55–59	0.2002	0.1027	1,714,700	1,760,400	3,433	1,808
60–64	0.2045	0.1294	1,347,100	1,409,900	2,755	1,824
Total (30–64)			12,347,000	12,588,800	8,335	6,114
			All: 24,935,800		All: 14,449	

Source: prevalence of dementia (Harvey *et al.*, 2003), population statistics (Office for National Statistics).

England and Wales for 5-year age bands according to prevalence estimates calculated from a relatively small population sample in England (Harvey *et al.*, 2003) and population data for 2005. Demographic changes in the next 30 years, with a substantial increase in the proportion of people in the 'old old' age groups, mean that prevalence of dementia is set to more than double in the next 30–50 years (Wancata *et al.*, 2003).

4.5   AETIOLOGY

Some risk factors are common to most types of dementia and others are specific to particular types. The summary below refers to dementia or a specific diagnostic category as appropriate to the evidence. Risk factors can be considered as genetic, environmental and genotypic. Genetic and genotypic risk factors will modify an individual's reaction to those environmental risk factors to which he or she is exposed.

4.5.1   Genetic factors

At least three genes with multiple mutations can be identified for familial young-onset AD, all of which are rare (Hardy, 1996; Schellenberg *et al.*, 1991; Cruts *et al.*, 1998).

- A family history of late-onset AD or VaD is associated with an increased risk of developing the condition in any individual, but no single chromosomal abnormality has been identified to account for this.
- Discrete chromosomal abnormalities account for some cases of frontotemporal degeneration (Spillantini *et al.*, 1998).
- Down's syndrome is the most common genetic disorder and is the result of a chromosomal abnormality. The risk of developing AD is significantly higher for those with Down's syndrome than the general population (Rabe *et al.*, 1990). The risk rises with increasing age, but the age of onset is considerably younger than in the general population (Visser *et al.*, 1997; Tyrell *et al.*, 2001).

Apolipoprotein E is a polymorphic lipoprotein found in the brain. Its role is unclear, though it has been implicated in repair of the nerve sheath (Mann *et al.*, 1996). There are three common variants of the gene that codes for ApoE. These are known as ApoE ε 2, ApoE ε 3 and ApoE ε 4. The ApoE ε 4 allele has been identified as a risk factor for the development of late-onset AD in particular and reduces the age at which one could expect to develop the condition (Strittmatter *et al.*, 1993; Poirier *et al.*, 1993). However, the effect is not equal across different racial groups (Tang *et al.*, 1996). Possession of the ApoE *e* 4 allele is not causative of AD on its own but tends to modulate when and whether the disease will become manifest under the influence of other aetiological factors (Kuusisto *et al.*, 1994; Skoog *et al.*, 1998).

4.5.2   Environmental factors

The risk of developing dementia rises with increasing age (Jorm *et al.*, 1987; Hofman *et al.*, 1991; Copeland *et al.*, 1992; Boothby *et al.*, 1994). Age may be a risk factor in itself or may reflect the effect of increasing time during which other factors can exert their influence.

Cardiovascular risk factors are smoking (Ott *et al.*, 1998), high blood pressure (Lindsay *et al.*, 1997), diabetes (Desmond *et al.*, 1993) and hyperlipidaemia (Moroney, 1999a). All of these are independent risk factors for the development of VaD and predispose to the development of atherosclerosis, which is associated with dementia of all clinical types (Hofman *et al.*, 1997). These risk factors also predispose to acute stroke, which is well established as a risk factor for the development of dementia (Tatemichi *et al.*, 1992, 1993). Smoking (Launer *et al.*, 1999; Prince *et al.*, 1994), high blood pressure (Stewart *et al.*, 1999; Skoog *et al.*, 1996) and diabetes mellitus (Leibson *et al.*, 1997) are all independent risk factors for the development of AD.

Earlier evidence linked an increased risk of developing AD with a history of depression earlier in life. More recent general population studies have identified an increased risk of all dementias with a past history of severe psychiatric problems, schizophrenia and depression being the most common diagnoses found (Cooper & Holmes, 1998).

Although earlier work described an association between head injury and AD (Mortimer *et al.*, 1985; Mayeux *et al.*, 1993), a more recent meta-analysis did not support these findings (Launer *et al.*, 1999). There is also currently no evidence for a causative link between occupational exposure to solvents or lead and the development of AD (EURODEM studies). While it is clear that ingestion of aluminium can be neurotoxic, it is unclear whether it is responsible for the chronic neurodegeneration of AD (Doll, 1993; Altmann *et al.*, 1999). Clustering of cases of AD in industrial areas could point to an environmental toxin not yet identified (Whalley *et al.*, 1995).

High educational attainment or higher premorbid IQ has been shown across different cultures to exert a protective effect against the development of dementia (Canadian Study of Health and Ageing, 1994; Zhang *et al.*, 1990; Schmand *et al.*, 1997; Snowdon *et al.*, 1996).

Research into the aetiology of dementia is confounded by the current classification systems (ICD-10 and DSM-IV-TR), which have been based on end-stage pathological findings that assume, in part, aetiology. Often an individual may have been given a clinical diagnosis of a particular type of dementia but, on post mortem examination, there can be a mixture of the pathological characteristics of AD, DLB and VaD. The relationship of these different pathological processes to each other and their roles in causing the cognitive decline experienced by people with dementia remains to be fully explained.

4.6 DETECTION AND ASSESSMENT

4.6.1 Detection

The changes that occur in cognition, emotion or capabilities as possible early signs of dementia can be recognised by the person him or herself and/or his or her family and friends, general practitioner (when he or she consults about other problems), or nursing or social care staff (providing services in his or her home or in a residential institution).

Detection of the early changes of dementia syndromes may occur when the person affected or those around him or her actively seek help, usually, but not exclusively, from his or her general practitioner. It may also occur when professionals become suspicious of changes in the individual, even when the individual and others around him or her are not concerned. A third route to recognition is through revelatory moments, for example when the sudden incapacity of a carer reveals the dementia processes in the person concerned, for whose cognitive losses the carer had compensated. These three routes to recognition of dementia create their own problems of investigation, diagnosis and disclosure, which will be discussed further in this guideline.

Detection of dementia, particularly in its early stages, depends on pattern recognition, deductive reasoning and accumulation of diagnostic evidence from multiple sources. These processes tend to be iterative and may be relatively prolonged. Factors inhibiting the detection process include denial on the part of affected individuals, families and professionals, and limited impact on families of changes in the individual, as well as limited awareness of the dementia syndromes and limited diagnostic skills amongst practitioners in different disciplines. Dementia syndromes can emerge as changes in cognition, emotion or capability, and their manifestation is influenced by the personality of the person affected. Delays in recognition can occur because of the difficulties in distinguishing novel changes from pre-existing characteristics or behaviour traits.

There is as yet no simple, accurate and cost-effective method for identifying individuals with early dementia syndromes through population screening, although there may be a case for targeted screening of sub-populations.

4.6.2   Assessment and diagnosis

Diagnosis of dementia syndromes can be a prolonged iterative process, particularly in the early stages of the condition. The time from first symptoms to diagnosis can be as much as 12 months, for a number of reasons.

The usual components of the diagnostic process in a primary-care setting are:
- the individual's self-report of changes in memory, capability or mood
- informant histories that support self-report and add significant new details of changes
- exclusion of depression and delirium as primary pathologies, using the information from the personal and informant histories
- measurable cognitive losses, using a standardised instrument
- absence of 'red flag' symptoms suggesting alternative diagnoses (for example, urinary incontinence or ataxia in apparent early dementia).

By custom, a number of other conditions that can induce cognitive impairment are excluded at this stage by blood tests, including vitamin B_{12} deficiency, hypothyroidism, diabetes and disorders of calcium metabolism.

Further clarification of the extent and probable cause of a dementia syndrome requires more complex cognitive function testing (and so referral to a specialist memory assessment service) and/or CT scanning (following referral to specialist care).

Disclosure of the emerging diagnosis is a complex and sensitive task, and all professional groups find this difficult. However, the rising public awareness of AD means that discussion about the possible causes of changes in cognition can begin earlier in the diagnostic process.

Needs assessment of the person with dementia, and of his or her family, are more commonly carried out in specialist services or by social services, than in primary care.

4.6.3   Assessment in learning disabilities and dementia

'Learning disability' is a term used almost exclusively in the United Kingdom to cover the ICD-10 categories for mental retardation (F70–79) in people of all ages. The two main components are low cognitive ability (defined as a full-scale IQ of less than 70) and diminished social competence characterised by impairment of skills that becomes apparent during the developmental period (that is, before the age of 18 years). IQ is used to define four categories of severity (mild, moderate, severe and profound). People with learning disabilities have a higher than expected rate of both physical and mental health problems. A catalogue of special diagnostic criteria, the DC-LD, has been produced for psychiatric disorders in this population to complement ICD-10 (Royal College of Psychiatrists, 2001). Other practice guidelines for diagnosis of mental health problems in learning disability also exist (Deb *et al.*, 2001).

The White Paper *Valuing People* (Department of Health, 2001a) estimated that there were more than 1.4 million people with learning disabilities in England. Of these people, 210,000 have severe and profound learning disabilities (of whom 12% are older people). The White Paper suggested that the number of people with severe learning disabilities of any age would increase by approximately 1% per year for the next 15 years, for various reasons.

Although the National Service Framework for Older People sets out a framework for services for older people (Department of Health, 2001b), the White Paper *Valuing People* (Department of Health, 2001a) points out that the ageing process for people with learning disabilities may begin much earlier and that planning for the needs of older people with learning disabilities may need to include a more extended population, perhaps from age 50 years upwards. It was assumed that local Partnership Boards would ensure coordination between learning disability services and older people's services so that people can use services most appropriate to their needs. In particular, people at risk of developing young-onset AD, such as people with Down's syndrome, were mentioned, and the White Paper stated that the Government will expect learning disability services to work with specialist mental health services to ensure that appropriate supports are provided for younger people with learning disabilities suffering from dementia.

People with Down's syndrome are at risk of developing AD about 30–40 years earlier than the rest of the population, although lifetime risk may not be different (Holland *et al.*, 1998).

The prevalence of dementia in people with learning disabilities without Down's syndrome is generally found to be two or three times that expected in people over 65 (Patel *et al.*, 1993; Cooper, 1997), although at least one study did not concur (Zigman *et al.*, 2004). Single-photon emission computed tomography (SPECT) scan findings in people with Down's syndrome who do not meet the criteria for clinical dementia are often abnormal and resemble the changes associated with AD in the rest of the population (Deb *et al.*, 1992; Kao *et al.*, 1993), so such testing is of limited diagnostic value, and for the most part the diagnosis of dementia in this population relies on history and observation.

Deterioration in functioning and other features that may suggest the onset of dementia might also occur in people with learning disabilities as a result of visual or hearing impairments, or other physical conditions that can, for example, impair mobility. The differential diagnosis of decline has to be very wide because there may be problems communicating with the person with the condition. People with Down's syndrome are at special risk throughout life of developing thyroid disease, particularly hypothyroidism, which can present with deterioration and dementia-like features. Partly for these reasons, *Valuing People* emphasised the role of health facilitation, involving regular health checks, in primary care services.

A particular challenge is ascertaining cognitive decline in people with learning disabilities whose performance might naturally fall outside the reference range for most psychological tests, although there have been attempts at consensus statements (Aylward *et al.*, 1997). The MMSE is generally unhelpful when used with people with Down's syndrome, although the Cambridge Cognitive Examination (CAMCOG) may be useful (Hon *et al.*, 1999). Other attempts at adapting tools developed in the general population include the modified Cambridge Examination for Mental Disorders of the Elderly (CAMDEX) (Ball *et al.*, 2004). A test battery proposed by an international working party in 2000 (Burt & Aylward, 2000) includes, among other items, two informant-based questionnaires that are widely used, the Dementia Questionnaire for Mentally Retarded Persons (DMR) devised by Evenhuis (Evenhuis *et al.*, 1990; Evenhuis, 1996) and Gedye's Dementia Scale for Down Syndrome (DSDS) (Gedye, 1995). The DSDS, although developed particularly for use in people with Down's syndrome, can also be useful in diagnosing dementia in the non-Down's population with learning disabilities. It should only be administered by a clinical psychologist or psychometrician. The DSDS is generally useful for diagnosis, whereas the DMR seems to be sensitive to change and can be used to track the progress of dementia over time. The DMR can be administered by non-psychologists. Changes in general condition can also be monitored using Dalton's Brief Praxis Test (BPT) (Dalton & Fedor, 1998), which some clinicians find useful to record on video so that changes over time can be better observed.

The diagnosis of dementia in people with learning disabilities is therefore a multi-stage process. Firstly, carers may note deterioration in functioning, or else deterioration is noted as a result of screening the population at risk. Secondly, alternative causes of the person's presentation must be investigated and excluded in a systematic way. This will involve checks of vision, hearing and mobility, together with general health screening including thyroid function tests. Consideration must be made as to whether the symptoms are related to stress, recent life events such as bereavement, or another intercurrent mental health problem. When screening for sensory problems, it is important to use tests appropriate for the population concerned, for example optometry in people with learning disabilities may be best carried out using the Cardiff Acuity Test (Adoh & Woodhouse, 1994; Johansen *et al.*, 2003). If no other causes are identified, or if after identifying such problems and treating them, there is still cause for concern, the third stage is to carry out more specific dementia assessment tests such as the DSDS, DMR and BPT; where dementia is diagnosed, the progress of the condition may continue to be monitored using the DSDS and BPT. At the time of diagnosis, an assessment using the Assessment of Motor and Process Skills (AMPS) (Fisher, 2003), carried out by an occupational therapist, may be used as part of the development of an appropriate care plan.

4.6.4 Social care assessment

The assessment of a person with dementia for social services (social care) rests on the powers given to local authorities under the NHS and Community Care Act 1990. Local authority policies and practices vary and few social workers or care managers employ standardised assessment tools (Challis & Hughes, 2002). Thresholds for entitlement to social care services have also varied but the Fair Access to Care (FAC) initiative (Department of Health, 2003) is now prompting greater uniformity of eligibility criteria. Examples of people with dementia are used in this Department of Health guidance to illustrate how local authorities must prioritise their services; some of these are provided by the local authority, but the majority are commissioned from the independent sector.

The single assessment process is not yet fully under way and various local models are emerging (Glasby, 2004), revealing the variations in assessment practices. The Department of Health is developing a Common Assessment Framework that builds on the Single Assessment Framework (Department of Health, 2006a). The initial contact or first screening process may trigger a specialist or comprehensive community care assessment or mental health assessment by social services. Where an individual may be in need of community care services, they should receive a comprehensive community care assessment which is likely to involve multidisciplinary contribution of information, from the GP or community nurse for example. The duty to conduct an assessment is not dependent on whether the individual is likely to be entitled to services or on his or her financial circumstances. As a result of the assessment, a package of care services may be put in place, with attention being given to the person's wishes where possible. A small but growing number of carers and people with dementia choose to use direct payments, where they receive cash instead of care services and use this cash to purchase their own support. This may expand if the new proposals of the White Paper 2006 (Department of Health, 2006a) are put into place, extending direct payments (and piloting individual budgets) in scale and scope.

Part of the assessment by social services involves an assessment of the individual's capital and income, since social care in the UK is means tested (with some variation in Scotland). Such financial assessments generally include advice or assistance with claims for financial benefits for the individual or the carer. Evidence from campaigning groups indicates that this process is difficult and stigmatising and that under-funding of the social care system is considerable (Social Policy on Ageing Information Network, 2001).

Other assessments may be made of individuals' health needs and mental health problems arising from their dementia. These impact on the assessment of care. First, an assessment of eligibility for NHS-funded continuing care may determine that the NHS should have full or partial responsibility for care funding, rather than the local authority or individual. The establishment of a national framework for continuing care is currently under review. Evidence from carers collected by the Alzheimer's Society (2005) shows that many carers find this system unfair and complex, and individuals may find it helpful to seek independent advice from the voluntary sector. Second, if a person's mental heath is placing him or her at risk of severe harm to self or others, an assessment under the Mental Heath Act 1983 may be carried out by the local authority approved social worker, who follows a code of practice and national procedures. Social care provided under this Act is not means tested. Other assessments that may create nuances in the care provided include risk assessments and adult protection assessments; these are likely to be locally determined.

Social-care assessment of people with dementia is therefore a 'hierarchy' – the bulk of social services resources, including assessment, is now spent on intensive home support and residential provision (Sutherland, 1999), with less support of those who have only minor or emerging impairment related to their dementia (although many people with mild dementia are assessed because of physical problems or disabilities). Some social-care assessments involve community equipment services and occupational therapists, who may carry out their own assessments to determine individuals' needs for aids and equipment, and advice about housing and environmental issues.

However, many people with dementia remain outside social services assessments as their income or capital is high enough to exclude them from support (Challis *et al.*, 2000). While social services are obliged to undertake assessments, there is evidence that they do not offer them to people who will have to make their own arrangements; as a result, rehabilitation and other needs remain unmet (Challis *et al.*, 2000). When a person's assets have reduced to the point where they qualify for financial support, an assessment will follow, but self-funding residents in long-term care settings may pay substantially more for their care than other residents (Wright, 2003).

Within local social care services, each provider is likely to have its own assessment process, whether formal or informal. This will assess the suitability of the person with dementia for its support, for example, to have a volunteer befriender, to take up a place in a day centre or to have a telephone alarm service. The complexity of local variations is frequently reported as difficult and frustrating by carers of people with dementia (Audit Commission, 2000).

Assessment for social-care support for carers themselves largely falls under the Carers (Recognition and Services) Act 1995 and the Carers (Equal Opportunities) Act 2004. These Acts lay a duty on local authorities to offer carers an assessment of their needs, to work collaboratively with other agencies and to take account of carers' wishes and circumstances. Review of the impact of the 1995 Act confirms the lack of a standardisation of assessments and the difficulty of meeting carers' needs, with many care managers not undertaking such assessments or feeling that they have little to offer (Seddon & Robinson, 2001). Respite and short-break care have emerged as the most likely services to be offered following an assessment (Arksey *et al.*, 2004) and carers of people with dementia are often positive about these services. Other triggers for full or comprehensive community care assessment are admission to hospital or a carer's illness, or death. When events such as these precipitate a change in an individual's circumstances, urgent assessment may be necessary to address his or her changing needs. Adult services departments (or local authorities/councils with social services responsibilities) may also be 'fined' if they delay the discharge from hospital of a person with dementia.

4.7 RISK, ABUSE AND NEGLECT

4.7.1 Vulnerability of people with dementia

The vulnerability of people with dementia to abuse and neglect is widely recognised (Compton *et al.*, 1997; Bond *et al.*, 1999; Bonnie & Wallace, 2003), although incidence, prevalence and precise risk factors are not well established (House of Commons Health Committee, 2004a). Practitioners working with people with dementia are required to follow policy and practice guidance (Department of Health/Home Office, 2000) that requires multi-agency responses for the protection of vulnerable adults from abuse. Training in the protection of vulnerable adults is not mandatory but is seen as good practice for people working in dementia services (Manthorpe *et al.*, 2005), and while we do not know what precise forms of training are effective, it is reported to lead to better identification of abuse (a random controlled trial by Richardson and colleagues (2002) provides good evidence of this). Agreed multi-agency policy and practice guidance is available at local level and identifies the approaches to be taken when abuse or neglect are suspected.

A national recording system for referrals of adult abuse has been piloted (Department of Health, 2005b), which found that older people with mental health problems were among those referred to local authorities' adult protection systems; a variety of interventions were adopted, although information on the outcomes is not available. Recommendations from a series of high-profile inquiries into care settings in hospitals (for example, Rowan Ward, Department of Health/Care Services Improvement Partnership, 2005) are relevant to commissioners, regulatory bodies and practitioners in seeking to lower the risk of abuse. The law in this area is developing and the Mental Capacity Act 2005 introduces a new criminal offence of ill treatment or neglect of a person who lacks capacity.

4.7.2 Impact of dementia on sexual relationships

Dementia can affect the sexual relationship between the person with dementia and his or her partner, who frequently plays the major care-giving role, in both heterosexual and homosexual partnerships. The sexual interests and attitudes of the person with dementia may change (Hanks, 1992). He or she may become less interested in sex, fail to respond to or reject expressions of affection by his or her partner or not demonstrate affection (Harris & Weir, 1998; Kuhn, 1994). People with dementia who continue to be sexually interested may experience sexual difficulties due to physical problems or because of the effects of dementia on their short-term memory, concentration and cognitive sequencing (Kuhn, 1994; Davies *et al.*, 1998).

Both the person with dementia and the carer may feel unloved, just at the time when they would normally expect emotional support from their partner as they learn to cope with the illness. This lack of support may cause feelings of rejection in one or both partners, leading to feelings of depression, despair, frustration and anger. However, where an intimate relationship can be maintained, this may help the partnership to endure (Davies *et al.*, 1998). As something the person with dementia and his or her partner can share together, intimacy may enable the person with dementia to both maintain his or her role identity and give something of value to his or her partner (Kuhn, 1994; Davies *et al.*, 1998). For the carer, intimacy may be an important source of support and a means of coping with his or her partner's devastating illness (Ballard, 1995).

Although sexual apathy is the most likely change in the sexual behaviour, some people with dementia at some stage develop an increased sex drive (Harris & Weir, 1998). When increased sexual behaviour occurs, it may be one of the more difficult problems encountered by a couple living with one partner's dementia (Kuhn, 1994). The person with dementia may behave without any apparent feeling or consideration for his or her partner, who may be emotionally and physically exhausted by the caring role and may find it difficult to respond to the person with dementia's sexual demands (Kuhn, 1994). Where the person with dementia's partner attempts to regulate the frequency of sex, this may cause conflict (Kuhn, 1994).

As dementia progresses, the person with dementia's partner may seek to avoid sex because the person with dementia no longer seems like a lover or spouse (Hanks, 1992; Kuhn, 1994). Partners of people with dementia may feel distressed about sexual overtures from someone who no longer knows their name or at times does not recognise who they are (Davies *et al.*, 1992), or may no longer find their partner sexually desirable due to the intimate tasks required in helping with toileting, washing and maintaining hygiene (Hanks, 1992). Partners of people with dementia may also experience worry and guilt about intimacy because they feel that the person with dementia cannot fully consent or participate in sex (Hanks, 1992; Kuhn, 1994).

If the person with dementia lives in a care home, opportunities for partners to express physical affection may be severely limited by the lack of privacy, as people may feel embarrassed to hold hands or kiss in public or to have sex in the resident's room. The lack of intimacy may cause frustration and anger in the person with dementia, which could contribute towards periods of behaviour that challenges while at the same time causing his or her partner to feel even more lonely and miserable.

4.8   DISCLOSURE/STIGMA

Assessment and reaching a conclusion about the diagnosis leads to a point where this information should be shared with the person with dementia. This is especially challenging in dementia for a number of reasons:

- the difficulty of accurate diagnosis
- the challenge of imparting 'bad news'
- uncertainty about whether or not the person will understand what is being said
- uncertainty about whether or not the person will retain what is said
- lack of follow-up support.

Studies, in which people with dementia have been invited to tell the story of how they reached a memory assessment service and what the assessment process felt like, indicate that this is not an easy journey for them (Keady & Gilliard, 2002). Often, they have been aware of their memory difficulties for some time before sharing this information with others (usually, but not always, their close family). This awareness may occur in quite private activities, like doing crossword puzzles. In the meantime, those who are closest to the person may also have been aware of the difficulties but have fought shy of sharing their concerns. Disclosing their concerns to each other is often what triggers a visit to the GP and referral to a memory assessment service (Keady & Gilliard, 2002).

People have reported that their visits to the memory assessment service can also be quite an ordeal (Keady & Gilliard, 2002). This is often like no other outpatient clinic. The doctor may speak to the carer separately from the person being assessed, leading to suspicion about what is being said. The assessment process itself may prove embarrassing, even humiliating. People report that they are aware that some of the questions are simple and feel foolish that they are unable to answer. They may establish strategies for managing this (Keady & Gilliard, 2002).

Whilst recognising that most people are seeking to make sense of what is happening to them, it is important to acknowledge that some will find it hard to listen to their diagnosis and there will be some who will not want to be told at all. They know they have a problem with their memory and that they are not able to function as they once did or as their peers do. They want to know what is wrong with them, and they need the clinician to be honest with them. Telling someone that he or she has a memory problem is only telling him or her what he or she already knows. People should be told their diagnosis as clearly and honestly as possible.

The moment of sharing the diagnosis may not be comfortable for any of those concerned – neither the clinician, nor the person with dementia, nor his or her carer (Friel McGowan, 1993). Without this knowledge, people cannot begin to make sense of what is happening, nor can they plan effectively for their future. They should be given a choice of treatments and need information about practical support and entitlements, like Lasting Powers of Attorney and advance decisions to refuse treatment (more information can be found in Section 4.9.4 and in the Mental Capacity Act 2005 [The Stationery Office, 2005]). They will want to make decisions about how they spend their time before life becomes more difficult for them (for example, visiting family abroad).

Following the disclosure of the diagnosis, people with dementia and their families may want further support and opportunities for talking. Pre- and post-assessment counselling services should be part of the specialist memory assessment service. Recent work (Cheston *et al.*, 2003a) has shown the value of psychotherapeutic support groups for people with dementia, allowing them space to share their feelings with others. Joint interventions with the person with dementia and family carers, such as family therapy, recognise the fact that the diagnosis does not impact on just one person but on a whole family system (Gilleard, 1996). Other services have used volunteer 'befrienders' to maintain contact with people who are newly diagnosed and who can offer both practical support and information together with a 'listening ear'. People with early dementia are also taking responsibility for their own support by forming groups, which may meet regularly or may be virtual networks using the internet (see, for example, www.dasninternational.org).

Sensitivity is required in ensuring that information about the diagnosis is given in a way that is easily understood by the person concerned and acceptable to the family. Gentle questioning at an early stage will help to ascertain what people can, and want, to be told. There is much we can learn from earlier work on sharing the diagnosis with people with cancer (for example, Buckman, 1996). It is especially important to be aware of different cultural sensitivities and the stigma that dementia holds for many people. This can range from subjective feelings of shame to a real exclusion from community and family life. Age and ethnicity are both factors in the sense of stigma associated with a diagnosis of dementia (Patel *et al.*, 1998).

4.9   BASIC LEGAL AND ETHICAL CONCEPTS IN CONNECTION WITH DEMENTIA CARE

4.9.1   Introduction

The ethical problems that arise in the context of dementia mainly relate to autonomy, which is compromised in dementia to varying degrees. Respect for autonomy is recognised as a key principle in health and social care (Beauchamp & Childress, 2001). Many of the ethical tensions that arise in looking after people with dementia do so because of, on the one hand, the requirement that autonomy ought to be respected and, on the other, the reality of increasing dependency, where this entails a loss of personal freedom.

Person-centred care is a means of respecting personal autonomy wherever it is threatened (Kitwood, 1997). As Agich has stated, 'Autonomy fundamentally importantly involves the way individuals live their daily lives; it is found in the nooks and crannies of everyday experience' (Agich, 2003).

Hence, respecting the person's autonomy will involve day-to-day interactions and will be achieved if the person with dementia is not positioned in such a way as to impede his or her remaining abilities. Such 'malignant positioning' can be the result of inappropriate psychosocial structures. The fundamental way to combat this tendency, which undermines the person's selfhood, is to encourage good-quality communication (Kitwood, 1997; Sabat, 2001).

Another way in which selfhood might be undermined is through structural or procedural barriers to good-quality care, and service providers should take an active role in promoting the individual's autonomy and his or her legal and human rights. Furthermore, services may discriminate against people with dementia if eligibility criteria are drawn up in such a way as to exclude them or because of an assumption that people with dementia cannot benefit from a service because staff lack confidence and skills in working with this group. Discrimination may also occur if a service does not offer people with dementia the support they may need in order for them to be able to make use of the service. The Disability Discrimination Acts (1995 and 2005), which include dementia within the definition of disability, aim to end the discrimination that many disabled people face in their everyday lives by making direct or indirect discrimination against disabled people unlawful in a range of areas including access to facilities and services and buying or renting property.

The discussion that follows will briefly focus on human rights, consent, capacity and confidentiality.

4.9.2   Human rights

Human rights are enshrined, as far as the United Kingdom is concerned, in the *Convention for the Protection of Human Rights and Fundamental Freedoms* (Council of Europe, 2003). The relevant UK legislation is the Human Rights Act 1998, which came into force in 2000. The principle of respect for autonomy is implicit throughout the Convention. A number of the articles of the Convention are potentially relevant to people with dementia. For example, Article 2 asserts that everyone has a right to life, Article 3 prohibits torture, but also "inhuman or degrading treatment", and Article 8 concerns the right to respect for the person's private and family life.

Article 5 asserts the right of people to liberty and security. It states that "No one should be deprived of his liberty", except in very specific circumstances. It also asserts that if someone is deprived of his or her liberty, there should be recourse to a court. Article 5 was central to the 'Bournewood' case. The European Court declared, amongst other things, that the man concerned (who had a learning disability) had been deprived of his liberty, in contravention of Article 5 (see Department of Health, 2004, for further information).

The crucial distinction to emerge from the case was that between *deprivation* of liberty and *restriction* of liberty. Whilst the former is illegal, except insofar as there are legal safeguards of the sort provided by the Mental Health Act 1983 (HMSO, 1983), the latter may be permissible under the sort of circumstances envisaged by Section 6 of the Mental Capacity Act 2005 (TSO, 2005). This discusses using restraint as a proportionate response to the possibility of the person suffering harm. Guidance on the distinction between 'restriction' and 'deprivation' of liberty has been provided by the Department of Health and the National Assembly for Wales (Department of Health, 2004).

4.9.3   Consent

In brief, for consent to be valid it must be:
● informed
● competent
● uncoerced
● continuing.

Each of these concepts requires interpretation and judgement, as none of them is entirely unproblematic (Department of Health, 2001a). For instance, people can be more or less informed. The 'Sidaway' case (1984) established that the legal standard as regards informing a patient was the same as for negligence (see the 'Bolam case', 1957). In other words, the person should be given as much information as a 'responsible body' of medical opinion would deem appropriate. However, since then, there has been a shift away from a professional-centred standard towards a patient-centred standard. In the 'Pearce' case (1998), one of the Law Lords declared that information should be given where there exists 'a significant risk which would affect the judgement of a reasonable patient'.

Department of Health guidelines (Department of Health, 2001c) have pointed out that, although informing patients about the nature and purpose of procedures may be enough to avoid a claim of battery, it may not be sufficient to fulfill the legal duty of care. There may be other pieces of information relevant to the individual patient that it would be negligent not to mention. Hence the General Medical Council (GMC)'s insistence that doctors should do their best 'to find out about patients' individual needs and priorities' (GMC, 1998). The GMC guidance goes on to say: 'You should not make assumptions about patients' views'.

These points are very relevant when it comes to consent in the context of dementia. It should be kept in mind that consent is not solely an issue as regards medical procedures. The 'nooks and crannies of everyday experience' (Agich, 2003) – what to wear or to eat, whether to go out or participate in an activity and whether to accept extra home or respite care – are all aspects of life to which the person with dementia may or may not wish to consent. If the person has capacity with respect to the particular decision, but does not wish to consent, he or she should be supported in making an autonomous decision.

4.9.4   Decision-making capacity

In England and Wales, a lack of capacity has been defined thus:

> '... *a person lacks capacity in relation to a matter if at the material time he is unable to make a decision for himself in relation to the matter because of an impairment of, or a disturbance in the functioning of, the mind or brain'* (Mental Capacity Act 2005 [TSO, 2005, Section 2]).

A person is further defined as unable to make a decision if he or she is unable:

'*(a)* *to understand the information relevant to the decision,*

(b) *to retain this information,*

(c) *to use or weigh that information as part of the process of making the decision, or*

(d) *to communicate his decision (whether by talking, using sign language or any other means)' (Mental Capacity Act 2005 [TSO, 2005, Section 3(1)]).*

The Mental Capacity Act 2005 (TSO, 2005), which will apply in England and Wales[31], sets out a framework for making decisions for people who are unable to make decisions for themselves. Its detailed provisions, along with its Code of Practice (currently in draft form [DCA, 2005]), should be referred to by all those involved in such decision making. In outline, the main provisions of the Act:

- offer a definition of lack of capacity (Sections 2–3)
- outline a process for the determination of a person's best interests (Section 4)
- create Lasting Powers of Attorney, which allow a person to appoint a donee to make decisions about his or her health and welfare (Sections 9–14)
- establish the Court of Protection in a new form, with powers to make declarations and appoint deputies in difficult cases or where there are disputes concerning decisions about a person's health and welfare (Sections 15–23)
- bring under statute and clarify the law regarding advance decisions to refuse treatment (Sections 24–26)
- set out safeguards concerning research with people who lack the capacity to consent (Sections 30–34)
- outline the requirement to appoint an independent mental capacity advocate if the person who lacks capacity requires 'serious medical treatment' or a change in long-term accommodation but lacks anyone else, other than those engaged in his or her care or treatment, to offer support or advice (Sections 35–41).

The SCIE practice guide on assessing the mental health needs of older people outlines the key dimensions of the Mental Capacity Act 2005 (SCIE, 2006) and the Department of Health is currently preparing a code of practice to support the implementation of the Act.

4.9.5 Confidentiality

People with dementia, no less than any others, have a right to expect that information given in confidence to professionals will be kept confidential. Guidance from professional bodies (for example, GMC, 2004; Royal College of Psychiatrists, 2006a) outlines the circumstances under which confidential information can be shared. These circumstances tend to be extreme, such as when public safety is threatened. Generally speaking, however, if a professional intends to break confidence this should be discussed with the

---

[31]The Mental Capacity Act 2005 is on the statute book but not yet introduced. It will come into force in April 2007.

person concerned and his or her agreement should be sought. This remains true when the person has dementia. An example of this sort of situation is when the professional feels it necessary to inform the Driver and Vehicle Licensing Agency (DVLA) that the person has a condition that may impair his or her ability to drive. In these circumstances, good practice suggests that, in the first instance, the person should be encouraged to contact the DVLA him- or herself. Thus, from an ethical point of view the issue of confidentiality in dementia care illustrates the delicate balance that has to be maintained between respecting the person's autonomy and recognising the complex ways in which people in a society are mutually dependent and inter-related (Hughes & Louw, 2002).

4.10   TREATMENT AND CARE OF PEOPLE WITH DEMENTIA IN ENGLAND AND WALES

4.10.1   Detection, recognition and referral

There is evidence of delays in the recognition of dementia syndromes in primary care, and of sub-optimal management, although there is also anecdotal evidence that diagnostic skills have improved in the last decade. Delays in recognition are due to a variety of factors, including the complex and variable ways in which cognitive impairment shows itself; the person with dementia and his or her family's reluctance to acknowledge changes in cognition and behaviour as problematic and to seek help; and professional attribution of changes to 'normal ageing' or other explanations (De Lepeleire & Heyrman, 1999; van Hout *et al.*, 2000).

General practitioners describe themselves as under-skilled in the recognition and management of dementia syndromes, and a significant minority believe care of people with dementia is the responsibility of specialist services (Audit Commission, 2000). However, there is also evidence that general practitioners' diagnostic skills for dementia are better than reported and that the main difficulties lie with disclosure of the diagnosis in the early stages (De Lepeleire *et al.*, 1998; De Lepeleire & Heyrman, 1999) and with management of behaviour changes in the later stages of the disease.

A perception that specialist services are absent or unresponsive can inhibit the recognition of dementia syndromes (Iliffe *et al.*, 2006); the development of dementia collaboratives can address and may modify this perception.

Postgraduate professional development programmes are available to support dementia education in the community, of which at least one has been shown to change recognition rates in a randomised controlled trial (Downs *et al.*, 2006).

4.10.2   Assessment and coordination of care

The organisational arrangements for needs assessment and case management of people with dementia are highly variable, with decisions about key-worker roles being decided according to local resource availability and priorities. The consequence of this local variation is that there is no comprehensive system of case management comparable to that of other long-term conditions like diabetes or asthma, and individuals may not receive the assessments and care that they need, particularly at the earlier stages of the disease. The new contract for general practice now includes targets for dementia care within its quality outcomes framework, so there is a link between performance in dementia care and remuneration. However, this is as yet only limited and does not extend to details of concordance with diagnostic and management guidelines.

The involvement of family members or others as organisers and advocates may determine how much care and support is available. Voluntary organisations can play an important educational, advisory and support role. For example, they often provide or signpost sources of support such as benefits advice and advice about eligibility for continuing care, but many individuals with dementia are not in contact with them. While in some areas voluntary organisations either do not have a presence or do not provide a full range of services, some organisations do provide national helplines that people with dementia and carers can use to access information and advice or support.

However, there are a variety of disciplines with expertise in dementia care in many communities, from social work to community nursing, and these skills need to be mobilised if assessment and care coordination are to be optimised. There is an argument for developing a generic system of case management for people with dementia, using locally available skills to create the kind of multidisciplinary assessment and management team needed (Challis *et al.*, 2002). The widespread involvement of general practitioners in this re-engineering of services would probably require further change in the GP contract.

4.10.3   Pharmacological treatment

Dementias have often been regarded as untreatable, with the exception of dementias of uncommon aetiology such as that caused by folic acid deficiency. However, careful assessment and the development of comprehensive multidisciplinary care plans to address personal, social, medical and behavioural problems associated with dementia have become the mainstay of treatment and care programmes in the delivery of high-quality care for people with dementia and their carers.

The search for more specific treatments began in the 1980s and 1990s with the introduction of codergocrine mesylate, which was used as an adjunct in the management of elderly people with mild to moderate dementia. Naftidrofuryl oxalate was introduced for the management of cerebral vascular disorders and thought to be of relevance in the treatment of VaD. However, neither of these drugs proved to be particularly effective in the treatment of any form of dementia and both fell into disuse.

New approaches to the pharmacological treatment of dementia, and in particular to AD, began with the introduction of the acetylcholinesterase inhibitors, which inhibit the breakdown of acetylcholine, a neurotransmitter thought to be important in the chemical basis of a number of cognitive processes including memory, thought and judgement. Acetylcholine was also thought to be involved in some behavioural disturbances, although this is speculative. Acetylcholinesterase inhibitors used in clinical practice include rivastigmine, donepezil and galantamine.

More recently, memantine has been introduced for the treatment of moderate to severe AD, again primarily used for its effect upon cognition, although some behavioural effects have been noted. Memantine works primarily through its action upon glutamate transmission and more specifically on particular subtypes of receptors within glutamate systems particularly related to memory (N-methyl-D-aspartate [NMDA] receptors).

Dosing of medication in Alzheimer's disease

Donepezil is the simplest drug to use, being a tablet given once a day and having only two different doses (5 mg and 10 mg), both of which are considered to be effective doses. Rivastigmine is given twice daily with morning and evening meals. There are four capsule strengths: 1.5 mg, 3 mg, 4.5 mg and 6 mg. Dosing commences with 1.5 mg twice daily, whilst the effective dose is 3–6 mg twice daily. Galantamine is also given twice daily (preferably with the morning and evening meal) as tablets, beginning at 4 mg and increasing to 8 mg and 12 mg. The effective dose is 8–12 mg twice a day. More recently, a once-daily formulation of galantamine has been made available with capsules to be taken in the morning, preferably with food, beginning at 8 mg and increasing to 16 mg and 24 mg.

In 2001, a NICE technology appraisal (TA019) recommended that these drugs should be made available as a component of the management of people with mild and moderate AD whose score on the MMSE was 12 or above. The appraisal advised that drug therapy should be initiated by a specialist following assessment, which should include tests of cognitive, global and behavioural functioning and of activities of daily living; general practitioners should only take over prescribing under an agreed shared-care protocol. Treatment should only be continued in people with dementia where, usually 2–4 months after reaching the maintenance dose of the drug, there was an improvement or no deterioration in the MMSE score, together with evidence of global improvement on the basis of behavioural and/or functional assessment. Assessment should be repeated every 6 months, and the drugs should normally only be continued with an MMSE score of above 12 and where the individual's global, functional and behavioural condition remains at a level where the drugs are still considered to be having a 'worthwhile effect'.

At the same time as developing this guideline, NICE undertook a fresh technology appraisal (and a review of the existing guidance TA019), examining the use of donepezil, rivastigmine, galantamine and memantine in the treatment of AD. The Guideline Development Group did not have any responsibility for the development of the technology appraisal. Nevertheless, its recommendations were incorporated into this guideline when the technology appraisal was finalised (where one of these recommendations appears, it is indicated as NICE, 2006).

4.10.4 Physical healthcare

Coexistent medical problems are very common in people with dementia. Most people with dementia are elderly and are therefore likely to suffer from other illnesses, both acute and chronic. It is very important not to assume that every physical or mental problem a person with dementia experiences arises because of the dementia (Jones, 2000). Elderly people with dementia frequently have other therapeutically important medical conditions. Problems such as urinary incontinence or increased confusion can arise for a number of reasons. One prospective study of 200 elderly outpatients with dementia identified 248 other medical diagnoses in 124 of them; 92 of the diagnoses were new (Larson *et al.*, 1986).

Coexistent medical problems require careful management. Another illness can increase a person's confusion either temporarily or chronically. Drugs used to treat other conditions may themselves be responsible for worsening cognition. Whilst other medical problems may have an adverse effect on the quality of life for people with dementia and carers, their over-zealous treatment, particularly at the end stage of dementia may be distressing as well. The existence of dementia may require modification in the treatment of other medical conditions. For example, dementia appears to be a significant independent determinant of non-treatment with aspirin or warfarin when otherwise indicated for the prevention of recurrent stroke (Moroney *et al.*, 1999b). In addition, there is an understandable reluctance to use warfarin in people with a condition like AD if compliance cannot be guaranteed because of the risk of overdosage, which may lead to haemorrhage.

Medical problems and their treatment can be aggravated by the inability of a person with dementia to report his or her own symptoms, so that regular review is essential. This becomes especially important when there has been acute deterioration in either cognition or behaviour. Common conditions may present in an atypical or non-specific manner. For example, a significant association between an impaired mental test score and atypical presentation of myocardial infarction has been observed (Black, 1987). It is also easy to overlook standard health measures such as an annual immunisation against influenza and regular eye checks.

The physical health problems that are a common feature of increasing longevity pose an additional difficulty for people with dementia. The presence of dementia increases the risk of delirium with any concurrent physical illness (Elie *et al.*, 1998). Delirium can cause increased confusion, behavioural problems and sleep disturbance. The delirium or the underlying physical problem will frequently precipitate an admission to a general hospital for physical treatment and this poses a further challenge for those with dementia and the services trying to care for them. For the person with dementia, he or she is unwell, possibly more confused and moved from familiar surroundings into a strange and frightening environment.

In a typical general hospital of 500 beds, 330 of those beds will be occupied by older people (Department of Health, 2001b), of whom 102 will have dementia (Royal College of Psychiatrists, 2005a). For inpatients in a General Hospital, dementia is an independent predictor of poor outcome, including increased mortality, increased length of stay, loss of function and higher rates of institutionalisation (Holmes & House, 2000).

Improving outcomes has important implications for people with dementia and the utilisation of resources. For instance, in a population of people with hip fracture, care from an intensive, specialist, multidisciplinary rehabilitation team achieved a reduction in length of stay in those with mild to moderate dementia. Those with mild impairment were as successful at returning to independent living as those without dementia (Nightingale *et al.*, 2001). Such a team would increase the awareness, in general hospital staff, of the problems associated with dementia. Through education and training, the team could facilitate the acquisition of basic skills in assessment and treatment.

Admission to a general hospital may be the first opportunity to identify dementia and all staff need to be able to recognise the symptoms, give information and advice to patients and carers, and be able to refer for a specialist assessment.

4.10.5 Psychological interventions

Psychological interventions for people with dementia have a long history. An evaluation of the effects of a variety of activities on people who would now be described as having dementia was published nearly 50 years ago (Cosin *et al.*, 1958). One theory likened the experience of dementia to sensory deprivation, with the person typically receiving little stimulation, whether at home or in an institution (Bower, 1967). Stimulation programmes of various kinds were developed and are still evident in the widespread use of music and other forms of sensory stimulation in dementia care. The disorientation typically observed in dementia was also targeted early on through the development in the US of reality orientation programmes, which did appear to be associated with small improvements in cognitive function (Taulbee & Folsom, 1966; Brook *et al.*, 1975; Woods, 1979). This approach led to widespread use of orientation aids and signposting in most dementia care facilities.

There are a wide range of psychological interventions currently provided in the UK for people with dementia, but their availability varies greatly. In the early stages of dementia, individual psychological treatment may be offered; this may focus on enhancing adjustment and mood, using cognitive behavioural therapy (CBT) (Scholey & Woods, 2003) or life review, and/or on strategies to improve memory, using a cognitive rehabilitation approach (Clare, 2003). In some areas, group activities for people in the early stages of dementia may be offered, with a similar range of goals (Cheston *et al.*, 2003a; Kipling *et al.*, 1999).

Interventions for people in the later stages may include a variety of group activities, including cognitive stimulation, reminiscence, music, and arts and crafts (Spector *et al.*, 2003; Holden & Woods, 1995; Gibson, 2004). These may be offered in day-care centres or in care homes. Well-being and quality of life are the aims here, helping the person to participate in enjoyable activities, often in a social context, and to be engaged with others rather than withdrawn into an inner world.

Increasingly, the intervention is provided personally in day-to-day contact with the person with dementia, whether through a family carer or a care worker. Psychological approaches to maintaining the person's self-care abilities and independence have been developed and involve good communication skills, prompting and providing just enough help for the person to complete the task for him- or herself (Woods, 1999). Training and support are needed for carers and care workers to be able to put these approaches into practice. This is also the case when the carer or care worker finds aspects of the person's behaviour difficult to manage. Behavioural approaches aim to help in finding ways of understanding where the problem lies and responding to the difficulty; sometimes, difficult behaviour can be averted by the carer or care worker modifying his or her approach or changing something in the environment (Moniz-Cook *et al.*, 2003). Although guidelines recommend that such behavioural management approaches be pursued before considering the prescription of psychotropic medication (Howard *et al.*, 2001), this is often not the case in practice.

In the late stages of dementia, sensory stimulation is the primary form of psychological intervention. The aim is often to provide relaxing stimulation and to reduce agitation and distress (multi-sensory stimulation equipment is widely used for this purpose); hand massage and aromatherapy are sometimes offered (Baker *et al.*, 1997; Burns *et al.*, 2002). Music and supported contact with trained pet dogs and other animals are other forms of stimulation that are available in a number of centres.

Whilst interventions with individuals or groups are important, a need for the whole care setting to support and facilitate a psychological approach is often highlighted. For example, changes to the regime of care in a care home will arguably have a much greater impact on the well-being of residents than a once-weekly group session (Brane *et al.*, 1989). Such a change involves changes in attitudes and behaviour, and sometimes changes to the physical as well as the social environment. The principles of person-centred care, as set out by Kitwood (1997) have achieved a broad consensus of support in dementia care in the UK, but it is readily acknowledged that their implementation is a challenge for those responsible for the management of care. Dementia care mapping is one observational method that has been developed to assist in helping care workers and managers to reflect on and develop their practice (Brooker *et al.*, 1998). Staff training and supervision are key issues in the implementation of a psychological approach, with a need in many settings to retain staff so that a consistent approach may be developed.

Psychological interventions for family carers are available in many areas. These include individual psychological treatment (such as CBT) for depression and anxiety in the significant proportion of carers where the difficulties of providing care contribute to a mental health problem (Marriott *et al.*, 2000). Individual work on problem-solving and coping skills may also be available. Groups for family carers are widely available and encompass a broad range of models of intervention, from the psychotherapeutic to peer support (Pusey & Richards, 2001). Interventions need to be geared to the different stages of the care-giving career, with particular issues arising for those carers where the person with dementia has been admitted to a long-term care facility and some requiring support after the death of the person.

Joint interventions with the person with dementia and family carers are now developing. These include applications of family therapy (Gilleard, 1996) and groups where people with dementia and family carers are involved together. The aims of this work may include improving the quality of the relationship, which potentially has an impact on quality of life and well-being for all concerned.

4.10.6   Social care

Social care covers all the different types of support that people of all ages may need to live as independently, safely and fully as possible, provided by local councils, private companies and voluntary organisations. It covers a diverse range of services, including care homes, sheltered housing, respite or short-break care, day services, home care and meals services, and often operates alongside other services, such as health or housing.

Most people with dementia are able to live in their own homes for most of their lives, and most care is given by families. Between 36% and 53% of people with mild to moderate dementia live in the community, and 35% of those with high-level needs live at home supported by carers (Melzer *et al.*, 1997, cited Parsons, 2001). The ability to provide care usually depends on proximity, and co-resident care is where the greatest intensity of care takes place. In most cases, this means care by a spouse or partner (Tinker, 2000), and requests for additional support from services are often precipitated by the ill health of carers (Parsons, 2001). The ensuing process of assessing need, planning and implementing a combination of services is referred to as 'care management'. An overriding objective for social-care service commissioners is to maintain people in their own home for as long as possible, including intensive home care schemes (Department of Health, 2001b & Department of Health/Care Services Improvement Partnership 2005). Thus, social care for dementia has largely centred on the deployment of domiciliary (home care) support, respite or short-break care and day care to support carers to cope with the increasing disability of people living with dementia or, if people live alone or have no carers, to support them in independent living for as long as possible. These services may be supplemented by adaptations to the home, undertaken by local councils, housing agencies or private providers, to reduce risks associated with failing memory and increasing disorientation. As well as providing physical care, home-based services should aim to provide a positive experience for the person with dementia, with opportunities for him or her to continue with his or her preferred activities.

Very sheltered housing with enhanced facilities, such as 24-hour care on site and provision of some meals, is another service option when people's needs are too great to be met through domiciliary support. When this is not sufficient, a move to residential care may be considered. Long-term residential care is usually prioritised for people with physical or persistent non-cognitive symptoms, such as behaviour that challenges. Shortage of places and greater life expectancy has led to higher concentrations in care homes of more frail and disabled older people and more people with dementia. At the same time, residential care work has remained low in status, with little training, and there are few homes led by staff with professional qualifications (Means, 2000). Nevertheless, as expectations of more person-centred approaches to dementia care develop, there is a little evidence of more diversified and personalised approaches to residential care (Judd *et al.*, 1997, cited Marshall, 2001).

Various issues have emerged in social care for people with dementia that have been under-recognised (Stanley & Cantley, 2001) in whatever setting care is delivered; these include recognition of the needs of people from black and ethnic minorities, including those for whom English is not a first language; the complexities of working alongside people with learning difficulties and dementia; managing behaviour that challenges in residential and day services, including 'wandering'; and ensuring the protection of people living with dementia from abuse and neglect.

4.10.7   Current care allowances

A diagnosis of dementia will have an impact on a person's financial status due to the extra costs arising from the illness and, in some circumstances, on the carer's financial status as well, as he or she may, for instance, have to work part-time or take early retirement to undertake full-time care.

Financial assistance is available to people with dementia and their carers from the state, the local council and the NHS. The main state benefits for people with dementia are Attendance Allowance for people aged 65 and over and Disability Living Allowance for people under the age of 65, neither of which is related to income or savings. People with dementia aged 60 and over with state pensions and/or low incomes may qualify for Pension Credit. People with dementia below the age of 60 who are unable to work full time may be entitled to Incapacity Benefit or Income Support. Carers who are unable to work full time because they are caring for a person with dementia for at least 35 hours a week may apply for Carer's Allowance, but it can only be claimed once the person with dementia's Attendance Allowance or Disability Living Allowance has been agreed. To qualify for Carer's Allowance, the carer must be on a low income (currently the level is less than £84 per week) and not in education for more than 21 hours per week. A carer cannot receive Carer's Allowance for more than one disabled person and two carers cannot share the allowance.

The allowances available to people with dementia differ depending on their living circumstances, for example living alone, living alone but with a carer who claims Carer's Allowance, living with a partner who provides care or living with a carer who is not a partner. Other allowances include exemption from council tax for people living alone who receive either Attendance Allowance or Disability Living Allowance (where they live with one other person, then a 25% discount can be claimed), Housing Benefit, and other grants and assistance (for example, grants from the Social Fund to purchase essential kitchen appliances or pay for adaptations or repairs to the home, Community Care Grants and help with health costs). Assistance with travel costs to and from hospital appointments may be available from the NHS.

Both the person with dementia and the carer need to be made aware of the long term implications of the illness on the management of their finances and property and should be encouraged to seek advice concerning Lasting Power of Attorney (more information can be found on the Department for Constitutional Affairs website).

Advice on benefits and other financial support can be obtained from council benefits officers and benefits advisers at voluntary organisations. Some social workers and nurses may be able to offer advice but this is not usually their role.

4.10.8   Inpatient dementia services

The central tenet of this guideline is that people with dementia should be assessed and treated as far as possible within their own, familiar environment and exercising as much choice and self-determination as possible. Brodaty and colleagues (2003c) suggests that with skilled teams in the community, such as outreach services and crisis resolution and home treatment teams, less than 1% of people with dementia should require treatment in an inpatient unit. However, inpatient services may be required to assess and treat people with dementia in the following circumstances:

● the person with dementia is severely disturbed and is required to be contained for the safety of his- or herself and/or others, including those liable to be detained under the Mental Health Act 1983
● assessment in a community setting is not possible, for example where a person with dementia has complex physical and psychiatric problems.

The role of the inpatient unit is to provide a safe environment, staffed by clinicians who are trained in the care of people with dementia, the assessment and management of those with behaviour that challenges and the management of aggression and violence. Admission to an inpatient unit should have a clear objective that is shared from the outset with the person with dementia, the carer and the multidisciplinary team. When the objective has been achieved, there should be an efficient discharge process, supported by community resources.

Given the high incidence of physical morbidity within the client group (see Section 4.10.4), an inpatient assessment unit for people with dementia is best placed on a district general hospital site to give prompt access to physical care when needed. Ideally the unit would be staffed by dual-trained nursing staff and/or would be managed jointly by physicians for the care of the elderly and old age psychiatrists. There should be full multidisciplinary input to the inpatient service including physiotherapy, occupational therapy, speech and language therapy, and psychological therapy to ensure a multi-skilled approach for people with dementia. Careful consideration should be given to the physical design of the unit, taking into account recommendations given in Section 5.4.3, with a high proportion of single rooms and a safe, low-stimulation area available for the management of those who are severely disturbed. Given the high level of need, the units should have no more than 12 residents.

Inpatient units should also act as a source of expertise to offer advice and provide training to other areas of the service in the management of behavioural and psychological symptoms of dementia.

4.11   PALLIATIVE CARE, PAIN RELIEF AND CARE AT THE END OF LIFE FOR PEOPLE WITH DEMENTIA

4.11.1   Introduction

The definition of palliative care emphasises its 'total' nature, encompassing not only physical symptoms, but also the psychological, social and spiritual aspects of non-curable diseases. The aim is to achieve 'the best quality of life for patients and their families' from an early point in the disease (World Health Organization (WHO), 1990). NICE has produced a manual on improving supportive and palliative care for adults with cancer (NICE, 2004a) and, although this manual is focused on services for adult patients with cancer and their families, it may inform the development of service models for other groups of patients. The NICE manual recommends three tools to support high-quality care for end of life: the Gold Standards Framework (see www.goldstandardsframework.nhs.uk/) (Thomas, 2003), the Liverpool Care Pathway for the dying patient (see www.lcp-mariecurie.org.uk/) (Ellershaw & Wilkinson, 2003) and the Preferred Place of Care Plan (see www.cancerlancashire.org.uk/ppc.html). The NHS End of Life Care Programme aims to improve care at the end of life for all and the programme website (http://eolc.cbcl.co.uk/eolc/) provides good practice, information and resources including links to the three tools recommended by the NICE palliative care manual (NICE, 2004a).

There is now considerable interest in the notion of palliative care for older people and in dementia (House of Commons Health Committee, 2004b; Hughes *et al.*, 2005a; WHO, 2004; National Council for Palliative Care, 2006). Retrospective case-note studies in the UK in psychiatric and acute hospital wards have suggested there is inadequate palliative care for people with dementia (Lloyd-Williams 1996, Sampson *et al.*, 2006). In a retrospective survey of carers (McCarthy *et al.*, 1997), the most commonly reported symptoms suffered by the person with dementia in the last year of life were confusion (83%), urinary incontinence (72%), pain (64%), low mood (61%), constipation (59%) and loss of appetite (57%). More recent research from the USA continues to paint a picture of sub-optimal palliative care for people with dementia in nursing homes and in hospital (Mitchell *et al.*, 2004a; Mitchell *et al.*, 2004b; Aminoff & Adunsky 2004). A similar picture emerges from a more recent synthesis of the research evidence (Davies, 2004), and a survey of care more generally for people with dementia in private and NHS facilities in the UK leaves little room for optimism (Ballard *et al.*, 2001). Given the need for improvement in terms of quality of care and the lack of evidence to support arguments concerning what constitutes good-quality palliative care in dementia, the need for further research is paramount (Bayer, 2006).

4.11.2   Defining palliative care in dementia

Palliative care can be thought of as a spectrum ranging from the palliative care approach to specialist palliative care (Addington-Hall, 1998). The palliative care approach should be integral to all clinical practice involving chronic, terminal disease and equates to good-quality person centred care in dementia (Hughes *et al.*, 2005b). Specialist palliative care, especially care in the last few days of illness, will be much the same in dementia as it is in cancer (NICE, 2004a). Most people with dementia die in long-term care or in hospitals, with only about 19% dying at home (Kay *et al.*, 2000) and very few using hospices (McCarthy *et al.*, 1997). Between the palliative care approach and specialist palliative care lie palliative interventions, which are non-curative treatments aimed at improving symptoms and signs of distress in order to maximise quality of life. In dementia, an area of focused intervention might be in the field of the behavioural and psychological signs of dementia (BPSD).

4.11.3   Specific issues at the end of life in dementia

The issue of the definition of palliative care in dementia is not without consequence. For instance, whilst it seems intuitively clear that the palliative care approach is applicable, a recent systematic review found little evidence to support its use in dementia (Sampson *et al.*, 2005). The reviewers commented, however, that the result might reflect ethical difficulties surrounding such research, prognostic uncertainty and the lack of clear outcome measures. In addition, there may be specific issues (some of which are dealt with below) relevant to palliative care where the evidence base is to be found elsewhere.

4.11.4   Ethics and the end of life in dementia

Palliative care in dementia raises many difficult ethical issues (Purtilo & ten Have, 2004). In order to deal with ethical dilemmas appropriately, clinicians must rely on background ethical or moral theories. For instance, the doctrine of double effect states that it is lawful to pursue treatments where bad effects can be foreseen but are not intended. A less contentious doctrine, which informs much of palliative care, is that of ordinary and extraordinary means. This suggests that where there is a lack of proportion between the proposed intervention and the likely clinical benefit, either because the intervention is too burdensome or lacking in efficacy, there is no moral obligation to pursue the treatment (Jeffrey, 2001). Some of the difficult issues to do with care at the end of life are dealt with in professional guidance (for example, see *Withholding and Withdrawing Life-Prolonging Treatments: Good Practice in Decision-Making*, GMC, 2002, and Section 3.9.4 of the 2005 Mental Capacity Act).

The possibility of diverse and disputed values in the area of end-of-life care suggests the applicability within this field of values-based medicine (VBM) (Fulford, 2004). VBM can be regarded as a complement to evidence-based medicine, but with the emphasis on weighing up contrasting values, in addition to the weighing up of evidence that is a necessary part of good medical practice (Woodbridge & Fulford 2004).

4.11.5   Artificial nutrition and hydration

Swallowing problems become increasingly noticeable as dementia worsens, with the possibility of aspiration pneumonia in the severer stages (Feinberg *et al.*, 1992). Nasogastric and percutaneous endoscopic gastrostomy tubes would seem to provide a safer way to feed people with severe dementia and dysphagia. However, a review of the evidence in 1999 found no relevant randomised clinical trials comparing tube feeding and oral feeding. On the basis of the available data, the reviewers concluded that the best evidence did not support the use of tube feeding in dementia (Finucane *et al.*, 1999). Ethical commentary, making use of this review, concluded that, although there may be individual cases in which tube feeding is not futile, 'balancing the risks and benefits leads to the conclusion that [feeding tubes] are seldom warranted for patients in the final stages of dementia' (Gillick, 2000). More recent research continues to support such views (Sanders, 2004; Alvarez-Fernández *et al.*, 2005). A palliative approach and the use of advance directives decrease reliance on tube feeding (Monteleoni & Clark, 2004). The alternative is to manage dysphagia conservatively, using food thickeners with appropriate posture and feeding techniques. Locally implemented protocols exist but require further evaluation (Summersall & Wight, 2005). More recently, NICE published a guideline on nutritional support that includes recommendations for artificial nutrition and hydration (see NICE guideline no. 32, *Nutrition Support in Adults: Oral Nutrition Support, Enteral Tube Feeding and Parenteral Nutrition*, www.nice.org.uk/cg032niceguideline).

4.11.6   Fever and infection

Pneumonia remains a common cause of death in people with dementia (Chen *et al.*, 2006). The use of antibiotics to treat fever or intercurrent infections is controversial and under-researched in dementia. Some research shows no difference in the mortality rate of people receiving antibiotics and those receiving only palliative care (Fabiszewski *et al.*, 1990). Subsequent work has shown, in a controlled but non-randomised study, that aggressive treatment with antibiotics (as opposed to palliative measures such as antipyretics and analgesia) was associated with a worsening of dementia (Hurley *et al.*, 1996). A more recent study demonstrated substantial suffering caused by pneumonia, irrespective of antibiotic treatment, in people with dementia (van der Steen *et al.*, 2002). An associated concern is that transfer to hospital from long-term care homes for treatment of pneumonia may not be indicated because the outcome in hospital is poorer (Fried *et al.*, 1995; Thompson *et al.*, 1997).

Against this evidence, clinical experience suggests that the usefulness of antibiotics in a given situation ought to be determined by the specific circumstances: the severity of the dementia, comorbidity, immobility, nutritional status and the virility of the infection will all determine to what extent the use of antibiotics is warranted. In other branches of palliative care, there is evidence that, even in the terminal stages of illness, antibiotics can relieve the distress caused by infected bronchial secretions (Spruyt & Kausae, 1998; Clayton *et al.*, 2003).

4.11.7   Resuscitation

The evidence is that, in severe dementia, cardiopulmonary resuscitation (CPR) is unlikely to be successful. Furthermore, there is evidence from the US that most older people are against life-sustaining treatments, even when contemplating only the milder stages of dementia (Gjerdingen *et al.*, 1999). Outside the hospital setting, the chances of survival following CPR are very slim and the procedures themselves are burdensome (Awoke *et al.*, 1992; Zweig, 1997; Conroy *et al.*, 2006). Even in hospital, CPR is three times less likely to be successful in cognitively impaired patients compared with cognitively intact patients: the success rate is almost as low as it is in metastatic cancer (Ebell *et al.*, 1998). The futility and burdensome nature of CPR in this population, therefore, indicates a lack of proportion between the treatment and the likely outcome. This suggests that it would be reasonable to regard CPR as an extraordinary treatment, which there would be no moral imperative to pursue in someone with severe dementia. Further discussion of the issues around resuscitation can be found in publications by the Resuscitation Council (www.resus.org.uk), including a joint statement on decisions relating to cardiopulmonary resuscitation from the British Medical Association, the Resuscitation Council (UK) and the Royal College of Nursing (Resuscitation Council (UK), 2001).

4.11.8   Pain

Amongst older people in long-term care, pain is a common symptom (Ferrell *et al.*, 1990; Sengstaken & King, 1993). There is evidence that pain goes undetected amongst people with dementia and in part this reflects difficulties with communication and the recognition of pain by clinicians (Marzinski, 1991; Ferrell *et al.*, 1995; Cook *et al.*, 1999). Along with problems of detection, there is increasing evidence of under-treatment (Horgas & Tsai, 1998; Morrison & Siu, 2000; Balfour & O'Rourke, 2003; Nygaard & Jarland, 2005).

The initial task is to detect pain. For people in the mild to moderate stages of dementia, clinicians should be aware of the possibility of pain and routinely enquire about it. There has been a tendency to use self-report pain scales where the person can still communicate (Closs *et al.*, 2002) and observational scales as verbal communication becomes more difficult. Research that takes into account the underlying physiology of pain suggests that observational scales should be used, whatever the cognitive status of the person (Scherder *et al.*, 2005).

A number of observational pain assessment tools now exist and these have been systematically reviewed (Zwakhalen *et al.*, 2006). The review was unable to recommend any particular scale unequivocally because they all showed only moderate psychometric properties. A further complexity exists because pain is only one cause of distress. There is a concern that pain assessment tools might detect distress caused by other factors (Regnard & Huntley, 2005). The need to consider, therefore, the possible relationships between pain, distress and BPSD is paramount (Cipher & Clifford, 2004; Zwakhalen *et al.*, 2006).

In principle, the management of pain in dementia should be much the same as it is in other branches of medicine; the cause of the pain should determine the treatment (Regnard & Huntley, 2005). The World Health Organization's analgesic ladder is a useful resource (WHO, 2006). In the final days of life, a palliative care pathway might encourage appropriate management of symptoms, including pain (Thomas, 2003; Ellershaw & Wilkinson, 2003). Non-pharmacological treatments might also be useful (for example, massage, aromatherapy and transcutaneous electrical nerve stimulation (TENS)); however, there is a lack of good-quality evidence to support the use of such means (Cameron *et al.*, 2003). It should not be forgotten that BPSD might be a manifestation of pain (Manfredi *et al.*, 2003; Chibnall *et al.*, 2005), but putative pain behaviour (that is, distress) might have some other cause, so blanket prescribing of analgesia would not be good practice.

4.11.9   Services to support palliative care in dementia

Services specifically designed to provide good-quality palliative care in dementia are few. There are several possible models but little research to support the use of one in particular (Sampson *et al.*, 2005). There is evidence from the US that both professionals and family members of people with dementia, especially if they have experience of terminal care, favour a palliative care approach (Luchins & Hanrahan, 1993). The question is how this might be provided (Evers *et al.*, 2002).

Ahronheim and colleagues (2000), in a randomised controlled study of 99 patients with severe dementia admitted to an acute hospital over the course of 3 years, found it difficult to effect a palliative care approach. They concluded that it would be better to identify patients prior to their arrival in an acute hospital.

In the US, dementia special care units (DSCU) have acted as specialist hospices (Volicer *et al.*, 1986). When the provision of care in the DSCU was compared with that in the traditional long-term care unit, the DSCU showed more evidence of advanced care planning and less invasive care, with lower costs (Volicer *et al.*, 1994). This study, however, was neither randomised nor blind. There are problems associated with the use of such units on a large scale (Hughes & Robinson, 2005).

The PEACE programme (Shega *et al.*, 2003) attempted to integrate palliative care into primary care from the time of the diagnosis until death. The focus was on advance care planning, symptom management (with special attention to pain, behavioural problems and depression), education, carer support, optimal use of community resources and improved coordination of care. The programme – neither randomised, nor controlled – relied upon two clinical nurse specialists. There are only preliminary results, but they suggest 'high rates of satisfaction with the quality of care, adequate pain control, appropriate attention to prior stated wishes, and patients dying in desired locations' (Shega *et al.*, 2003). Despite the support, however, carers still experienced significant stress. Family carers of people with dementia face particular stresses and it is known that their bereavement reactions are different in comparison with those bereaved through cancer (Albinsson & Strang, 2003).

Palliative care teams working in the community would help to keep people in their familiar surroundings, but there is still the problem of a lack of familiarity with dementia. If palliative care in dementia involves a broader role – with, for example, greater awareness of BPSD and its treatment – then specialist palliative dementia care nurses would be required (Robinson *et al.*, in press). Their role might be to coordinate care and a palliative approach wherever the person with dementia be located: in hospital, in long-term care or at home.

4.12   THE ECONOMIC COST OF DEMENTIA

Addressing the different aspects of care of people with dementia, and meeting the individual's needs and those of his or her carers, requires an extensive and complex network of health and social care services, as well as care provided informally by family and friends. The diversity of this network is illustrated by the cost estimates for dementia in the UK, ranging from £1 billion to over £14 billion per year. Bosanquet and colleagues (1998) estimated the annual cost of AD in the UK to be between £5.4 and £5.8 billion at 1996 prices, which included health and social care costs, social security, out-of-pocket expenses and the cost of providing informal care which was estimated using the equivalent formal wage rate. Lowin and colleagues (2001) estimated the annual societal cost to be between £7.06 and £14.93 billion at 1999 prices, dependent on prevalence, amount of informal care provided and the wage rate used to cost informal care.

McNamee and colleagues (2001) estimated the formal health and social care costs associated with dementia in England and Wales at £0.95 billion for men and £5.35 billion for women in 1994, rising at an expected £2.35 billion for men and £11.20 billion for women with dementia in 2031 (1994/95 prices). The increase in costs was attributed to an anticipated rise in the elderly population, especially women aged 80 years and above. The same study reported that if dementia prevalence rates declined smoothly over each decade by 0.5%, 1%, and 2% for people aged 75–79 years, 80–84 years and 85 years and over, respectively, then health and social care costs were likely to fall far below the initial projected estimate, reaching £1.01 billion for men and £5.77 billion for women with dementia in 2031. Likewise, if mental and physical functioning of people with dementia improved over time, as reflected in a hypothetical fall of 0.5 in overall MMSE and ADL scores, respectively per decade, then formal care costs were expected to drop at £1.65 billion for men and £7.87 billion for women with dementia. However, with a projected increase of 66% in the number of people with cognitive impairment between 1998 and 2031 (Comas-Herrera *et al.*, 2003), of which an estimated 72% will have AD (Ott *et al.*, 1995), the costs associated with formal care of people with dementia are expected to grow at even higher levels in the future than estimated figures.

The finding of McNamee and colleagues (2001) that the level of mental functioning is significantly associated with the costs of health and social care for people with dementia has been reproduced in a Swedish study that aimed at identifying the determinants of formal and informal care costs for people with AD (Jönsson *et al.*, 2006). The study found that the costs of community care for this population (which accounted for about half of total formal and informal care costs of AD in Sweden) increased sharply with increasing cognitive impairment, as expressed by declining MMSE scores. Informal care costs were also strongly associated with the level of disease severity. In contrast, the magnitude of medical care costs (inpatient and out-patient care and pharmaceuticals) was not substantially affected by the level of disease severity. The association between costs of care for people with AD and the level of cognitive impairment was confirmed both in comparisons across people with various levels of disease severity, as well as within patients with increasing severity over time. The study also demonstrated the significant influence of behavioural disturbances, measured with brief Neuropsychiatric Inventory (NPI) scores, on total costs of care. The latter finding has also been reported by Murman and colleagues (2002), who estimated that a one-point increase in the NPI score of people with AD would result in an annual increase of between $247 and $409 in total cost of care (2001 prices), depending on the value of unpaid care-giving.

Due to the nature of dementia, the majority of service provision falls on care rather than treatment, and with the large demand on time that care requires, it is unsurprising that informal care is identified as the main cost driver overall (Souetre *et al.*, 1999). Schneider and colleagues (2003) warn of the potential to significantly underestimate the total cost of care if informal care costs are not included, estimating that informal care accounts for up to 40% of the total cost of dementia. Caring for the person with dementia at home can mean that up to 75% of associated care costs are out-of-pocket expenses and informal care (Bosanquet *et al.*, 1998). Time invested in informal care-giving alone is estimated to account for on average 6.8 hours per day (Souetre *et al.*, 1999), 44 hours per week (Schneider *et al.*, 2002) and, for individuals with behaviour that challenges, 79% of the week (Kirchner *et al.*, 2000). The majority of time is taken up with general and domestic tasks and supervision that would otherwise be carried out by home care and mobile meals services. Based on the hourly rate for a Local Authority home care worker (Curtis & Netten, 2005), the substitution of informal care for formal care services is estimated at £15,885 per year. The potential cost savings of not employing formal care services will be considerable. Care provided by family carers enables many individuals to remain in their own home, delaying or preventing placement in residential care. With the additional cost of moving a person with AD into residential care calculated at up to £20,668 per year (Holmes *et al.*, 1998), alongside the monetary value placed on the care provided by family and friends, the potential cost savings provided by the informal carer are substantial. However, caring for people with dementia can be stressful and is associated with depression and anxiety that may reduce the quality of life of the carer. Moore and colleagues (2001) identified use of healthcare services as a component, albeit minor, of costs associated with informal care.

Due to the common late onset of the disease, the impact of lost productivity on industry associated directly with people with dementia is minimal, but the cost to industry due to caring is an important aspect. Souetre and colleagues (1999) estimated that, for those carers who had not reached retirement age, on average between 15 and 61 working days over a 3-month period were lost, depending on the severity of the condition. A study estimating the cost of AD to US business in 2002 found that absenteeism due to care-giving cost businesses $10 billion, productivity losses due to absenteeism cost $18 billion and the replacement cost of people taking early retirement to care for individuals cost $6 billion. The total cost associated with these factors of care-giving alone was $34.5 billion to US industry (Koppel, 2002). The largest component of direct carer costs was lost earnings due to early retirement, reduced working hours, refusing promotion, lateness and absence (Moore *et al.*, 2001).

Providing care for people with dementia requires a wide range of services from a wide range of sources. Although the exact economic cost of dementia is unknown because of the informal nature of a large amount of the care provided, it can be concluded that dementia has substantial economic implications.

4.13   HEALTH AND SOCIAL CARE RECOMMENDATIONS

4.13.1   Diversity, equality and language

4.13.1.1   People with dementia should not be excluded from any services because of their diagnosis, age (whether designated too young or too old) or coexisting learning disabilities. [For the evidence, see sections 4.6, 4.9 and 5.2.2]

4.13.1.2   Health and social care staff should treat people with dementia and their carers with respect at all times. [For the evidence, see sections 4.9 and 4.11]

4.13.1.3   Heath and social care staff should identify the specific needs of people with dementia and their carers arising from diversity, including gender, ethnicity, age (younger or older), religion and personal care. Care plans should record and address these needs. [For the evidence, see sections 4.2, 4.3, 4.9 and 4.10.6]

4.13.1.4   Health and social care staff should identify the specific needs of people with dementia and their carers arising from ill health, physical disability, sensory impairment, communication difficulties, problems with nutrition, poor oral health and learning disabilities. Care plans should record and address these needs. [For the evidence, see sections 4.6.3 and 4.10.4]

4.13.1.5   Health and social care staff, especially in residential settings, should identify and, wherever possible, accommodate the preferences of people with dementia and their carers, including diet, sexuality and religion. Care plans should record and address these preferences. [For the evidence, see sections 4.2, 4.9.1 and 4.10.6]

4.13.1.6   People who are suspected of having dementia because of evidence of functional and cognitive deterioration, but who do not have sufficient memory impairment to be diagnosed with the condition, should not be denied access to support services. [For the evidence, see sections 4.6.1, 4.6.2, 4.10.1, 4.10.2 and 6.4.2]

4.13.1.7   If language or acquired language impairment is a barrier to accessing or understanding services, treatment and care, health and social care professionals should provide the person with dementia and/or their carer with:
  ● information in the preferred language and/or in an accessible format
  ● independent interpreters
  ● psychological interventions in the preferred language. [For the evidence, see section 4.10.6]

4.13.2   Younger people with dementia

4.13.2.1   Younger people with dementia have special requirements, and specialist multidisciplinary services should be developed, allied to existing dementia services, to meet their needs for assessment, diagnosis and care. [For the evidence, see sections 4.1.1, 5.2.2 and 5.2.6]

4.13.3   People with a learning disability

4.13.3.1   Health and social care staff working in care environments where younger people are at risk of developing dementia, such as those catering for people with learning disabilities, should be trained in dementia awareness. [For the evidence, see sections 4.6.3, 5.2.2 and 6.5.2]

4.13.3.2   People with learning disabilities and those supporting them should have access to specialist advice and support regarding dementia. [For the evidence, see sections 4.6.3, 5.2.2 and 6.5.2]

4.13.4   Ethics, consent and advance decision making

4.13.4.1   Health and social care professionals should always seek valid consent from people with dementia. This should entail informing the person of options, and checking that he or she understands, that there is no coercion and that he or she continues to consent over time. If the person lacks the capacity to make a decision, the provisions of the Mental Capacity Act 2005 must be followed. [For the evidence, see sections 4.8, 4.9.1, 4.9.2, 4.9.3 and 4.9.4]

4.13.4.2   Health and social care professionals should inform people with dementia and their carers about advocacy services and voluntary support, and should encourage their use. If required, such services should be available for both people with dementia and their carers independently of each other. [For the evidence, see sections 4.8, 4.10.2, 6.5.4 and 6.5.5]

4.13.4.3   People with dementia should be given the opportunity to convey information to health and social care professionals involved in their care in a confidential manner. Professionals should discuss with the person any need for information to be shared with colleagues and/or other agencies. Only in exceptional circumstances should confidential information be disclosed to others without the person's consent. However, as dementia worsens and the person becomes more dependent on family or other carers, decisions about sharing information should be made in the context of the Mental Capacity Act 2005 and its Code of Practice. If information is to be shared with others, this should be done only if it is in the best interests of the person with dementia. [For the evidence, see sections 4.9.5 and 6.5.3]

4.13.4.4   Health and social care professionals should discuss with the person with dementia, while he or she still has capacity, and his or her carer the use of:

- advance statements (which allow people to state what is to be done if they should subsequently lose the capacity to decide or to communicate)
- advance decisions to refuse treatment[32]
- Lasting Power of Attorney (a legal document that allows people to state in writing who they want to make certain decisions for them if they cannot make them for themselves, including decisions about personal health and welfare)[33]
- a Preferred Place of Care Plan (which allows people to record decisions about future care choices and the place where the person would like to die)[34]. [For the evidence, see sections 4.8, 4.9.4 and 4.11.1]

4.13.5   Impact of dementia on personal relationships

4.13.5.1   At the time of diagnosis and when indicated subsequently, the impact of dementia on relationships, including sexual relationships, should be assessed in a sensitive manner. When indicated, people with dementia and/or their partner and/or carers should be given information about local support services. [For the evidence, see sections 4.7.2 and 6.5.4]

4.13.6   Risk of abuse and neglect

4.13.6.1   Because people with dementia are vulnerable to abuse and neglect, all health and social care staff supporting them should receive information and training about, and abide by the local multi-agency policy on, adult protection. [For the evidence, see section 4.7.1]

4.13.7   Care for people with dementia in an acute hospital facility

4.13.7.1   Acute and general hospital trusts should plan and provide services that address the specific personal and social care needs and the mental and physical health of people with dementia who use acute hospital facilities for any reason. [For the evidence, see sections 4.10.4 and 9.4.1]

4.13.7.2   Acute trusts should ensure that all people with suspected or known dementia using inpatient services are assessed by a liaison service that specialises in the treatment of dementia. Care for such people in acute trusts should be planned jointly by the trust's hospital staff, liaison teams, relevant social care professionals and the person with suspected or known dementia and his or her carers. [For the evidence, see sections 4.10.4 and 9.4.1]

---

[32]Under the provisions of the Mental Capacity Act 2005.
[33]Under the provisions of the Mental Capacity Act 2005.
[34]See www.cancerlancashire.org.uk/ppc.html.

4.13.8 Inpatient dementia services

4.13.8.1 As far as possible, dementia care services should be community-based, but psychiatric inpatient admission may be considered in certain circumstances, including if:
- the person with dementia is severely disturbed and needs to be contained for his or her own health and safety and/or the safety of others (in some cases, this might include those liable to be detained under the Mental Health Act 1983)
- assessment in a community setting is not possible, for example if a person with dementia has complex physical and psychiatric problems. [For the evidence, see section 4.10.8]

4.13.9 Palliative care and end of life issues

Dementia care should incorporate a palliative care approach from the time of diagnosis until death. The aim should be to support the quality of life of people with dementia and to enable them to die with dignity and in the place of their choosing, while also supporting carers during their bereavement, which may both anticipate and follow death[35].

4.13.9.1 Health and social care professionals working with people with dementia and their carers should adopt a palliative care approach. They should consider physical, psychological, social and spiritual needs to maximise the quality of life of the person with dementia and his or her family. [For the evidence, see sections 4.11.1 and 4.11.2]

4.13.9.2 Palliative care professionals, other health and social care professionals, and commissioners should ensure that people with dementia who are dying have the same access to palliative care services as those without dementia. [For the evidence, see sections 4.11.1, 4.11.2 and 4.11.9]

4.13.9.3 Primary care teams should ensure that the palliative care needs of people with dementia who are close to death are assessed and that the resulting information is communicated within the team and with other health and social care staff. [For the evidence, see sections 4.11.1 and 4.11.2]

4.13.9.4 Health and social care staff should encourage people with dementia to eat and drink by mouth for as long as possible. Specialist assessment and advice concerning swallowing and feeding in dementia should be available. Dietary advice may also be beneficial. Nutritional support, including artificial (tube) feeding, should be considered if dysphagia is thought to be a transient phenomenon, but artificial feeding should not generally be used in people with severe dementia for whom dysphagia or disinclination to eat is a manifestation of disease severity. Ethical[36] and legal[37] principles

---

[35]Information on good practice, resources, and tools to support end of life care are available at www.endoflifecare.nhs.uk/eolc.

[36]See General Medical Council, 2002.

[37]See the Mental Capacity Act 2005.

should be applied when making decisions about withholding or withdrawing nutritional support. [For the evidence, see section 4.11.5]

4.13.9.5   If a person with severe dementia has a fever, especially in the terminal stages, a clinical assessment should be undertaken. Simple analgesics, antipyretics and mechanical means of cooling the person may suffice. Antibiotics may be considered as a palliative measure in the terminal stages of dementia, but this needs an individual assessment. [For the evidence, see section 4.11.6]

4.13.9.6   Policies in hospitals and long-stay residential, nursing or continuing care units should reflect the fact that cardiopulmonary resuscitation is unlikely to succeed in cases of cardiopulmonary arrest in people with severe dementia. [For the evidence, see section 4.11.7]

4.13.9.7   In the absence of a valid and applicable advance decision to refuse resuscitation, the decision to resuscitate should take account of any expressed wishes or beliefs of the person with dementia, together with the views of the carers and the multidisciplinary team. The decision should be made in accordance with the guidance developed by the Resuscitation Council UK[38] and, if the person lacks capacity, the provisions of the Mental Capacity Act 2005. It should be recorded in the medical notes and care plans. [For the evidence, see section 4.11.7]

4.13.10   Pain relief

4.13.10.1 If a person with dementia has unexplained changes in behaviour and/or shows signs of distress, health and social care professionals should assess whether the person is in pain, using an observational pain assessment tool if helpful. However, the possibility of other causes should be considered. [For the evidence, see section 4.11.8]

4.13.10.2 The treatment of pain in people with severe dementia should involve both pharmacological and non-pharmacological measures. Non-pharmacological therapies should be used with the person's history and preferences in mind. [For the evidence, see section 4.11.8]

4.13.11   Assessment of carers' needs

4.13.11.1 Health and social care managers should ensure that the rights of carers to receive an assessment of needs, as set out in the Carers and Disabled Children Act 2000 and the Carers (Equal Opportunities) Act 2004[39], are upheld. [For the evidence, see section 4.6.4]

---

[38]See Resuscitation Council (UK), 2001.
[39]See Social Care Institute for Excellence, 2005.

5. HEALTH AND SOCIAL CARE SERVICES FOR PEOPLE WITH DEMENTIA AND THEIR CARERS

5.1 INTRODUCTION

This chapter considers care and support services for people with dementia and their carers. It is important to bear in mind that, while many people with dementia will want and need the same outcomes from services as their carers, in some cases their needs and wishes will be at variance with one another and may even conflict.

The evidence base focusing on service provision is slim. For example, there is little clear evidence to point towards benefits in terms of better outcomes for people with dementia and their carers from specialist rather than mainstream services, although there are collations of 'good practice'. It is also difficult to draw clear inferences from studies that attempt to assess the impact of an individual service or a way of organising services when other services and personal circumstances may have a greater impact on outcomes, perceptions and responses. Indeed, qualitative evidence on older people's perceptions of services suggests that what they find most important is the quality of the relationships that they experience with service providers. The evidence base on services is further limited in that the findings of research conducted in other countries may not be applicable to England and Wales, due to differences in the organisation and funding of care.

During the development of this guideline, the Department of Health published *Everybody's Business. Integrated Mental Health Services for Older Adults: a Service Development Guide* (Department of Health/Care Services Improvement Partnership, 2005)[40]. Although *Everybody's Business* and this guideline have different and distinct roles, this guideline has adopted *Everybody's Business* as the preferred source for guidance on service development and as a template for the planning, implementation and delivery of health and social care services for people with dementia and their carers. In this chapter we set out the reasoning behind this decision.

5.2 THE ORGANISATION AND PLANNING OF SERVICES

5.2.1 Introduction

The main emphasis of services for people with dementia is on promoting their independence and quality of life and, wherever practical and possible, supporting them

---

[40]Available from www.everybodysbusiness.org.uk.

and their carers in the community (Department of Health, 2001b). Social services therefore have a major role in providing support and services to people with dementia and their carers living in the community, along with supported housing options, including sheltered housing and residential care, for those needing more intensive care and support.

People with dementia and their carers generally access mainstream services and specialist mental health services through a referral by their general practitioner or primary care team. There is no common or generalisable pathway for access to services, so access can be a delayed and tortuous journey. Greater coordination and integration between health and social services and the provision of care management services are generally regarded as important steps to take if the delivery of support and services for people with dementia and their carers is to be improved. Involving service users and their carers is also central to quality improvement within health and social care, and is advocated by *Everybody's Business* (Department of Health/Care Services Improvement Partnership, 2005). In the health service, people with dementia and carers may be able to participate in service design through local patient and public involvement strategies.

Specialist mental health services are now in place in almost every mental health trust. Although there is no uniform style or model for the delivery of specialist mental health services for older people with dementia in the United Kingdom, the various models that have developed have done so through national guidance and the Royal Colleges encouraging patterns and levels of service provision (Audit Commission, 2000; Department of Health, 2001b; Royal College of Psychiatrists, 2005a). In general, specialist mental health services for older people are made up of community mental health teams, hospital-based assessment services, inpatient and day-hospital provision, and memory clinics. The specialist teams are often multidisciplinary in their composition, consisting of old age psychiatrists, mental health nurses, occupational therapists, social workers and psychologists (Royal College of Psychiatrists, 2005a). Teams may also have input from physiotherapists, pharmacists, speech and language therapists and support workers. The Royal College of Psychiatrists (2005a) identified the common features of an effective service as being a single entry-point system, case (or care) management, comprehensive assessment and a multidisciplinary team.

5.2.2   *Everybody's Business* – the Department of Health service development guide on integrated mental health services for older adults

Everybody's Business is a guide to current policy on key components of integrated mental health services for older people. Building on the service models outlined in the National Service Framework for Older People (Department of Health, 2001b), it identifies the foundations for a comprehensive mental health service for older people, with the objective that their needs and those of their carers are met wherever they are in the system, without encountering discrimination or barriers to access. *Everybody's Business* is aimed at commissioners and practitioners in health and social-care services who provide services for older people with mental health problems. It is the

Department of Health's intention that *Everybody's Business* and the accompanying web-based resources[41] should inform local discussions on commissioning services and develop understanding among those involved in planning services, as well as health and social-care practitioners, of how services can better meet the needs of older people with mental health problems.

While the dementia guideline and *Everybody's Business* were under development, the Department of Health development team and the GDG informed one another about their progress. Beyond that dialogue, *Everybody's Business* and the dementia guideline were developed through entirely separate processes with different and distinct roles – respectively to establish an agenda for the development of older people's mental health services and to provide recommendations on the care of people with dementia. On publication of *Everybody's Business*, it became clear that it covered the area of service guidance in the scope for the NICE-SCIE dementia guideline. As a result, SCIE and NICE took the decision that, with respect to the planning and organisation of health and social care services for people with dementia, this guideline adopt *Everybody's Business* as the preferred source for guidance on service development and as the template for the planning, implementation and delivery of health and social-care services for all people with dementia[42]. The grounds for this decision are outlined below.

The policy context
NICE-SCIE service guidance has to be developed within the context of Department of Health policy on the organisation and delivery of health and social care services. *Everybody's Business* provides a single source of current Department of Health good practice guidance on the development of a comprehensive range of services for older people with mental health problems.

The scope
The scope of *Everybody's Business* includes all of the key service domains identified by the dementia Guideline Development Group: primary care, home care, day services (including mainstream day services and specialist day care), housing (including sheltered housing and extra-care housing), assistive technology and telecare, care in residential settings, intermediate care, care in the general hospital, specialist mental health services (including community mental health teams), memory assessment services, psychological therapies and inpatient care. It pays particular attention to people with dementia and the special needs of younger people with dementia and people with learning disabilities with dementia.

The evidence base/limitation
A search for evidence on the best way to plan and organise services for people with dementia and their carers was carried out as part of the systematic review of the

---

[41] Available from www.everybodysbusiness.org.uk.
[42] It should be noted that Everybody's Business is specific to the English Department of Health. However, this guideline recommends that commissioners and providers of services in Wales should also use Everybody's Business for guidance and as a template.

literature and through the review of qualitative evidence. Few of the studies of services that look at outcomes for people with dementia and/or their carers made useful comparisons between services that allowed inferences to be drawn about the best and most effective ways of planning and organising services for people with dementia and their carers. There are also difficulties in determining whether effects can be attributed to the service. Furthermore, the applicability of evidence from non-UK research on health and social-care services for people with dementia is limited due to the different systems for organising and funding health and social care in other countries – particularly in the US and Scandinavia.

Given that the evidence base for recommendations on the planning and organisation of services for people with dementia and their carers is small (or non-existent in relation to some services) and generally of a poor quality or not easily applicable to the UK, any service recommendations provided by this guideline would be largely based on good practice, not good evidence. Because *Everybody's Business* provides a source of good practice guidance for services for people with dementia, this guideline has adopted *Everybody's Business* as its source of service guidance.

The audience
The primary role of NICE and SCIE guidance is to make recommendations directed at practitioners, whereas guidance in *Everybody's Business* is aimed at and applies to both commissioners and practitioners across all health and social-care service domains that may provide services for people with dementia. As the implementation of service recommendations may depend on action by the commissioners of services, *Everybody's Business* is therefore the more appropriate vehicle through which to promote service-level changes in the care of people with dementia.

Clarity
Signposting *Everybody's Business* is likely to promote a clearer message to service planners and commissioners than would be achieved through the creation of a separate source of guidance on the planning and organisation of services for people with dementia. Indeed, one reason for the development of *Everybody's Business* was to provide a unified source of guidance on service development for older people with mental health problems where before the service needs of this population had been addressed by a number of health and social-care policy documents, including the National Service Frameworks for older people and mental health.

5.2.3   Integrated health and social care services

People with dementia and their carers need support from a wide range of health and social services and, in principle, integrated services should lead to a simpler route to access services and a more coordinated delivery of services. Integration should also cut the number of professionals with whom people with dementia and their carers have to come into contact and remove the need for repeated assessments by different services. Furthermore, an integrated service should make more rational decisions about the funding of health and social care services, for example funding more intensive home support for people with dementia in order to avoid the need for admission to an acute hospital. At the current time, services can be integrated in a variety of ways; examples of integrated practices include collocation, shared notes and shared budgets.

Neither the systematic literature search nor the review of qualitative evidence identified evidence on the impact of integrated services on health and quality of life outcomes for people with dementia or their carers. Although one study describes a model of a specialist integrated dementia care service in the UK, it does not provide evidence on the effectiveness of integrated health and social care services, as care was provided by an integrated team to both the intervention and control groups (Challis *et al.*, 2002). However, two evidence-based studies (Brown *et al.*, 2003; Davey *et al.*, 2005) that address the impact of integrated services on outcomes for older people in the UK may have some relevance to people with dementia.

Brown and colleagues (2003) examined the impact of integrated health and social care teams on older people living in the community through a comparison of the effectiveness of such teams with more traditional arrangements over 18 months. Although no impact on service-user clinical outcomes was identified, two effects of the integrated teams were noteworthy. First, the response from referral to assessment was quicker. This led the authors to speculate that the integrated one-stop shop approach and better communication, understanding and exchange of information amongst different professional groups may have had an impact on the process of service delivery, with improvements in the initial stages of the process of seeking help and being assessed for a service. Secondly, although not statistically significant, a greater proportion of the group receiving care from the integrated teams went into residential care, which the authors suggest may be an unintended consequence of teams where a more medical model might predominate.

Brown and colleagues also interviewed the older people involved in the study to determine their perceptions of services. Most important was the quality of the relationships with service providers at every level of service delivery; respondents expressed little interest in who organised or delivered their services as long as they received what they felt they were entitled to. Rather than concluding that their findings do not support the integration of health and social care, Brown and colleagues suggest that the degree of integration in the teams studied may not have been sufficiently well-developed to make a difference to clinical outcomes.

Davey and colleagues (2005) compared the effectiveness of two different models of integration on outcomes for older people and concluded that outcomes are affected by a number of factors, one of which is cognitive function. The study suggests that it is therefore difficult to demonstrate the effects of services or the way they are organised; large-scale studies may be needed to detect any effects of even intensive mainstream services, such as home care, with the effects of less intensive services and integrated working likely to be more difficult to demonstrate.

Given that current policy on mental health services for older people promotes the integration of health and social care, research is needed to determine what impact integration has on outcomes for people with dementia and their carers. For future studies to be comparable and yield useful information on whether integration may deliver positive outcomes and on what features of integration have an impact on outcomes, there is therefore a need to develop consistent definitions of integrated working and its components that can be used in research.

5.2.4   Direct payments and individual budgets

Direct payments allow individuals to purchase their own care and equipment using cash payments that they receive from social services in lieu of community care services. Individual budgets, which are currently being piloted in a selected number of sites, differ in that they are sometimes notional amounts of money (rather than an actual transfer of cash) that are allocated to individuals to fund their care and equipment. Whilst older people are increasingly using direct payments to arrange their own care, only a small minority have so far taken up this option. People with dementia who choose to arrange their own care will require additional support to do so, including help with managing the financial aspects of arranging care and safeguards to protect them against potential exploitation or abuse. Individual budgets may therefore be a more appropriate route for people with dementia to achieve more flexible and individual care while avoiding the responsibilities of employment of assistants. However, for many people with dementia, the use of direct payments or individual budgets to arrange care will only be possible if carers are able to exercise choice and control over the services they receive on behalf of the person with dementia for whom they care.

5.2.5   Care management

Care management (referred to variously as 'case management' in the management of chronic diseases and more commonly as the 'Care Programme Approach' in some other areas of healthcare) involves four elements: the coordination of a full assessment, agreeing a care plan, arranging action to deliver services and reviewing changing needs.

The available evidence indicates that care management for people with dementia delivers improved outcomes for both the person and his or her carer, but because the models of care management that have been investigated vary, it is not possible to identify the most effective models or the individual components that contribute to their overall effectiveness. A UK study of care management for people with dementia (Challis *et al.*, 2002) found that care management delivered better outcomes and was more effective at maintaining people with dementia at home than standard community old age mental healthcare. Studies conducted in Finland (Eloniemi-Sulkkava *et al.*, 2001), Canada (Chu *et al.*, 2000) and the USA (Shelton *et al.*, 2001) similarly found evidence for potentially beneficial effects of care management for people with dementia and their carers. However, these studies do not establish that the benefits arise specifically from care management, as the schemes studied provide care management along with other interventions. A further US study (Seltzer *et al.*, 1992) demonstrates the potential for carers to take on the role of care manager, as family members trained to act as care managers were found to assume more responsibility for care management without experiencing any increase in burden.

Outcomes for people with dementia

Challis and colleagues (2002) found significant differences attributable to intensive care management in terms of quality of life and the needs of the person with dementia. At 6 months, people with dementia served by an intensive care management team were more satisfied with their home environment and had more improvement in social contact in comparison with those served by standard community old age services (both findings were statistically significant). At one year, the care management group continued to show significant improvement in social contact, in contrast to those receiving standard care.

Although at one year no difference was found in admission to institutional care, by the end of the second year there was an apparent positive effect of care management, with 51% of the care management group still at home (21% in institutional care, 28% deceased) compared with 33% of the control group (33% in institutional care, 35% deceased). Although the control group had a significant reduction in distressing behaviour at 6 months, the rate started at a higher level at baseline and was reduced to the mean of the care management group. No differences were found in levels of depression, frequency of activities at home or changes in dependency.

These positive outcomes appear attributable to care management, as the comparison group was referred to a similar community mental health team that provided an extensive service for older people with cognitive impairment, but without care management. The care management team benefited from the integration into the team of social services staff who had access to all relevant health and social care resources for people with dementia, caseloads of 20–25 cases and control over a devolved budget to provide services. Features of the care management scheme thought to be important to its effectiveness that were not available in the standard service included long-term contact with older people and their carers, relatively small caseloads and access to a significant range of other resources.

A randomised controlled trial of a nurse care management programme in Finland (Eloniemi-Sulkava *et al.*, 2001) provides more limited support for care management. The care management intervention was a 2-year systematic and comprehensive support programme delivered by a registered nurse with a public-health background who was given training, support and advice in dementia care from dementia care specialists. Care managers had access to the physician and they coordinated care, services and support for families and provided advocacy, support and annual training for the person with dementia and carers, as well as counselling, follow-up calls, home visits, assistance in arranging health and social care services, and 24-hour availability by mobile phone.

Eloniemi-Sulkava and colleagues focused on admission to long-term care. The care management programme had a statistically significant beneficial effect during the first months, with the rate of institutionalisation being lower in the support programme group than in a group receiving usual care. However, the difference between the groups decreased over time and benefits from care management did not persist at 2 years, when the number of people with dementia who had been admitted to institutional care did not differ between the groups. The effects of care management in delaying placement in institutional care were more marked in people with severe dementia, whereas in people with mild dementia institutionalisation was rare and there was little effect. The study suggests that care management interventions should be targeted at people with severe dementia with problems that threaten the continuity of community care and their carers. However, as a number of the elements of the care management programme are in themselves interventions for carers (support, education and counselling), its effects may be attributable to these additional components, rather than being a direct effect of care management.

Outcomes for carers

The UK and Finnish studies of care management interventions (Challis *et al.*, 2002; Eloniemi-Sulkava *et al.*, 2001) provide evidence that supports care management as an effective way of organising services for people with dementia that can have a positive impact across the whole range of outcomes, including well-being, quality of life, maintenance of independent living activities and delayed admission. However, in relation to admission to institutional care, the positive impacts of care management that the studies report appear contradictory. The UK study reports no effect on admission at 12 months, but an apparently beneficial effect at 24 months when a larger proportion of the care management group remained at home. In contrast, over the same follow-up time, the Finnish study found an opposite trend, with the rate of institutionalisation being significantly lower in the support programme group during the first months but with the benefit decreasing over time, such that by 12 months institutionalisation rates in the groups did not differ.

The UK study (Challis *et al.*, 2002) also provides evidence that care management resulted in more support and positive outcomes for carers in terms of outcomes of carer burden, carer well-being and symptom inventory. Statistically significant improved outcomes were observed for carers living with a person with dementia who received care management; they were given greater levels of support, expressed a reduced number of needs, and had reduced time input and felt burden. Half as many carers in the care management group showed severe symptoms on an indicator of stress (20% compared with 40%) as the control group, and the proportion of cases where the carer's level of distress constituted a serious risk was halved in the care management group, whereas there was no improvement in the control group. Additionally, the number of carers who could identify a service provider to whom they could turn increased in the care management group from just over two thirds to all carers at 12 months, but did not increase in the control group.

Gains for carers in the care management group only became apparent at 12 months, but the authors suggest that the care management service may be effective in delivering shorter-term benefits to some carers. They speculate that short-term benefits may have been obscured if some of the people with dementia referred in the early phase of the scheme had been retained at home for inclusion in the experimental service when in reality their carers were past the point where they could benefit from the enhanced support.

Other evidence on care management for people with dementia

Two North American studies provide further evidence that care management for people with dementia and their carers can result in better outcomes. A Canadian study of a comprehensive home care programme for people with early-stage AD and their carers (Chu *et al.*, 2000) found that institutionalisation was delayed for mild to moderately impaired people with dementia in the comprehensive home care programme compared with a control group. Carers in the home care group also felt less burdened at 6 months. The authors suggest that the beneficial effects were mostly attributable to the provision of care management to the treatment group, but they may have also been due to a range of interventions for carers delivered by the care management programme, such as counselling, skill training and education.

The second study, a randomised controlled trial conducted in the USA (Shelton *et al.*, 2001), compared the number of carers admitted to hospital from a group of people with dementia and carers who received care management with those in a group receiving usual care and found that there were significantly fewer admissions of carers in the care management group. Nurse care managers identified client and carer medical and psychosocial problems and service needs and developed care plans with the agreement of the carer and client. Although the authors were unable to identify which elements of care management might have contributed to the overall positive effect, they point to care management's focus on promoting and maintaining the health and safety of people with dementia and their families. The support provided by care management may have reduced the physical, emotional and psychological stress of caring and may also have given carers opportunities to identify their own health problems and to reinforce health maintenance behaviour.

Another US randomised controlled trial (Seltzer *et al.*, 1992) provides evidence that family members trained to act as care managers for elderly relatives with dementia can assume more responsibility for care management without any increase in their carer burden. Family members of two groups of elderly hospital patients (people with dementia and people needing haemodialysis) were assigned randomly to receive either systematic training in performing care management activities or services ordinarily provided by the hospital social work department. Care-management-trained family members performed significantly more care management tasks than control group family members, with no increase in their subjective or objective carer burden. These findings suggest that carers of people with dementia who choose to arrange services themselves (for example, through direct payments or individual budgets) might benefit from training in care management. Given the evidence that positive outcomes for people with dementia are associated with care management, training that results in carers taking a more active care management role might be beneficial to the person with dementia for whom they care.

While not measuring outcomes for people with dementia, a study of the effect of agitation and dementia-related behaviour problems on the use of care management time by older service users (Diwan & Phillips, 2001) has implications for the organisation and delivery of care management for people with dementia. Among the people with behaviours that challenge, those with greater functional ability consumed greater care management time, but most care management activity focused on service coordination rather than attempts to manage behaviour. Although the study population was not limited to people with dementia, among people with dementia, behaviours that challenge resulted in increased use of care management time. Diwan and colleagues suggest that care management programmes should consider case mix when allocating caseload size and that care managers should receive specific training on interventions to address behaviours that challenge.

Health economics evidence on care management for people with dementia

Challis and colleagues (2002) also evaluated the costs and effects of care management for people with dementia, compared with fragmented community services. The outcomes measured were destinational outcome, need, quality of care and quality of life of both the person with dementia and his or her carer, presented alongside the annual costs. The costs included in the analysis were for long-term care, community care services, hospital and GP care, professional visits (which include care managers), as well as out-of-pocket expenses, housing and care provided by family carers. Significant differences in outcomes between interventions were evident by 12 months. The care management group improved and maintained social contact, and carers experienced less burden and stress, a reduction in workload and an improved level of support. The care management group also experienced a greater proportion of people with dementia remaining in their own home in the long term.

The mean annual costs to society for care management were estimated at £35,992.28, whereas fragmented services were provided at the lower cost of £29,303.51[43]. The increased cost associated with care management, which fell mostly on social services, was mainly attributable to the cost of providing care management and additional home care and acute hospital care use. Some of the increased cost attributable to care management was offset by lower costs incurred by carers. However, due to the specialised nature of the scheme evaluated and other limitations on the transferability of the results to the wider UK setting, no firm conclusions can be drawn from the economic evidence. Details of the study characteristics and findings are presented in the form of evidence tables in Appendix 18.

5.2.6 Qualitative review

Evidence included

Twenty-five sources of evidence met the eligibility criteria set by the GDG. Fourteen were primary research: Aggarwal and colleagues (2003), Beattie and colleagues (2005), Davies and Nolan (2004), Gillies and Johnston (2004), Hubbard and colleagues (2003), Innes and colleagues (2005), Proctor (2001), and Walker and

---

[43]Updated to 2004/2005 prices using the Hospital and Community Health Services (HCHS) Pay and Prices inflation index (Curtis & Netten, 2005).

colleagues (2006) were published as journal articles and categorised as interview studies (all B3); Allan (2001) and Wilkinson and colleagues (2004) were published as reports and categorised as mixed-methods studies (B3); Stalker and colleagues (1999) was published as a report and categorised as an interview study (B3); Clarke (1999) was published as a journal article and categorised as a mixed-methods study (B3); Heiser (2002) was published as a journal article and categorised as a focus-group study (C1); and Walker and colleagues (1999) was published as a report and categorised as a mixed-methods study (B3). Five were case studies: Geppert (1998) and Husband (2000) were published as journal articles and categorised as interview studies (C2); Keady and colleagues (2004) was published as a journal article and categorised as a mixed-methods study; Maciejewski (1999) was published as a journal article and categorised as a focus-group study (C2); and Stokes (2004) was published as a journal article and categorised as an observation study (C2). Two were reviews: Arksey and colleagues (2004) was a systematic review but also involved a focus group and was published as a report (B3) and Bauld and colleagues (2000) was a literature review that was published as a journal article (B3). Two were descriptive accounts: Cantley and colleagues (2005) was published as a report (C2) and Gibson and colleagues (1995) was published as a report and categorised as an interview study (C2). Butterworth (1995) was a personal account and published as a journal article (U).

Key findings
Communication with people with dementia is possible (Allan, 2001), as is the engagement of moderate to severely impaired people with dementia in research, and conclusions can be drawn about their experiences and quality of life (Hubbard *et al.*, 2003). Some people with dementia want to be involved in service planning and can be supported to do so (Cantley *et al.*, 2005). Above all, people with dementia say that they want to continue leading an ordinary life (Allan, 2001) but are very concerned about stigma and may need support over self-esteem, not just practical problems (Husband, 2000). The evidence for benefit to people with dementia from the use of respite services and short-term breaks is limited and at times contradictory (Arksey *et al.*, 2004).

Carers constantly define and redefine their relationship with the person with dementia (Clarke, 1999). Risk and danger are common in dementia care, and carers spend much of their time supervising and controlling the care environment (Walker *et al.*, 2006). Services can arrive too little and too late to avoid carer distress (Butterworth, 1995), but providing a service will not in itself guarantee that it will be used (Geppert, 1998), and the extent of individual carers' involvement in care planning needs to be negotiated as their expectations differ (Walker *et al.*, 1999). Qualitative evidence from carers indicates that there are positive benefits from respite services and short-term breaks (Arksey *et al.*, 2004).

Control of services by people with dementia and carers is central to their positive evaluation of services (Innes *et al.*, 2005), and dementia services must be willing to invest in the resources to listen in a truly person-centred way (Proctor, 2001). Resistance to care, which is understandable in social terms, can be reduced by changes in professional behaviour (Stokes, 2004). Professionals should help foster a sense of self (Gillies & Johnston, 2004) and should be aware of power relationships

(Proctor, 2001). Community-based practitioners can support people with dementia and their carers through building up relationships, offering skills such as memory training, and helping with conflict resolution and care planning (Keady *et al.*, 2004). Community nurses working with people with dementia need greater role transparency, collaborative working styles and more preparation for practice (Keady *et al.*, 2004). Staff should be given support to enable them to consult with people with dementia (Allan, 2001), whilst accepting that measuring satisfaction with care is complex (Bauld *et al.*, 2000). Professional practice with people with dementia and their carers can be based on an empirically-grounded theoretical framework (Davies & Nolan, 2004). In relation to home care, high levels of satisfaction are associated with personalised support, attention to detail, staff with good manners and skilled help (Heiser, 2002). In care homes, where there can be high levels of inactivity and a lack of stimulation, residents' dissatisfaction may centre on their lack of choice and independence (Aggarwal *et al.*, 2003).

Marginalised groups within dementia services include people with early dementia who may not be known to services, rural populations that may have high levels of unmet needs and people with learning disabilities who develop dementia – provision of care for the latter group varies greatly (Beattie *et al.*, 2005; Gibson *et al.*, 1995; Maciejewski, 1999; Stalker *et al.*, 1999; Wilkinson *et al.*, 2004).

5.2.7 Evidence summary

The services that people with dementia and their carers need or choose to make use of, and the degree to which they benefit from those services, will largely depend on individual circumstances and preferences. It is therefore important that a full range of health and social services should be available and accessible to them, including alternatives to acute-hospital admission, such as those described in *Everybody's Business* (Department of Health/Care Services Improvement Partnership, 2005). While services aim to maintain people with dementia living as independently as possible for as long as possible, it may be better for people with dementia to access some supportive services, such as day centres and sheltered housing, earlier when they are more able and can develop relationships. Many people with dementia are supported by non-specialist services – from acute hospitals to home-help services and residential homes – and mainstream services therefore need to be aware of, and responsive to, the particular needs of people with dementia. This awareness should include an understanding that communication with people with dementia is possible.

There is quantitative evidence that care management is beneficial both to people with dementia and their carers. Care managers can identify an individual's needs, promote access to services and coordinate the delivery of health and social services, and respond to the developing needs of the person with dementia or his or her carer. Through their ongoing relationship with the person with dementia and his or her carer, care managers may be better able to communicate with the person with dementia and enable him or her to exercise the control over services that the qualitative evidence suggests they want.

5.3   DESIGN OF LIVING AND CARE ENVIRONMENTS

5.3.1   Introduction

Minimum standards for the physical environment of residential homes are set out in *National Minimum Standards: Care Homes for Older People* (Department of Health, 2002). Existing guides to the design of living environments for people with dementia make a range of recommendations, which are largely based on agreed good practice rather than empirical evidence (Day *et al.*, 2000). Though principally aimed at residential care environments for people with dementia, many of the principles of design may also be relevant to day centres and adaptations to a person's own home. The use of traditional and familiar designs is suggested on the grounds that if bedrooms, bathrooms and living rooms resemble rooms in a private residence then people with dementia will be more likely to remember what the rooms are for and will be more able to find their way around the care home environment. Simplified environments are also recommended.

Good practice regarding the design of environments for people with dementia includes incorporating features that support special orientation and minimise confusion, frustration and anxiety, such as better-quality ward environments, reality orientation cues and high light levels. Tactile wayfinding cues, good lighting and windows allowing daylight to enter, as well as views of external landmarks, may all help people with dementia to find their way around the indoor environment. Colours may also be used to assist with orientation, although the use of colour coding as a navigation aid may be too complex for people with dementia to understand. Highly visible toilets that act as a prompt may potentially reduce levels of incontinence. Providing moderate levels of environmental stimulation is also recommended, for example through murals rather than plain walls and accessible areas such as indoor courtyards or outdoor areas with therapeutic features and which allow residents the opportunity to explore in safety.

Features that are not recommended include large multi-purpose rooms, dead-end corridors and institutional environments that may contribute to confusion. Coarse-textured floor coverings can be difficult for people with dementia to walk on, and shiny floors can be misinterpreted as wet and slippery. Sharp colour or pattern contrasts can be misinterpreted as changes in level by people with impaired depth perception, and highly patterned surfaces (such as chessboard squares or repetitive lines) and poor colour or textural contrasts between walls and floors can cause dizziness or confusion.

Some design features may be better for some individuals with dementia but detrimental to others. For example, good practice guides to care home design recommend both simplified environments and moderate levels of environmental stimulation – environments that offer opportunities for stimulation and exploration may enhance the quality of life of some people with dementia, but others may find such environments overstimulating, disorienting and confusing.

More research is needed to develop a better and more evidence-based understanding of how environments can best serve the needs of people with dementia and promote their well-being and quality of life. It is notable that the review of qualitative evidence identified one relevant source of evidence, which described primary research using interview and observational methods and concluded that user involvement in environmental redesign is useful and provides insights. While some studies have investigated how environments can be better designed for people with dementia, most are small. A limitation shared by a number of the studies on environmental design features to assist people with dementia is that the care settings compared differ in factors other than the design, such as staff training, activity programming and ethos.

5.3.2 Overall size

Evidence from US studies on the impact of the size of assisted-living facilities on the quality of life of residents with dementia is equivocal; findings do not point to clear benefits associated with either small or large residential homes. No relationship was found between facility size and quality of life in a study of 134 residents with dementia living in 22 assisted-living facilities (Samus *et al.*, 2005), whereas an earlier study of 131 people with dementia living in ten assisted-living facilities (Kuhn *et al.*, 2002) found that residents living in large non-dementia-specific sites with 40 to 63 residents fared better with respect to quality of life and diversity of interactions and activities than those living in small dementia-specific sites with 10 to 28 residents. In any event, the interpretation of associations between residential home size and residents' quality of life is difficult; residents in large homes might experience care in small units with a homely environment and larger facilities might also be favoured if they offer greater access to specialist staff and therapeutic services or more opportunities to engage in activities.

5.3.3 Unit size

The research evidence indicates that smaller units accommodating fewer residents are beneficial to people with dementia (Day *et al.*, 2000). Studies indicate that larger units are associated with worse outcomes for residents with dementia in terms of agitation, intellectual deterioration, emotional disturbance, territorial conflicts, space invasion and aggressiveness towards other residents (Annerstedt 1994; Sloane *et al.*, 1998; Morgan & Stewart, 1998). By contrast, smaller units are associated with gains that include less anxiety and depression, greater mobility, increased supervision and interaction between staff and residents, increased social interaction between residents, higher motor functioning, improved or maintained activities of daily living (ADLs) and less use of antibiotic and psychotropic drugs (Annerstedt, 1993; Annerstedt, 1997; McAllister & Silverman, 1999; McCracken & Fitzwater, 1989; Moore, 1999; Netten, 1993; Skea & Lindesay, 1996). According to one study (Annerstedt 1993), smaller units for residents with dementia were also associated with gains for both residents' family members (lower levels of strain and better attitudes to dementia care) and staff (greater competence, more knowledge in dealing with dementia and greater job satisfaction). Smaller units may promote better outcomes for people with dementia because residents are less likely to experience overstimulation and also encounter fewer people (Day *et al.*, 2000). However, some of the apparent benefits of smaller units may be attributable to factors other than unit size.

5.3.4   Home-like and less institutional environments

Guides to the design of residential homes for the care of people with dementia generally recommend creating home-like environments that are domestic and familiar, rather than institutional, in character and there is some evidence that people with dementia benefit from caring environments that are more home-like in character. Environments characterised as having a home-like ambiance have personalised rooms, home-like furnishings and natural elements incorporated into the design. A number of studies suggest that such environments promote well-being among residents, as they are associated with improved intellectual and emotional well-being, enhanced social interaction, reduced agitation, reduced trespassing and exit seeking, greater preference and pleasure, and improved functionality of older adults with dementia and other mental illnesses (Annerstedt, 1994; Cohen-Mansfield & Werner, 1998; Kihlgren *et al.*, 1992; McAllister & Silverman, 1999; Sloane *et al.*, 1998).

Compared with those in traditional nursing homes and hospitals, residents in non-institutional settings are less aggressive, preserve better motor functions, require lower usage of tranquilising drugs and have less anxiety. Relatives also report greater satisfaction and less burden associated with non-institutional facilities (Annerstedt, 1997; Cohen-Mansfield & Werner, 1998; Kihlgren *et al.*, 1992), and staff also prefer less institutional environments (Cohen-Mansfield & Werner, 1998). The promotion of quality of life and well-being may also be enhanced through the incorporation of features that take account of a person's cultural and ethnic background.

However, non-institutional design requires supportive care-giving in order to be effective. An ethnographic study found that the therapeutic potential of the home-like environment was undermined by inflexible and formal ('institutional') care-giving practices (Moore, 1999). Mortality and decline rates for residents with dementia do not significantly improve in non-institutional settings when compared with traditional settings (Annerstedt, 1994; Phillips *et al*, 1997; Wimo *et al.*, 1993), and non-institutional environments are associated with some negative effects on people with dementia, including greater restlessness and more disturbances (Elmståhl *et al.*, 1997; Kihlgren *et al.*, 1992; Wimo *et al.*, 1993). These negative effects may be a consequence of residents in less institutional settings asserting their independence more, as well as increased disorientation and deterioration of diet.

5.3.5   Eating arrangements and design of dining areas

A recent study of 407 people with dementia in long-term residential care (Reed *et al.*, 2005) found that food and fluid intake at mealtimes was higher when dining rooms

127

had non-institutional features, such as tablecloths, where meals were not eaten from trays, and where meals were served in dining areas rather than residents' rooms. Gains in social interaction and eating behaviour were also found when residents dined together at small tables instead of dining from trays while seated in chairs arranged along the walls in a study of 21 residents in a mental hospital, 19 of whom had dementia (Melin & Gotestam, 1981). The increased social interaction followed from arranging the dining routine in such a way as to increase communication – for example, residents dining at tables had to serve themselves from serving dishes.

5.3.6   Design features to deliver, inform and support orientation

Limited evidence supports the use of design features that aim to give information to care home residents with dementia on orientation or wayfinding, that is, helping them find their way around their living quarters. On the whole, such features are simple and inexpensive, and there are no indications that they cause any harm. For example, one study looked at the effect of a large clock and a sign with large lettering identifying mealtimes hung in the dining area of a special care unit for people with dementia (Nolan & Mathews, 2004). The aim of the intervention was to decrease residents' agitation around mealtimes (particularly repetitive questions and requests for information) and to facilitate more pleasant interactions between residents and between residents and staff. When compared with baseline observations, repetitive food-related questions were reduced.

Studies on wayfinding design features (for example, Passini *et al.*, 2000) conclude that wayfinding decisions have to be based on environmental information that is readily accessible and enables people with dementia to proceed from one decision point to another. Even people with severe cognitive deterioration were able to reach some destinations. Positive design features that supported wayfinding included visual access to destinations, which increased the use of the destinations, and signage. Signs had an important function by creating redundancy in wayfinding and communication and by compensating for losses in memory and spatial understanding. Unhelpful design features included monotonous architecture and a lack of reference points (both of which rendered wayfinding difficult), floor patterns and dark lines or surfaces (which could cause people with dementia to experience disorientation and anxiety) and lifts (which were a major anxiety-causing barrier). A small randomised controlled trial found that the combination of a location map and behavioural training provided to residents over the course of a month helped people with dementia find their way, although this effect was not sustained 3 months later (McGilton *et al.*, 2003). Observations of three residents of a special care unit for people with dementia indicate that placing a portrait-type photograph of them as a young adult and a sign stating their name outside their bedrooms helped them to find their room (Nolan *et al.*, 2001).

Orientation is also enhanced through simple modifications to furniture that may help people with dementia locate their clothes when dressing. Wardrobes divided into two halves, one side locked for storage and the other presenting only the clothes to be worn in the appropriate order, minimise rummaging and thus support ADLs such as independent dressing (Namazi & DiNatale Johnson, 1992).

5.3.7   Gardens and outdoor environments for people with dementia

Literature on the design of residential homes also proposes that the well-being and quality of life of people with dementia living in residential homes is enhanced by free access to gardens. Gardens are presumed to provide opportunities for retreat, sensory stimulation, socialisation, exercise and activities in an environment that is safe and controlled but non-institutional (Detweiler *et al.*, 2002). Gardens may also give people with dementia in residential care a sense of the outside world and of still being part of it. However, few studies have investigated whether people with dementia benefit from access to a garden and no studies attempt to identify the design features that might make gardens most beneficial or rewarding to people with dementia.

A study on the effects of access to a 'wander garden' on the behaviour of people with dementia living in residential homes (Mather *et al.*, 1997) compared the behaviour of ten people with dementia for 1 week at the summer peak time for garden use with behaviour in winter when garden access was not possible. No significant differences in aggressive behaviour were found between seasons, but when the garden was accessible there was a non-significant reduction in overall disruptive behaviour and sleep disruption for the residents who spent more time in the garden. In the winter, residents had less physical contact with other residents, slept more and looked out of the window more than when they had access to the garden. Mather and colleagues suggest that the increased physical contact with other residents in summer resulted from decreased stress levels secondary to the increased personal space afforded by the garden.

Detweiler and colleagues (2002) suggest that gardens should provide a place where a person with dementia can spend time without fear of becoming disoriented or lost.

Several reasons are proposed for believing that access to a garden may have a positive effect on the well-being and quality of life of people with dementia living in residential homes: garden environments are reminiscent of life prior to institutionalisation and may help to promote memories and stimulate conversation with visitors; gardens allow access to a greater range of stimuli and choices, as well as opportunities for exercise and gardening activities that may be beneficial to physical and mental health; gardens may provide a peaceful setting for retreat from communal areas of the home and a place for residents to wander that is less stressful than in the home; access to natural light in an outdoor environment might promote a better sense of time and an improved sleep–wake cycle; observation of the seasons might promote improved orientation in time; and the option of going into the garden and opportunities to engage in activities there may increase feelings of autonomy and self-esteem and may alleviate frustrations caused by restricted freedom of movement (Detweiler *et al.*, 2002),

However, the potential benefits from access to a garden may change with the progression of a person's dementia – in the early stages, gardens may stimulate physical and mental function by promoting sensory activity, whereas in later stages they may promote an awareness outside of the self and create sensations of immediate pleasure. The potential for a person with dementia to enjoy and benefit from access to a garden may therefore be dependent on the individual and his or her dementia – for some, the garden environment might be overstimulating and cause confusion and disorientation.

Detweiler and colleagues (2002) suggests a range of design considerations for gardens used by people with dementia: access via resident-activated doors offering residents the choice to leave the indoor environment; division of the outdoor space into discrete units for activities or retreat, with no open and unstructured spaces that could be disorienting; paths designed to encourage movement that are wide enough to allow people (including those in wheelchairs) to pass; a covered perimeter walkway allowing exercise in bad weather; sheltered chairs and benches that are arranged to encourage socialisation; plants and safe water features that promote stimulation of all the senses; raised garden beds to promote tactile stimulation and gardening activity; and familiar plants and environmental features that may remind people with dementia of old routines and pleasures and draw them to the garden. Features to make a garden safe for people with dementia include windows allowing clear vision of all points of the garden from the home, to allow staff to monitor activity at a glance, a secure perimeter wall that may be high enough to keep the attention of residents on the garden, and level and safe surfaces that minimise the risk of falling and can be negotiated by residents in wheelchairs. Toxic plants or garden chemicals should not be used.

Research to identify garden features that are most pleasurable and beneficial to people with dementia would be of value to promote a more evidence-based approach to garden design. However, as noted by Day and colleagues in their review of empirical research into the design of care environments for people with dementia (Day *et al.*, 2000), not all design guidance requires validation from empirical research as some features of the residential home environment are arguably 'inalienable rights' – it might be considered that all people with dementia in residential care should have the option to spend time in a safe outdoor environment.

5.3.8   Qualitative review

Evidence included
One source of evidence met the eligibility criteria set by the GDG. Torrington and colleagues (2006) was primary research, published as a report and categorised as a mixed interview and observational study (B3).

Key findings
User involvement in environmental redesign is also useful and has the potential to provide rich insights (Torrington *et al.*, 2006).

5.3.9   Evidence summary

The principles of the design of care homes and other caring environments for people with dementia are largely based on theory but have some support from empirical research. The aim of design principles is to maximise the abilities of people with dementia while minimising negative features of the environment. When considering environmental design, it is important to be aware that individual requirements will vary both according to the individual's personal history, culture and religion, and the degree of his or her impairment.

5.4 HEALTH AND SOCIAL CARE RECOMMENDATIONS

5.4.1 Management and coordination of care

5.4.1.1 Health and social care staff should ensure that care of people with dementia and support for their carers is planned and provided within the framework of care management/coordination.[44] [For the evidence, see sections 4.10.2 and 5.2.5]

5.4.1.2 Care managers and care coordinators should ensure that care plans are based on an assessment of the person with dementia's life history, social and family circumstance, and preferences, as well as their physical and mental health needs and current level of functioning and abilities. [For the evidence, see sections 4.2, 4.3, 5.2.5 and 5.2.6]

5.4.1.3 Care managers and care coordinators should ensure the coordinated delivery of health and social care services for people with dementia. This should involve:

- a combined care plan agreed by health and social services that takes into account the changing needs of the person with dementia and his or her carers
- assignment of named health and/or social care staff to operate the care plan
- endorsement of the care plan by the person with dementia and/or carers
- formal reviews of the care plan, at a frequency agreed between professionals involved and the person with dementia and/or carers and recorded in the notes.[45] [For the evidence, see sections 4.10.2, 5.2.1, 5.2.2, 5.2.3 and 5.2.5]

5.4.2 Funding arrangements for health and social care

5.4.2.1 Care managers/care coordinators should explain to people with dementia and their carers that they have the right to receive direct payments and individual budgets (where available). If necessary, people with dementia and their carers should be offered additional support to obtain and manage these. [For the evidence, see section 5.2.4]

---

[44]Care management/care coordination involves four elements: the coordination of a full assessment, agreeing a care plan, arranging action to deliver services, and reviewing changing needs within the framework of the single assessment process.

[45]Time periods for review of care plans are stipulated by Care Programme Approach guidance and the Department of Health (2003).

5.4.2.2   People with dementia and their carers should be informed about the statutory difference between NHS care and care provided by local authority
social services (adult services) so that they can make informed decisions
about their eligibility for NHS Continuing Care. [For the evidence, see
section 4.6.4]

5.4.3   Environmental design for people with dementia

5.4.3.1   When organising and/or purchasing living arrangements or care home
placements for people with dementia, health and social care managers
should ensure that the design of built environments meets the needs of
people with dementia[46] and complies with the Disability Discrimination
Acts 1995 and 2005, because dementia is defined as a disability within the
meaning of the Acts. [For the evidence, see sections 4.9.1 and 5.3]

5.4.3.2   When organising and/or purchasing living arrangements and/or care home
placements for people with dementia, health and social care managers
should ensure that built environments are enabling and aid orientation.
Specific, but not exclusive, attention should be paid to: lighting, colour
schemes, floor coverings, assistive technology, signage, garden design, and
the access to and safety of the external environment. [For the evidence, see
section 5.3]

5.4.3.3   When organising and/or purchasing living arrangements and/or care home
placements for people with dementia, health and social care managers
should pay careful consideration to the size of units, the mix of residents,
and the skill mix of staff to ensure that the environment is supportive and
therapeutic. [For the evidence, see section 5.3]

5.4.4   Integrated health and social care

5.4.4.1   Health and social care staff should use the Department of Health's publication *Everybody's Business. Integrated Mental Health Services for Older
Adults: a Service Development Guide* (www.everybodysbusiness.org.uk)
in conjunction with this guideline as a framework for the planning, implementation and delivery of:
* primary care
* home care
* mainstream and specialist day services
* sheltered and extra-care housing
* assistive technology and telecare
* mainstream and specialist residential care

---

[46]See, for example, Judd *et al*, 1997.

- intermediate care and rehabilitation
- care in general hospitals
- specialist mental health services, including community mental health teams, memory assessment services, psychological therapies and inpatient care. [For the evidence, see section 5.2.2]

5.4.4.2   Health and social care managers should coordinate and integrate working across all agencies involved in the treatment and care of people with dementia and their carers, including jointly agreeing written policies and procedures. Joint planning should include local service users and carers in order to highlight and address problems specific to each locality. [For the evidence, see sections 5.2.1, 5.2.2, 5.2.3 and 5.2.5]

5.4.4.3   Health and social care professionals should ensure that people with dementia and their carers are given up-to-date information on local arrangements (including inter-agency working) for health and social care, including the independent and voluntary sectors, and on how to access such services. [For the evidence, see sections 4.2, 4.6.4, 4.10.2, 4.10.5, 4.10.6 and 6.5.4]

5.4.5   Practical support and services

5.4.5.1   Health and social care managers should ensure that carers of people with dementia have access to a comprehensive range of respite/short-break services. These should meet the needs of both the carer (in terms of location, flexibility and timeliness) and the person with dementia and should include, for example, day care, day- and night-sitting, adult placement and short-term and/or overnight residential care. Transport should be offered to enable access to these services if they are not provided in the person's own home. [For the evidence, see sections 4.6.4, 5.2.6 and 9.5.6]

5.4.5.2   Respite/short-break care of any sort should be characterised by meaningful and therapeutic activity tailored to the person with dementia and provided in an environment that meets their needs. Providing this in the person's own home should be considered whenever possible. [For the evidence, see section 5.2.6]

6. PREVENTION, EARLY IDENTIFICATION, ASSESSMENT AND DIAGNOSIS OF DEMENTIA

6.1 INTRODUCTION

Prevention of dementia syndromes would have a huge impact on large numbers of individuals and on society as a whole. Primary prevention, to avert early pathological changes, or secondary prevention, to delay pathological processes, are strategies that seem worthwhile pursuing. To do this, we must understand the factors that increase the risk of developing dementia and those that appear to be protective. Earlier identification of dementia may allow secondary prevention interventions, as well as early mobilisation of support and resources. To achieve earlier identification, we need to understand the ways in which cognitive function in dementia syndromes diverges from normal ageing processes. Diagnosis of dementia and its subtypes is often a complex process in which practitioners need to consider personal and informant histories, cognitive function testing and exclusion of other organic and psychological disorders. The importance of structural and functional neuroimaging is debated, as are the respective roles of primary- and secondary-care specialists in the diagnostic process. This step-wise process of reaching a diagnosis of dementia may involve assessment by a number of different professionals over a period of time. The process may raise difficult questions about how to discuss the possible or actual diagnosis, with whom and when. The experience of this assessment process may influence the way in which the person with dementia and his or her family or other carers assimilate and accommodate themselves to the diagnosis, and professional skills in managing the assessment process are therefore of great importance.

6.2 PREVENTION

6.2.1 Introduction

Prevention of dementia must remain an ultimate goal. Even a delay in onset of dementia would effectively be a preventive strategy, since it has been estimated that delaying the onset of dementia by 5 years would half its prevalence (Jorm *et al.*, 1987). Possible preventive strategies for dementia require consideration of:
- knowledge about risk factors for dementia and its subtypes
- the extent to which such risk factors are modifiable
- evidence that modification of these risk factors does indeed result in subsequent reduction in the incidence of dementia.

Current practice
There is no systematic public-health strategy for the prevention of dementia in the UK.

The evidence base/ limitations
The evidence base for the prevention of dementia is largely restricted to observational case control and cohort studies. The only prospective randomised controlled trials in prevention are of antihypertensive medication, hormone replacement therapy and statin therapy.

6.2.2   Non-modifiable risk factors for dementia

Age
Advancing age remains the single biggest risk factor for developing AD, VaD and DLB, though it should be noted that some less common causes of dementia (for example, FTD, CJD and Huntington's disease) are more common in mid life rather than at older ages (Harvey *et al.*, 2003). Prevalence rates for AD double every 4.5 years after the age of 65 and those for VaD double every 5.3 years, leading to a steady increase with advancing age (Jorm & Jolley, 1998). Rates may stabilise at around 50–60% when people reach their mid 90s, but there are insufficient studies of 'very old' people to know this with any degree of certainty. Clearly age is not a modifiable risk factor.

Learning disabilities
The ageing process for people with learning disabilities may begin much earlier than for the general population; people with Down's syndrome are at risk of developing a dementia of Alzheimer type about 30–40 years earlier than the rest of the population, and most researchers have found the prevalence of dementia in people with learning disabilities without Down's syndrome is also raised to two or three times that expected in those aged over 65 years.

Gender
Prevalence studies show higher rates of dementia in women than men, especially for AD (Rocca *et al.*, 1991). Rates for VaD are higher in men, though women tend to catch up at older ages. In part, the substantial difference (approximately 2:1) in prevalence between women and men in AD is due to women generally living longer than men. However, most, though not all, incidence studies also confirm higher rates of new cases in women, suggesting additional factors are involved. The reasons for the apparent increased susceptibility of women to develop AD are not clear, though a number of theories, including loss of oestrogens, have been proposed (but see section below on hormone replacement therapy) (Geerlings *et al.*, 2001).

Genotype

Several autosomal dominant forms of young-onset AD have been described, including mutations in the amyloid precursor protein, presenilin 1 and presenilin 2 genes. Such cases are rare (accounting for only about 1% of all AD) and characteristically have an age of onset below 55 years (Morris, 2005), although this may vary depending on the specific site of mutation (Lippa *et al.*, 2000). Genetic testing after appropriate counselling can be provided for such individuals and for non-affected members of their families. In relation to late-onset AD, the main genetic risk factor described thus far is possession of the apolipoprotein E4 allele, which shows a dose effect and has a major impact in terms of bringing forward the age at which dementia develops (Cedazo-Minguez & Cowburn, 2001). It is also likely to be a risk factor for VaD and DLB (Hebert *et al.*, 2000; Singleton *et al.*, 2002). However, at least 50% of late-onset AD develops without the apoE4 allele, making it difficult to interpret the results of such tests for diagnostic purposes). Undoubtedly, genetic factors are important in late-onset AD and may explain up to half the liability to develop the disorder (Pedersen *et al.*, 2004). Many other putative genetic risk factors have been described, but require further replication before they can definitively be accepted. There is much interest in potential therapeutic avenues that may be based on an understanding of the molecular changes caused by genetic factors associated with dementia, but apart from the possibility of pre-natal genetic diagnosis for known autosomal dominant cases, no modification of genetic risk factors is possible at the current time.

6.2.3 Potentially modifiable risk factors for dementia

Alcohol consumption

Excessive alcohol consumption is an established risk factor for dementia (Saunders *et al.*, 1991). There is consistent evidence from epidemiological studies that moderate alcohol consumption is associated, both cross-sectionally and in prospective studies, with lower rates of cardiovascular disease, cerebrovascular disease and dementia (including Alzheimer's and vascular disease) than either heavy drinking or abstinence (Letenneur, 2004). There is no consistent evidence that one type of alcoholic drink, for example, red wine, is more protective than another (Letenneur, 2004). These associative studies are not a basis on which to advise consumption of alcohol, though they do imply that drinking within the recommended range (up to 14 units per week for women and up to 21 units for men) is unlikely to increase risk of dementia.

Smoking

Large prospective epidemiological studies have established that smoking is a risk factor for dementia in general and AD in particular (Ott *et al.*, 1998), contradicting cross-sectional studies that had suggested that smoking may be protective (Wang *et al.*, 1999). Smoking is clearly a major risk factor for cardiovascular and cerebrovascular disease, and as such increases the risk of stroke and VaD.

Obesity

A number of recent prospective studies have supported an association between raised body mass index in mid life and subsequent increased risk of dementia in general and AD in particular (Gustafson *et al.*, 2003; Kivipelto *et al.*, 2005). Obesity also puts individuals at increased risk of developing type 2 diabetes, which is itself a risk factor for cerebrovascular disease and subsequent development of dementia (Ott *et al.*, 1999; Biessels *et al.*, 2006). No prospective studies have been undertaken to examine whether reducing obesity lowers risk of dementia.

Hypertension

Hypertension is a major risk factor for cardiovascular and cerebrovascular disease, including stroke, and antihypertensive treatment has been shown to reduce the incidence of both (Chalmers *et al.*, 2003; Sacco *et al.*, 2006; Williams *et al.*, 2002). Longitudinal epidemiological studies have also established hypertension in mid life to be a risk factor for the subsequent development of VaD and AD (Skoog *et al.*, 1996). Mid-life hypertension has also been associated with increased AD pathology at autopsy (Petrovitch *et al.*, 2000). Because of this, a number of prospective randomised controlled trials have investigated antihypertensive treatments in terms of possible reduction of dementia risk. A meta-analysis of such studies is reported by Feigin and colleagues (2005). Their analysis included four studies, details of which are provided in Appendix 15a. Study inclusion criteria varied; for example, the Perindopril Protection Against Recurrent Stroke Study (PROGRESS) (Tzourio *et al.*, 2003) included those with a history of stroke or transient ischaemic attack, whilst the other three studies included those with hypertension. Results are shown in Figure 1. Individually, the only study reporting a positive outcome was the SYST-EUR study (Forette *et al.*, 1998) of a dihydropyridine calcium-channel blocker (nitrendipine), and this showed an approximate halving of the number of dementia cases (mostly a reduction in AD) in the treatment group compared to placebo, though numbers developing dementia were small (21 cases in the treatment group and 43 in the control group). Overall, when the four studies are combined, the effect size shows a non-significant trend (relative risk [RR] = 0.80, 95% confidence interval [CI], 0.63–1.02) to a reduction in dementia in treated subjects. This suggests that antihypertensive treatment may be a promising avenue for prevention of dementia, including AD and VaD, but that further studies are required. It will also be important for future studies to distinguish between potential specific pharmacological effects of the agent under consideration (for example, an action on calcium channels) and the effects of lowering blood pressure itself. It should also be remembered that there are already many evidence-based reasons for treating hypertension apart from reducing dementia risk, including reducing cardiovascular and cerebrovascular events.

Hypercholesterolaemia

Raised cholesterol level has been implicated as a risk factor in the development of dementia in some (Jick *et al.*, 2000) but not all (Rea *et al.*, 2005) studies. Not only is it a recognised risk factor for stroke, itself a major risk factor for VaD, but raised cholesterol has also been associated with the development of AD. Scott and Laake

Figure 1: Risk of dementia or cognitive decline reported in trials of antihypertensive drugs (data from Feigin *et al.*, 2005)

Review: Dementia: Q2.2 Prevention
Comparison: 01 Antihypertensive drugs
Outcome: 01 Risk of dementia or cognitive decline

Study or sub-category	Treatment n/N	Control n/N	RR (random) 95% CI	Weight %	RR (random) 95% CI
01 Participants with hypertension					
SCOPE	175/4893	182/4869		35.23	0.96 [0.78, 1.17]
SHEP	21/2365	31/2371		13.40	0.68 [0.39, 1.18]
Syst-Eur	21/1485	43/1417		14.67	0.47 [0.28, 0.78]
Subtotal (95% CI)	8743	8657		63.31	0.70 [0.45, 1.11]
Total events: 217 (Treatment), 256 (Control)					
Test for heterogeneity: Chi² = 7.14, df = 2 (P = 0.03), I² = 72.0%					
Test for overall effect: Z = 1.51 (P = 0.13)					
02 Participants with stroke or transient ischaemic attack					
PROGRESS	193/3051	217/3054		36.69	0.89 [0.74, 1.07]
Subtotal (95% CI)	3051	3054		36.69	0.89 [0.74, 1.07]
Total events: 193 (Treatment), 217 (Control)					
Test for heterogeneity: not applicable					
Test for overall effect: Z = 1.22 (P = 0.22)					
Total (95% CI)	11794	11711		100.00	0.80 [0.63, 1.02]
Total events: 410 (Treatment), 473 (Control)					
Test for heterogeneity: Chi² = 7.28, df = 3 (P = 0.06), I² = 58.8%					
Test for overall effect: Z = 1.83 (P = 0.07)					

0.1   0.2   0.5   1   2   5   10

Favours treatment   Favours control

(2001) reviewed epidemiological studies examining the association between statin therapy and a reduced incidence of AD, but could not exclude bias as responsible for the observed associations. In terms of biomarkers, statin use has not been demonstrated to have any effect on serial brain measurement of hippocampal volume or amyloid biomarkers in plasma (Hoglund *et al.*, 2004). A community-based prospective cohort study (Li *et al.*, 2004) found that, while cross-sectional analysis revealed an apparent protective effect of previous statin use, prospective data showed no effect of statin use on subsequent development of either dementia in general or specifically AD. A similar finding was reported from the Canadian Study of Health and Aging (Rea *et al.*, 2005). The PROSPER study (Shepherd *et al.*, 2002) compared pravastatin to placebo and found a significantly reduced risk of coronary disease in treated subjects but no effect on cognitive function or stroke. In the heart protection study (HPSCG, 2002), there were no differences between simvastatin and placebo groups after 5 years' treatment in terms of rates of dementia or rates of cognitive impairment. A preliminary study suggests a possible beneficial effect in established AD (Sparks *et al.*, 2005) and further trials are ongoing. NICE recently published guidance on the initiation of statin therapy in adults with clinical evidence of cardio-vascular disease and in adults considered to be at risk of cardiovascular disease (NICE, 2006).

Head injury
A number of epidemiological studies have shown that head injury sufficient to cause loss of consciousness increases the risk (an approximate doubling) of subsequent dementia (Guo *et al.*, 2000; Plassman *et al.*, 2000). A possible biological mechanism has been suggested by the finding that after acute head injury, cerebrospinal fluid (CSF) and brain amyloid levels are elevated (Olsson *et al.*, 2004), though not all studies have supported this (Jellinger, 2004) and a meta-analysis of 15 epidemiological studies concluded that the risk was only apparent for males (Fleminger *et al.*, 2003).

Low folate and raised homocysteine levels
Raised homocysteine levels, associated with low folate intake and low folate levels, have been associated with increased risk of cardiovascular and cerebrovascular disease and increased risk of dementias, including AD (Seshadri *et al.*, 2002). There is much current interest in whether supplementation with B_{12} and/or folate (to reduce homocysteine levels) may prevent the development of dementia and perhaps slow its progression. Although results to date have been negative (Malouf *et al.*, 2003), further studies are ongoing and results are awaited with interest.

Hormone replacement therapy
The apparent increased vulnerability of women to develop AD, together with findings from a number of epidemiological studies that past use of hormone replacement therapy (HRT) was associated with a decreased risk of dementia and AD, have prompted great interest in the possibility that HRT may delay or prevent the onset of dementia

in general and AD in particular. A Cochrane review on the effects of HRT on cognitive function in cognitively intact post-menopausal women found little evidence that oestrogen therapy enhanced overall cognitive functioning (Hogervorst *et al.*, 2002). More recently, Low and Anstey (2006) conducted a meta-analysis of 26 studies (17 cross-sectional, five longitudinal observational and four RCTs) on the association between HRT and cognition in cognitively intact post-menopausal women. A further analysis was made of 18 studies on HRT and risk of dementia. The results suggest that there is no consistent benefit in favour of HRT and there may be an inverse relationship between study design and effect size. For example, a large prospective RCT (the Women's Health Initiative Memory Study) involving 4,532 post-menopausal women over the age of 65 and randomised to combined oestrogen or placebo found, not only that hormone replacement was not protective, but that it substantially increased the risk of dementia of any cause and cognitive decline (Shumaker *et al.*, 2004). Rates of dementia were approximately doubled in the group receiving HRT.

Depression
The relationship between depression and dementia is a complex one. Rates of depression are increased in those with dementia, while depression can sometimes be an early prodrome or manifestation of a dementing illness (Jorm, 2000). In addition, those with depression have a variety of cognitive impairments, sometimes severe enough to mimic dementia, whilst depression has also been examined as a risk factor for dementia. A meta-analysis, which included seven case controls and six prospective studies, found an approximately doubling of subsequent risk of dementia in those with a history of depression (Jorm, 2000). However, there was insufficient evidence to determine the hypothesis by which this relationship occurred, which may be a) that depression is an early prodrome of dementia, b) both depression and dementia have shared risk factors (environmental or genetic), c) depression itself, or some changes associated with it (inflammatory, cortisol toxicity), increase subsequent risk of dementia. The MIRAGE study (Green *et al.*, 2003) showed that depression does not simply appear to represent a prodrome of dementia, in that even depressive episodes occurring 25 years before the onset of cognitive impairment increase the risk of dementia. There are no prospective studies that have examined whether reducing depression subsequently reduces dementia risk.

Non-steroidal anti-inflammatory drugs
A number of studies, prompted by the inflammatory hypothesis of AD (McGeer & McGeer, 1999), have investigated whether the use of non-steroidal anti-inflammatory drugs (NSAIDs) may prevent subsequent development of dementia in general and AD in particular. A meta-analysis by De Craen and colleagues (2005) included 25 case control and cohort studies and showed that studies including prevalent and incident dementia cases showed a decreased risk of dementia in those using anti-inflammatory drugs, but not when cognitive decline was used as the clinical endpoint. The risk reduction of NSAIDs in preventing dementia or cognitive impairment was 50% in retrospective studies involving existing dementia cases, 20% in prospective studies

examining new dementia cases and was absent when cognitive decline alone was used as the endpoint. To explain this, the authors suggested that many of the reported beneficial effects of NSAIDs may result from various forms of recall, prescription and publication biases. Other reviews (for example, Szekely *et al.*, 2004) have suggested that duration of exposure may be important, with studies showing a duration of 2 years or more affording most benefit. The MIRAGE study (Yip *et al.*, 2005) suggested a particular benefit among apoE4 carriers. A systematic review and meta-analysis of nine studies of NSAIDs showed significant reduction in subsequent risk of AD, especially for long-term use (over 2 years) (Etminan *et al.*, 2003a). There was no effect in eight studies of aspirin. However, NSAIDs can have significant side effects, especially in older people. Whilst NSAIDs may yet have a role in prevention, further research is needed to establish dose, drug and duration of potential benefits, with careful consideration of potential risks. Effects need to be confirmed in prospective double blind, randomised trials.

Antioxidants

Because oxidative damage has been associated with pathological changes of dementia and AD (Retz *et al.*, 1998), it has long been hypothesised that antioxidants may provide some protection to the ageing brain in terms of reducing radical oxygen species and the damage they can cause. This has led to studies of antioxidants, particularly vitamin C (ascorbic acid) and vitamin E (D-alpha-tocopherol acetate in doses of 400 iu or more daily), both for AD and as a possible preventative measure. However, large-scale randomised controlled trials have not been undertaken and prospective observation studies examining this issue have come to differing conclusions (Boothby & Doering, 2005; Zandi *et al.*, 2004; Luchsinger *et al.*, 2003). Other evidence suggests that use of high doses of vitamin E for more than a year may be associated with an increase in all-cause mortality (Miller *et al.*, 2005) and increase the incidence of heart failure in those with diabetes mellitus or pre-existing vascular disease (Lonn *et al.*, 2005). The conclusion of a recent comprehensive review is that, in the absence of prospective, randomised controlled trials documenting benefits that clearly outweigh risks, vitamin E should not be recommended for primary or secondary prevention of AD or other dementias (Boothby & Doering, 2005). It further concludes that, although the risks of taking high doses of vitamin C are lower than those for vitamin E, there is no consistent efficacy data supporting its use.

Exercise

Exercise has many recognised benefits, including beneficial effects on the cardiovascular system and bone density and effects on well-being and mood, as well as potentially increasing social interaction when undertaken in a group setting. Some evidence suggests an association between physical activity in mid life and decreased risk of dementia and AD later in life. A population-based study over 21 years showed that physical activity at least twice a week (defined as 20–30 minutes in duration and causing breathlessness and sweating) was associated with a reduced risk of dementia and AD (roughly a halving of risk) (Rovio *et al.*, 2005). However, no randomised controlled trials have yet been undertaken to investigate whether starting to engage in exercise for those who currently do not will reduce their risk of developing dementia. In summary, engagement in physical activity lasting 20–30 minutes at least twice a week in mid life has been associated with decreased subsequent risk of dementia and AD. However, there is insufficient evidence to recommend physical activity specifically as a preventive measure for dementia, though there are many other reasons to encourage moderate exercise in everyone.

Education and mental stimulation

There is evidence that low educational attainment is associated with subsequent development of dementia (Valenzuela & Sachdev, 2005), but interpretation of this finding remains unclear, because whether this represents a true increased risk, or alteration of the threshold at which dementia becomes apparent, is uncertain. Of greater interest, is whether participation in cognitively stimulating activities can reduce the subsequent incidence of AD or other dementias (that is, the 'use it or lose it' hypothesis). A prospective study over 4.5 years showed that people participating in common cognitive activities had a decreased rate of subsequently developing AD (Wilson *et al.*, 2002). However, such observations would also be compatible with the 'cerebral reserve' hypothesis, whereby those of higher ability, who would be more likely to engage in mentally stimulating activities, would also be at decreased risk of subsequently developing dementia. Randomised controlled trials have demonstrated cognitive benefits of cognitive training, which last up to 2 years, but without effect on measures of everyday functioning (Ball *et al.*, 2002). Verghese and colleagues (2003) also found that participation in cognitively demanding leisure activities may protect against dementia. Over a median follow-up period of 5.1 years, the authors found that reading, playing board games, playing musical instruments and dancing were associated with a reduced risk of dementia. Similar results were found when AD and VaD were analysed separately. Whilst there are many reasons to encourage engagement in such activities, further studies to assess possible protective effects of cognitive activities on risk of dementia are needed.

6.2.4   Other risk factors for dementia

Other factors have been suggested as potential risk factors for dementia but await more definitive evidence. These include atrial fibrillation (Ott *et al.*, 1997) and the consumption of saturated fats (Mental Health Foundation, 2006).

6.2.5   Evidence summary

Established non-modifiable risk factors for dementia in general and AD in particular include advancing age, genotype, female gender and having a learning disability. Established risk factors that are potentially modifiable include hypertension, excessive alcohol consumption, diabetes, depression and head injury. Other potentially modifiable risk factors may include obesity, raised homocysteine levels and raised cholesterol levels. Risk factors for VaD overlap with AD and include age, vascular risk factors (stroke, hypertension, diabetes and smoking) and apoE4 genotype. Protective factors for dementia may include prior long-term use of NSAIDs control of vascular risk factors, regular exercise and engagement in leisure and cognitively stimulating activities. However, thus far prospective randomised controlled trials have not clearly demonstrated that modification of risk factors leads to a reduction in dementia rates. Four RCTs of antihypertensive therapy showed a non-significant trend towards reduced dementia rates in treated subjects, two RCTs of statins found no effect and one study of HRT unexpectedly found increased dementia rates in treated people.

6.2.6   Health economics evidence

No evidence was identified by the systematic literature search on the cost effectiveness of interventions that can prevent or delay the onset of dementia.

6.3   EARLY IDENTIFICATION

6.3.1   Identifying dementia early

Population studies of ageing and cognition suggest that impairment in multiple cognitive domains is observable several years before a diagnosis of AD and other dementias is made. In these epidemiological studies, the observed cognitive deficit is not qualitatively different from that seen in 'normal' ageing, suggesting continuity rather than discontinuity in the shift from 'normal' ageing to pre-clinical dementia (Bäckman *et al.*, 2004). Global cognitive deterioration occurs early, affecting episodic memory, executive functioning, verbal ability, visuospatial skills, attention and perceptual speed (Bäckman *et al.*, 2004). There is no evidence as yet that these changes are detectable in individuals in clinical encounters.

Precise diagnosis of AD and other dementias in their early phases would be aided by an understanding of the initiating neurobiological events and the development of specific cognitive paradigms or biomarkers (DeKosky, 2003).

Longitudinal studies suggest that the magnitude of cognitive impairment may remain relatively constant for a period of several years. This phase corresponds to the clinical concept of 'mild cognitive impairment' (MCI), in which the individual has subjective symptoms (predominantly of memory loss) and measurable cognitive deficits but without significant impairment in usual activities of everyday life. There is a considerable overlap in cognitive performance between 'normal' ageing and this stable phase (Small *et al.*, 2003).

At this stage, stringent tests of episodic memory are the best current neuropsychological predictors of subsequent conversion from MCI to AD at group level.

Imaging techniques can identify early brain changes, both structural and metabolic, but no single technique if used as a screening test can accurately identify individuals with MCI who will subsequently develop AD or other dementias (Nestor *et al.*, 2004).

A combination of neuropsychological testing and neuroimaging improves the diagnostic accuracy of predicting cognitive decline in people in the MCI phase over that achieved with either modality alone (Chong & Sahadevan, 2003). However, the tools for identifying the early changes of AD and other dementias are outpacing the therapeutic options and so the usefulness of such very early 'pre-clinical' diagnosis currently remains uncertain (Chang & Silverman, 2004).

Although an evidence-based approach to case finding and case management can be described, a systematic review of the literature on early identification of dementia states that there is insufficient evidence of benefit to justify population screening in primary care (Boustani *et al.*, 2003).

In AD, the stable phase ends with a precipitous decline in cognitive function, lasting between 2 and 5 years, in which semantic memory (the store of facts and general knowledge) and implicit memory (the non-conscious influence of past experience on subsequent performance) also become degraded (Spaan *et al.*, 2003). Other dementia subtypes will follow different paths, for example, difficulties in attention and executive function will be prominent in VaD, language disturbances in types of fronto-temporal dementia, and motor features and psychosis in DLB. People presenting with language disturbance may benefit from access to specialist speech and language therapy assessment and therapy within the multidisciplinary team at this early stage.

There is some evidence from the United States that early recognition and active therapy at this point (when early dementia can be diagnosed) delays the subsequent need for nursing home care and reduces the risk of misdiagnosis and inappropriate management (Chang & Silverman, 2004).

Earlier recognition of dementia syndromes can assist people with dementia and their families by dispelling anxiety about changes in memory, thinking, mood or behaviour and allowing mobilisation of resources that will be needed in the future. However, there are multiple obstacles to earlier diagnosis, both in terms of public awareness and professional understanding of dementia, which are still less than optimal (Iliffe *et al.*, 2002). Earlier recognition of dementia syndromes would have major resource, training and organisational implications for multidisciplinary working, services and inter-agency working if the development of 'care gaps' is to be avoided (Manthorpe *et al.*, 2003).

Personal awareness of changes in cognitive function in people with AD and other dementias is associated with better treatment outcomes from cognitive rehabilitation, but awareness can be difficult to assess, since individuals with AD may deny problems in one context but report awareness of them in another (Clare, 2004).

An evidence-based educational intervention using adult learning principles a nd conducted in the practice can improve diagnostic rates of dementia syndromes in general practice. Decision-support software designed to assist diagnostic and management thinking also improves recognition rates for dementia (Downs *et al.*, 2006).

6.3.2   Evidence summary

The shift from 'normal' ageing to pre-clinical dementia appears to occur slowly and there is no evidence as yet that this change is detectable in individuals in clinical encounters. The magnitude of cognitive impairments that do emerge may remain relatively constant for a period of several years. The individual does have subjective symptoms (predominantly of memory loss) and measurable cognitive deficits, but without significant impairment in usual activities of everyday life. At present, tests of episodic memory are the best neuropsychological predictors of subsequent conversion from pre-clinical to clinical dementia. Imaging techniques can identify early brain changes, both structural and metabolic, but no single technique if used as a screening test can accurately identify individuals with pre-clinical dementia who will subsequently develop clinical dementia. The means of identification of the early changes of dementia syndromes are developing more rapidly than the therapeutic options and so the usefulness of such very early pre-clinical diagnosis currently remains uncertain. There is insufficient evidence of benefit to justify population screening in primary care. The stable pre-clinical phase ends with a sharp decline in cognitive function, its length being dependent on the subtype of dementia. There is some evidence that early recognition and active therapy at this point (when early dementia can be diagnosed) delays the subsequent need for nursing home care and reduces the risk of misdiagnosis and inappropriate management.

6.3.3   Health economics evidence

No economic evidence was identified regarding the early identification of dementia.

6.4   DIAGNOSIS AND ASSESSMENT

6.4.1   Introduction

Many conditions apart from dementia can present with cognitive impairments, most commonly delirium, depression, side effects of medication, other psychiatric illnesses, substance misuse and medical conditions like hypothyroidism, or intracerebral infections or space-occupying lesions. A careful and comprehensive assessment with appropriate investigations is therefore necessary to arrive at a diagnosis of dementia.

Current practice
Diagnosis of a dementia syndrome may often be appropriately made in primary care, though the knowledge and expertise to make a subtype-specific diagnosis resides in specialists. Most specialists undertake a broadly similar assessment in terms of history, mental state and use of routine blood tests, but use of other diagnostic tests

(for example, imaging) varies considerably. Several different sets of diagnostic criteria exist, which are used to varying extents by different clinicians.

The evidence base/limitations
Current practice is largely based on cross-sectional and cohort studies that have assessed the usefulness of investigations in the clinical diagnosis of dementia and the accuracy of clinical diagnostic criteria as judged by autopsy verification. Definitive conclusions regarding the 'added value' of certain diagnostic tests over others are limited by the paucity of studies that assess investigations against autopsy in a truly blinded fashion and the relatively few studies that have directly compared one diagnostic test against another.

6.4.2   Diagnosis

As detailed in Chapter 4, dementia is a clinical diagnosis that is made when acquired cognitive deficits in more than one domain, representing a decline from a previously higher level of functioning, interfere with social and/or occupational functioning. Other features, including behavioural changes and symptoms such as depression, delusions and hallucinations, are commonly present. Dementia can result from a number of single or combined causes; it is usually progressive and can in some circumstances be reversible (for example, when due to a space-occupying lesion or infective or metabolic process).

Several different diagnostic criteria for dementia exist and have been shown to have good reliability (Knopman *et al.*, 2001). The Diagnostic and Statistical Manual of Mental Disorders, third edition revised (DSM-IIIR; American Psychiatric Association, 1987) definition of dementia includes as an absolute requirement an impairment in memory, whilst the tenth edition of the International Classification of Diseases (ICD-10; World Health Organization, 1992) definition requires multiple cognitive disturbances, including memory. Such definitions are often appropriate for the dementia seen in AD, when memory is nearly always affected, but are not always appropriate for other disorders including VaD, FTD and DLB when memory is not predominantly impaired (O'Brien *et al.*, 2003; Neary *et al.*, 1998; McKeith *et al.*, 1996, 2005).

As a result, a person may not meet ICD-10 or DSM-IIIR criteria for dementia because of an absence of memory impairment, despite having multiple acquired cognitive domains representing a decline from a previous level of functioning and causing social and/or occupational impairment.

6.4.3   Diagnostic criteria for subtypes of dementia

A number of different clinical diagnostic criteria have been proposed for the main subtypes of dementia.

Alzheimer's disease

Several sets of diagnostic criteria for AD exist, including:

● ICD-10
● Diagnostic and Statistical Manual of Mental Disorders, fourth edition text revision (DSM-IV-TR; American Psychiatric Association, 2000)
● National Institute of Neurological and Communicative Disorders and Stroke and the Alzheimer's Disease and Related Disorders Association (NINCDS/ADRDA) criteria (McKhann *et al.*, 1984).

The most widely studied in terms of predictive ability are the DSM and the NINCDS/ADRDA criteria, while the NINCDS/ADRDA criteria have almost universally been adopted for entry into therapeutic trials. Both the DSM-IIIR criteria for dementia of Alzheimer type and the NINCDS/ADRDA criteria for probable AD have reasonable sensitivity (mean 81%) and specificity (mean 70%), while the NINCDS/ADRDA diagnosis of possible AD has higher sensitivity (mean 83%) at the price of loss of specificity (mean 48%) (Knopman *et al.*, 2001). The diagnostic accuracy of the NINCDS/ ADRDA criteria, their ability to subdivide into probable and possible AD and their widespread use in clinical therapeutic trials make them the preferred criteria for clinical diagnosis.

Vascular dementia

Criteria for the diagnosis of VaD include:

● ICD-10
● DSM-IV-TR
● National Institute of Neurological Disorders and Stroke/Association Internationale pour la Recherche et l'Enseignement en Neurosciences (NINDS–AIREN) criteria (Roman *et al.*, 1993)
● the Modified Hachinski Ischaemic Score (MHIS; Hachinski *et al.*, 1975; Rosen *et al.*, 1980)
● the ischaemic VaD criteria proposed by the state of California Alzheimer's Disease Diagnostic and Treatment Centers (ADDTC) (Chui *et al.*, 1992).

Criteria for subcortical ischaemic VaD have also been proposed (Erkinjuntti *et al.*, 2000). As judged by pathology, sensitivity with all criteria tends to be low, around 50%, while specificity is good, around 85% (Gold *et al.*, 2002). Therapeutic studies have generally used the NINCS/AIREN criteria, making them the preferred criteria for clinical diagnosis. However, neither these nor criteria for AD deal adequately with the issue of mixed dementia, which may be the most common subtype in clinical practice. In assessing people with possible dementia, clinicians will often be faced with difficulty, since many people may not fulfil strict criteria for a single subtype such as VaD or AD.

Dementia with Lewy bodies

Consensus diagnostic criteria for DLB exist (McKeith *et al.*, 1996) and have been prospectively validated (McKeith *et al.*, 2000b). In common with other criteria for diagnosis of subtypes of dementia, the criteria for DLB have low sensitivity (around 50%) but high specificity (Litvan *et al.*, 2003; McKeith *et al.*, 2005). Sensitivity for possible DLB criteria appears higher, but has been the subject of few investigations. These criteria have recently been reviewed and amended based on clinical expert discussion and review of the latest research evidence (McKeith *et al.*, 2005). The consensus criteria have been almost universally adopted for use in all clinical research and therapeutic studies and are the criteria of choice. It should be noted that DLB may form part of a spectrum of Lewy body dementias, which would include dementia seen in Parkinson's disease (PDD). DLB and PDD are separated in current diagnostic criteria by the duration of parkinsonian features (if present), which has to be more than one year before onset of dementia for PDD and less than one year for DLB.

Frontotemporal dementia
Two sets of diagnostic criteria for FTD have been proposed:
● the Lund-Manchester criteria (Neary *et al.*, 1998)
● the NINDS Work Group on Frontotemporal Dementia and Pick's Disease (McKhann *et al.*, 2001).

The Lund-Manchester criteria recognise three main syndromes, FTD, progressive nonfluent aphasia and semantic aphasia. The NINDS Work Group criteria recognise two main presentations, frontal (behavioural) and temporal (language). Neither set has been prospectively validated against autopsy.

Mixed dementia
Many people with dementia will have mixed disease; indeed the community-based Cognitive Function and Ageing Study showed that this was common in older people (MRC/CFAS, 2001). In such cases, until further evidence emerges to suggest otherwise, it is pragmatic to consider the clinical condition that best fits. For example, someone with mixed dementia whose dementia is predominantly thought to be due to AD would likely best be supported and managed as someone with AD. This is the approach taken by NICE in its technology appraisal of drugs for AD[47].

6.4.4   Assessment

Diagnosis of a dementia syndrome can often be made in primary care, though if diagnosis is in doubt, referral to a specialist (old age psychiatrist, neurologist, physician in healthcare of older people or specialist GP, as deemed appropriate) should be undertaken. In most cases, subtype-specific diagnosis of the type of dementia will be required and people should be referred to a specialist with expertise in the differential diagnosis of the condition. Other reasons for referral to a specialist at any stage of dementia may include the presence of other behavioural changes and symptoms, especially if severe and non-responsive to initial treatment, or the need to access expertise or special investigations, services or treatments (for example, medication

---

[47]For further information see www.nice.org.uk/guidance/TA111.

for the treatment of dementia) only available within secondary care. Agreed referral pathways between primary and secondary care should be in place for people with dementia, as recommended in the National Service Framework for older people (Department of Health, 2001b).

History

Diagnosis of dementia can only be made after a thorough assessment consisting of history, cognitive and mental state examination, physical examination and appropriate investigations. A detailed history from the person and, as the person may not be able to give a fully accurate history, a history from a relative or someone who knows the person well should be obtained, including the history of the presenting complaint, past medical and psychiatric history, medication use, drug or alcohol history, family medical and psychiatric history, a history of changes in personality or behaviour and assessment of changes in abilities to undertake everyday tasks. Useful standardised informant-administered assessment measures include the Informant Questionnaire on Cognitive Decline in the Elderly (IQCODE) (Jorm & Jacomb, 1989) and measure of activities of daily living such as the Bristol Activities of Daily Living Scale (BADL) (Bucks *et al.*, 1996).

Physical examination

A physical examination (including basic neurological examination) can detect evidence of physical disorders that can cause cognitive impairment, as well as other features that are important in making an accurate diagnosis, including the presence of focal neurological signs and motor features such as parkinsonism.

Mental state examination

A mental state examination should examine for the presence of psychiatric disorders that may cause diagnostic confusion with dementia (in particular depression) and also for associated non-cognitive symptoms that may be associated with dementia, including delusions, misidentifications and hallucinations that may have impact on diagnosis and management (Royal College of Psychiatrists, 2005b); Scottish Intercollegiate Guidelines Network, 2006).

Cognitive testing

   Brief cognitive assessment

In order to make a clinical diagnosis of a dementia, cognitive assessment is essential. The aim of this is to determine which, and to what extent, different cognitive domains are affected. As dementia represents a change from the person's previous level of function, life long intellectual and educational attainment provides the context for current performance. Cognitive assessment includes testing attention and concentration, orientation, immediate and delayed memory, and higher cortical function including praxis, perception, language and executive function.

    There are several standardised screening tests for the initial assessment of dementia that may be helpful adjuncts. The most widely used is the 30-item Mini Mental State Examination (MMSE), widely used in old age psychiatry and which takes

149

around 5 minutes to complete. Others include the Newcastle Mental Test Score; the 7-minute screen (Meulen *et al.*, 2004); the clock drawing test, useful for assessing praxis and executive function (Sunderland *et al.*, 1989); the General Practitioner Assessment of Cognition (GPCOG) (Brodaty *et al.*, 2002), which helpfully includes a brief informant rating as well as cognitive items; and the 6-Item Cognitive Impairment Test (6-CIT) (Brooke & Bullock, 1999), used in general practice. Advantages of standardised scales include the facts that norms are available, that severity of cognitive impairment can be quantified and easily communicated to others, that they serve as a useful baseline from which future change (for example, deterioration in the case of suspected dementia or improvement on medication or when delirium/depression resolves) can be accurately determined. Potential limitations, particularly of the MMSE, include associations with education level and sensitivity to depression (Orrell *et al.*, 1992). There is some variance in terms of reliability, particularly when standardised instructions and procedures are not followed. These screening measures may be misleading with those with either high or low premorbid ability and with certain types of dementia (especially FTD and VaD). They do not generally adequately reflect important cognitive functions, such as executive function. There are also difficulties in their use with people with language impairment or sensory difficulties, or who are being tested in a second language. Where English is not the person's first language, the use of an interpreter should be considered; where a screening test has been translated into the person's first language, this should be utilised, so the interpreter may focus on the person's responses (see for example, Gangulai *et al.*, 1995; Kabir & Herlitz, 2000; Lindesay *et al.*, 1997; Rait *et al.*, 1997; Rait *et al.*, 2000; Rowland *et al.*, 2006). Published cut-off points to assist in the diagnosis of dementia should be interpreted cautiously, in view of the many other factors involved and the possibility of high false-positive rates (White *et al.*, 2002). Cognitive impairment is not a good predictor of behavioural disturbance and carer stress, so only forms a part of the assessment needed.

Neuropsychological assessment

For those with mild or questionable impairment, and in other selected cases to assist with specific subtype diagnosis and differential diagnosis and to inform management, more comprehensive standardised cognitive assessments (for example, Cambridge Cognitive Examination – Revised (CAMCOG-R) (Roth *et al.*, 1998; Williams *et al.*, 2003), Addenbrooke's Cognitive Examination (ACE) (Mathuranath *et al.*, 2000), Alzheimer's Disease Assessment Scale cognitive subscale (ADAS-cog) (Rosen *et al.*, 1984), Middlesex Elderly Assessment of Mental State (MEAMS) (Golding, 1989) and Repeatable Battery for the Assessment of Neuropsychological Status (RBANS) (Randolph, 1998)) may be needed. This would usually be undertaken as part of specialist referral. These more detailed assessments might form the first part of a full and detailed neuropsychological assessment by a clinical psychologist. Where there is also a significant impairment of language, an assessment by a speech and language therapist will contribute to the overall neuropsychological assessment. Such testing may provide important information regarding diagnosis and management, with specific comparisons made with predicted life-long levels of attainment and ability, but, if diagnosis is unclear, also provides a baseline against which any future cognitive change can be measured. This may be particularly important in cases where cognitive change has been identified but does not meet the diagnostic criteria for dementia, as in MCI.

Hentschel and colleagues (2005) provide evidence that a neuropsychological assessment (using the Consortium to Establish a Registry for Alzheimer's Disease (CERAD) battery of tests) adds to the basic neuropsychiatric evaluation, with the initial diagnosis being changed in a significant number of cases. This occurs mainly at the borderline between 'no dementia' and 'dementia'. In contrast, magnetic resonance imaging (MRI) scanning tends to change the subtype of dementia, rather than influence decisions about its presence. This suggests that neuropsychological assessment and MRI scanning may be complementary in the added value they provide to diagnostic assessment.

Blood tests and other investigations
There is no universal consensus on the appropriate diagnostic battery that should be undertaken in those with suspected dementia. However, a review of 14 guidelines and consensus statements found considerable similarity in recommendations (Beck *et al.*, 2000). The main reason for undertaking investigations in a person with suspected dementia is to exclude a potentially reversible or modifying cause for the dementia and to help exclude common misdiagnoses including delirium. However, it should be noted that in recent studies the prevalence of reversible dementias is low. Clarfield (2003) reviewed 39 studies of over 7,000 cases and found potentially reversible causes in 9%, though only 0.6% of cases actually reversed. A recent consensus document from the Royal College of Psychiatrists recommends full blood count, erythrocyte sedimentation rate (ESR) or C-reactive protein (CRP), vitamin B_{12}, folate, thyroid function, urea and electrolyte, calcium, liver function and glucose tests, with blood tests for syphilis, lipids and HIV listed as 'optional' (Royal College of Psychiatrists, 2005b). The recent Scottish Intercollegiate Guidelines Network (SIGN) dementia guideline (SIGN, 2006) does not recommend any specific blood tests and indicates that they should be selected 'on clinical grounds according to history and clinical circumstances'.

Other investigations may include neuroimaging and cerebrospinal fluid analysis, but these are likely to be undertaken as part of further assessment for subtype diagnosis by a specialist with experience of differential diagnosis of the condition.

Structural neuroimaging
The two main forms of structural imaging are computed tomography (CT) and MRI. Local access to each varies considerably, while some forms of scanning are appropriate for some people and not others (for example, some find MRI scanning claustrophobic or have contraindications such as pacemakers or metallic implants). MRI is more costly than CT but superior in terms of anatomical visualisation of structural lesions, infarcts and white-matter pathology.

There are two main reasons for undertaking structural imaging in people with suspected dementia. The first is to exclude an intracerebral lesion (for example, a space-occupying or subdural lesion, or normal pressure hydrocephalus) as a cause for the cognitive impairment. Systematic reviews have suggested that between 2.2 and 5% of cases with suspected dementia had conditions that required structural neuroimaging to assist with diagnosis (Chui & Zhang, 1997; Clarfield, 2003).

Though such lesions can sometimes be suspected on clinical grounds by factors such as atypical history, early neurological signs, seizure, disturbance and short duration – factors that may prioritise those who undergo imaging if resources are limited (Royal College of Psychiatrists, 2005b) – a systematic review of six different clinical prediction rules for neuroimaging in dementia showed that most had poor sensitivity and all low specificity (Gifford *et al.*, 2000).

The second use of structural imaging is to inform the subtype-specific diagnosis of dementia, in particular differentiating AD from VaD and FTD. Reported sensitivities and specificities in this regard vary depending on the method (that is, visual rating, volumetric or voxel based) and the anatomical area studied. A systematic review of over a hundred studies found several structural imaging measures, which clearly separated groups with AD, including early-stage, from controls, with overlap between groups of less than 6% for the hippocampus (Zakzanis *et al.*, 2003). Similar changes in hippocampus and/or entorhinal cortex have been found, on a group basis, to differentiate those with mild impairment who subsequently progress to AD from those who remain stable (Jack *et al.*, 1999; Stoub *et al.*, 2005). Serial MRI scanning may also identify early brain changes before clinical onset of dementia (Scahill *et al.*, 2002). Such brain imaging changes are not absolutely diagnostic in any individual but may be used to inform clinical judgement regarding diagnosis and likelihood of progression.

However, such structural imaging changes are less helpful in distinguishing AD from other types of dementia, including VaD and DLB, where atrophy of the hippocampus also occurs, albeit to a lesser extent than in AD (Barber *et al.*, 1999). In FTD, frontal lobe atrophy may be seen on CT and MRI but, while this is a fairly specific marker, it can lack sensitivity. VaD is associated with a number of cerebrovascular changes, including cortical infarcts, lacunes and extensive white-matter lesions (Roman *et al.*, 1993). Many lesions can be seen on CT, but MRI has greater sensitivity to detect small vascular lesions and subcortical white-matter change.

There is much variability in methods of analysis and reporting of such MR images, and some techniques (such as volumetric) are very time consuming to apply in clinical practice; further work is needed to harmonise and standardise methods on analysis and reporting of clinical CT and MRI studies before such methods could be widely adopted clinically.

Functional imaging

Single-photon emission computed tomography (SPECT) and positron emission tomography (PET)

Both perfusion hexamethylpropyleneamine oxime (HMPAO) SPECT and 2-[18F] fluoro-2-deoxy-D-glucose (FDG) PET can offer valuable information in the assessment and diagnosis of those with suspected dementia. A systematic review of diagnostic accuracy of HMPAO SPECT found pooled sensitivity of 77.1% and specificity of 89% in the separation of AD from normal comparison groups, with sensitivity of 71% and specificity of 76% separating AD from VaD, and sensitivity of 71% and specificity of 78% in separation from FTD (Dougall *et al.*, 2004). In a comparison with clinical criteria (as judged by pathological verification), clinical criteria were found to be more sensitive in detecting AD than SPECT (81% versus 74%), but SPECT provided higher specificity against other types of dementia than clinical criteria (91% versus 70%) (Dougall *et al.*, 2004). This supports the view that SPECT can be helpful in selected cases in the differentiation of AD, in particular from FTD and VaD. Other studies have suggested that perfusion SPECT is particularly helpful when there is diagnostic uncertainty, for example, in cases of possible as opposed to probable AD (Jagust *et al.*, 2001).

Another form of SPECT imaging, iodine I 123-radiolabeled 2beta-carbomethoxy-3beta-(4-iodophenyl)-N-(3-fluoropropyl) nortropane (FP-CIT) has been licensed for the investigation of suspected parkinsonism and shows high sensitivity and specificity in separating cases of Parkinson's disease from disorders such as essential tremor (Benamer *et al.*, 2000). DLB is associated with nigrostriatal degeneration, even in people without clinical parkinsonism, and studies have suggested high sensitivity and specificity (one against autopsy verification) in terms of distinguishing AD from DLB (Walker *et al.*, 2002; O'Brien *et al.*, 2004; Ceravolo *et al.*, 2004). Detection of degeneration of the dopaminergic system in people with dementia has been incorporated into the latest consensus diagnostic criteria for DLB (McKeith *et al.*, 2005). As such, FP-CIT SPECT may give useful information in people suspected of having DLB.

PET scanning has been shown to improve the sensitivity and specificity of clinical criteria in much the same way as SPECT, and sensitivities of around 90% and specificity of 70% have been reported in pathological verification studies (Mosconi, 2005; Patwardhan *et al.*, 2004). FDG PET may show some superiority over perfusion SPECT in detecting AD (Mielke & Heiss, 1998) but currently PET is not widely available in the UK and remains an expensive and invasive investigation.

Other neuroimaging techniques

Functional MRI, MR spectroscopy, diffusion weighted MR and other techniques have been investigated in the assessment and diagnosis of those with dementia. Other specific ligands and imaging markers are being developed, such as PET amyloid imaging (Klunk *et al.*, 2004). Group differences between AD and other types of dementia have been reported for many of these modalities. However, their high cost, limited availability and lack of evidence base mean they cannot be recommended for clinical use at the current time.

Role of cerebrospinal fluid and other biomarkers

There is much interest in the possible development of tests, both in cerebrospinal fluid (CSF) and blood, for use in AD to allow earlier and more accurate diagnosis. Most studies to date that have been undertaken on CSF biomarkers include tau, phosphorylated tau and beta-amyloid 1-42. These three biomarkers have high sensitivity to differentiate AD from normal ageing, depression and some forms of dementia (for example, alcohol related) but have much lower specificity against other dementias, including FTD, DLB and VaD (Andreasen & Blennow, 2005). Some recent reports have suggested high sensitivity and specificity in relation to determining progression of those with mild cognitive impairment to AD but not other types of dementia. However, the majority of studies come from specialist centres, making widespread interpretation of results difficult, and there remain concerns and difficulties about reliability and standardisation of assays between different laboratories (Wiltfang *et al.*, 2005). It also remains to be seen whether lumbar puncture to obtain CSF would be widely acceptable to people with dementia as a routine investigation. The 14-3-3 protein is associated with rapid neuronal loss and in most studies has been shown to have high sensitivity and specificity (both >90%) for CJD (Hsich *et al.*, 1996).

EEG

Many studies have investigated the ability of the electroencephalogram (EEG) to separate AD from normal ageing (Jonkman, 1997) and, less commonly, other causes of dementia (Walker *et al.*, 2000). Many rely on complex quantitative techniques, which are not applicable clinically. The resting EEG is often diffusely abnormal in dementia and may not be useful as a routine investigation. However, its use in selected cases can be helpful. Abnormal EEGs have been described in delirium (gross slowing) (Jacobson & Jerrier, 2000) and CJD (triphasic spikes) (Poser *et al.*, 2000), while in FTD, EEG is reported to be normal (Neary *et al.*, 1998).

Brain biopsy

In highly selected cases, a brain biopsy, usually of non-dominant frontal cortex, may sometimes be considered necessary when a treatable disorder, such as an infective, metabolic or inflammatory condition, is suspected but which cannot be diagnosed by other means. A retrospective study showed that this produced a diagnosis in 57% of cases, with 11% of people having complications such as bleeding or seizures (Warren *et al.*, 2005). However, it should be noted that even in this highly selected group referred for biopsy, yields of reversible causes of dementia were low (around 10%).

6.4.5 Evidence summary

Standardised and widely accepted criteria exist for the diagnosis of subtypes of dementia including AD, VaD, DLB and FTD. These generally have high specificity but sensitivity can be low, and none deals adequately with those who have mixed causes of dementia. In those with suspected dementia, the most frequent reasons for misdiagnosis include delirium, depression, metabolic and endocrine disorders and other intracerebral pathologies. A standardised cognitive assessment tool is a useful adjunct to cognitive testing. Routine screening for syphilis and HIV is not indicated. CT scanning can detect most gross intracerebral pathology, but MRI has superior sensitivity and is preferred where available. Neuropsychological assessment can be helpful, especially in early cases, to help determine whether dementia is present or not. Blood-flow SPECT or FDG PET can detect functional changes in AD and be useful in differentiating AD, FTD and VaD. Dopaminergic SPECT or PET can detect nigrostriatal degeneration *in vivo* and can differentiate DLB and Parkinson's disease from AD and VaD. CSF examination shows changes in AD, including increased levels of tau and phosphorylated tau and reduced levels of Abeta 1-42, though the role of these measurements in diagnosis and monitoring of AD and other dementias remains to be determined. The 14-3-3 protein shows a high sensitivity and specificity for the diagnosis of CJD. The resting EEG shows non-specific abnormalities in most types of dementia but is relatively normal in FTD and shows specific abnormalities in some cases of CJD. Brain biopsy may be considered appropriate in highly selected cases and can contribute in a minority of cases to accurate diagnosis that alters management.

6.4.6   Health economics evidence

Five studies were identified that addressed the cost effectiveness of neuroimaging tests for the diagnosis of dementia. Four studies, three in a US setting and one in a European setting, compared a range of neuroimaging tests to a standard examination that involved medical history, cognitive and functional assessment, laboratory tests and an MRI (McMahon *et al.*, 2000 & 2003; Silverman *et al.*, 2002; Moulin-Romsee *et al.*, 2005). One study, LaFrance and colleagues (1998), compared dynamic susceptibility contrast MRI to SPECT. Characteristics and results of all studies are presented in the form of evidence tables in Appendix 18.

The diagnostic procedures and primary outcome measures were considered not relevant to the UK setting.

6.5   EXPERIENCE OF ASSESSMENT PROCESS

6.5.1   Introduction

The diagnosis of dementia is often a step-wise process in which the person with dementia is assessed by different professionals. The experience of this assessment process may influence the way in which the person with dementia and his or her family or other carers assimilate and accommodate to the diagnosis. Professionals involved in assessment and diagnosis of dementia need to understand the potential impact of the ways in which they respond to questions, offer and share information and provide support during the assessment process.

Professionals working with people with dementia can find the process of reaching a diagnosis difficult, because they may have to respond to anxiety, distress and disbelief on the part of the individual and those around him or her. Many professionals express concerns about how and when to convey the diagnosis, and to whom. This review of qualitative research evidence gives some guidance to assist practitioners in these tasks.

6.5.2 Sharing the diagnosis

The majority of people with mild dementia wish to know of their diagnosis (Pinner & Bouman, 2003; De Lepeleire *et al.*, 2004), and all practitioners should assume that the diagnosis will be discussed with the person with dementia, unless there are clear reasons not to do so. The benefits of sharing a diagnosis include ending uncertainty, confirming suspicions, increasing understanding of problems, giving access to support, promoting positive coping strategies, facilitating planning and fulfilment of short-term goals (Bamford *et al.*, 2004; Pratt & Wilkinson, 2003; Husband, 1999, 2000; Smith & Beattie, 2001).

People who have been informed of their diagnosis sometimes report that this disclosure process is badly handled, that little information is provided or that little or no follow-up occurs (Clare, 2004). A systematic review of the literature about sharing the diagnosis of dementia suggests that non-sharing of information or vague information about it is experienced as confusing, upsetting and difficult for some people with dementia and their families (Bamford *et al.*, 2004).

However, there is also some evidence that clinicians do discuss disclosure carefully with people with suspected dementia and their families, to establish the best approach and what the person wishes to be told. During the assessment and diagnostic process, people should routinely be asked if they wish to know the diagnosis and with whom this should be shared (Pratt & Wilkinson, 2003; Pinner & Bouman, 2003).

Adjustment to the diagnosis of dementia is easier if the social context is supportive. Continuing support for people receiving a diagnosis is the responsibility of primary care. Necessary skills may include being able to anticipate and respond to shock, fear and grief.

People with severe dementia are often not given their diagnosis, although family carers are likely to receive it (Fahy *et al.*, 2003). There may be issues around lack of insight and difficulties in retaining information, which make conveying information about diagnosis difficult if not impossible in such situations. However, this should be assessed and, wherever possible, responded to on an individual basis. There should be no automatic assumption that diagnosis should not be conveyed to the individual simply because of the perceived severity of dementia.

People with learning disabilities should be told their diagnosis of dementia; those supporting them should have access to specialist clinical advice and support about information sharing (Kerr & Wilkinson, 2005).

Clinicians may find the work of sharing the diagnosis with the individual and providing support difficult and may require their own support with such therapeutic work (Arber & Gallagher, 2003).

6.5.3 Confidentiality

Issues regarding confidentiality (that is, the question of with whom information is shared) should be addressed with people with dementia at the time of diagnosis and throughout their subsequent assessments or reviews (also see Section 4.9.5). Records and care plans should routinely note information about sharing agreements, outlining interprofessional exchange and communications with others, including carers, and the rare circumstances when such steps might need to be breached (for example, with regard to issues such as driving, safety and risk) (Pinfold *et al.*, 2004; Tracy *et al.*, 2004).

6.5.4   Support and information

For people with newly diagnosed dementia and members of their family, accurate details of local support should be available in primary and secondary care, social care and voluntary and community settings (Audit Commission, 2000; Cornwall County Council, 2005). Information is most useful if people with dementia have been involved in its compilation and presentation, and examples of good practice should be adapted for local situations (McKillop & Wilkinson, 2004; Scottish Action on Dementia[48]).

Family members should have access to information and advice from sources that are able to address their different concerns, which may be different to those antici- pated by clinicians (Gely-Nargeot *et al.*, 2003). People with financial problems may find care-giving particularly difficult and may benefit from early referral to financial or debt advice agencies (Schneider *et al.*, 1999). People with dementia who also have another mental health problem, such as depression, may need particular and individ- ualised help to access support (Manthorpe & Iliffe, 2005). Information for children in families where a member has dementia should be available, particularly for children and young people who act as carers. Voluntary sector organisations are a major source of information for people with dementia and their families, but their resources are often limited and capacity-building is necessary at local level (Manthorpe *et al.*, 2003).

When working with people from minority communities where terms like demen- tia may not be widely known, practitioners should develop or draw on specialist support and publications (Bowes & Wilkinson 2003; Adamson, 2001).

6.5.5   Assessment and support

Assessment experiences can induce shame and distress and can lead to people trying to maintain their sense of identity, and this can be perceived as 'covering up' or loss of insight (Keady *et al.*, 1995; Cheston *et al.*, 2003a, 2003b). Support groups for people with newly diagnosed dementia promote well-being. These may be experien- tial group therapy, allowing people to explore the experience of dementia in a safe, supportive and secure setting (Cheston, 1996; Cheston & Jones, 2000; Cheston *et al.*, 2003a, 2003b). Family therapy services show promise at helping people with

---

[48]www.alzscot.org.

dementia and their families where psychiatric problems exist (in the person with dementia or his or her family) that are beyond the skills of primary care practitioners (Benbow *et al.*, 1993).

Delays in referrals to diagnostic and assessment services are experienced as stressful by relatives of people with dementia (Sperlinger & Furst, 1994). Continuity of care matters and services that facilitate continuity of contact and support are appreciated by people with dementia and their carers, who dislike discontinuity associated with hospital-based services and prefer community-based assessment services (Timlin *et al.*, 2005).

At all stages of contact with services, advocacy for people with dementia should be available but at present is widely variable in scale and scope (Cantley *et al.*, 2003).

6.5.6   Evidence summary

The majority of people with mild dementia wish to know of their diagnosis. All practitioners should assume that the diagnosis will be discussed with the person with dementia, unless there are clear reasons not to do so. Failure to share or provision of vague information about the diagnosis is experienced as confusing. There should be no automatic assumption that diagnosis should not be conveyed to the individual simply because of the perceived severity of dementia. Adjustment to the diagnosis of dementia is easier if the social context is supportive and continuing support for people receiving the diagnosis is the responsibility of primary care.

Family members should have access to information and advice from sources that are able to address their different concerns, which may be different to those anticipated by clinicians. Accurate details of local support should be available in primary and secondary care, social care and voluntary and community settings for people with newly diagnosed dementia and members of their family. Assessment experiences can induce shame and distress and can lead to people trying to maintain their sense of identity, and this can be perceived as 'covering up' or loss of insight. Services that facilitate continuity of contact and support are appreciated by people with dementia and their carers.

6.6   HEALTH AND SOCIAL CARE RECOMMENDATIONS

6.6.1   Risk factors, screening and genetic counselling

6.6.1.1   General population screening for dementia should not be undertaken. [For the evidence, see section 6.3]

6.6.1.2   In middle-aged and older people, vascular and other modifiable risk factors for dementia (for example, smoking, excessive alcohol consumption, obesity, diabetes, hypertension and raised cholesterol) should be reviewed and, if appropriate, treated. [For the evidence, see sections 4.5.2 and 6.2]

6.6.1.3   Healthcare professionals working with people likely to have a genetic cause for their dementia (for example, familial autosomal dominant AD or FTD, CADASIL, or Huntington's disease) should offer to refer them and their unaffected relatives for genetic counselling. [For the evidence, see sections 4.5.1 and 6.2.2]

6.6.1.4   Regional genetic services should provide genetic counselling to people who are likely to have a genetic cause for their dementia and their unaffected relatives. [For the evidence, see sections 4.5.1 and 6.2.2]

6.6.1.5   If a genetic cause for dementia is not suspected, including late-onset dementia, genotyping should not be undertaken for clinical purposes. [For the evidence, see sections 4.5.1 and 6.2.2]

6.6.2   Preventive measures

6.6.2.1   The following interventions should not be prescribed as specific treatments for the primary prevention of dementia:
- statins
- hormone replacement therapy
- vitamin E
- non-steroidal anti-inflammatory drugs. [For the evidence, see sections 4.5.2 and 6.2.3]

6.6.2.2   For the secondary prevention of dementia, vascular and other modifiable risk factors (for example, smoking, excessive alcohol consumption, obesity, diabetes, hypertension and raised cholesterol) should be reviewed in people with dementia and, if appropriate, treated. [For the evidence, see sections 4.5.2 and 6.2.3]

6.6.3   Early identification of dementia

6.6.3.1   Primary healthcare staff should consider referring people who show signs of MCI[49] for assessment by memory assessment services to aid early identification of dementia, because more than 50% of people with MCI later develop dementia. [For the evidence, see sections 4.1.1 and 6.3]

6.6.3.2   Those undertaking health checks as part of health facilitation for people with learning disabilities should be aware of the increased risk of dementia in this group. Those undertaking health checks for other high-risk groups, for example those who have had a stroke and those with neurological conditions such as Parkinson's disease, should also be aware

---

[49]MCI is a syndrome defined as cognitive decline greater than expected for an individual's age and education level, which does not interfere notably with ADLs. It is not a diagnosis of dementia of any type, although it may lead to dementia in some cases.

of the possibility of dementia. [For the evidence, see sections 4.1.1, 4.1.4, 4.5.2, 4.6.3, 6.2.2 and 6.2.3]

6.6.3.3   Memory assessment services that identify people with MCI (including those without memory impairment, which may be absent in the earlier stages of non-Alzheimer's dementias) should offer follow-up to monitor cognitive decline and other signs of possible dementia in order to plan care at an early stage. [For the evidence, see sections 4.1.1, 4.6.1, 4.6.2 and 6. 3]

6.6.4   Recognition

6.6.4.1   A diagnosis of dementia should be made only after a comprehensive assessment, which should include:
● history taking
● cognitive and mental state examination
● physical examination and other appropriate investigations
● a review of medication in order to identify and minimise use of drugs, including over-the-counter products, that may adversely affect cognitive functioning. [For the evidence, see sections 4.1.1, 4.1.2, 4.6.1, 4.6.2, 4.6.3 and 6.4]

6.6.4.2   People who are assessed for the possibility of dementia should be asked if they wish to know the diagnosis and with whom this should be shared. [For the evidence, see section 6.5.2]

6.6.4.3   Clinical cognitive assessment in those with suspected dementia should include examination of attention and concentration, orientation, short and long-term memory, praxis, language and executive function. As part of this assessment, formal cognitive testing should be undertaken using a standardised instrument. The MMSE has been frequently used for this purpose, but a number of alternatives are now available, such as the 6-CIT, the GPCOG and the 7-Minute Screen. Those interpreting the scores of such tests should take full account of other factors known to affect performance, including educational level, skills, prior level of functioning and attainment, language, and any sensory impairments, psychiatric illness or physical/neurological problems. [For the evidence, see section 6.4.4]

6.6.4.4   Formal neuropsychological testing should form part of the assessment in cases of mild or questionable dementia. [For the evidence, see section 6.4.4]

6.6.5   Investigation

6.6.5.1   A basic dementia screen should be performed at the time of presentation, usually within primary care. It should include:
● routine haematology

- biochemistry tests (including electrolytes, calcium, glucose, and renal and liver function)
- thyroid function tests
- serum vitamin B_{12} and folate levels. [For the evidence, see section 6.4.4]

6.6.5.2 Testing for syphilis serology or HIV should not be routinely undertaken in the investigation of people with suspected dementia. These tests should be considered only in those with histories suggesting they are at risk or if the clinical picture dictates. [For the evidence, see section 6.4.4]

6.6.5.3 A midstream urine test should always be carried out if delirium is a possibility. [For the evidence, see section 6.4.4]

6.6.5.4 Clinical presentation should determine whether investigations such as chest X-ray or electrocardiogram are needed. [For the evidence, see section 6.4.4]

6.6.5.5 Cerebrospinal fluid examination should not be performed as a routine investigation for dementia. [For the evidence, see section 6.4.4]

6.6.6 Diagnosis of subtypes

6.6.6.1 A diagnosis of subtype of dementia should be made by healthcare professionals with expertise in differential diagnosis using international standardised criteria (see Table 6). [For the evidence, see section 6.4]

6.6.6.2 Structural imaging should be used in the assessment of people with suspected dementia to exclude other cerebral pathologies and to help establish the subtype diagnosis. MRI is the preferred modality to assist with early diagnosis and detect subcortical vascular changes, although CT scanning could be used. Specialist advice should be taken when interpreting scans in people with learning disabilities. [For the evidence, see section 6.4.4]

Table 6: Diagnostic criteria for dementia

Type of dementia	Diagnostic criteria
AD	Preferred criteria: NINCDS/ADRDA. Alternatives include ICD-10 and DSM-IV
VaD	Preferred criteria: NINDS-AIREN. Alternatives include ICD-10 and DSM-IV
DLB	International Consensus criteria for DLB
FTD	Lund-Manchester criteria, NINDS criteria for FTD

161

6.6.6.3   HMPAO SPECT should be used to help differentiate AD, VaD and FTD if the diagnosis is in doubt. People with Down's syndrome may show SPECT abnormalities throughout life that resemble those in Alzheimer's disease, so this test is not helpful in this group. [For the evidence, see section 6.4.4]

6.6.6.4   If HMPAO SPECT is unavailable, FDG PET should be considered to help differentiate between AD, VaD and FTD if the diagnosis is in doubt. [For the evidence, see section 6.4.4]

6.6.6.5   FP-CIT SPECT should be used to help establish the diagnosis in those with suspected DLB if the diagnosis is in doubt. [For the evidence, see section 6.4.4]

6.6.6.6   CSF examination should be used if CJD or other forms of rapidly progressive dementia are suspected. [For the evidence, see section 6.4.4]

6.6.6.7   EEG should not be used as a routine investigation in people with dementia. [For the evidence, see section 6.4.4]

6.6.6.8   EEG should be considered if a diagnosis of delirium, FTD or CJD is suspected, or in the assessment of associated seizure disorder in those with dementia. [For the evidence, see section 6.4.4]

6.6.6.9   Brain biopsy for diagnostic purposes should be considered only in highly selected people whose dementia is thought to be due to a potentially reversible condition that cannot be diagnosed in any other way. [For the evidence, see section 6.4.4]

6.6.7   Mixed dementias

6.6.7.1   Many cases of dementia may have mixed pathology (for example, AD and VaD or AD and DLB). Unless otherwise stated in this guideline, such cases should be managed according to the condition that is thought to be the predominant cause of dementia. [For the evidence, see section 6.4.3]

6.6.8   Specialist services for dementia assessment

6.6.8.1   Memory assessment services (which may be provided by a memory assessment clinic or by community mental health teams) should be the single point of referral for all people with a possible diagnosis of dementia. [For the evidence, see section 4.6.2]

6.6.8.2   Memory assessment services should offer a responsive service to aid early identification and should include a full range of assessment, diagnostic, therapeutic, and rehabilitation services to accommodate the needs of people with different types and all severities of dementia and the needs of their carers and family. [For the evidence, see sections 4.6.2, 4.8 and 6.4]

6.6.8.3   Memory assessment services should ensure an integrated approach to the care of people with dementia and the support of their carers, in partnership with local health, social care, and voluntary organisations. [For the evidence, see sections 5.2.2 and 5.2.3]

6.6.9   Addressing needs that arise from the diagnosis of dementia

6.6.9.1   The experience of the diagnosis of dementia is challenging both for people with dementia and family members and for healthcare professionals, so healthcare professionals should make time available to discuss the diagnosis and its implications with the person with dementia and also with family members (usually only with the consent of the person with dementia). Healthcare professionals should be aware that people with dementia and family members may need ongoing support to cope with the difficulties presented by the diagnosis. [For the evidence, see sections 4.1.2, 4.1.3, 4.1.4, 4.2, 4.3, 4.6.1, 4.6.2, 4.7.2, 4.8, 4.10.2, 6.1, 6.3, 6.5, 9.2 and 9.5]

6.6.9.2   Following a diagnosis of dementia, health and social care professionals should, unless the person with dementia clearly indicates to the contrary, provide them and their family with written information about:
● the signs and symptoms of dementia
● the course and prognosis of the condition
● treatments
● local care and support services
● support groups
● sources of financial and legal advice, and advocacy
● medico-legal issues, including driving
● local information sources, including libraries and voluntary organisations.
Any advice and information given should be recorded in the notes. [For the evidence, see sections 4.8 and 6.5]

6.6.9.3   Healthcare professionals who regularly diagnose dementia and discuss this with people with the condition and carers should consider mentoring or providing clinical supervision to less experienced colleagues. [For the evidence, see sections 4.8, 6.5.1 and 6.5.2]

7. THERAPEUTIC INTERVENTIONS FOR PEOPLE WITH DEMENTIA – COGNITIVE SYMPTOMS AND MAINTENANCE OF FUNCTIONING

7.1 INTRODUCTION

There are a number of possible ways to group and categorise interventions in dementia care, for example, by the type of treatment approach used. In this and the following chapter, the main grouping is by the therapeutic goal, with three major domains highlighted: the maintenance of function, including cognitive functions, the management of behaviours that challenge and the reduction of comorbid emotional disorders. Each of these three areas has the aim of improving the quality of life and well-being of the person with dementia, which may in turn impact on the well-being of those providing care. In this chapter, we look at the evidence for the effectiveness of interventions designed to enhance and increase functioning; in the following chapter, the aim of therapy is to reduce depression or agitation or to modify other distressing symptoms of dementia – although potentially this may also be achieved by improving function in other areas.

This chapter focuses specifically on outcomes for the person with dementia, whilst in Chapter 9 interventions directed at carers, whose experience of the effects of dementia is often equally important, are discussed in detail. However, with regard to the intervention reviewed in this chapter, where relevant effects on carers have been documented, these will be highlighted here.

Cognitive symptoms are, of course, recognised as the core of any definition of dementia, and interventions targeting them have been the subject of much research and interest. However, the link between improving cognitive symptoms and maintaining day-to-day function is also key. In considering the efficacy of interventions in this chapter, it is this broader effect that must be the eventual goal.

This chapter includes discussion of both pharmacological and non-pharmacological approaches. The potential range of non-pharmacological 'interventions' in dementia care is vast and would include the day-to-day interactions of carers with the person with dementia, the impact of the physical and social environment and all manner of informal 'therapies', ranging from art sessions to contact with animals. Evaluating the effects of such different types of interventions alongside each other is a relatively new endeavour and some caution is required, especially when the double-blind RCT is taken as the gold standard (Woods, 2003). In particular:

- While the pharmacological intervention can be conveniently packaged and standardised, with a measured dose, non-pharmacological interventions can be more difficult to evaluate. The same label may be used for an intervention in different studies, but it may comprise quite different components. Non-pharmacological interventions have rarely used a standardised treatment manual; any such manual would, in any case, need to take on board the range of individual differences between people with dementia if it were to be seen as a credible approach.
- Double-blind studies are seldom possible, as the person with dementia or carer will be perfectly aware of which intervention he or she is receiving, although it is feasible to ensure that assessors are unaware of group allocation. While it is sometimes possible to design placebo interventions, assuring that those delivering them do so with the same enthusiasm as for the intervention being evaluated is problematic.

Although some interventions can be offered for a discrete period of time, such as half an hour per day, many others involve intervention at the level of the care setting or in the general approach or interactive style of those providing care. Cluster randomised designs would be appropriate for evaluating interventions at care-setting level, but require considerable resources. Where the intervention is designed to be delivered through carer interaction, a key step is to ensure that any training provided is effective in producing the required type and quality of interactions.

7.2   STRATEGIES FOR PROMOTING INDEPENDENCE

7.2.1   Introduction

Promoting independence is important at all stages of dementia and is used in this guideline to mean facilitating performance of or engagement in as much activity as is reasonable and tolerable for the individual. Though the level of independence will change with the stage of dementia and other illnesses, a balance across personal care and productive, leisure, social and spiritual activities is important for quality of life and well-being.

As function deteriorates, it is not uncommon for people with dementia to withdraw from more complex activity and social environments and for others to want to perform tasks for them. However, the literature suggests that functioning in activities of daily living often deteriorates below what would be expected by the illness alone (Tappen, 1994; Beck *et al.*, 1997). Therefore the person with dementia, care providers, family and friends should consider opportunities to maintain an active life and social roles and to promote independence beginning in the early stages of the condition. When exploring appropriate activities, it is also important to consider the right level of stimulation and challenge for the individual. The complexity of activity and level of engagement will change; however, it should not be assumed that the person with dementia does not retain abilities to perform an activity. Individualised and creative ways need to be explored to maximise the use of an individual's strengths well into the later stages of dementia. Social networks, voluntary services, communities, and health and social services can play an important role in socially including people and maximising independence at all stages of illness.

7.2.2 Interventions for promoting independence

There is little research from which to draw clear conclusions on specific interventions for promoting independence. The following is, therefore, a summary of good practice. Interventions should be selected and implemented based on the needs and strengths of the individual. It is important to note that any one person may benefit from any combination of strategies listed below. Further information about each of the primary-level studies referenced below can be found in Appendix 15b.

Communication

Communication is at the core of all effective psychological interventions, and communication strategies adapted to the individual's needs and abilities are the main building blocks to maximising skills and ensuring the least amount of dependency care. People with dementia also need to have their vision and hearing tested and the most appropriate aid available for use when interacting (Oddy, 2003).

Good communication means attending to cues which are often non-verbal and using language and sentence structure that matches the individual's level of comprehension, sensory abilities and culture (Oddy, 2003). Trying out different phrases and words to find the ones that elicit the best response and adapting tone and rate of speech can make the difference between the person with dementia performing a task with a verbal prompt and the care giver carrying out the task for the person.

As well as using verbal and body language, communication may need to take written or pictorial form (Oddy, 2003), such as memory books. Memory books consist of individualised images and simple statements that the person with dementia and care giver can use to aid the individual's recall and the quality and frequency of communication (Bourgeois *et al.*, 2001).

Where a person with dementia has a specific communication problem, individualised advice regarding appropriate strategies will be needed from a speech and language therapist.

ADL skill training

Literature and current practice suggest that for people with dementia activities of daily living (ADL) skill training can promote independence in personal care tasks (for example, dressing, feeding and washing) and maximise the use of skills and participation in their own care. The training can also lead to less disruption during ADL performance and reduce carer stress (Tappen, 1994; Beck *et al.*, 1997; Rogers *et al.*, 1999). However, more research is required.

ADL skill training involves assessing people's abilities, impairments and their task performance to understand the underlying physical, psychosocial and neurological factors (Tappen, 1994; Beck *et al.*, 1997). The intervention may involve analysing the results of the assessment to develop individualised programmes for enabling people to perform as many of their ADL tasks as possible themselves (Tappen, 1994; Beck *et al.*, 1997; Pool, 2002). The programmes include graded assistance, which means the care giver providing the least amount of assistance needed at each step to complete the task. Strategies may include verbal or visual cues, demonstration, physical guidance, partial physical assistance and problem solving (Beck *et al.*, 1997).

Professionals trained in assessments and care planning with ADLs can devise ADL skill training programmes for use by carers and/or care staff.

Activity planning

The principles of ADL skill training can be applied across various activities beyond personal care. Identifying the person's strengths and challenges and his or her level of performance can contribute to plans for establishing a wider range of activities. Care providers and the person with dementia should also consider preferences, interests and life histories in order to create meaningful activity plans (Kolanowski *et al.*, 2005; Pool, 2002). The Pool Activity Level instrument provides guidance on individualising activity plans to maximise a person's performance in individual- or group-based activities (Pool, 2002). The Enriched Opportunities Programme (Brooker & Woolley, in press) demonstrates what can be achieved in care homes. This involved individualised assessment, working with individuals to identify types of occupation and activity that were most likely to lead to well-being and a programme of activity that was rich, integrated with the local community, flexible and practical. Management and staff training issues also needed to be addressed.

Assistive technology

Assistive technology is a broad term defining 'any item, piece of equipment, product or system, whether acquired commercially, off the shelf, modified or customised, that is used to increase, maintain or improve functional capabilities of individuals with cognitive, physical or communication disabilities' (Marshall, 2000). The function of this technology is wide ranging, with many products and systems currently available through commercial suppliers or social services. It is not within the scope of this guideline to evaluate or recommend any one piece of assistive technology, but to consider the technology more broadly as an intervention for people with dementia.

Adaptive aids (including low-level technology) and environmental modifications

Adaptive aids and environmental modifications to promote safety and independence in performing a broad range of ADLs are in common use. Adaptive aids can range from memory aids to bathing equipment and are aimed at minimising the impact of physical, cognitive and sensory deficits. Similarly, low-level technology (for example, lights attached to a movement sensor) is widely used in adaptive aids to minimise risk without the need for action by the user. Low-level technology can stand alone without the need for sophisticated computer and telecommunications systems (Cash, 2003). Environmental modifications can be as simple as visual prompts and signs or as complex as structural changes to the home, such as shower installations. Prior to installing equipment as a permanent or sole option, the person's underlying impairments should be assessed and consideration given to the effect of any treatment or rehabilitation of underlying physical, cognitive and sensory impairments. The provision of an adaptive aid and low-level technology should consider the person with dementia and carer in his or her own environment and be based on the individual's need; there should be follow-up to evaluate its utility for meeting that need. Information for the purpose and proper use of adaptive aids should be provided.

Memory aids such as calendars, diaries, schedules of daily routine, memory books or electronic devices are often introduced into the individual's routine in the earlier stages of dementia (Bourgeois *et al.*, 2003). However, some clinicians find combining memory aids with memory training exercises (such as spaced retrieval or cueing hierarchy) can improve the independent use of the aids and also benefit people into the moderate stages of dementia (Bourgeois *et al.*, 2003). Memory aids need to be introduced in collaboration with the user to find the most appropriate aid for him or her and consideration given to how the user can best utilise the aid. An intervention may not work at first or in isolation, so it is useful to think about the whole person in his or her environment before stopping it. For example, Dooley and Hinojosa (2004) note that combining adaptive aids with carer education and environmental modifications contributed to improved outcomes in independence for people with dementia and reduced stress for their carers.

Telecare

Telecare, the delivery of care from a distance to an older person living at home through computers and telecommunications systems, 'involves a range of services including virtual visiting, reminder systems, home security, and social alarm systems with the overall aim of avoiding hospitalisation and aiding ageing in place' (Magnusson *et al.*, 2004). People with dementia may be able to live safely and independently, minimising potential risks (Department of Health, 2005a). A telecare package may involve monitoring activity patterns to detect any changes that may warn of potential health changes or of an event such as a fall (Magnusson *et al.*, 2004). Responsive alarms can detect risks by monitoring motion (for example falls) and the presence of fire and gas and triggering a warning to a response centre or carer (Department of Health, 2005a).

The significant benefit of telecare for a person with dementia is that many devices are passive so the individual does not need to remember where they are or how to use them (Cash, 2003). Telecare is one intervention that can be implemented alongside but not replacing care provision (Department of Health, 2005a). Guidance suggests that benefits can be gained by keeping people with dementia at the centre of the development and application of technology (taking into account ethical considerations) and involving them in a partnership working with services and care providers (Cash, 2003; Magnusson *et al.*, 2004).

Initial findings support the use of assistive technology in aiding people to stay in the community longer, thereby delaying moves to higher dependency care (Cash, 2003), but further research is needed before any firm conclusions can be drawn (Magnusson *et al.*, 2004). The Department of Health has published a few useful guides for establishing telecare in local communities (for example, Department of Health, 2005a).

Exercise/promoting mobility

Although conclusions cannot be drawn from current research on the benefits of a specific exercise programme, it is widely accepted that exercise is important for the health of people with dementia (Oddy, 2003). Many benefits are stated to occur – ranging from improved continence to slowing loss of mobility and improving or slowing loss in strength, balance and endurance levels – with overall improved physical functioning in comparison with people not receiving exercise (Oddy, 2003; Schnelle *et al*, 2002; Shimada *et al.*, 2003; Worm *et al.*, 2001; Chandler *et al.*, 1998). Exercise is also widely used in preventing falls (see NICE, 2004b).

The literature is wide and varied, with descriptions of both standardised group and individualised exercise programmes, which are widely used in practice. Such programmes may involve walking, gait training, resistance training or strengthening exercises, balance and endurance training (Tappen *et al.*, 2000; Chandler *et al.*, 1998; Shimada *et al.*, 2003; Worm *et al.*, 2001). Some reports recommend the use of walking and conversation simultaneously to improve compliance to the exercise (Tappen *et al.*, 2000). Combining exercise with other interventions, such as continence care (Schnelle *et al.*, 2002) and behavioural management techniques (Teri *et al.*, 2003), is also of interest (see below). Teaching care providers effective strategies to encourage exercise and avoid behavioural problems associated with increased activity may make exercise training most effective (Teri *et al.*, 2003).

Exercise is best implemented with the individual's abilities in mind, and relevant healthcare professionals should determine risk and devise suitable programmes. Risk should not necessarily represent a barrier to people with dementia receiving opportunities for exercise.

Rehabilitation programmes for people with dementia
The Department of Health and independent bodies report that people with dementia are often excluded from rehabilitation programmes because of the nature of the condition (Department of Health, 2003; The Nuffield Institute, 2002). However, there is evidence that they can benefit equally well from rehabilitation-based services, particularly community services (Department of Health, 2003; Nuffield Institute, 2002). Promoting and maintaining cognitive skills and mobility and independence in wider ADLs is possible (Oddy, 2003; Beck *et al.*, 1997; Tappen, 1994; Bourgeois *et al.*, 2003).

Good quality rehabilitation programmes take into account the whole person at the centre of care in his or her environment and are tailored to the individual's assessed needs, strengths and limitations. This process is no different for people with dementia, although programmes may need to be adapted to compensate for cognitive, perceptual or mood elements. In addition, tailoring programmes to meet the needs of the individual may require time, adaptive aids, communication strategies and organising staff in a different way (Department of Health, 2003). Many of the interventions described in this chapter can be used in a rehabilitation programme. Care givers and care staff may perceive a greater degree of risk in encouraging greater independence in some areas of the person with dementia's life. Support in considering the balance of risks and benefits in these instances can be helpful.

Combining interventions
One intervention is often not enough because people with dementia do not only experience cognitive impairment, but often physical, emotional and social concerns as

well. There is literature on interventions targeting multiple aspects of the person, his or her carers and environment in order to address the complexity of supporting people with dementia (Dooley & Hinojosa, 2004; Gitlin *et al.*, 2003; Graff *et al.*, 2003; Teri *et al.*, 2003). For example, occupational therapy for people with dementia consists of a combination of environmental modification, adaptive aids, problem-solving strategies, skill training and carer/care provider education and training (Gitlin *et al.*, 2003; Dooley & Hinojosa, 2004; Graff *et al.*, 2003). By combining interventions, care providers and professionals are more likely to succeed in promoting the independence of an individual than with the use of one intervention alone (Gitlin *et al.*, 2003; Graff *et al.*, 2003; Dooley & Hinojosa, 2004). Physical health difficulties may contribute to loss of independence, and it is essential that such difficulties are assessed and treated appropriately. Collaborative working between psychiatry and geriatric medicine as part of a multidisciplinary approach would help to achieve this.

An example of combining interventions for promoting and maintaining independence with toileting

Toileting is often an important issue. All avenues should be assessed and relevant interventions tried before concluding that incontinence is permanent and in need of full care and/or incontinence pads. There are often treatable causes that can be uncovered by medical investigation. Observation of the situation is essential to determine the right strategies to maximise independence in toileting. Specialist advice can also be obtained through nursing services, and many communities have specialist continence advisors. The following strategies may be combined:

- ADL skill training can be used if the person is having difficulty initiating or performing steps to the task. Understanding the person's underlying difficulties in cognitive, physical and sensory areas can lead to effective care planning for overcoming these difficulties. The task of toileting should be broken down to find where the person may need intervention, beginning with the least invasive form of intervention first (for example, verbal prompts, gestures and visual cues) and leading to physical guidance. The person may need regular prompting to use the toilet at regular intervals.
- Communication strategies should be considered to find the best way to prompt the person to use the toilet at regular intervals or at moments when the person indicates need. Familiar phrases or words should be explored or gestures or pictures used.
- If the individual needs assistance finding the toilet (appropriate signage and visual cues), environmental modifications should be considered. Appropriate adaptive aids should be considered to ensure that the toilet is physically accessible and can be used with ease. Contrasting colours may help the person differentiate the toilet from the wall behind it. A commode placed in a visible location in the person's room may provide a prompt and reduce physical exertion, particularly at night.
- Exercise can be used to strengthen legs and arms, and abdominal and pelvic floor muscles to improve control, and may improve endurance and ability getting to and using the toilet.

7.2.3 Qualitative review

Evidence included
Two sources of qualitative evidence on the experiences of people with dementia and their carers of strategies for promoting the independence of people with dementia met the eligibility criteria set by the GDG: a non-experimental study with evidence from professionals, carers and people with learning disabilities and dementia (Stalker *et al.*, 1999) and primary research involving 15 people with dementia and with evidence from professionals, people with dementia and carers (Woolham & Frisby, 2002).

Key findings
An evaluation of a home assistive technology package for people with dementia found that the technology worked on the whole, and that family members and professionals felt it reduced risks and helped to maintain the independence of the person with dementia (Woolham & Frisby, 2002). A study involving people with learning disabilities and dementia, along with their key worker and relatives, that explored how far people with learning disabilities and dementia were involved in making decisions and choices in their own lives found wide variations (Stalker *et al.*, 1999). The findings indicate that staff training and development is needed to ensure that care environments enable people with dementia and learning disabilities to exercise choice and control over their everyday lives, and so maximise their independence.

7.2.4 Evidence summary

Ultimately, promoting independence with someone or for oneself is dependent upon opportunities for doing so. Continual engagement in life's roles and activities is a means in itself for maintaining independence; however, as dementia progresses, some aspects will inevitably become more difficult. By finding out about the person through spending time with him or her, asking family and friends and conducting holistic assessments and observations to keep information current, services and care providers can continually shape interventions to maximise independence. By including the person with dementia and using information from a variety of sources, staff can devise and use a variety of techniques to promote independence in a meaningful way. Promotion of independence means the involvement of the person in his or her ADLs, communities and care, treating him or her with respect, preserving dignity and looking for the abilities and strengths within the person.

Qualitative evidence on the experience of people with dementia and carers points to the contribution that assistive technology can make by reducing risks and promoting independence. Other qualitative evidence highlights the importance of promoting independence for people with dementia and learning difficulties, who should have the opportunity to exercise choice and control over their everyday lives.

7.3   MAINTENANCE OF COGNITIVE FUNCTION: PSYCHOLOGICAL INTERVENTIONS

7.3.1   Introduction

Rigorous evaluations of non-pharmacological interventions are at an early stage of development, in relation to the maintenance of cognitive function. The creativity and enthusiasm of practitioners in the field has often not been followed up by systematic assessment of outcomes, and so a section such as this, which aims to draw together the evidence base, cannot do justice to the range and diversity of interventions that have been developed.

Three major types of approach with a cognitive focus have been delineated (Clare & Woods, 2004). These are:

1. Cognitive stimulation, which entails exposure to and engagement with activities and materials involving some degree of cognitive processing, usually within a social context and often group based, with the emphasis on enjoyment of activities.
2. Cognitive training, which involves specific training exercises geared to specific cognitive functions. It includes practice and repetition, may be computer-assisted and may be individual or group based.
3. Cognitive rehabilitation, which is always individually tailored, involving working on personal goals, often using external cognitive aids and with some use of learning strategies; it is carefully targeted.

Particularly in relation to cognitive rehabilitation approaches, there is a strong tradition of evaluation through series of single case studies, using experimental designs. Individualised, tailored rehabilitation programmes, targeting the goals selected by the person with dementia and his/her carers, are increasingly being developed and used, and show some promise (Clare & Woods, 2004).

Other approaches in this section include reminiscence work, characterised by use of memory triggers, prompting discussion of remote memories, which may be individual or group based; 'snoezelen', which involves stimulation of a number of senses using aromas, hand massage and other tactile stimulation, visual light displays and atmospheric music and sounds; and validation therapy, a group-based approach which encourages communication at an emotional level in a safe, facilitative environment.

Multi-sensory stimulation is most typically used with people with moderate to severe dementia, whereas the other approaches are more appropriate for mild to moderate dementia. Reminiscence work is probably the most commonly used of these approaches in the UK. In its previous manifestation, as 'reality orientation', cognitive stimulation was widely used, but concerns arose over its inflexible, insensitive application. Current projects emphasise the importance of a person-centred approach as a basis for any of these interventions.

The main emphasis here is on cognitive change, with reference to ADLs and quality of life as an important context for the clinical significance of any changes in cognition. In Chapter 8, other outcomes are considered for these approaches.

7.3.2 Databases searched and inclusion/exclusion criteria

Information about the databases searched and the inclusion/exclusion criteria used for this section of the guideline can be found in Table 7.

Table 7: Databases searched and inclusion/exclusion criteria

Electronic databases	AMED, BNI, CINAHL, COCHRANE, EMBASE, MEDLINE, PsycINFO, AgeInfo, AgeLine, ASSIA, CareData, HMIC, PAIS International, SIGLE, Social Services Abstracts, Social Work Abstracts, SSCI
Date searched	Database inception to March 2006; table of contents September 2004 to 5 May 2006
Study design	RCT
Patient population	People with AD/VaD/DLB/PDD/FTD/other dementias (subcortical, mixed dementias)
Interventions	-Memory training (for example, procedural memory stimulation) -Cognitive rehabilitation -Life review -Reminiscence -Validation therapy -Snoezelen (multi-sensory stimulation, for example aromatherapy and massage) -Creative arts therapy (for example, dance and music) -Cognitive stimulation (reality orientation) -Animal-assisted therapy
Outcomes	-Cognitive functioning (for example, MMSE, ADAS-Cog) -ADL test score (for example, ADL, IADL, BGP, NOSGER) -Admission to hospital/care home -Subjective improvement in quality of life -Global rating scale (for example, CIBC-Plus, CGIC, SCAG, GDS) -Side effects (for example, ESRS, TESS, targeting abnormal kinetic effects)

7.3.3   Studies considered[50]

We conducted a new systematic search for RCTs that assessed the efficacy of the specified psychological interventions for people with dementia (see Table 8).

Nineteen trials met the guideline eligibility criteria, providing data on 1,132 participants. Of these, one (MORGAN2000) was unpublished and 18 were published in peer-reviewed journals between 1979 and 2004. In addition, 39 studies were excluded from the analysis (further information about both included and excluded studies can be found in Appendix 15c).

7.3.4   Psychological interventions for the treatment of cognitive symptoms of dementia

Evidence from critical outcomes and overall quality of evidence are presented in Table 9. The full evidence profiles and associated forest plots can be found in Appendix 16 and Appendix 20, respectively. The single study of cognitive rehabilitation (LOEWENSTEIN2004) did not present appropriate data to be included in the table. However, the results do not provide any evidence that cognitive rehabilitation improves cognition, ADLs or quality of life when compared to an active control (mental stimulation).

7.3.5   Combination treatment – cognitive stimulation in combination with acetylcholinesterase inhibitors

Onder and colleagues (2005) evaluated the effects of 6 months of cognitive stimulation, delivered by family carers, on people with mild to moderate Alzheimer's disease who had been stabilized on donepezil for at least 3 months compared with a control group who received donepezil alone. Of a total of 156 randomised, the mean age was 75.8 years, 72% were women and 137 people completed the trial. With regard to cognitive symptoms, there was a statistically significant advantage to the combined treatment group on the MMSE (SMD = -0.39, 95% CI, -0.73 to -0.05) and ADAS-Cog (SMD = -0.44, 95% CI, -0.77 to -0.10).

Chapman and colleagues (2004) evaluated the effects of cognitive stimulation on people with mild to moderate Alzheimer's disease receiving donepezil compared with a control group who received donepezil alone. The cognitive-communication stimulation intervention consisted of 8 weekly sessions delivered to groups of six to seven participants by a trainer, followed by monthly contacts with participants on an individual basis. All participants in the study had been on a stable dose of donepezil for at least 3 months. Of a total of 54 randomised participants, the mean age was 76.4 years, 54% were women and 41 completed the trial. With regard to cognitive symptoms, there was a benefit from combined treatment as the donepezil-plus-cognitive-stimulation

---

[50]Here, and elsewhere in the guideline, each study considered for review is referred to by a study ID in capital letters (primary author and date of study publication, except where a study is in press or only submitted for publication, then a date is not used).

Table 8: Study information table for trials of psychological interventions in people with dementia

	Cognitive rehabilitation versus active control	Cognitive stimulation (reality orientation) versus standard care	Life review and reminiscence versus no treatment	Reminiscence versus social contact
Total no. of trials (total no. of participants)	1 (44)	6 (299)	5 (122)	1 (71)
Study ID	LOEWENSTEIN 2004	BAINES1987 BREUIL1994 FERRARIO1991 SPECTOR2003 WALLIS1983 WOODS1979	BAINES1987 GOLDWASSER 1987 LAI2004 MORGAN2000 THORGRIMSEN 2002	LAI2004
Diagnosis	Probable or possible AD (NINDS-ADRDA)	Moderate to severe impairment of cognitive function according to the CAPE (BAINES1987) AD, M-ID, PDD; DSM-III (BREUIL1994)	Moderate to severe impairment of cognitive function according to the CAPE (BAINES1987) Clinical diagnosis of dementia (GOLDWASSER1987)	Unspecified dementia DSM-IV

Continued

175

Table 8: *(Continued)*

	Cognitive rehabilitation versus active control	Cognitive stimulation (reality orientation) versus standard care	Life review and reminiscence versus no treatment	Reminiscence versus social contact
		Unspecified dementia; MMSE or DSM-IV (FERRARIO1991, SPECTOR2003, WALLIS1983)	Unspecified dementia DSM-IV (LAI2004)	
		Wechsler Memory Scale (WOODS1979)	Mild to moderate dementia, CDR (MORGAN2000)	
			Unspecified dementia (THORGRIMSEN2002)	
Baseline severity: mean (SD)	MMSE: ~24	MMSE: ~14.5 (SPECTOR2003 only)	MMSE: 8.3 to 13	MMSE: 8.3 to 10.7
Treatment length	12 to 16 weeks	4 to 24 weeks	4 to 18 weeks	6 weeks
Age (years)	76.4 (mean)	70 to 85.3	76.2 to 85.7	85.7

	Memory training versus active control	Memory training versus waitlist control	Memory training versus social support	Computerised memory training versus social support
Total no. of trials (total no. of participants)	2 (71)	3 (117)	1 (43)	1 (35)
Study ID	CAHN-WEINER2003 DAVIS2001	CORBEIL1999 KOLTAI2001 QUAYHAGEN2000	QUAYHAGEN2000	HEISS1994
Diagnosis	AD (NINDS-ADRDA) (CAHN-WEINER2003, DAVIS2001)	Possible or probable AD (CORBEIL1999)	AD (NINDS-ADRDA), MI-D, PDD	AD (NINDS-ADRDA)
		Mild to moderate dementia (CDR) (KOLTAI2001)		
		AD (NINDS-ADRDA), MI-D, PDD (QUAYHAGEN2000)		
Baseline severity: mean (SD)	MMSE: 21.84 to 25.1	MMSE: ~24.75 (KOLTAI2001 only)	–	MMSE: ~20.39
Treatment length	5 to 6 weeks	5 to 12 weeks	8 weeks	6 months
Age (years)	71 to 76.9	73 to 74.2	73	67

Continued

Table 8: *(Continued)*

	Multi-sensory (snoezelen) versus active control	Validation therapy versus standard care	Validation therapy versus social contact
Total no. of trials (total no. of participants)	1 (27)	2 (80)	1 (60)
Study ID	BAKER2003	ROBB1986 TOSELAND1997	TOSELAND 1997
Diagnosis	AD, VaD, mixed dementia	70% unspecified dementia (ROBB1986) Unspecified dementia (TOSELAND1997)	Unspecified dementia
Baseline severity: mean (SD)	MMSE: ~8.05	–	–
Treatment length	4 weeks	36 to 52 weeks	52 weeks

Table 9: Summary evidence table for trials of psychological interventions versus control in people with dementia – cognitive symptoms

	Cognitive stimulation (reality orientation) versus standard care	Life review and reminiscence versus no treatment	Reminiscence versus social contact
Total no. of trials (total no. of participants)	6 (299)	5 (122)	1 (71)
Study ID	BAINES1987 BREUIL1994 FERRARIO1991 SPECTOR2003 WALLIS1983 WOODS1979	BAINES1987 GOLDWASSER1987 LAI2004 MORGAN2000 THORGRIMSEN 2002	LAI2004
Evidence profile table number (Appendix 16)	Table A16-5	Table A16-2	Table A16-6
Overall quality of evidence	Moderate	Low	Moderate
Benefits			
Cognitive symptoms	Various measures: SMD −0.40 (−0.63 to −0.18) K = 6, N = 319	Various measures: SMD −0.27 (−0.67 to 0.13) post-treatment K = 4, N = 103	MMSE: SMD −0.21 (−0.67 to 0.26) post-treatment K = 1, N = 71

Continued

179

Table 9: *(Continued)*

	Cognitive stimulation (reality orientation) versus standard care	Life review and reminiscence versus no treatment	Reminiscence versus social contact
		SMD −0.50 (−0.92 to −0.07) follow-up K = 3, N = 93	SMD −0.55 (−1.02 to −0.08) follow-up K = 1, N = 71
Activities of daily living	—	MDS-ADL: SMD −0.04 (−0.52 to 0.45) K = 1, N = 66	MDS-ADL: SMD 0.13 (−0.34 to 0.59) post-treatment K = 1, N = 71 SMD −0.07 (−0.54 to 0.39) follow-up K = 1, N = 71
Quality of life	QoL-AD: SMD −0.39 (−0.68 to −0.11) K = 1, N = 201	Life Satisfaction Index: SMD −0.15 (−0.91 to 0.61) post-treatment K = 2, N = 27 SMD −0.48 (−1.25 to 0.29) follow-up K = 2, N = 27	WIB: SMD −0.06 (−0.53 to 0.41) post-treatment K = 1, N = 71 SMD −0.09 (−0.56 to 0.37) follow-up K = 1, N = 71

	Memory training versus active control	Memory training versus waitlist control	Memory training versus social support	Computerised memory training versus social support
Total no. of trials (total no. of participants)	2 (71)	3 (117)	1 (43)	1 (35)
Study ID	CAHN-WEINER2003 DAVIS2001	CORBEIL1999 KOLTAI2001 QUAYHAGEN2000	QUAYHAGEN2000	HEISS1994
Evidence profile table number (Appendix 16)	Table A16-1	Table A16-8	Table A16-9	Table A16-10
Overall quality of evidence	Low	Low	Moderate	Low
Benefits				
Cognitive symptoms	MMSE: SMD −0.01 (−0.65 to 0.63) K = 1, N = 37	MMSE: SMD −0.34 (−1.21 to 0.54) K = 1, N = 22	Memory and behaviour problem checklist: SMD 0.00 (−0.59 to 0.60) K = 1, N = 43	MMSE: SMD −0.04 (−0.70 to 0.63) K = 1, N = 35
Activities of daily living	SMD −0.15 (−0.82 to 0.52) K = 1, N = 34	—	—	—
Quality of life	Quality of life assessment by patient SMD −0.29 (−0.94 to 0.36) K = 1, N = 37	PGCMS: SMD −0.11 (−0.78 to 0.55) K = 1, N = 36		

Continued

181

Table 9: *(Continued)*

	Multi-sensory stimulation (snoezelen) versus active control	Validation therapy versus standard care	Validation therapy versus social contact
Total no. of trials (total no. of participants)	1 (127)	2 (80)	1 (60)
Study ID	BAKER2003	ROBB1986 TOSELAND1997	TOSELAND1997
Evidence profile table number (Appendix 16)	Table A16-4	Table A16-3	Table A16-7
Overall quality of evidence	Moderate	Moderate	Moderate
Benefits			
Cognitive symptoms	MMSE: SMD 0.01 (−0.38 to 0.39) K = 1, N = 106	MSQ: SMD −0.24 (−1.11 to 0.62) K = 1, N = 21	MSQ: SMD 0.12 (−0.46 to 0.71) K = 1, N = 45
Activities of daily living	–	–	MOSES: SMD −0.12 (−0.71 to 0.47) K = 1, N = 45
Quality of life	–	–	–

group maintained their level of performance on the MMSE over 1 year, while the donepezil-only group showed a statistically significant decline from baseline (donepezil plus cognitive stimulation: mean change in MMSE = −1.25, 95% CI, −2.78 to 0.28; control group: mean change in MMSE = −2.14, 95% CI, −4.18 to −0.10).

Bottino and colleagues (2005) evaluated the effects of a 5-month programme of weekly group cognitive rehabilitation sessions on mildly impaired people with probable Alzheimer's disease receiving rivastigmine compared with a control group who received rivastigmine alone. All participants in the study had been on rivastigmine for at least 2 months. Of a total of 13 randomised participants, the mean age was 73.7 years and 69% were women. All 13 completed the trial. With regard to cognitive symptoms, there was a statistically significant benefit from combined treatment on the MMSE (mean MMSE before treatment: combined treatment group=23.50, SD 3.27; control group=21.29, SD 3.82, no statistical difference; mean MMSE after treatment: combined treatment group=24.33, SD 3.14; control group=19.86, SD 3.67, statistically significant, p=0.047).

Cahn-Weiner and colleagues (2003) evaluated the efficacy of six group sessions of memory training (cognitive training) delivered by an instructor over a period of 6 weeks on people with probable Alzheimer's disease, compared with a control group that attended 6 weekly sessions where educational information pertaining to aging and dementia was presented. All participants were taking an acetylcholinesterase inhibitor (donepezil). Of a total of 34 randomised participants, the mean age was 76.9 years, 59% were women and 29 people completed the trial. No significant effects of the intervention were detected on any of the outcome measures of cognitive function.

7.3.6   Health economics evidence

One economic study was identified that assessed the cost-effectiveness of cognitive stimulation therapy (CST) (Knapp *et al.*, 2006). This was a UK study that compared CST to standard care for people with mild to moderate dementia. The objective of the study was to investigate the resource implications and cost-effectiveness of CST in care homes and day centres. The economic analysis was conducted alongside an RCT (Spector *et al.*, 2003).

The study adopted the perspective of the health and personal social services. Costs consisted of those associated with providing the CST intervention, including staff time, travel and equipment, as well as residential care and domestic housing costs, community services costs, and direct medical costs. Clinical outcomes corresponded to those of the study by Spector and colleagues. The primary outcome measure of the analysis was cognition as measured by the MMSE; quality of life, as measured by the QoL-AD, was a secondary outcome measure. The time horizon of the analysis was 8 weeks, which is considered a limitation of the study but corresponded with the length of the CST programme.

The mean weekly cost per person in the CST group was £45.18 higher compared with the respective cost per person in the control group. The difference was statistically significant (p = 0.037). However, there was a difference of £28.53 at baseline weekly cost per person between the two groups (with the CST group being more expensive), as measured over 8 weeks before the intervention started. An analysis of covariance (ANCOVA), carried out to adjust for the baseline cost difference between the groups, reduced the significance of the follow-up difference in costs between groups ($p = 0.076$). Regarding clinical outcomes, there was a significant improvement for people in the CST group relative to controls on both the MMSE and the QoL-AD. The incremental cost-effectiveness ratio (ICER) for the cognition outcome was £75.32 per additional point on the MMSE, calculated using a mean cost difference of £45.18 and mean outcome difference of 0.6 in favour of CST. For the quality of life outcome, the ICER was £22.82 per additional point of QoL-AD, based on the same mean cost difference and a mean outcome difference of 1.98 in favour of CST.

Further analysis was carried out investigating the impact of group size on the cost-effectiveness of CST. Reducing the average group size from five to three people per group increased the ICER to £102.00 per additional MMSE point, and increasing the group size to seven people caused the ICER to decrease to £63.87 per additional MMSE point. The impact of group size on QoL-AD followed a similar pattern. It must be noted that the changes in the ICERs following an increase or reduction in group size were caused by changes in mean weekly costs per person in the CST group exclusively, as effectiveness results were assumed to remain the same regardless of the group size. However, this may not be true, as clinical outcomes may differ when smaller or larger groups receive the intervention. Subgroup analysis found no difference in results between care homes and day centres. Details of the study are provided in the form of evidence tables in Appendix 18.

The evidence suggests that, in the UK, providing cognitive stimulation therapy alongside usual care for people with mild to moderate dementia in both care homes and day-care centres is likely to be more cost effective than usual care alone.

7.3.7 Qualitative review

Evidence included

Four sources of qualitative evidence on experiences of people with dementia and their carers of psychosocial interventions for the maintenance of cognitive function met the eligibility criteria set by the GDG: primary research involving six people with dementia, three carers and three care staff (Alm *et al.*, 2004); a systematic review (Bates *et al.*, 2004); a case study with evidence from one person with early dementia and a carer (Clare *et al.*, 2003); and primary research with evidence from people with dementia and carers (Spector *et al.*, 1999).

Key findings

Qualitative evidence on the experiences of people with dementia and their carers supports the potential value of a range of psychosocial approaches aimed at maintaining cognitive function. An evaluation of a therapeutic programme for people with dementia involving 12 people with dementia (six receiving standard care and six receiving the intervention) indicates that therapy resulted in a positive effect on friendship (Spector *et al.*, 1999). Spector and colleagues also report that therapy participants reported enjoying the sessions and wishing that they could continue. Quantitative findings indicate that therapy improved cognition and reduced depression and anxiety in people with dementia and also resulted in improvements in carers' self-rated health status.

Findings from a pilot study of a project to develop a cognitive and communication aid for people with dementia indicate that prompts and stimulation from a computer may assist in reminiscence conversations (Alm *et al.*, 2004). People with dementia could enjoy reminiscence when stimulated by a multi-media reminiscence package; they had no difficulty touching the screen and the package maintained their interest – in particular, they liked local and personal pictures.

A single case study of a person with early dementia's experience of cognitive rehabilitation suggests that it can help people with dementia to make use of their remaining memory (Clare *et al.*, 2003). This case study points to further beneficial effects of cognitive rehabilitation for people with early Alzheimer's disease as the intervention was also reported to lift the person with dementia's distress and did not cause depression.

Finally, according to a systematic review of psychosocial interventions for people with milder dementia (including evidence from professionals, people with dementia and carers) cognitive stimulation (reality orientation) appears efficacious for people with mild dementia, but the value of other interventions is less clear (Bates *et al.*, 2004).

7.3.8   Evidence summary

There is now reasonable evidence to support the use of cognitive stimulation approaches with people with mild to moderate dementia. Importantly, there are now indications of improvements in quality of life to accompany the well-established (modest) improvements in cognitive function. The importance of appropriate, respectful, person-centred carer attitudes in the implementation of these approaches has been highlighted in the largest, and most successful, trial to date.

Cognitive stimulation appears to add to the effects of donepezil in both mild and moderate Alzheimer's disease.

Cognitive training has generally not been associated with benefits beyond the particular tasks trained. There is insufficient evidence to evaluate fully the effects of reminiscence therapy and cognitive rehabilitation in relation to cognitive function in dementia.

7.4   ACETYLCHOLINESTERASE INHIBITORS OR MEMANTINE FOR THE TREATMENT OF COGNITIVE SYMPTOMS OF NON-ALZHEIMER DEMENTIA

7.4.1   Introduction

Acetylcholinesterase inhibitors (donepezil, galantamine, rivastigmine) are licensed in the UK for the symptomatic treatment of mild to moderately severe Alzheimer's disease. Memantine was originally licensed for moderately severe to severe Alzheimer's disease, but the licence was extended in November 2005 and now covers moderate to severe Alzheimer's disease. Donepezil is a reversible inhibitor of acetylcholinesterase, galantamine is a reversible inhibitor of acetylcholinesterase and also has nicotinic receptor agonist properties, and rivastigmine is a reversible non-competitive inhibitor of acetylcholinesterases and also inhibits butyrylcholinesterase. Memantine is an N-methyl-D-aspartate (NMDA)-receptor antagonist that affects glutamate transmission.

Apart from rivastigmine, no drugs are currently licensed for the symptomatic treatment of people with VaD, DLB, FTD or other dementias (subcortical or mixed dementias), although people with these forms of dementia suffer similar problems associated with cognitive symptoms and loss of daily living skills. Rivastigmine is licensed for the symptomatic treatment of mild to moderately severe dementia in patients with idiopathic Parkinson's disease.

If the underlying neurochemical deficit is similar, irrespective of the aetiology of the cognitive impairment, then it is possible that acetylcholinesterase inhibitors or memantine would produce a similar symptomatic effect in other types of dementia. It is therefore important to establish as far as possible from the evidence available whether there is a significant clinical improvement to be gained by treatment with acetylcholinesterase inhibitors or memantine in the other forms of dementia.

The clinical and cost-effectiveness of donepezil, galantamine and rivastigmine for mild to moderately severe AD, and memantine for moderately severe to severe AD are the subject of a NICE technology appraisal[51] and so will not be reviewed here. The clinical and cost-effectiveness of donepezil, galantamine, rivastigmine, and memantine for PDD are covered in another NICE guideline[52] and so will not be reviewed here.

Current practice

Acetylcholinesterase inhibitors and memantine are currently prescribed in dementia, other than Alzheimer's type, as part of a clinical trial or at clinical discretion without licence.

The evidence base/limitations

There are no studies of the use of acetylcholinesterase inhibitors or memantine for the treatment of FTD. A treatment response in VaD is difficult to measure because there is no linear progression of deterioration and a longer period of follow-up is probably required to differentiate between treatment and placebo groups. The scales used in the studies considered were devised for use in Alzheimer's type dementia and there are subtle differences in the nature of the deficits in the two conditions. Studies of MCI are included in this section because of the relatively high rate of progression from the amnestic form of MCI to dementia.

7.4.2   Databases searched and inclusion/exclusion criteria

Information about the databases searched and the inclusion/exclusion criteria used for this section of the guideline can be found in Table 10.

---

[51]For further information see www.nice.org.uk/guidance/TA111.
[52]For further information see www.nice.org.uk/guidance/CG35.

Table 10: Databases searched and inclusion/exclusion criteria

Electronic databases	AMED, BNI, CENTRAL, CINAHL, Embase, Medline, PsycINFO
Date searched	Database inception to March 2006; table of contents September 2004 to 5 May 2006
Study design	RCT (efficacy, acceptability, tolerability, adverse events) Observational study (adverse events)
Patient population	VaD/DLB/FTD/other dementias (subcortical, mixed dementias)/MCI/Down's syndrome and other learning disabilities plus dementia
Interventions	Donepezil, galantamine, rivastigmine, memantine
Outcomes	– Improvement on a score of a cognitive function test (for example, MMSE, ADAS-Cog) – Improvement on ADL test score (for example, ADL, IADL, BGP, NOSGER) – Reduction in carer stress (for example, CBS) – Delay in time to 24-hour care – Subjective improvement in quality of life – Global rating scale (for example, CIBC-Plus, CGIC, SCAG, GDS) – Side effects (for example, ESRS, TESS, targeting abnormal kinetic effects) – Leaving the study early

7.4.3   Studies considered[53]

We conducted a new systematic search for studies that assessed the efficacy and/or safety of donepezil, galantamine, rivastigmine (acetylcholinesterase inhibitors) or memantine (NMDA-receptor antagonist) (see Table 11).

Ten trials met the guideline eligibility criteria, providing data on 5,894 participants. Of these, two were unpublished and eight were published in peer-reviewed journals between 2000 and 2005. In addition, 22 studies were excluded from the analysis (further information about both included and excluded studies can be found in Appendix 15d).

7.4.4   Acetylcholinesterase inhibitors or memantine for the treatment of cognitive symptoms of non-Alzheimer dementia or mild cognitive impairment

Evidence from critical outcomes and overall quality of evidence are presented in Table 12. The full evidence profiles and associated forest plots can be found in Appendix 16 and Appendix 20, respectively.

---

[53]Here, and elsewhere in the guideline, each study considered for review is referred to by a study ID in capital letters (primary author and date of study publication, except where a study is in press or only submitted for publication, then a date is not used).

Table 11: Study information table for trials of acetylcholinesterase inhibitors or memantine versus placebo in people with non-Alzheimer dementia

	Acetylcholinesterase inhibitors (maximum dose) versus placebo for VaD	Acetylcholinesterase inhibitors (minimum dose) versus placebo for VaD	Memantine versus placebo for VaD
Total no. of trials (total no. of participants)	3 (1,811)	2 (1,219)	2 (867)
Study ID (drug)	BLACK2003 (donepezil 10 mg/day) ERKINJUNTTI2002 (galantamine 24 mg/day) WILKINSON2003 (donepezil 10 mg/day)	BLACK2003 WILKINSON2003 (donepezil 5 mg/day)	ORGOGOZO2002 WILCOCK2002 (memantine 10 mg/day)
Diagnosis	VaD*	VaD	VaD
Diagnostic tool	NINDS-AIREN, NINDS-ADRDA	NINDS-AIREN	DSM-III-R/NINDS-AIREN/HIS $\geq$ 4, NINDS-AIREN/MIS $\geq$ 5
Baseline severity: mean range	MMSE: 20.5 to 21.8	MMSE: 20.5 to 21.8	MMSE: 16.9 to 17.6
Treatment length: mean range	24 weeks	24 weeks	28 weeks
Age: mean range	38 to 95 years old	38 to 95 years old	

*ERKINJUNTTI2002 included participants (48%) with AD with cerebrovascular disease.

Continued

Table 11: *(Continued)*

	Acetylcholinesterase inhibitors versus placebo for DLB	Acetylcholinesterase inhibitors versus placebo for MCI
Total no. of trials (total no. of participants)	1 (120)	2 (1,039) donepezil and 2 (2,057) galantamine
Study ID (drug)	MCKEITH2000A (rivastigmine 12 mg/day)	PETERSEN 2005 SALLOWAY 2004 (donepezil 10 mg/day) GAL-INT-11 GAL-INT-18 (galantamine 16 mg/day)
Diagnosis	DLB	Amnestic subtype of MCI
Diagnostic tool (donepezil)	Consensus guidelines for DLB[54]	MMSE ≥ 24*
Baseline severity: mean range	MMSE: 17.85	MMSE: 27.3 to 27.5 (donepezil)
Treatment length: mean range	20 weeks	24 to 156 weeks (donepezil) 104 weeks (galantamine)
Age: mean range	57 to 87 years old	55 to 90 years old (donepezil) ≥50 (galantamine)

*In addition, all participants had a documented memory complaint representing a change from previous functioning, and their global Clinical Dementia Rating (CDR) score was required to be 0.5, with memory box scores of 0.5 or 1, no more than two box scores other than memory rated as high as 1 and no box score rated greater than 1.

[54]McKeith *et al.*, 1996.

Table 12: Summary evidence table for trials of acetylcholinesterase inhibitors or memantine versus placebo in people with non-Alzheimer dementia or MCI – cognitive symptoms

	Donepezil, galantamine, rivastigmine (acetylcholinesterase inhibitors; maximum dose) versus placebo for VaD	Memantine (NMDA antagonist) versus placebo for VaD	Rivastigmine (acetylcholinesterase inhibitors) versus placebo for DLB
Total no. of trials (total no. of participants)	3 (1,811)	2 (867)	1 (120)
Study ID (drug)	BLACK2003 (donepezil) ERKINJUNTTI2002 (galantamine) WILKINSON2003 (donepezil)	ORGOGOZO2002 WILCOCK2002	MCKEITH2000A
Baseline severity: mean range	MMSE: 20.5 to 21.8	MMSE: 16.9 to 17.6	MMSE: 17.85
Treatment length: mean range	24 weeks	28 weeks	20 weeks
Evidence profile table number (Appendix 16)	Table A16-20	Table A16-22	Table A16-23
Overall quality of evidence	Moderate	Moderate	Moderate
Benefits			
Cognitive symptoms	ADAS-Cog: SMD −0.39 (−0.53 to −0.24) K = 2, N = 748	ADAS-Cog: SMD −0.24 (−0.41 to −0.06) K = 1, N = 527	MMSE: difference in change score favouring drug, p .072 K = 1, N = not reported

Global functioning	Improved or no change on CIBIC-Plus: NNTB 34 (NNTH 17 to ∞ to NNTB 9)* K = 1, N = 389	Improved or no change on CIBIC-Plus: NNTB 15 (NNTH 25 to ∞ to NNTB 6) K = 1, N = 288	Good, moderate or minimal improvement on CGC-Plus: treatment effect favours drug, p 0.085 K = 1, N = not reported
Activities of daily living	ADFACS: SMD −0.17 (−0.32 to −0.04) K = 2, N = 760	NOSGER: SMD −0.08 (−0.25 to 0.09) K = 2, N = 525	Power of attention: SMD −0.52 (−0.96 to −0.08) K = 1, N = 83
Number converting to dementia	–	–	–
Risks			
Leaving the study early due to adverse events	NNTH 10 (8 to 15) K = 3, N = 1,405	NNTH 100 (NNTH 20 to ∞ to NNTB 34) K = 2, N = 900	NNTH ∞ K = 1, N = 120
Any adverse events	NNTH 12 (7 to 50) K = 3, N = 1,405	NNTH 50 (NNTH 13 to ∞ to NNTB 25) K = 2, N = 900	NNTH 7 (4 to 34) K = 1, N = 120
Serious adverse events	–	NNTB 25 (NNTH 100 to ∞ to NNTB 13) K = 2, N = 900	NNTH 50 (NNTH 7 to ∞ to NNTB 10) K = 1, N = 120
Individual adverse events	See Appendix 16	See Appendix 16	See Appendix 16

*Further information about how to interpret the confidence intervals associated with NNTB/H can be found in Altman (1998).

Continued

191

Table 12: *(Continued)*

	Donepezil (acetylcholinesterase inhibitor) versus placebo for MCI	Galantamine (acetylcholinesterase inhibitor) versus placebo for MCI
Total no. of trials (total no. of participants)	2 (1,039)	2 (2,057)
Study ID (drug)	PETERSEN2005, SALLOWAY2004	GAL-INT-11, GAL-INT-18
Baseline severity: mean range	MMSE: 27.3 to 27.5	–
Treatment length: mean range	24 to 156 weeks	104 weeks
Evidence profile table number (Appendix 16)	Table A16-24	Table A16-25
Overall quality of evidence	Moderate	High
Benefits		
Cognitive symptoms	ADAS-Cog: SMD –0.20 (–0.34 to –0.06) K = 2, N = 774	By 24 months: ADAS-Cog: SMD –0.03 (–0.12 to 0.06) K = 2, N = 1,903
Global functioning	Minimal or moderate improvement on CGIC-MCI: NNTB 13 (NNTH 20 to ∞ to NNTB 5)* K = 1, N = 199	By 24 months: CDR sum of boxes: SMD –0.11 (–0.20 to –0.02) K = 2, N = 1,903
Activities of daily living	ADCS MCI-ADL: SMD –0.21 (–0.38 to –0.04)	–

Number converting to dementia	By 12 months: RR 0.43 (0.25 to 0.75), NNTB 13 (7.1 to 33.3); by 36 months: NNTB 34 RR 0.88 (0.66 to 1.18) (NNTH 25 to ∞ to NNTB 3.7) K = 1, N = 512	K = 1, N = 512 By 24 months: RR 0.78 (0.64 to 0.95), NNTB 25 (12.5 to 100) K = 2, N = 1,903
Risks		
Leaving the study early due to adverse events	NNTH 7 (5 to 17) K = 1, N = 270	NNTH 8 (7 to 11) K = 2, N = 1,903
Any adverse events	NNTH 7 (5 to 17) K = 1, N = 269	NNTH 34 (16.7 to ∞) K = 2, N = 1,903
Serious adverse events	NNTB 100 (NNTH 20 to ∞) K = 1, N = 269	Mortality: NNTH 100 (50 to ∞), RR 9.22 (1.71 to 49.66) to NNTB 25) K = 2, N = 1,903
Individual adverse events	See Appendix 16	See Appendix 16

*Further information about how to interpret the confidence intervals associated with NNTB/H can be found in Altman (1998).

7.4.5 Qualitative review

Evidence included

No sources of evidence were found that met the eligibility criteria set by the GDG relating specifically to the experience of treatment of non-Alzheimer dementia with acetylcholinesterase inhibitors or memantine. Qualitative evidence on the experiences of people with dementia and their carers of the use of medication for dementia was identified, but as this may include evidence from people with Alzheimer's disease it is discussed elsewhere (see Section 7.7).

7.4.6 Evidence summary

In people with VaD, acetylcholinesterase inhibitors (donepezil 5 or 10 mg/day, galantamine 24 mg/day for 24 weeks) when compared to placebo in three trials produced a small treatment effect on cognition (on average, about two points on the ADAS-Cog), which was not shown to have any clinically significant benefit to the person with dementia (in terms of global functioning or ADLs). Evidence suggested an increased risk of adverse events, particularly anorexia and cramps (although serious adverse events are unlikely). The evidence suggests that at high doses the potential benefits are unlikely to outweigh the increased risk of adverse events. When given at lower doses, adverse events are less likely; therapeutic responses are not diminished, but are still unlikely to outweigh the potential increased risk of adverse events.

In two trials of memantine (10 mg/day for 28 weeks) in people with VaD, although the overall risk of adverse events was relatively low, there was an increased risk of constipation and any clinical improvement was very limited (on average, less than two points on the ADAS-Cog). As with donepezil and galantamine, there was no clinically significant benefit to the person with dementia (in terms of global functioning or ADL). Therefore, any potential benefits are unlikely to outweigh the potential increased risk of adverse events.

In people with DLB, there was one trial of rivastigmine (up to 12 mg/day for 20 weeks) versus placebo. The primary outcome measures in this study were a computerised cognitive assessment and a measure of psychotic symptoms derived from a four-item subscore of the neuropsychiatric inventory (NPI). Evidence from the latter will be discussed in Chapter 8. Results from the cognitive test suggest that rivastigmine may produce benefits in terms of ADLs. Secondary outcomes point to benefits in cognitive symptoms and global functioning, but the study's relatively small sample size limits the conclusions that can be drawn. Adverse events were described as mild to moderate and were mainly cholinergic in nature (for example, nausea). The evidence suggests that an increased risk of serious adverse events is unlikely. Therefore, there is currently insufficient evidence to determine whether the potential benefits with regard to cognitive symptoms outweigh the potential risks.

In people with MCI, two trials of donepezil (10 mg/day for 24 weeks or 156 weeks) and two trials of galantamine (16 mg/day for 104 weeks) were considered. Although in the first 12 months of treatment with donepezil there was a significant reduction in the number of cases converting to dementia, this was not sustained over 36 months. Evidence suggests an increased risk of adverse events and in the two trials of galantamine there was an, as yet unexplained, increase in the risk of mortality. Therefore, for both these drugs the potential benefits are unlikely to outweigh the increased risks of adverse events.

7.5 MEDICINES OTHER THAN ACETYLCHOLINESTERASE INHIBITORS/ MEMANTINE FOR THE TREATMENT OF COGNITIVE SYMPTOMS OF DEMENTIA

7.5.1 Introduction

Apart from acetylcholinesterase inhibitors and memantine, a number of other putative compounds or popular remedy preparations have been suggested or investigated. In addition, the potential for developing compounds that modify the disease process in the dementias is exciting, as our knowledge of the underlying pathological changes is growing dramatically.

Acetylcholinesterase inhibitors increase the availability of acetylcholine in the synapse. An alternative approach utilising the same system would be to increase the efficiency of the post-synaptic cholinergic receptors, both muscarinic and nicotinic, by the use of agonists or modulators (for a recent review, see Standridge, 2005). No satisfactory compound has, as yet, been discovered that combines adequate clinical efficacy together with acceptable tolerability.

Ginkgo biloba is a widely available and popular preparation sold in Europe and elsewhere for 'cerebral insufficiency'. There are many different agents in the extract, produced from the maidenhair tree, and the potential mechanisms of action include vasoactive effects, antiplatelet activity, increasing neurone tolerance to anoxia and prevention of membrane damage caused by free radicals.

Antioxidants, such as vitamin E, have the theoretical potential to reduce concentrations of free radicals, which appear to be involved in the process of neurodegeneration seen in all the dementias.

Anti-inflammatory agents might appear potentially useful because an inflammatory and immunological response has been shown to contribute to the formation of neuritic plaques and neurofibrillary tangles, but these compounds have significant adverse effects, particularly in elderly populations.

The evidence for older compounds currently available in the UK or Europe, like hydergine, piracetam and naftidrofuryl, will also be included in the review if relevant studies are found.

Current practice
Those products that are available to purchase over the counter or via the internet are taken at the discretion of the individual, who may also seek professional advice. Those preparations currently available on prescription but not licensed for the treatment of dementia should only be prescribed as part of a clinical trial.

7.5.2   Databases searched and inclusion/exclusion criteria

Information about the databases searched and the inclusion/ exclusion criteria used for this section of the guideline can be found in Table 13.

7.5.3   Studies considered

We conducted a new search for systematic reviews of RCTs that assessed the efficacy and/or safety of medicine other than acetylcholinesterase inhibitors or memantine for the treatment of cognitive symptoms of dementia (Table 14). Where a recent systematic review of adequate quality was found, we searched for more recent RCTs relevant to the review.

Eight systematic reviews and three new trials met the guideline eligibility criteria, providing data on 10,512 participants (further information about the new trials can be found in Appendix 15e).

Table 13: Databases searched and inclusion/exclusion criteria

Electronic databases	AMED, BNI, CENTRAL, CINAHL, EMBASE, HMIC, MEDLINE, PsycINFO
Date searched	Database inception to March 2006; table of contents September 2004 to 5 May 2006
Study design	Systematic review of RCTs (efficacy, acceptability, tolerability, side effects), observational study (adverse events)
Patient population	People with AD/VaD/DLB/PDD/FTD/other dementias (subcortical, mixed dementias)/MCI
Interventions	Vitamin E, vitamin B_{12}, folate (folacin, folic acid), sage (salvia officinalis, salvia lavendulafolia), ginkgo biloba, nicergoline, nimodipine, hydergine, indomethacin
Outcomes	– Improvement on a score of a cognitive function test (for example, MMSE, ADAS-Cog) – Improvement on ADL test score (for example ADL, IADL, BGP, NOSGER) – Reduction in carer stress (for example CBS) – Delay in time to 24-hour care – Subjective improvement in quality of life – Global rating scale (for example CIBC-Plus, CGIC, SCAG, GDS) – Side effects (for example ESRS, TESS, targeting abnormal kinetic effects)

Table 14: Study information table for trials of other medicines versus placebo in people with dementia – cognitive symptoms

	Vitamin E (alpha-tocopherol) versus placebo	Vitamin B$_{12}$ versus placebo	Folic acid versus placebo
Total no. of trials (total no. of participants)	1 (341)	2 (42)	3 (179 + one study reported an small unspecified number of participants)
Study ID	SR: Tabet *et al.*, 2000 RCTs: none eligible	SR: Malouf & Areosa Sastre, 2003 RCTs: none	SR: Malouf *et al.*, 2003 RCTs: none eligible
Diagnosis	AD	AD / dementia	Dementia or cognitive impairment
Baseline severity: mean range	MMSE: 11.3 (SD = 5.7) [vitamin E] 13.3 (SD = 4.9) [PLB]	Moderate to severe dementia on MMSE	MMSE > 12
Dose	2,000 IU total daily dose divided into two doses	10/50/1000 mcg/day	2 to 15 mg/day
Treatment length mean range	24 months	1 to 5 months	2 to 3 months (one study unreported period)

Continued

197

Table 14: *(Continued)*

	Salvia officinalis versus placebo	Ginkgo biloba versus placebo	Nicergoline versus placebo
Total no. of trials (total no. of participants)	1 (39)	33 (3,278) + 1 new RCT (123)	11 (1,260) + 1 new RCT (346)
Study ID	SR: none RCTs: AKHONDZADEH2003	SR: Birks & Grimley-Evans, 2002 RCTs: VANDONGEN2003	SR: Fioravanti & Flicker, 2001 RCTs: WINBLAD2001A
Diagnosis	AD	Dementia of any type or age-related cognitive impairment	Dementia or cognitive impairment
Baseline severity: mean range	Mild to moderate dementia (ADAS-Cog $\geq$ 12 and CDR $\leq$ 2)	New RCT: MMSE 18.7 (SD 4.6) (PLB); 18.0 (SD 4.9) (ginkgo biloba)	New RCT: MMSE 18.7 (SE 0.2) (nicergoline); 18.5 (SE 0.2) (PLB)
Dose	Salvia officinalis extract 60 drops/day	80 to 600 mg/day	40 to 60 mg/day
Treatment length: mean range	4 months	3 to 52 weeks	4 to 104 weeks

	Nimodipine versus placebo	Hydergine versus placebo	Indomethacin versus placebo
Total no. of trials (total no. of participants)	14 (3,166)	19 (1,470)	1 (44)
Study ID	SR: López-Arrieta & Birks, 2002 RCTs: none	SR: Olin *et al.*, 2000 RCTs: none	SR: Tabet & Feldman, 2002 RCTs: none
Diagnosis	Dementia	Dementia	AD
Baseline severity: mean range	–	–	–
Dose	90/180 mg/day	1.5 to 7.5 mg/day	100 to 150 mg/day
Treatment length: mean range	12 to 26 weeks	9 to 60 weeks	26 weeks

7.5.4 Other medicines versus placebo for the treatment of cognitive symptoms of dementia

Evidence from critical outcomes and overall quality of evidence are presented in Table 15. The full evidence profiles can be found in Appendix 16.

7.5.5 Qualitative review

Evidence included
We found no sources of evidence that met the eligibility criteria set by the GDG relating specifically to the experience of treatment with other medicines in people with dementia.

7.5.6 Evidence summary

Evidence from systematic reviews of RCTs suggests that for vitamin E (2,000 IU total daily dose divided into two doses for 24 months), nimodipine (90/180 mg/day for 12 to 26 weeks), folic acid (2 to 15 mg/day, for 1 to 3 months) and indomethacin (100 to 150 mg/day for 6 months) the increased risk of adverse events outweighs any potential benefit to people with dementia.

There is currently insufficient evidence from RCTs to determine whether vitamin B_{12} (10/50/1000 mcg/day for 1 to 5 months), sage (salvia officinalis extract 60 drops/day for 4 months), nicergoline (40 to 60 mg/day for 4 to 104 weeks) and hydergine (1.5 to 7.5 mg/day for 9 to 60 weeks) have benefits that outweigh any risk of adverse events.

One systematic review reported evidence from 33 RCTs of ginkgo biloba (80 to 600 mg/day for 3 to 52 weeks) versus placebo in 3,278 participants with dementia. We also identified one new RCT not included in the systematic review, which included 123 participants randomised to ginkgo (160 to 240 mg/day) or placebo. The evidence suggests that the benefits of ginkgo may outweigh a low risk of adverse events. However, because the meta-analysis was based on a completer analysis and a variety of measures of cognition, it is difficult to determine the clinical importance of the observed effects.

7.6 MEDICINES THAT CONTROL RISK FACTORS FOR VASCULAR DEMENTIA FOR THE TREATMENT OF COGNITIVE SYMPTOMS OF DEMENTIA

7.6.1 Introduction

In VaD, concurrent physical illnesses such as hypertension, diabetes, heart disease and hypercholesterolaemia will be treated with recommended drugs for the management of these problems. It is assumed that the control of the comorbid conditions

Table 15: Summary evidence table for other medicines versus placebo in people with dementia – cognitive symptoms

	Vitamin E versus placebo	Vitamin B_{12} versus placebo	Folic acid versus placebo
Total no. of trials (total no. of participants)	1 (341)	2 (42)	3 (~179)
Study ID	SR: Tabet et al., 2000 RCTs: none eligible	SR: Malouf & Areosa Sastre, 2003 RCTs: none	SR: Malouf et al., 2003 RCTs: none eligible
Overall quality of evidence	Tabet et al., 2000 (Allocation concealment: category A)	Malouf & Areosa Sastre, 2003 (Allocation concealment: category A or B)	Malouf et al., 2003 (Allocation concealment: category A or B)
Benefits			
Cognitive symptoms	–	ADAS-Cog: SMD 0.01 (–1.18 to 1.19) K = 1, N = 11	ADAS-Cog: SMD 0.08 (–0.26 to 0.43) K = 1, N = 133
Global functioning	Survival time to the first of four endpoints; death, institutionalisation, loss of two out of three basic ADLs or decline of global CDR from 2 to 3: RR 0.47, P = 0.001[1]	–	–

Continued

201

Table 15: *(Continued)*

	Vitamin E versus placebo	Vitamin B$_{12}$ versus placebo	Folic acid versus placebo
Activities of daily living	–	–	Bristol ADL: SMD –0.14 (–0.48, 0.20) K = 1, N = 134
Risks			
Leaving the study early due to adverse events	–	–	–
Any adverse event	Dental treatment: RR 3.04 (0.13 to 73.45) Fall: RR 3.04 (1.02 to 9.01) Syncope: RR 2.03 (0.53 to 7.81)	No adverse events were reported during the trials	No adverse events were reported during the trials
Serious adverse events	Data only available from non-dementia populations[2]	–	–

[1] Cox proportional hazards model and controlling for baseline MMSE.

[2] Reported by Boothby & Doering (2005) – the pooled all-cause mortality risk difference was 39 mortalities per 10,000 persons (95% CI 3 to 74 per 10,000; p = 0.035). A greater incidence of heart failure was detected in the vitamin E group versus placebo (RR 1.13; 95% CI 1.01 to 1.26; p = 0.03).

	Salvia officinalis versus placebo	Ginkgo biloba versus placebo	Nicergoline versus placebo
Total no. of trials (total no. of participants)	1 (39)	33 (3,278) + 1 new RCT (123)	11 (1,260) + 1 new RCT (346)
Study ID	SR: none RCTs: AKHONDZADEH2003	SR: Birks & Grimley-Evans, 2002 RCTs: VANDONGEN2003	SR: Fioravanti & Flicker, 2001 RCTs: WINBLAD2001A
Overall quality of evidence	SIGN 1 ++	Birks & Grimley-Evans, 2002 (Allocation concealment: category A or B) VANDONGEN2003 (SIGN 1+)	Fioravanti & Flicker, 2001 (Allocation concealment: category A) WINBLAD2001A (SIGN 1+)
Benefits			
Cognitive symptoms	ADAS-Cog: SMD −5.38 (−6.91 to −3.84) K = 1, N = 30	Cognition (completer analysis only): SMD −0.17 (−0.32 to −0.02) (24 weeks any dose) K = 5, N = 715	ADAS-Cog: SMD −0.11 (−0.32 to 0.10) K = 2, N = 342
		SMD −0.41 (−0.69 to −0.13) (52 wks <200 mg/day) K = 1, N = 200	MMSE: SMD −0.57 (−0.82 to −0.32) K = 3, N = 161

Continued

Table 15: *(Continued)*

	Salvia officinalis versus placebo	Ginkgo biloba versus placebo	Nicergoline versus placebo
		New RCT: Syndrome Kurz Test (cognitive functioning): mean change from baseline (SD): −1.2 (3.8) PLB	New RCT: ADAS-Cog: mean change from baseline (SE): −0.17 (0.55) (nicergoline); 1.38 (0.57) (PLB)
Global functioning	CDR-SB: SMD −2.34 (−3.26 to −1.41) K = 1, N = 30	−0.8 (4.1) ginkgo 160 + 240 −0.7 (4.4) ginkgo 160 −1.0 (3.9) ginkgo 240 CGI: RR 1.32 (1.03 to 1.69) (24 weeks >200 mg/day) K = 1, N = 156	CGI: RR 2.09 (1.71 to 2.54) K = 6, N = 809
Activities of daily living	–	SMD −0.25 (−0.49 to 0.00) (24 weeks any dose) K = 3, N = 449 SMD −0.41 (−0.71 to −0.11) (52 weeks <200 mg/day) K = 1, N = 177 New RCT: NAI-NAA (German gerontopsychological measure of ADL): mean change from baseline (SD): −1.4 (5.5) PLB −1.4 (4.8) ginkgo 160 + 240 −1.2 (4.9) ginkgo 160 −1.5 (4.8) ginkgo 240	–

Risks	Vomiting (N = 3 sage; N = 1 PLB); dizziness (N = 1, N = 1); wheezing (N = 2, N = 0); agitation (N = 1, N = 6); abdominal pain (N = 2, N = 0); nausea (N = 1, N = 0)	RR 0.91 (0.65 to 1.29) (24 weeks) K = 11, N = 1,062	–
Leaving the study early due to adverse events	–	–	New RCT: 8.5% nicergoline, 8.3% placebo
Any adverse event	–	–	RR 1.24 (1.04 to 1.48) K = 9, N = 1,314
Serious adverse events	–	–	–

Continued

Table 15: *(Continued)*

	Nimodipine versus placebo	Hydergine versus placebo	Indomethacin versus placebo
Total no. of trials (total no. of participants)	14 (3,166)	19 (1,470)	1 (44)
Study ID	SR: Lopez-Arrieta & Birks, 2002 RCTs: none	SR: Olin et al., 2000 RCTs: none	SR: Tabet & Feldman, 2002 RCTs: none
Baseline severity: mean range	–	–	–
Treatment length: mean range	12 to 26 weeks	9 to 60 weeks	26 weeks
Overall quality of evidence	López-Arrieta & Birks, 2002 (Allocation concealment: category B, D)	Olin et al., 2000 (Allocation concealment: category A, B, D)	Tabet & Feldman, 2002 (Allocation concealment: no details reported in primary study)
Benefits			
Cognitive symptoms	Cognitive function: SMD –0.08 (–0.19 to 0.02) [24 weeks/ 90 mg]; K = 4, N = 1,343 SMD –0.19 (–0.31 to –0.06) [24 weeks/ 180 mg] K = 1, N = 970	Comprehensive rating: SMD –0.38 (–0.55 to –0.21) K = 8, N = 533	ADAS-Cog: SMD 0.72 (–0.04 to 1.49) K = 1, N = 24

Global functioning	CGI-Global: SMD 0.05 (−0.06 to 0.17) [24 weeks/ 90 mg] K = 2, N = 1,163 SMD −0.08 (−0.21 to 0.05) [24 weeks/ 180 mg] K = 1, N = 970	% Improved: RR 1.98 (1.55 to 2.51) K = 9, N = 393	—
Activities of daily living	SMD 0.12 (−0.23 to 0.00) [24 weeks/ 90 mg] K = 3, N = 1,228 SMD −0.08 (−0.21 to 0.04) [24 weeks/ 180 mg] K = 1, N = 970	—	—
Risks			
Leaving the study early due to adverse events	RR 1.34 (0.86 to 2.09) [24 weeks/ 90 mg] K = 2, N = 1,244 RR 1.14 (0.71 to 1.73) [24 weeks/ 180 mg] K = 1, N = 1,101	—	RR: 3.33 (0.8 to 13.95) K = 1, N = 44

Continued

Table 15: *(Continued)*

	Nimodipine versus placebo	Hydergine versus placebo	Indomethacin versus placebo
Any adverse event	RR 0.84 (0.72 to 0.99) [24 weeks/ 90 mg] K = 3, N = 1,470 RR 0.85 (0.71 to 1.83) [24 weeks/ 180 mg] K = 1, N = 1,101	Adverse events were not reported in a systematic manner in most trials, therefore making formal comparison difficult.	–
Serious adverse events	RR 1.41 (0.96 to 2.06) [24 weeks/ 90 mg] K = 3, N = 1,503 RR 1.94 (1.10 to 3.45) [24 weeks/ 180 mg] K = 1, N = 1,101	–	–

reduces the risk of further cerebral damage, but there is no assumption that there will be any effect on cognitive function.

7.6.2   Databases searched and inclusion/exclusion criteria

Information about the databases searched and the inclusion/ exclusion criteria used for this section of the guideline can be found in Table 16.

7.6.3   Studies considered

We conducted a new search for systematic reviews (and more recent RCTs) that assessed the efficacy and/or safety of drugs used to control risk factors for VaD (Table 17 and Table 18), more specifically, drugs for hypertension, drugs that control glucose levels for people with diabetes, antiplatelet treatment, statins and other cholesterol-lowering drugs, and xanthine derivatives.

Table 16: Databases searched and inclusion/exclusion criteria

Electronic databases	AMED, BNI, CENTRAL, CINAHL, EMBASE, HMIC, MEDLINE, PsycINFO
Date searched	Database inception to March 2006; table of contents September 2004 to 5 May 2006
Study design	RCT (efficacy, acceptability, tolerability, side effects); observational study (adverse events)
Patient population	People with VaD
Interventions	Drugs for hypertension, drugs that control glucose levels for people with diabetes, antiplatelet treatment, statins and other cholesterol-lowering drugs, xanthine derivatives (for example, pentoxifylline, propentofylline)
Outcomes	– Age-adjusted incidence of dementia – Rate of cognitive decline (for example, MMSE, ADAS-Cog) – Rate of decline on ADL test score (for example, ADL, IADL, BGP, NOSGER) – Reduction in carer stress (for example, CBS) – Delay in time to 24-hour care – Subjective improvement in quality of life – Global rating scale (for example, CIBC-Plus, CGIC, SCAG, GDS) – Side effects (for example, ESRS, TESS, targeting abnormal kinetic effects)

Table 17: Study information table for trials of drugs that control VaD risk factors versus placebo for the treatment of cognitive symptoms

	Antihypertensive drugs versus placebo	Drugs that control glucose levels for people with diabetes versus placebo	Antiplatelet drugs (aspirin) versus placebo
Total no. of trials (total no. of participants)	–	None applicable (no new RCTs)	None applicable (no new RCTs)
Study ID	None applicable	Existing review: Areosa Sastre & Grimley Evans, 2003	Existing review: Rands et al., 2000
Baseline severity: mean range	–	–	–
Treatment length: mean range	–	–	–

Table 18: Study information table for trials of drugs that control VaD risk factors versus placebo for the treatment of cognitive symptoms

	Statins and other lipid-lowering drugs versus placebo	Xanthine derivatives (propentofylline) versus placebo
Total no. of trials (total no. of participants)	None applicable (no new RCTs)	7 studies of VaD/AD, but data for VaD only extracted from 1 RCT (87)
Study ID	Existing review: Etminan et al., 2003b	Existing review: Frampton et al, 2003 + EMEA refusal of marketing authorisation[55] RCT: Marcusson (EPSG)[56]
Baseline severity: mean range	–	–
Treatment length:	–	12 months

---

[55]www.emea.eu.int/pdfs/human/opinion/014699EN.pdf.
[56]Marcusson et al., 1997.

Four systematic reviews and one new trial met the guideline eligibility criteria. However, only one review and one trial reported appropriate data on the outcomes of interest.

7.6.4 Drugs that control vascular dementia risk factors versus placebo for the treatment of cognitive symptoms

Evidence from critical outcomes is presented in Table 19.

7.6.5 Qualitative review

Evidence included
We found no sources of evidence that met the eligibility criteria set by the GDG relating to the experience of treatment with drugs that control VaD risk factors.

7.6.6 Evidence summary

In the studies reviewed, cognitive symptoms, global functioning and ADLs were not reported as outcome measures of the research, except for propentofylline, but the evidence was of poor quality. There is therefore currently no evidence to suggest that these treatments, for conditions deemed to be vascular risk factors, have any beneficial effect on cognitive symptoms. The quality of the evidence for propentofylline is low and the benefits marginal, so these are unlikely to outweigh the risk of adverse events.

7.7 QUALITATIVE EVIDENCE ON THE EXPERIENCES OF PEOPLE WITH DEMENTIA AND THEIR CARERS OF MEDICATION FOR THE TREATMENT OF DEMENTIA

The evidence reviewed concerning the effectiveness of pharmacological interventions for dementia has primarily been derived from systematic synthesis and meta-analysis of randomised controlled trials. Typically, this approach measures outcomes for people with dementia, and sometimes for their carers, in terms of a range of instruments such as scales or questionnaires from which quantified data can be derived. A limitation of this approach is that in most cases the results contain little reportage of the direct voice of people with dementia and their carers. To complement this analysis, a search was made for qualitative research that reported in their own words the views of people with dementia and their carers on the experience of receiving pharmacological treatment and its outcomes.

7.7.1 Evidence included

Four sources of qualitative evidence on the experiences of people with dementia and their carers of the use of medication for people with dementia met the eligibility

Table 19: Summary evidence table for trials of drugs that control VaD risk factors versus placebo for the treatment of cognitive symptoms

	Antihypertensive drugs versus placebo	Drugs that control glucose levels for people with diabetes versus placebo	Antiplatelet drugs (aspirin) versus placebo	Statins and other lipid-lowering drugs versus placebo	Xanthine derivatives (propentofylline) versus placebo
Total no. of trials (total no. of participants)	–	None applicable (no new RCTs)	None applicable (no new RCTs)	None applicable (no new RCTs)	7 studies of VaD/AD, but data for VaD only extracted from 1 RCT (87)
Study ID	None applicable	Existing review: Areosa Sastre & Grimley Evans, 2003	Existing review: Rands et al., 2000	Existing review: Etminan et al., 2003b	Existing review: Frampton et al., 2003 + EMEA refusal of marketing authorisation[57] RCT: Marcusson (EPSG)[58]
Baseline severity: mean range	–	–	–	–	–
Treatment length: mean range	–	–	–	–	12 months
Overall quality of evidence	–	–	–	–	Very low due to missing data

Benefits					
Cognitive symptoms	–	–	–	SKT (change from baseline) at 12 months: SMD −0.49 (−0.61 to −0.04)	
Global functioning	–	–	–	CGI (change from baseline) at 12 months: SMD −0.26 (−0.69 to 0.16)	
Activities of daily living	–	–	–	NAB (change from baseline) at 12 months (includes AD &/or VaD): SMD −0.32 (−0.59 to −0.04)	
Risks					
Leaving the study early due to adverse events	–	–	–	By end of treatment at 12 months (AD &/or VaD): RR 1.38 (0.66 to 2.90)	
Any adverse event	–	–	–	By end of treatment at 12 months (AD &/or VaD): RR 1.99 (1.28 to 3.08)	
Serious adverse events	–	–	–	Death by end of treatment at 11 to 12 months (AD &/or VaD): RR 2.03 (0.38 to 10.90)	

[57] www.emea.eu.int/pdfs/human/opinion/014699EN.pdf.
[58] Marcusson et al., 1997.

213

criteria set by the GDG: a descriptive account (C1) with evidence from one carer (Anon, 2002), a questionnaire survey (B3) involving 64 carers (Bayer, 1994), case studies (C1) with evidence from people with dementia and carers (Davis & Davis, 2005), and a multi-centre survey (B3) in which 176 people caring for older relatives (including some people with dementia) were interviewed (Smith *et al.*, 2003).

7.7.2   Key findings

Evidence from 64 carers of people with dementia attending a memory clinic who completed questionnaires that explored their views on dementia drugs indicates that carers value them (Bayer, 1994). According to carers' responses, they feel that benefits from dementia drugs are evident at the earliest stages of dementia and they also think that dementia drugs are needed at very early stages when any improvement in, or stabilisation of, the person with dementia's condition can be appreciated. Most carers feel that the benefits of medication for dementia should be discernible for about 6 months, and if not it is not worth taking the drug, but those carers less in touch with people with dementia thought the benefits of drugs should last about 1 year.

Another survey of people caring for older relatives explored their attitudes to and experiences of managing medication for them (Smith *et al.*, 2003). While not focussed on dementia care, the survey did include carers of people with dementia and furthermore appears relevant as many carers reported having to remind care recipients and help them with medication. Smith and colleagues interviewed 176 people caring for older relatives and found that they had worries about medication that need to be addressed. The survey suggests that more attention should be given to what is a stressful issue for some carers – this might be achieved if carers' needs are explored at regular medication reviews and through pharmacists giving information about medication to carers.

Two personal accounts are also relevant. One documenting the physical and mental difficulties and exhaustion experienced by one carer of a person with dementia reports that home helps and respite were much appreciated, and that medication was used to help settle the person with dementia at night (Anon, 2002). A second personal account from a person with dementia and a carer relates experiences of the diagnosis of dementia and of rehabilitation, and reports that medication for the person with dementia was stopped because of side effects (Davis & Davis, 2005). This case study points to a need for the experiences of the person with dementia and carers to be taken into consideration when managing medication.

Alzheimer's Society survey of people with dementia and carers
An Alzheimer's Society survey of people's experiences of dementia medication found that three quarters of respondents – including people with dementia, carers and professionals – were largely positive and felt that dementia medication was to some degree beneficial (Alzheimer's Society, 2004). This survey did not use qualitative methodology, but is noteworthy as the number of respondents was high (of over 4,000 respondents, 2,889 had experience of at least one medication used for the treatment of dementia) and there is a paucity of other evidence on the experiences of people with dementia and their carers of medication for dementia.

7.7.3 Conclusion

Apart from four publications relating carers' experiences, which made brief comment on the role of drug treatment, this transpired to be an undeveloped field of research. Given the magnitude of public response to policy changes in relation to the availability of treatment for dementia, the dearth of well-conducted qualitative research would appear to be a potential priority for future funding. Responses to a survey conducted by the Alzheimer's Society indicate that many people with dementia and many carers experience beneficial effects from drug treatment for dementia using acetylcholinesterase inhibitors or memantine.

Evidence on the experiences of people with dementia and carers indicates that, when managing medication, the feelings of the person with dementia and carers should be taken into consideration, including their feelings about whether side effects are tolerable.

7.8 RESEARCH RECOMMENDATIONS

7.8.1 Cognitive stimulation and/or acetylcholinesterase inhibitors in Alzheimer's disease

For people with AD, are cognitive stimulation (activities involving cognitive processing; usually in a social context and often group-based, with an emphasis on enjoyment of activities), acetylcholinesterase inhibitors (donepezil, galantamine or rivastigmine) or combined treatment clinically and cost effective in terms of cognition, global functioning, ADLs and quality of life when compared with placebo over 6 months?

Why this is important

No randomised studies have directly compared cognitive stimulation with an acetylcholinesterase inhibitor, and few randomised studies have compared the combination with an acetylcholinesterase inhibitor alone in people with mild-to-moderate AD. Evidence suggests that cognitive stimulation is effective in people with dementia, but it is difficult to compare the magnitude of the effect with that of acetylcholinesterase inhibitors.

7.9 HEALTH AND SOCIAL CARE RECOMMENDATIONS

7.9.1 Promoting and maintaining independence of people with dementia

7.9.1.1 Health and social care staff should aim to promote and maintain the independence, including mobility, of people with dementia. Care plans should address ADLs that maximise independent activity, enhance function, adapt and develop skills, and minimise the need for support. When writing care plans, the varying needs of people with different types of dementia should be addressed. Care plans should always include:
- consistent and stable staffing
- retaining a familiar environment

- minimising relocations
- flexibility to accommodate fluctuating abilities
- assessment and care-planning advice regarding ADLs, and ADL skill training from an occupational therapist
- assessment and care-planning advice about independent toileting skills; if incontinence occurs all possible causes should be assessed and relevant treatments tried before concluding that it is permanent
- environmental modifications to aid independent functioning, including assistive technology, with advice from an occupational therapist and/or clinical psychologist
- physical exercise, with assessment and advice from a physiotherapist when needed
- support for people to go at their own pace and participate in activities they enjoy. [For the evidence, see section 7.2]

7.9.1.2   When developing a care plan for a person with a learning disability newly diagnosed with dementia, an assessment using the AMPS[59] should be considered. The DMR[60] and BPT[61] should be considered for monitoring change in function over time. [For the evidence, see section 4.6.3]

7.9.2   Non-pharmacological interventions for cognitive symptoms and maintaining function

7.9.2.1   People with mild-to-moderate dementia of all types should be given the opportunity to participate in a structured group cognitive stimulation programme. This should be commissioned and provided by a range of health and social care staff with appropriate training and supervision, and offered irrespective of any drug prescribed for the treatment of cognitive symptoms of dementia. [For the evidence, see section 7.3]

7.9.3   Pharmacological interventions for the cognitive symptoms of Alzheimer's dementia[62]

7.9.3.1   The three acetylcholinesterase inhibitors donepezil, galantamine and rivastigmine[63] are recommended as options in the management of people

---

[59]The AMPS should be carried out by someone with formal training in its use.

[60]Evenhuis *et al.*, 1990.

[61]Dalton & Fedor, 1998.

[62]The GDG has not had any responsibility for the development of the NICE technology appraisal on the clinical and cost effectiveness of donepezil, galantamine and rivastigmine for mild to moderate Alzheimer's disease and memantine for moderate to severe Alzheimer's disease (for further information see www.nice.org.uk). Nevertheless, following NICE protocol, the technology appraisal recommendations have been incorporated verbatim into this guideline (where one of these recommendations appears, it is indicated as NICE TA 2006).

[63]The guidance applies to the marketing authorisation held for each drug at the time of the appraisal.

with AD of moderate severity only (that is, those with an MMSE score of between 10 and 20 points), and under the following conditions. **[NICE TA 2006]**

- Only specialists in the care of people with dementia (that is, psychiatrists including those specialising in learning disability, neurologists, and physicians specialising in the care of the elderly) should initiate treatment. Carers' views on the patient's condition at baseline should be sought.
- Patients who continue on the drug should be reviewed every 6 months by MMSE score and global, functional and behavioural assessment. Carers' views on the patient's condition at follow-up should be sought. The drug should only be continued while the patient's MMSE score remains at or above 10 points and their global, functional and behavioural condition remains at a level where the drug is considered to be having a worthwhile effect. Any review involving MMSE assessment should be undertaken by an appropriate specialist team, unless there are locally agreed protocols for shared care.

7.9.3.2   Although it is recommended that acetylcholinesterase inhibitors should be prescribed only to people with AD of moderate severity, healthcare professionals should not rely on the MMSE score in certain circumstances. These are:

- in those with an MMSE score greater than 20, who have moderate dementia as judged by significant impairments in functional ability and personal and social function compared with premorbid ability
- in those with an MMSE score less than 10 because of a low premorbid attainment or ability or linguistic difficulties, who have moderate dementia as judged by an assessment tool sensitive to their level of competence
- in people with learning disabilities
- in people who are not fluent in spoken English or in the language in which the MMSE is applied. [For the evidence, see sections 4.6.3 and 6.4.4]

7.9.3.3   For people with learning disabilities, tools used to assess the severity of dementia should be sensitive to their level of competence. Options include:

- CAMCOG[64]
- CAMDEX[65]
- DMR
- DSDS[66], which can be useful in diagnosis of dementia in people with learning disabilities who do not have Down's syndrome. [For the evidence, see section 4.6.3]

7.9.3.4   When the decision has been made to prescribe an acetylcholinesterase inhibitor, it is recommended that therapy should be initiated with a drug

---

[64]Hon *et al.*, 1999.
[65]Ball *et al.*, 2004.
[66]Gedye, 1995.

with the lowest acquisition cost (taking into account required daily dose and the price per dose once shared care has started). However, an alternative acetylcholinesterase inhibitor could be prescribed where it is considered appropriate having regard to adverse event profile, expectations around concordance, medical comorbidity, possibility of drug interactions, and dosing profiles. **[NICE TA 2006]**

7.9.3.5   Memantine is not recommended as a treatment option for people with moderately severe to severe AD except as part of well-designed clinical studies. **[NICE TA 2006]**

7.9.3.6   People with mild Alzheimer's disease who are currently receiving donepezil, galantamine or rivastigmine, and people with moderately severe to severe Alzheimer's disease currently receiving memantine, whether as routine therapy or as part of a clinical trial, may be continued on therapy (including after the conclusion of a clinical trial) until they, their carers and/or specialist consider it appropriate to stop. **[NICE TA 2006]**

7.9.4   Pharmacological interventions for the cognitive symptoms of non-Alzheimer dementias and mild cognitive impairment

7.9.4.1   For people with vascular dementia, acetylcholinesterase inhibitors and memantine should not be prescribed for the treatment of cognitive decline, except as part of properly constructed clinical studies. [For the evidence, see section 7.4]

7.9.4.2   For people with MCI, acetylcholinesterase inhibitors should not be prescribed, except as part of properly constructed clinical studies. [For the evidence, see section 7.4]

8. THERAPEUTIC INTERVENTIONS FOR PEOPLE WITH DEMENTIA – NON-COGNITIVE SYMPTOMS AND BEHAVIOUR THAT CHALLENGES

8.1   INTRODUCTION

Although it is the cognitive features of dementia that are its defining characteristic, other aspects contribute in large measure to the difficulties experienced, by both the person with dementia and the people that support him or her. Often these non-cognitive symptoms are described as neuropsychiatric symptoms or 'behavioural and psychological symptoms of dementia' (BPSD), terms that include delusions, hallucinations, depression, anxiety, apathy and a range of behaviours, such as aggression, wandering, disinhibition and agitation. It is suggested that these behaviours may occur in up to 90% of people with AD (Robert *et al.*, 2005). Prevalence rates for features such as anxiety, apathy and depression are consistently high.

In this chapter, the term 'behaviour that challenges' is used to describe those aspects that are often viewed as a comorbid emotional disorder. This term may be taken to encompass a wide range of difficulties often experienced by people with dementia and which may have an effect on those who provide care; such behaviour includes aggression, agitation, wandering, hoarding, sexual disinhibition, apathy and disruptive vocal activity such as shouting.

In many cases, these difficulties directly reflect the distress that the person with dementia might be experiencing (for example, if he or she is agitated). The reactions of others to such behaviour may also lead to secondary discomfort and distress for the person with dementia, or the person may be given medication (with the potential for adverse side effects) as a result of the behaviour. Behaviour that challenges has frequently been associated with higher levels of strain and distress in family carers (Donaldson *et al.*, 1997) and is a common precipitant of admissions to institutional care. In care homes such behaviour may be a key factor in staff seeking specialist care, admissions to hospital or transfer to an alternative care home. This area is one of crucial significance in dementia care for all concerned – people with dementia, family carers and paid care staff.

It should be noted that the various categorisations of behaviour, such as those listed above, encompass a wide range of types of behaviour, arising for a multitude of different reasons (Hope & Fairburn, 1990; Ware *et al.*, 1990). For example, wandering may be a determined effort to escape from a care home or a search for something or someone, or a result of restless agitation, boredom or need for exercise. Its impact may be greater at 3 a.m. than during the day. Treatment approaches would need to reflect the range of possible causes of the behaviour, and professionals should always ask the vital question of whether the behaviour is a serious problem and, if so, for whom. To simply see such behaviour as a symptom of dementia would be to miss the evident psychosocial factors, which interact with biological factors and influence greatly the presenting picture. Rather than clustering symptoms together, the key to individually tailored interventions will be to delineate the factors leading to a particular behaviour in a particular context – whether these be physical, social, environmental or psychological.

8.2   NON-PHARMACOLOGICAL INTERVENTIONS FOR BEHAVIOUR THAT CHALLENGES

8.2.1   Introduction

Behaviour that challenges arises in the context of a particular care environment. Although in some cases such behaviour may not be viewed as a problem by those providing care, the association between carer strain and difficult behaviour has been noted above. There is also the possibility that a stressed carer behaves in ways that elicit more difficult behaviour from a person with dementia (Woods, 2001). This may mean that the target for therapeutic intervention will at times be the attributions, attitudes and interactions of carers, rather than the behaviour itself.

Although some general approaches have been evaluated in relation to their effect on behaviour that challenges, the need for individually tailored approaches is widely recognised. General approaches have aimed primarily to reduce agitation, by offering calming stimulation, or distraction, or re-setting circadian rhythms. The need to adapt the intervention to the unique circumstances of the person with dementia and his/her care environment is one reason why single case study research has proved popular in this field; in this way, the intervention can be tailored to the person's individual difficulties and an appropriate treatment plan developed. The challenge for research in this area is to carry out larger scale studies, whilst retaining the focus on an individualised approach.

Currently in the UK, while guidelines urge non-pharmacological management of agitation as a first-line intervention (Howard *et al.*, 2001), in practice, this is rarely attempted. The skills needed for individualised assessment and intervention are rare, and most referrals come at a crisis point where it is difficult for carers to take on board a different approach, as their own levels of distress have reached breaking point. Mental health professionals with the requisite skills are available in some areas, and training is widely available in the basics of managing behaviour that challenges for care staff and family carers.

8.2.2   Databases searched and inclusion/exclusion criteria

Information about the databases searched and the inclusion/exclusion criteria used for this section of the guideline can be found in Table 20.

Table 20: Databases searched and inclusion/exclusion criteria

Electronic databases	AMED, BNI, CINAHL, COCHRANE, EMBASE, MEDLINE, PsycINFO, AgeInfo, AgeLine, ASSIA, CareData, HMIC, PAIS International, SIGLE, Social Services Abstracts, Social Work Abstracts, SSCI
Date searched	Database inception to March 2006; table of contents September 2004 to 5 May 2006
Study design	RCT
Patient population	People with AD/VaD/DLB/PDD/FTD/other dementias (subcortical, mixed dementias) and behaviour that challenges (including aggression, agitation, disinhibition [sexual], apathy, wandering, disruptive vocalisations, eating disorders, hoarding, psychosis, sleep disturbance)
Interventions	– Psychological interventions (including reality orientation, validation therapy, reminiscence)
	– Behavioural interventions* – Occupational/structured activities – Environmental interventions/modifications – Sensory enhancement/relaxation – Social contact – Staff training – Medical/nursing care interventions (including bright-light therapy/ sleep interventions, pain management, hearing aids, removal of restraints) – Combination therapies – Interventions involving working with carers – Multi-sensory stimulation (snoezelen) – Psychodrama – Subjective barriers to prevent wandering

*The search was widened to include all study designs.

8.2.3 Studies considered[67]

We conducted a new systematic search for RCTs that assessed the efficacy of psychological, behavioural or other interventions for the management of behaviour that

---

[67]Here, and elsewhere in the guideline, each study considered for review is referred to by a study ID in capital letters (primary author and date of study publication, except where a study is in press or only submitted for publication, then a date is not used).

challenges (see Table 21). For the purposes of the guideline, behavioural management was reviewed separately.

For the review of psychological and other interventions, 17 RCTs met the guideline eligibility criteria, providing data on 767 participants. Of these, all were published in peer-reviewed journals between 1986 and 2005. In addition, 94 studies were excluded from the analysis (further information about both included and excluded studies can be found in Appendix 15f). For the review of behavioural management, six controlled studies met eligibility criteria (Beck *et al.*, 2002;

Table 21: Study information table for trials of psychological and other interventions in people with dementia – management of behaviour that challenges

	Aromatherapy versus placebo	Cognitive stimulation (reality orientation) versus standard care	Light therapy versus placebo
Total no. of trials (total no. of participants)	2 (1 cluster randomised) (93)	3 (72)	4 (114)
Study ID	BALLARD2002B SMALLWOOD2001	BAINES1987 FERRARIO1991 WALLIS1983	ANCOLIISRAEL 2003 FONTANAGASIO 2003 LYKETSOS1999 MISHIMA1998
Diagnosis	Severe dementia (CDR stage 3) Severe dementia (by a consultant psychiatrist)	Moderate to severe impairment of cognitive function according to the CAPE (BAINES 1987)	AD (NINDS-ADRDA) (ANCOLIISRAEL 2003) AD, VaD, DLB, PDD (CERAD) (FONTANAGASIO 2003)
		Unspecified dementia; MMSE or DSM-IV (FERRARIO1991, WALLIS1983)	AD, VaD (DSM-IV) (LYKETSOS 1999, MISHIMA1998)
Treatment length	2 to 4 weeks	4 to 24 weeks	10 days to 4 weeks

Table 21: (*Continued*)

	Light therapy versus standard care	Multi-sensory stimulation versus active control	Music therapy versus control
Total no. of trials (total no. of participants)	1 (70)	2 (143)	1 (30)
Study ID	DOWLING2005	BAKER2003 HOLTKAMP1997	GROENE1993
Diagnosis	AD (NINDS-ADRDA)	AD, VaD, mixed dementia (BAKER2003) Unspecified dementia DSM III-R (HOLTKAMP 1997)	AD (DSM III-R)
Treatment length	10 weeks	3 days to 4 weeks	15 weeks

Table 21: (*Continued*)

	Reminiscence versus no treatment	Reminiscence versus standard care	Validation therapy versus social support	Validation therapy versus standard care
Total no. of trials (total no. of participants)	3 (91)	1 (71)	1 (60)	2 (80)
Study ID	BAINES1987 LAI2004 THORGRIM-SEN2002	LAI2004	TOSELAND 1997	ROBB1986 TOSELAND 1997

Continued

Table 21: (*Continued*)

	Reminiscence versus no treatment	Reminiscence versus standard care	Validation therapy versus social support	Validation therapy versus standard care
Diagnosis	Moderate to severe impairment of cognitive functioning, DSM-IV diagnosis of dementia, unspecified dementia	Clinical diagnosis of dementia or DSM-IV	Unspecified dementia	Unspecified dementia
Treatment length	6 to 18 weeks	6 weeks	52 weeks	36 to 52 weeks

Gormley *et al.*, 2001; Lichtenberg *et al.*, 2005; McCurry *et al.*, 2005; Teri *et al.*, 2000, 2005a) and several case studies were also identified. Because meta-analysis was not possible, these studies are reviewed narratively.

8.2.4   Psychological interventions versus control in people with dementia – management of behaviour that challenges

Evidence from critical outcomes and overall quality of evidence are presented in Table 22. The full evidence profiles and associated forest plots can be found in Appendix 16 and Appendix 20, respectively.

8.2.5   Behavioural management approaches for people with dementia

Behavioural management emerged as one of the stronger non-pharmacological approaches in a recent wide-ranging systematic review (Livingston *et al.*, 2005), where it appeared 'to have lasting effectiveness for the management of dementia-associated neuropsychiatric symptoms'. However, it is notable that the best evidence for the effects of behavioural approaches comes from studies targeting comorbid depression and anxiety in dementia (see Section 8.3). The evidence in relation to behaviour that challenges is less extensive, and some of the most compelling evidence comes from series of single case studies. These have reported, using rigorous single-case experimental methodology, individually tailored behavioural interventions, based on a careful assessment and understanding of the behaviour in question, its function and maintaining factors. Although not successful in every case, they demonstrate the value of an in-depth, individualised behavioural approach in responding to complex

Table 22: Summary evidence table for trials of psychological and other interventions in people with dementia – management of behaviour that challenges

	Aromatherapy versus placebo	Cognitive stimulation (reality orientation) versus standard care	Light therapy versus placebo
Total no. of trials (total no. of participants)	2 (1 cluster randomised) (93)	3 (72)	4 (114)
Study ID	BALLARD2002B SMALLWOOD 2001	BAINES1987 FERRARIO1991 WALLIS1983	ANCOLIISRAEL 2003 FONTANAGASIO 2003 LYKETSOS1999 MISHIMA1998
Evidence profile table number (Appendix 16)	–	Table A16-14	Table A16-18
Overall quality of evidence	Moderate	Moderate	Moderate
Benefits			
General behaviour	–	Various measures: SMD −0.19 (−0.78 to 0.40) K = 3, N = 48	
Neuro-psychiatric symptoms	NPI: WMD −15.80 (−24.37 to −7.22)*	–	NPI: Endpoint SMD −0.66 (−1.87 to 0.56) K = 1, N = 13
Aggressive behaviour	CMAI: WMD −3.27 (−7.62 to 1.80)*	–	–
Agitation	CMAI: WMD −11.08 (−19.95 to −2.21)*	–	Agitated Behaviour Rating Scale – morning BLT: endpoint SMD 0.12 (−0.46 to 0.70) K = 1, N = 46
Other outcomes	–	–	Change in sleep: Endpoint SMD −0.08 (−1.26 to 1.10) K = 1, N = 13

*Results from BALLARD2002B reported by Thorgrimsen and colleagues (2003).

Table 22: (*Continued*)

	Light therapy versus standard care	Multi-sensory stimulation versus active control	Music therapy versus control
Total no. of trials (total no. of participants)	1 (70)	2 (143)	1 (30)
Study ID	DOWLING2005	BAKER2003 HOLTKAMP1997	GROENE1993
Evidence profile table number (Appendix 16)	Table A16-19	Table A16-12	Table A16-17
Overall quality of evidence	Moderate	Moderate	Moderate
Benefits			
General behaviour	–	CAPE behaviour rating scale: SMD = − 0.07 (−0.45 to 0.30) K = 2, N = 111	–
Aggressive/ problem behaviour	–	–	–
Agitation	–	–	–
Other behavioural outcomes	–	–	Not wandering: SMD −0.73 (−1.48 to 0.01) K = 1, N = 30
	Sleep time (mins) – morning bright light: SMD 0.03 (−0.57 to 0.63) K = 1, N = 46	BMD – active/ disturbed subscale: SMD −0.03 (−0.43 to 0.38) K = 1, N = 93	

	Reminiscence versus no treatment	**Reminiscence versus social contact**	**Validation therapy versus social support**	**Validation therapy versus standard care**
Total no. of trials (total no. of participants)	3 (91)	1 (71)	1 (60)	2 (80)
Study ID	BAINES1987 LAI2004 THORGRIM-SEN2002	LAI2004	TOSELAND 1997	ROBB1986 TOSELAND 1997
Evidence profile table number (Appendix 16)	Table A16-15	Table A16-16	Table A16-13	Table A16-11
Overall quality of evidence	Moderate	Moderate	Moderate	Moderate
Benefits				
General behaviour	CAPE Behaviour Rating Scale: post-treatment SMD −0.45 (−1.42 to 0.52) K = 2, N = 20	–	–	–
Aggressive/ Problem behaviour	Problem Behaviour Rating Scale: post-treatment SMD −0.18 (−1.42 to 1.07) K = 2, N = 10	–	CMAI-observer rated: aggressive behaviour SMD 0.14 (−0.45 to 0.73) K = 1, N = 45	CMAI-observer rated: aggressive behaviour SMD 0.34 (−0.24 to 0.93) K = 1, N = 45

Continued

Table 22: *(Continued)*

	Reminiscence versus no treatment	Reminiscence versus social contact	Validation therapy versus social support	Validation therapy versus standard care
Agitation	–	–	CMAI-observer rated: verbally agitated: SMD 0.02 (−0.57 to 0.61) K = 1, N = 45	CMAI-observer rated: verbally agitated: SMD 0.36 (−0.23 to 0.95) K = 1, N = 45
Other behavioural outcomes	Holden Communication Scale: post-treatment SMD −0.23 (−1.15 to 0.68) K = 2, N = 20	Social Engagement Scale: post-treatment SMD 0.27 (−0.87 to 1.41) K = 1, N = 71	Withdrawal: SMD −0.12 (−0.71 to 0.47) K = 1, N = 44	Withdrawal: SMD −0.10 (−0.68 to 0.49) K = 1, N = 45

behaviour that challenges, such as aggression, uncooperative behaviour and disruptive vocalisations (for example, Bird *et al.*, 1995; Moniz-Cook *et al.*, 2001, 2003; Buchanan & Fisher, 2002). The intervention typically involves working through others, either family carers or paid care workers. It may, inevitably, involve elements of training and support. For example, Bourgeois and colleagues (1997) report a behavioural intervention with seven family carers, each caring for a person with dementia reported to repeat him- or herself persistently. The approach involved an individualised cueing system; there was a clear reduction in 'repetitive verbalisations' where the carer implemented the system consistently, in comparison with matched controls.

A few randomised controlled trials (RCTs) have been reported, involving people with dementia living in the community, supported by a family carer. Gormley and colleagues (2001) randomly allocated 62 carers to either receive four individual sessions on behavioural management of aggression, or to have discussion sessions. Carers in the intervention group tended to rate aggression as lower in their relative after the intervention.

Teri and colleagues (2000) examined the effects of behaviour management on agitation, in comparison with two types of medication (haloperidol and trazodone) and placebo. Behaviour management consisted of 11 sessions over approximately three months, and included a videotape training programme. Ninety of the 148 couples completed the study, which showed no statistically significant effects on agitation, compared with placebo, of the behaviour management or either of the drugs. Behaviour management was associated with less harmful side effects, however.

More recently, Teri and colleagues (2005a) evaluated the impact of 'community consultants', who were trained to teach family carers a behavioural treatment protocol. This included use of the A-B-C (antecedents-behaviour-consequences) model to assist in problem solving in relation to difficult behaviour. Although the main focus was on carer outcomes (significant reductions in depression, burden and reactivity to behaviour problems), a significant reduction in frequency and severity of care-recipient behaviour problems was also noted, and this was maintained at a 6-month follow-up (when 66 of the original 95 couples could be assessed).

Night-time disturbance and sleep problems were the focus of an RCT reported by McCurry and colleagues (2005). Thirty-six carers and people with dementia took part, and the behavioural approaches used included sleep hygiene education, daily walking and increased light exposure. People with dementia in the intervention group woke up less often at night and spent less time awake at night, in total. These improvements were maintained at a 6-month follow-up.

Controlled trials of behaviour management in care homes appear to be even less common and are perhaps more likely to be classed as primarily 'training and education' interventions (for example, Proctor *et al.*, 1999; Fossey *et al.*, 2006) (see Section 9.4). Lichtenberg and colleagues (2005) report a comparison of two adjacent units, one of which received 'behavioural treatment' while the other continued with 'usual care'. The behavioural treatment included pleasant event scheduling, which is usually aimed at improving mood. However, there were no changes in depression in the intervention group, although there was a reduction in how troubling or difficult behaviour was reported to be (by staff) in the intervention group; both groups showed less frequency of difficult behaviour over time.

Beck and colleagues (2002) report a complex study where 179 people with dementia in nursing homes were allocated to receive either an activities of daily living (ADL) intervention or a psychosocial activity intervention, or the two treatments in combination or a placebo intervention or no intervention, over a 12-week period. No changes in disruptive behaviour were observed, but there was a statistically significant increase in positive affect associated with the active interventions. The authors acknowledge that their interventions did not specifically address factors that may have been contributing to disruptive behaviours and call for a more targeted approach.

8.2.6   Health economics evidence

No evidence was identified on the cost effectiveness of non-pharmacological interventions for the management of behaviour that challenges by the systematic literature search.

8.2.7   Qualitative review

Evidence included
Three sources of qualitative evidence on the experiences of people with dementia and their carers of non-pharmacological interventions for behaviour that challenges met

the eligibility criteria set by the GDG: a descriptive account of the experience of a carer of a person with dementia (Gibson, 2005) and two reports of primary research with evidence from people with dementia (Gillies, 2000; Pulsford *et al.,* 2000).

Key findings
An account of the experience of a carer suggests that doll therapy may be beneficial for some people with dementia, as the carer reported that having a doll tended to reduced the person with dementia's distress, helped promote his or her quality of life and eased the provision of personal care (Gibson, 2005). Two sources of qualitative evidence on the experience of people with dementia – one looking at how people with dementia cope (Gillies, 2000) and the other looking at how people with dementia respond to a therapeutic activity (Pulsford *et al.*, 2000) – suggest that it is important to avoid compounding feelings of failure and humiliation where people with dementia have difficulty with interventions, activities and games.

8.2.8   Evidence summary

There is no evidence that standardised approaches, such as validation, cognitive stimulation and reminiscence, reduce behaviour that challenges in people with dementia. In general, this is not the major objective of such approaches, although some improvements in mood have been noted. Little research is yet available regarding music-based approaches, multi-sensory stimulation and bright light therapy.

Aromatherapy in severe dementia has been evaluated in two controlled trials with some evidence of benefit in terms of reduced agitation and general neuropsychiatric symptoms.

The evidence that behaviour that challenges may be reduced using behavioural management largely derives from single case series, although there are some promising indications that family carers may be able to use a behavioural approach, including problem solving, with some success. The need for an individualised, tailored approach, given the range of challenging behaviour and the many factors associated with it, does seem clear.

Qualitative evidence suggests that it is important to avoid compounding feelings of failure and humiliation where people with dementia have difficulty with interventions, activities and games.

8.3   PSYCHOLOGICAL INTERVENTIONS FOR PEOPLE WITH DEMENTIA WITH DEPRESSION OR ANXIETY

8.3.1   Introduction

Depression and anxiety are commonly association with dementia (Ballard *et al.*, 1996a, b) but may be difficult to diagnose and may present with more general behavioural change. Depression can sometimes be precipitated or exacerbated by medications taken for other conditions (including beta-blockers, some other migraine treatments and some antiviral drugs) and any assessment of a change in mood state should consider this. Mood is of course also affected by life events such as bereavement and relocation and other factors such as the quality of the caring environment, which may be particularly relevant for people with dementia. Common sense would suggest that the assessment and initial management of depression and anxiety in dementia should first of all involve consideration of precipitating factors such as life events or concomitant medication and also the nature of the living situation, both physically and socially.

Where there is significant cognitive impairment, non-pharmacological interventions for mood disorders will necessarily involve carers as well as the person with dementia, and the general environment in which the person lives and is cared for needs to be taken into account. Such approaches may therefore also have outcomes for carers, both professional and non-professional, as well as the person with dementia. Although 'talking treatments' that rely on verbal language and skills may be available, the impairment of verbal ability by dementia raises the possibility of also using non-verbal approaches such as music or art, and animal assisted therapy.

Non-pharmacological interventions that might be used to help people with dementia and comorbid emotional disorders include cognitive behavioural therapy (CBT), multi-sensory stimulation, relaxation and animal-assisted therapies. Other approaches such as the creative and drama therapies are considered elsewhere in this review.

Cognitive behavioural therapy is a recognised treatment for depression and anxiety in general use, and mental health professionals from various disciplines may be trained in its use. In the early stages of dementia, CBT may be used in outpatient or other community settings and delivered by appropriately trained nurses or other mental health professionals, individually or in groups (Scholey & Woods, 2003; Kipling *et al.*, 1999). In later stages, and in nursing home situations, this is currently less likely to be available, although protocols for involving carers in CBT programmes specifically tailored for people with dementia have been reported (Teri 1994; Teri *et al.*, 1997).

Multi-sensory stimulation (also known as snoezelen therapy), involves active stimulation of senses using a special room with appropriate lighting, sound and equipment. It has a moderately wide use in nursing home and other care environments, and is often used with older people and those with dementia, although its main use has been with other groups such as those with learning disabilities.

Relaxation training may be carried out by occupational therapists, nurses or other trained staff. People with dementia, especially in early stages, may be trained to carry this out by themselves, and the skills for its use in individual cases may also be transferable to non-professional carers.

Animal-assisted therapy ('pet-assisted therapy') involves the use of companion animals to improve mood and well-being while providing an extra avenue for social interaction. Its current use is variable, though fairly widespread in both health and social care settings.

The evidence base/limitations
Although there is a wide evidence base for the use of CBT in the general population without dementia, there has been very little work specifically focusing on its use in

231

emotional disorders associated with dementia. Most research thus far has required the active participation of carers in any programme of treatment and often considers the outcome on the mood of the carer as well as the person with dementia. Where purely behavioural approaches are described, outcomes tend not to be described in relation to the severity or staging of dementia. Studies where severity of dementia is reported tend to also include other treatment variables such as psychotropic medication. It is therefore difficult to assess the effectiveness of CBT and related approaches in different stages of dementia. Evaluation of all the other treatment approaches considered in this section is hampered by an overall lack of controlled randomised studies, despite their widespread use in some cases.

8.3.2   Databases searched and inclusion/exclusion criteria

Information about the databases searched and the inclusion/exclusion criteria used for this section of the guideline can be found in Table 23.

Table 23:   Databases searched and inclusion/exclusion criteria

Electronic databases	AMED, BNI, CINAHL, COCHRANE, EMBASE, MEDLINE, PsycINFO, AgeInfo, AgeLine, ASSIA, CareData, HMIC, PAIS International, SIGLE, Social Services Abstracts, Social Work Abstracts, SSCI
Date searched	Database inception to March 2006; table of contents September 2004 to 5 May 2006
Study design	RCT
Patient population	People with AD/VaD/DLB/PDD/FTD/other dementias (subcortical, mixed dementias) and comorbid depression/anxiety
Interventions	– CBT – Multi-sensory stimulation – Relaxation/progressive relaxation training – Animal-assisted therapy
Outcomes	– Depression (for example, Cornell Scale for Depression in Dementia, HRSD) – Subjective improvement in self-reported mood and quality of life (for example, GDS) – Anxiety (for example, RAID)

8.3.3   Studies considered[68]

We conducted a new systematic search for RCTs that assessed the efficacy of psychological interventions for people with dementia and depression or anxiety (Table 24).

Two studies met the guideline eligibility criteria, providing data on 131 participants. Both studies were published in peer-reviewed journals between 1997 and 2003. In addition, eight studies were excluded from the analysis (further information about both included and excluded studies can be found in Appendix 15g).

8.3.4   Psychological interventions versus standard care in people with Alzheimer's disease with depression

Teri and colleagues (1997) specifically reported a CBT-based approach for treating depression occurring in people with AD. Treatment consisted of nine once-weekly sessions of 60 minutes each. There were two treatment arms. The first, 'behaviour therapy – pleasant events', involved teaching carers behavioural strategies for

Table 24: **Study information table for trials of psychological interventions in people with dementia with depression or anxiety**

	Psychological intervention versus standard care
Total no. of trials (total no. of participants)	2 RCTs (N = 131)
Study ID	BRODATY2003B TERI1997
Diagnosis	BRODATY2003B: 100% unspecified dementia (DSM IV), 40% depression (HRSD), 38% depression and psychosis (HRSD) TERI1997: 100% AD (NINDS-ADRDA), 75% major depressive disorder (DSM III-R), 25% minor depressive disorder (DSM III-R)
Baseline severity: mean (SD)	BRODATY2003B: Abbreviated Mental Test Score 3.29, HRSD 15.58. TERI1997: MMSE 16.5, Beck Depression Inventory 17.9
Treatment length	4–12 weeks

[68]Here, and elsewhere in the guideline, each study considered for review is referred to by a study ID in capital letters (primary author and date of study publication, except where a study is in press or only submitted for publication, then a date is not used).

improving the person's depression by increasing pleasant events and using behavioural problem-solving strategies to alter the contingencies that relate to depression and associated behaviour. The second, 'behaviour therapy – problem solving', used the same amount of therapist time but focused on problem solving for depressive behaviours of people with dementia that were of specific concern to the carers. These two treatments were compared with two control situations, one involved the provision of typical advice and support that might be available, and the other was a waitlist control with no contact with a therapist during the duration of the study. Seventy-two participants with both AD and depressive disorder (each diagnosed by standard clinical instruments) were recruited, together with their 88 carers, of whom 88% completed the study. This meant that the sizes of the four different groups were relatively small (ranging from 10 to 23). Participants were all living with their carers in the community, though no further description of severity or stage of dementia is given. Primary outcome measures included the Hamilton scale extracted from a Schedule for Affective Disorders and Schizophrenia (SADS) interview, and the Cornell Scale for Depression in Dementia (CSDD), with a carer-rated version of the Beck inventory being used as a secondary measure. Carer depression was also assessed using the SADS-derived Hamilton scale. Participants in both 'behaviour therapy – pleasant events' and 'behaviour therapy – problem solving' groups showed statistically significant improvement in depression symptoms compared to the two control conditions, and this improvement was maintained at 6 months. An unexpected finding was that carers in each of the treatment arms also showed significant improvement in their own depression scores, whereas those in the two control groups did not.

Brodaty and colleagues (2003b) reported a study investigating different models of service for people with AD with concomitant depression and/or psychosis. One model of service included the availability of psychological intervention for depression involving supportive therapy and encouraging participation in more pleasurable activities. It is difficult to comment on the findings specifically regarding psychological treatment for depression, however, in view of both the study design (evaluating aspects of service model rather than efficacy of individual treatment types) and the concomitant use of psychotropic medication.

8.3.5 Health economics evidence

The systematic literature search identified no evidence on the cost effectiveness of psychological interventions for comorbid emotional disorders.

8.3.6 Qualitative review

Evidence included
Four sources of qualitative evidence on the experiences of people with dementia and their carers of psychological interventions for comorbid emotional disorders met the eligibility criteria set by the GDG: a piece of primary research (B3) involving 20

people with dementia living in the community that looked at how they cope (Gillies & Johnston, 2004), a descriptive account of the experiences of a group of people with young-onset dementia and their views about services (The PROP Group, 2005), primary research with evidence from people with dementia and carers (Spector *et al.*, 1999), and a case study (C2) with evidence from professionals and a person with dementia (Sutton, 1994).

Key findings

Evidence from 20 people with dementia presented by Gillies and Johnston (2004) indicates that the emotional consequences of receiving a diagnosis of dementia can be severe, with many people experiencing feelings of failure and humiliation, although the findings also suggest that group work can help to reduce these feelings. This evidence has implications for both policy and services for people with dementia, in that it points to a need for the provision of more psychosocial support and indicates that it is important that services minimise disruption, seek continuity and have an awareness of the intense humiliation people with dementia may experience. According to another source (The PROP Group, 2005), people with young-onset dementia report experiences of feeling abandoned but value meeting in groups and appreciate group support and activities. Needs for resources for group and social activities are identified.

Qualitative findings from an evaluation of a therapeutic programme for people with dementia involving 12 people with dementia (six receiving standard care and six receiving the intervention) indicate that therapy resulted in a positive effect on friendship (Spector *et al.*, 1999). Spector and colleagues also report that therapy participants reported enjoying the sessions and wishing that they could continue. Quantitative findings indicate that therapy reduced depression and anxiety in people with dementia and also resulted in improvements in carers' self-rated health status. Finally, the potentially beneficial effects of psychotherapy for people with dementia are pointed to by a case study reporting that psychotherapy appeared to lessen the distress of a person with dementia (Sutton, 1994). Based on this report, there may be value in psychosocial interventions for people with dementia and these should be considered. A need to provide long-term support is also identified.

8.3.7 Evidence summary

There is limited evidence from one RCT, albeit with relatively small numbers, that a CBT-based approach may be helpful in treating depressive symptoms in people with AD, and this may also benefit carers who are actively involved in the treatment (see Chapter 9 for a complete review of interventions for carers). Nine once-weekly 1-hour sessions resulted in improvement that was maintained after 6 months. There is, however, a lack of information regarding the appropriateness of this approach at different stages of dementia.

Qualitative evidence on the experiences of people with dementia suggests that some people with dementia value meeting in groups for support and social activities, and that this has the potential to help to reduce the emotional impact of the diagnosis.

8.4 PHARMACOLOGICAL INTERVENTIONS FOR NON-COGNITIVE SYMPTOMS OF DEMENTIA AND COMORBID EMOTIONAL DISORDERS

8.4.1 Introduction

Those who develop one of the dementias are more likely than the general population to suffer from depression and/or psychosis (Robert *et al.*, 2005). These symptoms may be self-limiting or can be persistent and, if so, are usually treated with a pharmacological intervention.

The compounds that have been used (many off licence) include antipsychotics, antidepressants, anticonvulsants, benzodiazepines, adrenergic beta-blockers, acetylcholinesterase inhibitors, memantine and hypnotics. The potential benefits of using these drugs, such as reduced levels of depression and neuropsychiatric symptoms, must be weighed against the potential risk of side effects and serious adverse events. In particular, a number of these drugs may cause confusion or worsen cognition, especially drugs that have anticholinergic properties, for example antipsychotics and tricyclic antidepressants. The use of antipsychotic drugs appears to be associated with accelerated cognitive decline in people with AD (Holmes *et al.*, 1997; McShane *et al.*, 1997).

In March 2004, the Medicines and Healthcare products Regulatory Agency's (MHRA) Committee on Safety of Medicines (CSM) issued a safety warning about the atypical antipsychotic drugs risperidone and olanzapine (see Text Box 5)[69].

In 2006, the Royal College of Psychiatrists released a prescribing update for old age psychiatrists (Royal College of Psychiatrists, 2006b). This advice superseded earlier advice (Working Group, 2004), issued after the CSM safety warning, and aimed to clarify the issues and suggest good practice for old age psychiatrists in the UK on the use of atypical antipsychotics in people with dementia.

Advice on good practice is needed since there is a history of inappropriate use of antipsychotic drugs in people with dementia, 'for example, drugs given for the wrong reason (for example, for depression) or without any documented reason for the prescription; two or more antipsychotics prescribed at the same time; drugs given at too high a dose and for too long without reviewing the need or the dose (Oborne *et al.*, 2002; Waite, 2002)' (Royal College of Psychiatrists, 2006b).

In all situations, the most appropriate management should start with a full assessment (and this may sometimes benefit from the input of a specialist) to try and establish a cause for the symptoms and the impact of the symptoms on the person with dementia. A clear description of the problem, its severity, frequency and precipitating factors has to be established and this can only be done over a period of time in the absence of any behaviour-modifying medication. Problems such as pain, constipation, side effects of current medications and infection need to be excluded before any treatments are considered.

---

[69]Further information can be found at www.mhra.gov.uk.

Text Box 5: Safety warning regarding risperidone and olanzapine

---

CSM advice on balance of risks and benefits (9th March 2004)

'The CSM has advised that there is clear evidence of an increased risk of stroke in elderly patients with dementia who are treated with risperidone or olanzapine. The magnitude of this risk is sufficient to outweigh likely benefits in the treatment of behavioural disturbances associated with dementia and is a cause for concern in any patient with a high baseline risk of stroke.

Prescribing advice

- CSM has advised that risperidone or olanzapine should not be used for the treatment of behavioural symptoms of dementia.

- Use of risperidone for the management of acute psychotic conditions in elderly patients who also have dementia should be limited to short-term and should be under specialist advice (olanzapine is not licensed for management of acute psychoses).

- Prescribers should consider carefully the risk of cerebrovascular events before treating any patient with a previous history of stroke or transient ischaemic attack. Consideration should also be given to other risk factors for cerebrovascular disease including hypertension, diabetes, current smoking and atrial fibrillation.

Although there is presently insufficient evidence to include other antipsychotics in these recommendations, prescribers should bear in mind that a risk of stroke cannot be excluded, pending the availability of further evidence. Studies to investigate this are being initiated.

Patients with dementia who are currently treated with an atypical antipsychotic drug should have their treatment reviewed. Many patients with dementia who are disturbed may be managed without medicines'.

8.4.2 Databases searched and inclusion/exclusion criteria

Information about the databases searched and the inclusion/exclusion criteria used for this section of the guideline can be found in Table 25.

8.4.3 Studies considered[70]

We conducted a new systematic search for systematic reviews and RCTs that assessed the efficacy and/or safety of drugs used to treat the non-cognitive symptoms of

---

[70]Here, and elsewhere in the guideline, each study considered for review is referred to by a study ID in capital letters (primary author and date of study publication, except where a study is in press or only submitted for publication, then a date is not used).

Table 25: Databases searched and inclusion/exclusion criteria

Electronic databases	AMED, BNI, CENTRAL, CINAHL, EMBASE, HMIC, MEDLINE, PsycINFO, HMIC
Date searched	Database inception to March 2006; table of contents September 2004 to 5 May 2006
Study design	RCTs (efficacy outcomes/acceptability/tolerability/side effects) Observational studies (adverse events)
Patient population	People with dementia and depression/ psychosis/ apathy/ wandering/ sleep disturbance/ behaviour that challenges (including those associated with restlessness or over-activity, disordered communications [especially repetitive noisiness], disturbed behaviour [for example, aggression, sexual disinhibition, eating disorders and hoarding]).
Interventions	– Antipsychotics – Anxiolytics (benzodiazepines [sustained action: diazepam, alprazolam, chlordiazepoxide, clobazam, clorazepate; shorter-acting compounds: lorazepam and oxazepam]; buspirone; beta-blockers [for example propranolol, oxprenolol]; meprobamate (NOT recommended in BNF 48 [British Medical Association, 2004]) – Hypnotics (benzodiazepines [sustained action: nitrazepam and flurazepam; shorter-acting compounds: loprazolam, lormetazepam and temazepam]; non-benzodiazepines [zaleplon, zolpidem and zopiclone]; chloral and derivatives [limited role as hypnotics]; clomethiazole [chlormethiazole]; some antihistamines [such as diphenhydramine and promethazine] – Selegiline – Antimanic drugs [for example, carbamazepine, valproate, lithium, quetiapine] – Acetylcholinesterase inhibitors (donepezil, galantamine, rivastigmine) and memantine – Antidepressants (tricyclic and related antidepressants, for example, trazodone; SSRIs and atypical antidepressants)

dementia and/or comorbid emotional disorders (see Table 26, Table 27, Table 28, Table 29 and Table 30).

For the efficacy review of atypical antipsychotic drugs, 11 trials met the guideline eligibility criteria, providing data on 3,741 participants. Of these, two were

Table 26: Study information table for trials of antipsychotics versus placebo in people with AD, VaD or mixed dementia – non-cognitive symptoms of dementia (efficacy review)

	Aripiprazole versus placebo	Olanzapine versus placebo	Quetiapine versus placebo	Risperidone versus placebo
Total no. of trials (total no. of participants)	2 (464)	5 (1,598)	2 (252)	5 (1,905)
Study ID	CN138-005 DEDEYN2005	DEBERDT2005 DEDEYN2004 MEEHAN2002 STREET2000 STUDY F1D-MC-HGAO	BALLARD2005 TARIOT2006	BRODATY2003A DEBERDT2005 DEDEYN1999 KATZ1999 MINTZER2006
Diagnosis	AD	AD, VaD, mixed	AD, VaD	AD, VaD, mixed
Dose	Up to 15 mg/day	2.5 to 10 mg/day	50 to 100 mg/day	0.5 to 2 mg/day
Treatment length	10 weeks	6 to 10 weeks (NB, MEEHAN 2002 – IM olanzapine followed for 24 hours)	10 to 26 weeks	10 to 13 weeks
Age (years)	55 to 95 (range)	76.6 to 83.6 (range of means)	82.5 to 83.8 (range of means)	77.9 to 83.2 (range of means)

Table 27: Study information table for trials of antipsychotics versus placebo in people with AD, VaD or mixed dementia – non-cognitive symptoms of dementia (safety review)

	Aripiprazole versus placebo	Olanzapine versus placebo	Quetiapine versus placebo	Risperidone versus placebo
Total no. of trials (total no. of participants)	3 (951)	5 (1,858)	3 (791)	5 (2,087)
Study ID	SCHNEIDER2005	SCHNEIDER2005	SCHNEIDER2005	SCHNEIDER2005 MHRA2004
Diagnosis	AD with psychosis	Mixed	Mixed	AD, mixed
Dose	Up to 15 mg/day	2.5 to 10 mg/day	50 to 100 mg/day	0.5 to 2 mg/day
Treatment length	10 weeks	6 to 26 weeks	10 to 26 weeks	8 to 12 weeks
Age (years)	56 to 99 (range)	76.6 to 82.8 (range of means)	83.2 to 83.9 (range of means)	81 to 83.3 (range of means)

Table 28: Study information table for trials of acetylcholinesterase inhibitors or memantine versus placebo in people with AD – non-cognitive symptoms of dementia

	Acetylcholinesterase inhibitor (donepezil) versus placebo for AD	Acetylcholinesterase inhibitor (galantamine) versus placebo for AD	Memantine versus placebo for AD
Total no. of trials (total no. of participants)	5 (1,082)	2 (1,364)	3 (1,005)
Study ID (drug)	FELDMAN2001 HOLMES2004 NUNEZ2003 TARIOT2001A WINBLAD2001B	ROCKWOOD2001 TARIOT2000	MD-01 PESKIND2006 REISBERG 2003
Diagnosis	AD	AD	AD
Diagnostic tool	NINDS-ADRDA	NINDS-ADRDA	NINDS-ADRDA
Treatment length: mean range	12 to 52 weeks	12 to 21 weeks	24 to 28 weeks
Age (years): mean range	72 to 86	75 to 78	75 to 77

Table 29: Study information table for trials of acetylcholinesterase inhibitors or memantine versus placebo in people with VaD or DLB – non-cognitive symptoms of dementia

	Acetylcholinesterase inhibitors (donepezil/ galantamine) versus placebo for VaD	Acetylcholinesterase inhibitor (rivastigmine) versus placebo for DLB
Total no. of trials (total no. of participants)	3 (1,811)	1 (120)
Study ID (drug)	BLACK2003 (donepezil) ERKINJUNTTI2002 (galantamine) WILKINSON2003 (donepezil)	MCKEITH2000A (rivastigmine)

Continued

241

	Acetylcholinesterase inhibitors (donepezil/ galantamine) versus placebo for VaD	Acetylcholinesterase inhibitor (rivastigmine) versus placebo for DLB
Funding	Drug industry	Not reported
Diagnosis	VaD*	DLB
Diagnostic tool	NINDS-AIREN, NINDS-ADRDA	Consensus guidelines for DLB[71]
Treatment length: mean range	24 weeks	20 weeks
Age (years): mean range	38 to 95	57 to 87

*ERKINJUNTTI2002 included participants (48%) with AD with cerebrovascular disease.

Table 30: Study information table for trials of antidepressants or mood stabilisers versus placebo in people with dementia with depression or anxiety

	Antidepressants versus placebo	Mood stabilisers versus placebo
Total no. of trials (total no. of participants)	Efficacy analysis: 4 (137) Safety analysis: 6 (740)	5 (342)
Study ID	SR: Bains *et al.*, 2002 Included RCTs: Lyketsos *et al.*, 2003 (sertraline 25 to 150 mg/day) Petracca *et al.*, 1996 (clomipramine 100 mg/day) Petracca *et al.*, 2001 (fluoxetine 40 mg/day) Reifler *et al.*, 1989 (imipramine 83 mg/day) New RCTs: no more recent eligible trials found	SR: Sink *et al.*, 2005 Included RCTs: Tariot *et al.*, 1998 (carbamazepine 304 mg/day) Olin *et al.*, 2001 (carbamazepine 388 mg/day) Porsteinsson *et al.*, 2001 (divalproex sodium 826 mg/day) Tariot *et al.*, 2001b (divalproex sodium 1000 mg/day) Sival *et al.*, 2002 (rapid-acting sodium valproate 480 mg/day)

Continued

[71]McKeith *et al.*, 1996.

Table 30: (*Continued*)

	Antidepressants versus placebo	**Mood stabilisers versus placebo**
Diagnosis	DSM criteria for dementia or NINDS-ADRDA criteria for probable AD	AD, VaD or mixed dementia
Treatment length	6 to 12 weeks	3 to 6 weeks
Age	71 to 80 years old	

unpublished and nine were published in peer-reviewed journals between 1999 and 2005. For the safety review of atypical antipsychotics, two meta-analyses were utilised (Schneider *et al.*, 2005; MHRA, 2004). For the efficacy/safety review of acetylcholinesterase inhibitors/ memantine, 17 trials met the eligibility criteria, providing data on 6,962 participants. In addition, 20 studies were excluded from the analysis (further information about both included and excluded studies can be found in Appendix 15 h). For the efficacy/safety review of antidepressants, one systematic review was utilised (Bains *et al.*, 2002). For the efficacy/safety review of mood stabilisers, one systematic review was utilised (Sink *et al.*, 2005).

8.4.4 Antipsychotics versus placebo for people with dementia – non-cognitive symptoms of dementia

Evidence from critical outcomes (except individual adverse events) and overall quality of evidence are presented in Table 31 and Table 32. The full evidence profiles (including individual adverse events data) and associated forest plots can be found in Appendix 16 and Appendix 20, respectively.

8.4.5 Intramuscular antipsychotic or benzodiazepine versus placebo for the treatment of non-cognitive symptoms of dementia (in situations where there is a significant risk of harm due to behaviour that challenges)

Evidence from critical outcomes (except individual adverse events) and overall quality of evidence are presented in Table 33. The full evidence profiles (including individual adverse events data) and associated forest plots can be found in Appendix 16 and Appendix 20, respectively.

Table 31: Summary evidence table for trials of antipsychotics versus placebo in people with AD, VaD or mixed dementia – non-cognitive symptoms of dementia

	Aripiprazole (atypical antipsychotic) versus placebo for AD	Olanzapine (atypical antipsychotic) versus placebo for AD and VaD	Quetiapine (atypical antipsychotic) versus placebo for AD and VaD	Risperidone (atypical antipsychotic) versus placebo for AD	Haloperidol (conventional antipsychotic) versus placebo for AD and VaD*
Total no. of trials (total no. of participants)	2 (464)	5 (1,862)	1 (62)	5 (1,905)	5 (555) efficacy analysis 2 (482) safety analysis
Study ID	DEDEYN2005 CN 138-005	DEBERDT2005 DEDEYN2004 STREET2000 STUDY F1D-MC-HGAO	BALLARD2005 TARIOT2006	BRODATY2003A DEBERDT2005 DEDEYN1999 KATZ 1999 MINTZER2006	Lonergan et al., 2002 (review of agitation) SCHNEIDER2005 (safety analysis)
Baseline severity: mean (SD)	NPI total: ~40	NPI/NH total: 9.7 to 14.8	CMAI: ~59	BEHAVE-AD: 15.9 to 19.0	–
Treatment length	10 weeks	6 to 10 weeks	26 weeks	10 to 13 weeks	3 to 16 weeks
Evidence profile table number (Appendix 16)	Table A16-26 Table A16-33 Table A16-34	Table A16-27 Table A16-35 Table A16-36	Table A16-28 Table A16-37 Table A16-38	Table A16-29 Table A16-39 Table A16-40	–

Overall quality of evidence	High	Moderate	Moderate	High	Moderate
Benefits					
Neuropsychiatric symptoms	NPI or NPI-NH total: SMD −0.19 (−0.38 to −0.01) K = 2, N = 452	NPI/ BEHAVE-AD total: SMD −0.09 (−0.23 to 0.05) K = 4, N = 841	–	NPI/ BEHAVE-AD total: SMD −0.33 (−0.47 to −0.20) K = 3, N = 839	Behavioural symptoms: SMD −0.19 (−0.40 to 0.01)
Psychotic symptoms	NPI/NH psychosis: SMD −0.08 (−0.26 to 0.11) K = 2, N = 452	NPI/NH psychosis: SMD −0.05 (−0.21 to 0.11) K = 3, N = 636	–	NPI/NH psychosis: SMD −0.07 (−0.22 to 0.08) K = 2, N = 694	–
Aggressive behaviour/agitation	–	CMAI total aggressiveness: SMD −0.09 (−0.34 to 0.16) K = 1, N = 283	CMAI total: SMD 0.06 (−0.45 to 0.57) K = 1, N = 56	CMAI total aggressiveness: SMD −0.31 (−0.45 to −0.17) K = 3, N = 809	Aggression: SMD −0.31 (−0.49 to −0.13) Agitation: SMD −0.12 (−0.33 to 0.08)
Risks					
Leaving the study early due to adverse events	NNTH 34 (NNTH 10 to ∞ to NNTB 20)** K = 1, N = 208	NNTH 17 (11.1 to 33.3) K = 4, N = 1,390	–	NNTH 20 (12.5 to 100) K = 3, N = 1,252	NNTH 10 (5.6 to 50)

Death	NNTH 100 (NNTH 33.3 to ∞ to NNTB 100)	NNTH 100 (NNTH 33.3 to ∞)	NNTH 50 (NNTH 20 to ∞ to NNTB 100)	NNTH 100 (NNTH 50 to ∞ to NNTB 100)	NNTH 50 (NNTH 16.7 to ∞ to NNTB 100)
	Patient-years exposure: NNTH 10 (NNTH 4.3 to ∞ to NNTB 100)	Patient-years exposure: NNTH 13 (6.7 to 100)	Patient-years exposure: NNTH 6 (NNTH 2.9 to ∞ to NNTB 100)	Patient-years exposure: NNTH 17 (NNTH 7.1 to ∞ to NNTB 33.3)	—
Cerebrovascular adverse events	—	NNTH 100 (NNTH 50 to ∞)	—	NNTH 34 (NNTH 16.7 to ∞ to NNTB 100)	Versus olanzapine RR 1.1 (0.5 to 2.3); risperidone RR 1.4 (0.7 to 2.8)***

*Schneider et al. (1990) reviewed seven RCTs (252 people with dementia) that compared conventional antipsychotic drugs (haloperidol, thioridazine, thiothixene, chlorpromazine, trifluoperazine, acetophenazine (75 to 267 mg/day in chlorpromazine equivalents) to placebo. A meta-analysis of the primary outcome measures from each study found an SMD of −0.37 (p = .004) and an NNTB of approximately 6. In a further analysis of 11 RCTs comparing one antipsychotic with another, there was little difference between drugs.

**Further information about how to interpret the confidence intervals associated with NNTB/H can be found in Altman (1998).

***Data from observational study (Herrmann et al., 2004).

Table 32: Summary evidence table for trials of atypical antipsychotics versus placebo in people with AD – subgroup analysis: participants with AD and clinically significant psychotic symptoms

	Aripiprazole (atypical antipsychotics) versus placebo for AD and psychotic symptoms	Olanzapine (atypical antipsychotics) versus placebo for AD and psychotic symptoms	Risperidone (atypical antipsychotics) versus placebo for AD and psychotic symptoms
Total no. of trials (total no. of participants)	2 (464)	2 (1,146)	1 (494) Post-hoc analysis: 2 (419)
Study ID	CN 138-005 DEDEYN2005	DEDEYN2004 DEBERDT2005	DEBERDT2005 Post-hoc: BRODATY2003A KATZ1999
Baseline severity: mean (SD)	NPI psychosis total score (mean range): 10.39 to 12.69	NPI psychosis total score (mean range): 11.1 to 11.5 (DEBERDT2005 only)	NPI psychosis total score (mean range): 11.1 to 11.2 (DEBERDT2005 only) Post-hoc: BEHAVE-AD psychosis: 9.3 (BRODATY2003A only)
Treatment length	10 weeks	10 weeks	10 weeks
Evidence profile table number (Appendix 16)	Table A16-30	Table A16-31	Table A16-32
Benefits			
Neuro-psychiatric symptoms	NPI/NH total. SMD −0.19 (−0.38 to −0.01)	NPI/NH total: SMD −0.06 (−0.23 to 0.12)	NPI/NH total: SMD 0.13 (−0.12 to 0.38) Post-hoc: BEHAVE-AD total:

Continued

Table 32: (*Continued*)

	Aripiprazole (atypical antipsychotics) versus placebo for AD and psychotic symptoms	Olanzapine (atypical antipsychotics) versus placebo for AD and psychotic symptoms	Risperidone (atypical antipsychotics) versus placebo for AD and psychotic symptoms
			SMD −0.37 (−0.68 to −0.06) (reported for KATZ1999 only)
Psychotic symptoms	NPI/NH psychosis: SMD −0.08 (−0.26 to 0.11)	NPI/NH psychosis: SMD 0.00 (−0.17 to 0.18)	NPI/NH psychosis: SMD 0.09 (−0.16 to 0.34) Post-hoc: BEHAVE-AD psychosis: SMD −0.34 (−0.59 to −0.09)
Aggressive behaviour	–	CMAI total aggressiveness: SMD −0.09 (−0.34 to 0.16) (reported for DEBERDT2005 only)	CMAI total aggressiveness: SMD −0.14 (−0.39 to 0.11)

8.4.6   Acetylcholinesterase inhibitors or memantine for the treatment of non-cognitive symptoms of Alzheimer's disease, vascular dementia and mixed dementia

Evidence from critical outcomes and overall quality of evidence are presented in Table 34. The full evidence profiles and associated forest plots can be found in Appendix 16 and Appendix 20, respectively.

8.4.7   Acetylcholinesterase inhibitors for the treatment of non-cognitive symptoms of dementia with Lewy bodies

Evidence from critical outcomes (except individual adverse events) and overall quality of evidence are presented in Table 35. The full evidence profiles (including individual adverse events data) and associated forest plots can be found in Appendix 16 and Appendix 20, respectively.

Table 33: Summary evidence table for trials of IM olanzapine or IM lorazepam versus placebo for the treatment of non-cognitive symptoms of dementia (in situations where there is a significant risk of harm due to behaviour that challenges)

	IM olanzapine (atypical antipsychotic) versus placebo for AD and VaD	IM lorazepam (benzodiazepine) versus placebo for AD and VaD
Total no. of trials (total no. of participants)	1 (204)	1 (135)
Study ID	MEEHAN2002	MEEHAN2002
Baseline severity: mean (SD)	CMAI: 6.97	CMAI: 6.97
Treatment length	Immediate IM injection with 24-hour follow-up	Immediate IM injection with 24-hour follow-up
Evidence profile table number (Appendix 16)	Table A16-41 Table A16-42	Table A16-43 Table A16-44
Overall quality of evidence	Moderate	Moderate
Benefits		
Psychotic symptoms	PANSS-EC: 2-hour post-treatment SMD −0.49 (−0.83 to −0.14) K = 1, N = 133	PANSS-EC: 2-hour post-treatment SMD −0.48 (−0.82 to −0.13) K = 1, N = 134
Aggressive behaviour/ agitation	CMAI: 2-hour post-treatment SMD −0.32 (−0.67 to 0.02) K = 1, N = 133	CMAI: 2-hour post-treatment SMD −0.40 (−0.74 to −0.06) K = 1, N = 134
Risks		
Leaving the study early for any reason	RR 0.63 (0.22 to 1.84)	RR 0.86 (0.33 to 2.24)

Table 34: **Summary evidence table for trials of acetylcholinesterase inhibitors and memantine versus placebo in people with AD, VaD or mixed dementia – non-cognitive symptoms of dementia**

	Donepezil (acetylcholinesterase inhibitor) versus placebo for AD	Galantamine (acetylcholinesterase inhibitor) versus placebo for AD	Memantine (NMDA antagonist) versus placebo for AD	Donepezil/ galantamine (acetylcholinesterase inhibitors) versus placebo for VaD
Total no. of trials (total no. of participants)	5 (1,082)	2 (1,364)	3 (1,005)	3 (1,811)
Study ID	FELDMAN2001 HOLMES2004 NUNEZ2003 TARIOT2001A WINBLAD2001B	ROCKWOOD2001 TARIOT2000	MD-01 PESKIND2006 REISBERG2003	BLACK2003 (donepezil) ERKINJUNTTI2002 (galantamine) WILKINSON2003 (donepezil)
Baseline severity: mean (SD)	NPI: 11.78 to 21.0	NPI: 9.2 to 12.9	NPI: 21.4	–
Treatment length	12 to 52 weeks	12 to 21 weeks	24 to 28 weeks	24 weeks
Evidence profile table number (Appendix 16)	Table A16-45	Table A16-46	Table A16-47 Table A16-48	Table A16-49
Overall quality of evidence	Moderate	Moderate	Moderate	Low
Benefits				
Neuro-psychiatric symptoms	NPI total: SMD −0.31 (−0.45 to −0.18)	NPI total: SMD −0.13 (−0.27 to 0.00)	NPI total: SMD −0.16 (−0.28 to −0.03)	NPI total: SMD −0.21 (−0.41 to −0.01)

Psychotic symptoms	WMD −4.65 (−6.71 to −2.60)	WMD −1.41 (−2.90 to 0.07) K = 2, N = 879	WMD −2.49 (−4.49 to -0.40) K = 3, N = 935	WMD −2.20 (−4.32 to −0.08) (Note: galantamine only)
Aggressive behaviour/agitation	NPI-NH agitation/aggression: NNTB 6 (4 to 25)*, RR 1.59 (1.09 to 2.31)	–	–	–
Risks			
Leaving the study early due to adverse events	NNTH 100 (NNTH 17 to ∞ to NNTB 25)	NNTH 10 (NNTH 4 to ∞ to NNTB 12)	NNTB 34 (NNTH 50 to ∞ to NNTB 13)	NNTH 10 (8 to 15)
Number suffering agitation as an adverse event	NNTH 50 (NNTH 17 to ∞ to NNTB 10)	NNTB 100 (NNTH 17 to ∞ to NNTB 34)	NNTB 20 (12 to ∞)	–
Death	–	–	NNTB 100 (NNTH 100 to ∞ to NNTB 50)†	–
Cerebrovascular adverse events	–	–	–	–

*Further information about how to interpret the confidence intervals associated with NNTB/H can be found in Altman (1998).
†Data from www.fda.gcv/ohrms/dockets/ac/03/briefing/3979B1_04_FDA-Safety%20Review.pdf.

251

8.4.8   Combination treatment – cognitive stimulation in combination with acetylcholinesterase inhibitors

Onder and colleagues (2005) evaluated the effects of 6 months of cognitive stimulation, delivered by family carers, on people with mild to moderate AD who had been

Table 35: Summary evidence table for trials of rivastigmine versus placebo in people with DLB – non-cognitive symptoms of dementia

	Rivastigmine (acetylcholinesterase inhibitor) versus placebo for DLB
Total no. of trials (total no. of participants)	1 (120)
Study ID	MCKEITH2000A
Baseline severity: mean (SD)	–
Treatment length	20 weeks
Evidence profile table number (Appendix 16)	Table A16-50
Overall quality of evidence	Moderate
Benefits	
Neuropsychiatric symptoms	NPI total: SMD −0.28 (−0.67 to 0.12) K = 1, N = 100
Psychotic symptoms	NPI-4: SMD = − 0.28 (−0.67 to 0.12) K = 1, N = 100
Response to treatment (NPI-4)	NNTB 4 (3 to 13)* K = 1, N = 120
Risks	
Leaving the study early due to adverse events	NNTH ∞ K = 1, N = 120
Number suffering any adverse event	NNTH 7 (4 to 34)
Death	NNTB 50 (NNTH 17 to ∞ to NNTB 34)
Cerebrovascular adverse events	–

*Further information about how to interpret the confidence intervals associated with NNTB/H can be found in Altman (1998).

stabilised on donepezil for at least 3 months, compared with a control group who received donepezil alone. Of a total of 156 randomised, the mean age was 75.8 years, 72% were women, and 137 people completed the trial. With regard to non-cognitive symptoms, there was no statistically significant advantage to the combined treatment group on the NPI (SMD = -0.20, 95% CI, -0.54 to 0.13), although the confidence intervals do not preclude a difference between groups.

Chapman and colleagues (2004) evaluated the effects of cognitive stimulation on people with mild to moderate AD receiving donepezil compared with a control group who received donepezil alone. The cognitive-communication stimulation intervention consisted of 8 weekly sessions delivered to groups of six to seven participants by a trainer, followed by monthly contacts with participants on an individual basis. All participants in the study had been on a stable dose of donepezil for at least 3 months. Of a total of 54 randomised participants, the mean age was 76.4 years, 54% were women and 41 completed the trial. With regard to non-cognitive symptoms, there was a statistically significant advantage to the combined treatment group on the overall NPI caregiver distress score ($F(2, 78) = 4.05$, $p = 0.02$), although there was no significant effect of combined treatment on the overall NPI score. Statistically significant effects favouring combined treatment were also found for the NPI subscales Irritability (Severity Index) ($F(2, 78) = 5.14$, $p = 0.008$) and Irritability (Caregiver Distress) ($F(2, 78) = 8.20$, $p < 0.001$), with a trend for increased irritability for the donepezil-only group noted on the Irritability (Severity Index) measure ($p = 0.086$). For the NPI subscale of Apathy (Severity Index), a trend favouring combined treatment was found and the change scores for the combined treatment group approached significance ($p = 0.077$), suggesting reduced apathy over time.

8.4.9 Antidepressants or mood stabilisers versus placebo for the treatment of depression or anxiety in people with dementia

Evidence from critical outcomes is presented in Table 36.

8.4.10 Health economics evidence

Acetylcholinesterase inhibitors for the treatment of non-cognitive symptoms of AD

The NICE Technology Appraisal on the use of donepezil, galantamine, rivastigmine and memantine for the treatment of AD[72] incorporated a primary eco-nomic analysis based on a decision-analytic model to assess the cost effectiveness of acetylcholinesterase inhibitors added to usual care relative to usual care alone for the treatment of AD. According to the augmented base case of this analysis, undertaken by the NICE secretariat, the incremental cost-effectiveness ratios (ICERs) of donepezil, galantamine and rivastigmine plus usual care versus usual care alone were £54,000, £46,000 and

---

[72]For further information see www.nice.org.uk/guidance/TA111.

Table 36: Summary evidence table for trials of antidepressants or mood stabilisers versus placebo in people with dementia with depression or anxiety

	Antidepressants versus placebo	Mood stabilisers versus placebo
Total no. of trials (total no. of participants)	Efficacy analysis: 4 (137) Safety analysis: 6 (740)	5 (342)
Study ID	SR: Bains *et al.*, 2002 RCT: no more recent eligible trials found	SR: Sink *et al.*, 2005 RCT: no more recent eligible trials found
Treatment length: mean range	6 to 12 weeks	3 to 6 weeks
Benefits		
Depression/ anxiety symptoms	HRSD: SMD −0.20 (−0.55 to 0.15)* K = 4, N = 128 Cornell Scale for Depression in Dementia: SMD −0.79 (−1.41 to -0.17)* K = 1, N = 44	Carbamazepine: Agitation improved more in drug group than placebo in one study, but not other. Valproate: no difference between groups
Clinical global impression	RR 2.38 (1.28 to 4.44)* K = 1, N = 44	Carbamazepine: 77% (drug) versus 21% (PLB) improved (Tariot *et al.*, 1998); 56% (drug) versus 58% (PLB) improved (Olin *et al.*, 2001) Valproate: no difference between groups
Cognitive symptoms	MMSE: SMD 0.07 (−0.28 to 0.41)** K = 4, N = 128	–
Activities of daily living	SMD −0.05 (−0.40 to 0.30)* K = 4, N = 128	–

Continued

Table 36: (*Continued*)

	Antidepressants versus placebo	Mood stabilisers versus placebo
Risks		
Leaving the study early for any reason	RR 1.05 (0.66 to 1.68)** K = 5, N = 264	–
Number of adverse events	RR 1.21 (1.04 to 1.41)** K = 3, N = 791	Carbamazepine: 59% (drug) versus 29% (PLB) (Tariot *et al.*, 1998); 44% (drug) versus 67% (PLB) (Olin *et al.*, 2001) Valproate: Significantly more in drug group versus placebo (p = .03) (Porsteinsson *et al.*, 2001); study discontinued early due to significantly more adverse events in drug group (Tariot *et al.*, 2001b); 17% (drug) versus 2% (PLB) (Sival *et al.*, 2002)
Adverse event: nervous system	RR 6.98 (1.38 to 35.40)** K = 2, N = 65	–
Adverse event: gastrointestinal related	RR 2.57 (1.07 to 6.20)** K = 3, N = 791	–
Adverse event: dryness of mouth	RR 1.38 (1.04 to 1.84)** K = 3, N = 726	–
Adverse event: dizziness/falls	RR 1.33 (0.99 to 1.79)** K = 3, N = 918	–

*Favours treatment.
**Favours placebo.

£39,000 per QALY, respectively, when 70% of costs of institutional care were assumed to be met by the NHS and personal social services (PSS); these ICERs fell to £52,000, £38,000 and £32,000 per QALY, respectively, when the NHS/PSS were assumed to bear 100% of institutional care costs (Technical Report 1: Extra Work on Appraisal of Drugs for Alzheimer's Disease[73]). The augmented base case used a starting prevalence of psychotic symptoms in the study population of 10% and a 0% effect of acetyl-cholinesterase inhibitors on these symptoms. One-way sensitivity analyses were undertaken using increasing prevalence rates of psychotic symptoms in people with AD; two alternative rates were used: 30% and 50%. As expected, the base-case results were practically unaffected by this increase in the starting prevalence of psychotic symptoms when the estimate of the efficacy of acetylcholinesterase inhibitors on psychotic symptoms remained 0%. However, the results were sensitive to increases in the starting prevalence of psychotic symptoms in the study population when a 20% efficacy of acetylcholinesterase inhibitors on psychotic symptoms was used. The results of these one-way sensitivity analyses, undertaken on the augmented base case that assumed that NHS/PSS bore 100% of institutional costs, are provided in Table 37.

It can be seen that ICERs of all acetylcholinesterase inhibitors were reduced by approximately 23% when the prevalence of psychotic symptoms was raised from 10% to 50%, with the ICERs of galantamine and rivastigmine falling below £30,000 per QALY. ICERs were higher than those reported in the above table when NHS/PSS were assumed to bear the 70% of institutional costs. It must be noted that the estimates related to the prevalence and the effect of acetylcholinesterase inhibitors on psychotic symptoms were based on the use of risk equations that utilised scores of the Columbia University Scale for Psychopathology; the scale measures the presence of delusions, hallucinations and other specific behavioural signs occurring during the month prior to assessment.

The above results must be interpreted with extreme caution as suggested by the NICE secretariat, owing to scarce evidence and limitations in the methodology used to estimate prevalence of psychotic symptoms and efficacy of acetylcholinesterase inhibitors. Nevertheless, they indicate that, by extrapolating the results of the analyses to a population with even higher prevalence of psychotic symptoms, acetylcholinesterase inhibitors

Table 37: Results of one-way sensitivity analysis undertaken by the NICE secretariat on the augmented base case of the NICE Technology Appraisal on the use of donepezil, galantamine, rivastigmine and memantine for the treatment of AD, using an estimate of 20% efficacy of acetylcholinesterase inhibitors on psychotic symptoms and an assumption that 100% of institutional care costs are met by NHS/PSS (adopted from Technical Report 1)

Starting prevalence of psychotic symptoms	ICERs		
	Donepezil	**Galantamine**	**Rivastigmine**
10%	£48,000/QALY	£36,000/QALY	£29,000/QALY
30%	£42,000/QALY	£31,000/QALY	£25,000/QALY
50%	£37,000/QALY	£28,000/QALY	£22,000/QALY

[73]www.nice.org.uk/page.aspx?o=288356.

might be a cost-effective treatment for people with AD experiencing non-cognitive symptoms (that is, for a 100% prevalence of psychotic symptoms).

Acetylcholinesterase inhibitors for the treatment of non-cognitive symptoms of DLB
No evidence was identified from the systematic literature search on the cost effectiveness of acetylcholinesterase inhibitors for the treatment of non-cognitive symptoms of DLB. However, the use of acetylcholinesterase inhibitors for the treatment of non-cognitive symptoms of DLB was identified as an area with potential major resource implications. Therefore a primary economic analysis was undertaken based on a decision-analytic Markov model to evaluate the cost effectiveness of treating non-cognitive symptoms of DLB with acetylcholinesterase inhibitors added to standard care relative to standard care alone. The choice of acetylcholinesterase inhibitors assessed in the analysis depended on the availability of relevant efficacy data; therefore rivastigmine was the only acetylcholinesterase inhibitor assessed in the analysis.

The analysis adopted the perspective of health and social care services. Resource use estimates were based on published US data and further assumptions made by the GDG. Benefits were expressed as the total number of 20-week periods in improvement experienced by a person with DLB receiving rivastigmine or standard care alone over 5 years. Improvement was defined as a reduction in the NPI-4 score of at least 30% over a 20-week period. Effectiveness data were taken from McKeith and colleagues (2000a).

The base-case analysis demonstrated that rivastigmine was more effective than standard care alone, at a cost of £137 per additional 20-week period of improvement of non-cognitive symptoms. This value fell below the cost-effectiveness threshold of £30,000/QALY set by NICE[74], when the health benefit was translated into QALYs by assuming that a clinically significant improvement of non-cognitive symptoms reflected at least a 0.012 improvement in the overall health-related quality of life of people with DLB (on a scale of 0–1). This result was robust under a number of assumptions tested in sensitivity analysis. Overall, the results of the economic analysis indicate that acetylcholinesterase inhibitors are likely to be a cost-effective treatment option for people with DLB experiencing non-cognitive symptoms.

A detailed description of the economic analysis of the use of rivastigmine for the treatment of non-cognitive symptoms of DLB is provided in Appendix 17.

8.4.11   Qualitative review

Evidence included
No sources of evidence were found that met the eligibility criteria set by the GDG relating specifically to the experiences of people with dementia and their carers of the use of medication to treat non-cognitive symptoms of dementia and comorbid emotional disorders. Qualitative evidence on the experience of people with dementia

---

[74]www.nice.org.uk/page.aspx?o=201973.

and their carers of the use of medication for dementia was identified and, although this may include evidence on medication for non-cognitive symptoms and comorbid emotional disorders, it is likely to relate primarily to medication for cognitive symptoms and has been reviewed in Chapter 7 (see Section 7.7).

Alzheimer's Society survey of people with dementia and carers
Responses to the Alzheimer's Society survey of peoples' experiences of dementia medication indicate that people with dementia and carers attribute beneficial effects on non-cognitive symptoms to dementia medication (Alzheimer's Society, 2004). This survey did not use qualitative methodology, but is noteworthy as the number of respondents – including people with dementia, carers and professionals – was substantial (of over 4,000 respondents, 2,889 had experience of at least one medication used for the treatment of dementia) and there is a paucity of other evidence on the experiences of people with dementia and their carers of medication for non-cognitive symptoms of dementia.

8.4.12   Evidence summary

In people with AD or VaD, there is moderate- to high-quality evidence that atypical antipsychotic drugs (aripiprazole 15 mg/day for 10 weeks, olanzapine 2.5 to 10 mg/day for 6 to 10 weeks, quetiapine 50 to 100 mg/day for 26 weeks, risperidone 0.5 to 2 mg/day for 10 to 13 weeks) when compared with placebo produce small benefits in terms of reduced neuropsychiatric symptoms as measured by the total score on the NPI or BEHAVE-AD. However, there was insufficient evidence to establish the effect on psychotic symptoms, aggressive behaviour or agitation when measured separately, except for risperidone, which may reduce aggression. Conventional antipsychotics appear to produce similar benefits to the atypical antipsychotics, although there is a paucity of head-to-head trials. In a sub-analysis of trials that only included participants with clinically significant psychotic symptoms, there was little evidence to suggest greater treatment benefit.

With regard to safety, all antipsychotics studied appear to increase the risk of death when compared to placebo. Haloperidol, olanzapine and risperidone may also increase the risk of cerebrovascular adverse events, but evidence is lacking from studies of the other antipsychotics. Similarly, it is difficult to assess the incidence of individual side effects in all but olanzapine and risperidone. In these drugs, there is evidence of increased risk of somnolence, hostility, confusion, fever/flu syndrome, abnormal gait, urinary incontinence, asthenia and peripheral oedema when compared to placebo.

For people with DLB, we found no evidence from RCTs regarding the benefits or risks associated with antipsychotics. However, several observational studies have suggested that up to 50% of people with DLB may show marked sensitivity to both older and newer antipsychotics with an increase in mortality of two to three times[75].

In people with AD or VaD with clinically significant agitation, there is moderate-quality evidence suggesting that both antipsychotic drugs and benzodiazepine drugs

---

[75]See McKeith *et al*. (2004) and Sink *et al*. (2005) for further information.

administered by IM injection, when compared with placebo, may produce benefits in terms of reduced psychotic symptoms and aggression/agitation that outweigh the risk of adverse events. Given the paucity of evidence, it is unknown whether there is any difference between conventional and atypical antipsychotic drugs when administered by IM injection.

In people with AD, there is moderate-quality evidence suggesting that donepezil (10 mg/day for 12 to 52 weeks), when compared with placebo, produces benefits in terms of reduced neuropsychiatric symptoms and agitation/aggression that outweigh the risk of adverse events. There was insufficient evidence to determine whether galantamine (24 mg/day for 12 to 21 weeks), when compared with placebo, produces benefits in terms of neuropsychiatric symptoms that outweigh the risk of adverse events.

In people with AD, there is insufficient evidence to determine whether memantine (20 mg/day for 24 to 28 weeks) produces clinically important improvements in neuropsychiatric symptoms. In the studies included in the review, there was no evidence of increased risk of adverse events.

In people with VaD, there was insufficient evidence to determine whether acetylcholinesterase inhibitors (galantamine 24 mg/day for 24 weeks), when compared with placebo, produce benefits in terms of neuropsychiatric symptoms that outweigh the risk of adverse events.

In people with DLB, there was moderate-quality evidence to suggest that rivastigmine (12 mg/day for 20 weeks) may produce benefits in terms of improved psychotic symptoms that outweigh the risk of adverse events.

There is currently insufficient evidence to establish whether there is any advantage to combining cognitive stimulation with an acetylcholinesterase inhibitor to improve neuropsychiatric symptoms, although there may be an advantage to combination therapy in terms of reduced irritability in both the person with dementia and his or her carer.

In people with dementia who also have depression, there is some evidence that antidepressants, when compared with placebo, may produce benefits in terms of reducing depressive symptoms and improving general functioning (over 6 to 12 weeks) that outweigh the risk of adverse events. There is no evidence of serious adverse events, but there is a risk of side effects (nervous system and gastrointestinal related, dryness of mouth and dizziness/falls).

There is currently insufficient evidence to support the use of mood stabilisers.

8.5   RESEARCH RECOMMENDATIONS

8.5.1   Acetylcholinesterase inhibitors and memantine for the treatment of psychotic symptoms in dementia

For people with dementia who develop severe non-cognitive symptoms (psychosis and/or agitated behaviour causing significant distress), is an acetylcholinesterase inhibitor (donepezil, galantamine or rivastigmine) and/or memantine effective in improving quality of life and reducing non-cognitive symptoms/behaviour that

259

challenges when compared with placebo over 6 months, and is treatment cost effective in dementia and/or its subtypes?

Why this is important
Up to 75% of people with dementia may be affected by non-cognitive symptoms/behaviour that challenges. They are a leading cause of distress to carers and often lead to the institutionalisation of the person with dementia. Several studies have shown that acetylcholinesterase inhibitors may improve non-cognitive symptoms of dementia; however, the cost effectiveness of these drugs in the treatment of people with dementia with severe non-cognitive symptoms has not been established.

8.6 HEALTH AND SOCIAL CARE RECOMMENDATIONS

8.6.1 Non-pharmacological interventions for non-cognitive symptoms and behaviour that challenges

8.6.1.1 People with dementia who develop non-cognitive symptoms that cause them significant distress or who develop behaviour that challenges should be offered an assessment at an early opportunity to establish likely factors that may generate, aggravate or improve such behaviour. The assessment should be comprehensive and include:
- the person's physical health
- depression
- possible undetected pain or discomfort
- side effects of medication
- individual biography, including religious beliefs and spiritual and cultural identity
- psychosocial factors
- physical environmental factors
- behavioural and functional analysis conducted by professionals with specific skills, in conjunction with carers and care workers.

Individually tailored care plans that help carers and staff address the behaviour that challenges should be developed, recorded in the notes and reviewed regularly. The frequency of the review should be agreed by the carers and staff involved and written in the notes. [For the evidence, see sections 8.1 and 8.2]

8.6.1.2 For people with all types and severities of dementia who have comorbid agitation, consideration should be given to providing access to interventions tailored to the person's preferences, skills and abilities. Because people may respond better to one treatment than another, the response to each modality should be monitored and the care plan adapted accordingly. Approaches that may be considered, depending on availability, include:
- aromatherapy
- multi-sensory stimulation
- therapeutic use of music and/or dancing

- animal-assisted therapy
- massage.

These interventions may be delivered by a range of health and social care staff and volunteers, with appropriate training and supervision. The voluntary sector has a particular role to play in delivering these approaches. Health and social care staff in the NHS and social care, including care homes, should work together to ensure that some of these options are available, because there is some evidence of their clinical effectiveness. More research is needed into their cost effectiveness. [For the evidence, see section 8.2]

8.6.2 Pharmacological interventions for non-cognitive symptoms and behaviour that challenges

8.6.2.1 People with dementia who develop non-cognitive symptoms or behaviour that challenges should be offered a pharmacological intervention in the first instance only if they are severely distressed or there is an immediate risk of harm to the person or others. The assessment and care-planning approach, which includes behavioural management, should be followed as soon as possible (see recommendation 8.6.1.1). If distress and/or agitation are less severe, the interventions described in recommendations 8.6.1.2, 8.6.4.3 and 8.6.4.4 should be followed before a pharmacological intervention is considered. [For the evidence, see sections 8.2.1 and 8.4.1]

8.6.2.2 People with AD, VaD or mixed dementias with mild-to-moderate non-cognitive symptoms should not be prescribed antipsychotic drugs because of the possible increased risk of cerebrovascular adverse events and death.[76] [For the evidence, see sections 8.4.1, 8.4.4 and 8.4.12]

8.6.2.3 People with DLB with mild-to-moderate non-cognitive symptoms, should not be prescribed antipsychotic drugs, because those with DLB are at particular risk of severe adverse reactions. [For the evidence, see section 8.4.12]

8.6.2.4 People with AD, VaD, mixed dementias or DLB with severe non-cognitive symptoms (psychosis and/or agitated behaviour causing significant distress) may be offered treatment with an antipsychotic drug after the following conditions have been met.

- There should be a full discussion with the person with dementia and/or carers about the possible benefits and risks of treatment. In particular, cerebrovascular risk factors should be assessed and the possible increased risk of stroke/transient ischaemic attack and possible adverse effects on cognition discussed.
- Changes in cognition should be assessed and recorded at regular intervals. Alternative medication should be considered if necessary.

---

[76]In March 2004, the Medicines and Healthcare products Regulatory Agency's Committee on Safety of Medicines issued a safety warning about the atypical antipsychotic drugs risperidone and olanzapine, advising that these drugs should not be used for the treatment of behavioural symptoms of dementia. Further information is available from www.mhra.gov.uk.

- Target symptoms should be identified, quantified and documented.
- Changes in target symptoms should be assessed and recorded at regular intervals.
- The effect of comorbid conditions, such as depression, should be considered.
- The choice of antipsychotic should be made after an individual risk–benefit analysis.
- The dose should be low initially and then titrated upwards.
- Treatment should be time limited and regularly reviewed (every 3 months or according to clinical need).

For people with DLB, healthcare professionals should monitor carefully for the emergence of severe untoward reactions, particularly neuroleptic sensitivity reactions (which manifest as the development or worsening of severe extrapyramidal features after treatment in the accepted dose range or acute and severe physical deterioration following prescription of antipsychotic drugs for which there is no other apparent cause). [For the evidence, see sections 8.4.4, 8.4.12 and 9.4.1]

8.6.2.5   People with mild, moderate, or severe AD who have non-cognitive symptoms and/or behaviour that challenges, causing significant distress or potential harm to the individual, may be offered an acetylcholinesterase inhibitor if:
- a non-pharmacological approach is inappropriate or has been ineffective, and
- antipsychotic drugs are inappropriate or have been ineffective. [For the evidence, see sections 8.4.6, 8.4.10 and 8.4.12]

8.6.2.6   People with DLB who have non-cognitive symptoms causing significant distress to the individual, or leading to behaviour that challenges, should be offered an acetylcholinesterase inhibitor. [For the evidence, see sections 8.4.7, 8.4.10 and 8.4.12]

8.6.2.7   People with VaD who develop non-cognitive symptoms or behaviour that challenges should not be prescribed acetylcholinesterase inhibitors, except as part of properly constructed clinical studies. [For the evidence, see sections 8.4.6 and 8.4.12]

8.6.3   Behaviour that challenges requiring urgent treatment [77]

The control of behaviour that challenges becomes a priority if violence, aggression and extreme agitation threaten the safety of the person with dementia or others.

Managing risk

8.6.3.1   Health and social care staff who care for people with dementia should identify, monitor and address environmental, physical health and

---

[77]These recommendations were adapted by the dementia GDG from the NICE guideline on schizophrenia: www.nice.org.uk/guidance/CG1.

psychosocial factors that may increase the likelihood of behaviour that challenges, especially violence and aggression, and the risk of harm to self or others. These factors include:

- overcrowding
- lack of privacy
- lack of activities
- inadequate staff attention
- poor communication between the person with dementia and staff
- conflicts between staff and carers
- weak clinical leadership.

8.6.3.2   Health and social care staff should be trained to anticipate behaviour that challenges and how to manage violence, aggression and extreme agitation, including de-escalation techniques and methods of physical restraint.

8.6.3.3   Healthcare professionals who use medication in the management of violence, aggression and extreme agitation in people with dementia should:

- be trained in the correct use of drugs for behavioural control, specifically benzodiazepines and antipsychotics
- be able to assess the risks associated with pharmacological control of violence, aggression and extreme agitation, particularly in people who may be dehydrated or physically ill
- understand the cardiorespiratory effects of the acute administration of benzodiazepines and antipsychotics and the need to titrate dosage to effect
- recognise the importance of nursing people who have received these drugs in the recovery position and of monitoring pulse, blood pressure and respiration
- be familiar with and trained in the use of resuscitation equipment
- undertake annual retraining in resuscitation techniques
- understand the importance of maintaining an unobstructed airway.

Principles of pharmacological control of violence, aggression and extreme agitation

8.6.3.4   For people with dementia who are at significant risk to themselves or others because of violence, aggression and extreme agitation, immediate management should take place in a safe, low-stimulation environment, separate from other service users.

8.6.3.5   Drug treatments for the control of violence, aggression and extreme agitation should be used to calm the person with dementia and reduce the risk of violence and harm, rather than treat any underlying psychiatric condition. Healthcare professionals should aim for an optimal response in which agitation or aggression is reduced without sedation.

8.6.3.6   Violent behaviour should be managed without the prescription of high doses or combinations of drugs, especially if the person with dementia is elderly or frail. The lowest effective dose should be used.

8.6.3.7   Drugs for behavioural control should be used with caution, particularly if the person with dementia has been restrained, because of the following risks:
- loss of consciousness instead of sedation
- over-sedation with loss of alertness
- damage to the relationship between the person with dementia, their carers and the health and social care team
- specific issues related to age and physical and mental health.

8.6.3.8   People with dementia who have received involuntary sedation and their carers should be offered the opportunity to discuss their experiences and be provided with a clear explanation of the decision to use urgent sedation. This should be documented in their notes.

Route of drug administration

8.6.3.9   If drugs are necessary for the control of violence, aggression and extreme agitation, oral medication should be offered before parenteral medication.

8.6.3.10   If parenteral treatment is necessary for the control of violence, aggression and extreme agitation, the IM route should be preferred because it is safer than intravenous administration. Intravenous administration should be used only in exceptional circumstances.

8.6.3.11   Vital signs should be monitored after parenteral treatment for the control of violence, aggression and extreme agitation. Blood pressure, pulse, temperature and respiratory rate should be recorded at regular intervals agreed by the multidisciplinary team until the person with dementia becomes active again. If the person appears to be or is asleep, more intensive monitoring is required.

Intramuscular agents for behavioural control

8.6.3.12   If IM preparations are needed for behavioural control, lorazepam, haloperidol or olanzapine should be used. Wherever possible, a single agent should be used in preference to a combination.

8.6.3.13   If rapid tranquillisation is needed, a combination of IM haloperidol and IM lorazepam should be considered.

8.6.3.14   IM diazepam and IM chlorpromazine are not recommended for the management of behaviour that challenges in people with dementia.

8.6.3.15   If using IM haloperidol (or any other IM conventional antipsychotic) for behavioural control, healthcare professionals should monitor closely for dystonia and other extrapyramidal side effects. If side effects become distressing, especially in acute dystonic reactions, the use of anticholinergic agents should be considered. If using anticholinergic agents, healthcare professionals should monitor for deteriorating cognitive function.

8.6.4   Interventions for people with dementia with depression and/or anxiety

8.6.4.1   At the time of diagnosis of dementia, and at regular intervals subsequently, assessment should be made for medical comorbidities and key psychiatric features associated with dementia, including depression and psychosis, to ensure optimal management of coexisting conditions. [For the evidence, see sections 4.1.2, 6.4.2, 6.4.4, 8.2.1, 8.3.1, 8.4.1 and 9.1]

8.6.4.2   Care packages for people with dementia should include assessment and monitoring for depression and/or anxiety. [For the evidence, see sections 8.3.1 and 8.4.1]

8.6.4.3   For people with dementia who have depression and/or anxiety, cognitive behavioural therapy, which may involve the active participation of their carers, may be considered as part of treatment. [For the evidence, see section 8.3]

8.6.4.4   A range of tailored interventions, such as reminiscence therapy, multi-sensory stimulation, animal-assisted therapy and exercise, should be available for people with dementia who have depression and/or anxiety. [For the evidence, see section 8.3]

8.6.4.5   People with dementia who also have major depressive disorder should be offered antidepressant medication. Treatment should be started by staff with specialist training, who should follow the NICE clinical guideline *Depression: Management of Depression in Primary and Secondary Care*[78] after a careful risk–benefit assessment. Antidepressant drugs with anticholinergic effects should be avoided because they may adversely affect cognition. The need for adherence, time to onset of action and risk of withdrawal effects should be explained at the start of treatment. [For the evidence, see sections 8.4.1, 8.4.9 and 8.4.12]

---

[78]Available from www.nice.org.uk/CG023.

9. EDUCATION FOR PEOPLE WITH DEMENTIA, DEMENTIA CARE MAPPING, STAFF TRAINING AND INTERVENTIONS FOR CARERS OF PEOPLE WITH DEMENTIA

9.1 INTRODUCTION

This chapter is largely concerned with interventions that aim to educate, inform and shape understanding of dementia and care-giving practice. Although there are some pointers towards educational interventions for people with dementia, which might be seen as the beginning of a movement towards the person with dementia as 'expert patient', most of the research summarised relates to interventions for staff and family carers. This is undoubtedly related to the fact that it is only recently that the importance of the perspective of the person with dementia has been accorded due acknowledgement and recognition (Woods, 2001).

It has long been recognised that the attitudes, skills and knowledge of staff working with people with dementia have the potential to influence the person's well-being, quality of life and function. Training is often seen as the means by which changes in quality of care can be pursued, and there are an increasing number of opportunities for staff in dementia care to attend training courses, external and in-house, and to achieve an accredited level of competence in care under the vocational qualification framework. For example, the National Minimum Standards from the Care Standards Act 2000 included the requirement that from 2005 at least 50 per cent of the workforce in care homes for older people should be qualified to National Vocational Qualification (NVQ) Level 2 in Health and Social Care (although it should be noted that there is no requirement for the NVQ to specifically address dementia care).

However, there is evidence in many fields that training *per se* is not sufficient and that other changes are also required, for example, in staff support, supervision and reward, as well as in the organisational culture in which staff operate (for example, Burgio & Burgio, 1990). Staff are instrumental in the delivery of many of the non-pharmacological interventions described in Chapters 6 and 7, and when training interventions are evaluated in relation to changes in the people with dementia who are the care recipients, there is a grey area where interventions might be viewed either as involving staff training or representing a particular type of non-pharmacological intervention. There is certainly no doubt that for non-pharmacological interventions to be successfully implemented in care homes, hospital units and day-care facilities, careful attention must be given to the relevant staff factors. Dementia care mapping, as part of an audit process involving feedback to staff and action planning, is one approach which holds promise as a means of driving forward improvements in quality of care.

It was developed from the influential work of Kitwood (1997), in relation to person-centred care.

The contribution that family carers make to the support of people with dementia has also been widely acknowledged. Carers have moved from a position where they might be described as 'forgotten sufferers' or 'hidden victims' to one where there is universal recognition of how much the care of people with dementia depends upon them and of the potential costs involved in terms of increased risk of psychological distress (Donaldson *et al.*, 1998), physical health problems and increased mortality (Schulz & Beach, 1999). This has led to extensive literature on factors associated with carer stress and a number of attempts to evaluate some of the wide range of interventions and services that have been developed in response. Some evaluation studies have examined outcomes for carers in isolation from the situation of the person with dementia; some have considered the 'time taken to institutionalisation' as the critical variable in relation to the person with dementia, whilst evaluating stress or depression experienced by the carer. Few studies to date have attempted the more difficult task of evaluating the balance between outcomes for the carer and those for the person with dementia; if a 'good' outcome for one party (whether it be reduced stress or remaining at home) were to be at the expense of a 'poor' outcome for the other, the value of the intervention could reasonably be questioned. It is likely that in the future there will be a shift in emphasis to the care-giving relationship, with interventions aiming to enhance outcomes for the person with dementia and carers together.

9.2 EDUCATIONAL INTERVENTIONS FOR PEOPLE WITH DEMENTIA

9.2.1 Introduction

Since dementia now tends to be diagnosed earlier, a range of interventions have been made possible that had not previously been considered feasible. It is now recommended that the diagnosis be shared with the person with dementia (Department of Health, 2001d) and this draws attention to the necessity of responding to the need of the person for information about his or her condition, and his or her role in its management. The 'expert patient' role has come to the fore, with several studies drawing attention to the importance of listening to the voice of people with dementia. Although, at present, there appear to be few educational interventions that have been described, this is clearly an important area for development. However, it should be noted that education may implicitly form part of approaches aimed at adjustment and coping, such as individual work using a CBT approach with the intention of modifying the person's thoughts and fears about his or her condition (Husband, 1999) or the psychotherapeutic groups developed by Cheston and colleagues (Cheston *et al.*, 2003a & b). The absence of didactic teaching does not exclude the possibility of group members using a variety of sources to seek information, stimulated by discussion with other people with dementia in the group sessions.

The evidence base/limitations
Current practice in this area is not reliant on a strong evidence base, with no studies directly evaluating the impact of education and training for people with dementia on

knowledge and awareness. The few studies available have had different primary aims, although some extrapolation is possible.

9.2.2   Databases searched and inclusion/exclusion criteria

Information about the databases searched and the inclusion/ exclusion criteria used for this section of the guideline can be found in Table 38.

9.2.3   Studies considered[79]

The review team conducted a new systematic search for RCTs that assessed the efficacy of educational interventions (see Table 39).

Table 38: Databases searched and inclusion criteria

Electronic databases	AMED, BNI, CINAHL, COCHRANE, EMBASE, MEDLINE, PsycINFO, AgeInfo, AgeLine, ASSIA, CareData, HMIC, PAIS International, SIGLE, Social Services Abstracts, Social Work Abstracts, SSCI
Date searched	Database inception to March 2006; table of contents September 2004 to 5 May 2006
Study design	Quantitative and qualitative research
Patient population	People with AD/VaD/DLB/PDD/FTD/other dementias (subcortical, mixed dementias)
Interventions	Educational interventions – 1. Any programme involving interaction between information provider and person with dementia or family. 2. People with dementia and/or families are provided with support, information and management strategies. 3. To be considered as well defined, the educational strategy should be tailored to the need of individuals or families.
Outcomes	- Perceived benefit - Reduced distress - Greater knowledge - Better ability to access services

---

[79]Here, and elsewhere in the guideline, each study considered for review is referred to by a study ID in capital letters (primary author and date of study publication).

Table 39: Study information table for trials of educational interventions

	Educational intervention versus standard care
Total no. of trials (total no. of participants)	2 (221)
Study ID	CLARK2004 ELONIEMI2001
Diagnosis	AD, VaD, other dementias (DSM III-R)
Baseline severity: mean (SD)	CLARK2004: Not reported ELONIEMI2001: MMSE – intervention group 14.4, standard care group 15.3
Treatment length	1–2 years
Length of follow-up	Not reported
Age	CLARK2004: Not reported ELONIEMI2001: 79 years (mean), 65–97 years (range)

Two trials met the eligibility criteria set by the GDG (CLARKE2004, ELONIEMI2001), providing data on 221 participants. Both were published in peer-reviewed journals between 2001 and 2004. In addition, three studies were excluded from the analysis. The most common reason for exclusion was a lack of confirmed dementia diagnosis (further information about both included and excluded studies can be found in Appendix 15i).

Both included studies involved a comparison of educational interventions, but neither focused solely on the person with dementia. Two unpublished studies are also described as representing innovative practice, and reference is made to a further descriptive evaluation.

9.2.4 Educational interventions versus standard care

CLARKE2004 reports an evaluation over one year of the effects of telephone contact with care consultants employed through the Alzheimer's Association, in Cleveland, USA. The approach involved empowering people with dementia and their carers, developing an individualised care plan, based on strengths and resources, and often made use of other services provided by the Association, including education and training programmes, support groups and respite care. Participants in the control group had access to such services through the usual channels, but did not have the input from the care consultant. On average, participating families in the project group had ten telephone consultations during the year. Outcomes for 89 people with dementia who could be interviewed at the one-year evaluation included less embarrassment and isolation related to memory loss, and less difficulty coping. For more severely impaired people with dementia, there were also fewer consultations with physicians, less use of hospital services, and decreased depression and relationship strain. The authors acknowledge that more work is needed on the details of the intervention offered, although they suggest that the improvements in embarrassment and coping may have arisen from the educational component of the intervention.

ELONIEMI2001 conducted an RCT where the intervention comprised systematic, comprehensive support by a dementia family care coordinator over a 2-year period. This included an annual training course where the person with dementia and carer were admitted together to a rehabilitation centre for 10 days at the start of the project, followed by 5-day courses 1 year and 2 years later. The course was similar to the highly successful intervention for family carers reported by Brodaty and Gresham (1989), where carers and people with dementia were similarly admitted together for a 2-week period, which involved various training interventions. Although there was a strong educational component for the carers, the emphasis for the people with dementia was on a medical and psychological assessment, with group meetings to share feelings and experiences. The outcome reported (time to institutionalisation) showed some reduction in the intervention group in the early months of the study, but by 2 years there was no difference. No specific indication is given of the effects of the educational impact of the intervention.

Bird and colleagues (2004) report an evaluation of the 'Living with Memory Loss' project, provided by the Alzheimer's Association. This project offers six to eight 2-hour weekly group sessions to people in the early stages of dementia and their carers; for part of the time the people with dementia and carers meet together, but some time is also spent in separate groups. The programme is based on the pioneering support groups for people with early-stage dementia described by Yale (1995). Although some limited data are available from a naturalistic wait-list control group, essentially the outcomes compare participants' responses at three time points: before the group, immediately at the end of the group and 3 months later. Data on 84 people with dementia indicate a high level of enjoyment of the group (86.2% enjoyed the group all or most of the time), and 91.6% reported that it had helped them at least quite often. Depression levels, as assessed by the Leeds scale for the self-assessment of anxiety and depression, reduced significantly by follow-up. No change was noted on a crude (0–4) rating of insight, with most participants having a high level of awareness of their memory problems at the outset.

Zarit and colleagues (2004) report a similar ten-session programme for people in the early stages of dementia and their family carers, described as the 'Memory Club'; here, the evaluation related to participants' ratings of various aspects of the programme, which were all very positive.

Finally, a descriptive paper from the Cheston and colleagues study of group support for people with dementia (Watkins *et al.*, 2006) describes changes in awareness levels of participants in the groups, in addition to the changes in mood reported elsewhere. However, unlike the other available studies, this does focus solely on the person with dementia, rather than being confounded with the intervention for the family carer.

9.2.5 Health economics evidence

No studies were identified on the cost effectiveness of educational interventions for people with dementia.

9.2.6 Qualitative review

Evidence included
The qualitative review did not identify evidence on experiences of people with dementia and their carers of educational interventions for people with dementia.

9.2.7 Evidence summary

In relation to people with dementia, the evidence base for educational interventions is lacking at present. Education does appear to be a component of a few other programmes, which include a variety of other interventions, and of support groups, which have had a primary focus on outcomes of depression and anxiety rather than on knowledge and awareness.

9.3 DEMENTIA CARE MAPPING

9.3.1 Dementia care mapping for people with dementia

Dementia care mapping (DCM) is an observational method, developed by Kitwood and Bredin (Kitwood & Bredin, 1992), arising from the development of Kitwood's person-centred care approach (Kitwood, 1997). It involves as much as 6 hours' observation, recording every 5 minutes the main activity in which the person has been engaged and a subjective rating of the person's well-being during that period. Also recorded are any occasions when a carer shows one of a number of 'personal detractions', where the person with dementia is depersonalised, diminished or devalued in any way. DCM has many uses and continues to be developed. It can be used to help staff understand the experience of people of dementia in their care or simply to rate the quality of a care environment (Ballard *et al.*, 2001); it can also be used to provide feedback to staff and to assist in drawing up an action plan for change at both the level of the individual resident and the care setting as a whole (Lintern *et al.*, 2002). A further DCM evaluation can then be used to indicate where change has occurred and generate further ideas for action (Brooker *et al.*, 1998), in a repeated audit cycle. DCM is widely used in the UK and abroad, although the extent to which it is used systematically in an audit cycle is less clear, as is the most effective method of providing feedback and action planning.

Assisting staff in using a systematic approach to assessment and care planning may also be helpful in ensuring an individualised, person-centred approach, where

271

the whole range of needs is addressed, rather than simply the perceived problems (Barrowclough & Fleming, 1986; Reynolds *et al.*, 2000). There is a need for evaluation of the impact of these various approaches on outcomes relevant to the person with dementia; they represent a vehicle through which the evidence and best practice can be implemented in relation to those older people with dementia who are resident in a care home or hospital, or attend a day-care facility.

The research literature on the use of DCM has been recently reviewed by Brooker (2005). A number of studies have used DCM in the context of a cross-sectional survey, comparing different facilities or examining the association between well-being and the characteristics of residents. Others have used DCM as an indicator of the effect of an intervention, such as reminiscence or aromatherapy, or the discontinuation of neuroleptic medication. Six studies were identified by Brooker (2005) that used DCM data to change care practice in a developmental process. All the studies showed changes in DCM scores; the largest of these studies (Brooker *et al.*, 1998) reported on three annual DCM cycles for nine care settings, with statistically significant improvements on DCM well-being scores. Brooker emphasises that DCM is only likely to change care practice in the context of an organisational framework that is supportive of person-centred care and that research is needed using outcome measures of quality of life other than DCM, in order to adequately evaluate its impact as a vehicle of change.

No evidence has been identified in relation to people with dementia of the effects of other systematic approaches to inform care planning. Individualised care depends on careful, holistic assessment of the person with dementia and his/her situation, but evidence is lacking regarding how such an assessment might best be approached.

9.3.2   Qualitative review

Evidence included
Three sources of qualitative evidence on the experiences of people with dementia and their carers that met the eligibility criteria set by the GDG have some relevance to the use of observational approaches in the care of people with dementia: case studies with evidence from six people with dementia (Sperlinger & McAuslane, 1994), case studies with evidence from professionals (Stokes, 2004), and primary research with evidence from 308 people with dementia newly admitted to care homes and also from staff (Mozley *et al.*, 1999).

Key findings
Two sources identified in the qualitative review provide evidence that people with dementia can report on their experiences as users of services and also comment on their quality of life. The qualitative evidence therefore indicates that, along with the use of observational methods such as DCM, it is always important to attempt to elicit the views of people with dementia about care, services and interventions. According to evidence from primary research involving 308 people with dementia newly admitted to care

homes, even people with quite high levels of cognitive impairment can comment on their quality of life, the essential requirements being minimum levels of orientation, attention and language (Mozley *et al.*, 1999). These findings have implications for policy and practice as they indicate that people with dementia should be included in consultation – proxies should not be relied on and it is important both to make sure that advocates do not gloss over the need to consult people with dementia and to challenge those who exclude people with dementia. The importance of listening and giving time for consultation with people with dementia is also highlighted.

A similar message comes out of a source reporting on six case studies that demonstrate that it is possible to interview people with dementia, who can express discernible views and opinions and can have much to say (Sperlinger & McAuslane, 1994). Sperlinger and McAuslane note that the collection and interpretation of the views of people with dementia require care and suggest that good practice could include focus on a topic, repeat encounters, privacy, clarity and attention to analysis. The evidence from these case studies demonstrates that people with dementia should not be excluded from care planning, quality assessment and so on, as it is important and possible to involve them and find out what they want. These findings have implications for policy and practice – services need to recognise that people with dementia can make choices and express opinions and it is important that they allow the time necessary for effective consultation with people with dementia and if possible respond to their expressed wishes.

Support for the value of observational approaches in the care of people with dementia is provided by case studies, which demonstrate that aggressive resistance to care can be understood in social terms, and can be reduced by changes in professional behaviour (Stokes, 2004).

9.3.3   Health economics evidence

No economic studies on DCM were identified by the systematic literature search.

9.3.4   Evidence summary

The effectiveness of DCM in changing care practice in various care settings receives support from several studies, but further systematic research is required, with additional indices of the quality of care and well-being of people with dementia.

Evidence from the qualitative review indicates that care planning and assessments of the quality of care can be informed by people with dementia, including those with a relatively high degree of cognitive impairment, as they can express views and opinions about their care. Taking time to elicit the views of people with dementia about their care can be a valuable source of information about the quality of care and can be used to inform care planning.

9.4 MODELS OF TRAINING

9.4.1 Models of training for health and social care staff

Staff training is widely available in the UK (although care homes may have difficulty in releasing staff for training in non-pharmacological approaches, which would not be required as mandatory training), but there are suggestions that training on its own is not sufficient to bring about change without attention to organisational constraints and obstacles to change (Lintern *et al.*, 2002). Such constraints may prevent what has been learned in training sessions being implemented in the workplace. High rates of staff turnover also militate against the effectiveness of one-off training sessions. Implementation may be assisted by regular input from members of a specialist dementia service; thus, for many years in the UK, some old age mental health services have provided regular input to care homes and day-care units in the form of regular consultation sessions with old age psychiatrists, community mental health nurses, clinical psychologists or other team members.

The use of non-pharmacological interventions for the management of behaviour that challenges in residential care homes has long been recommended in professional and government policies. Furthermore, it is generally believed that training care workers to use non-pharmacological interventions improves their understanding of the causes of behaviour, improves staff attitudes towards people with dementia and increases job satisfaction, reducing absenteeism and staff turnover.

Training for management of behaviour that challenges
Rovner and colleagues (1996) aimed to reduce behaviour disorders in people with dementia in a 250-bed nursing home using a programme of structured activities, combined with staff education and guidelines for psychotropic medications. The activity programme included music, exercise, crafts, relaxation, reminiscences, word games and food preparation. A creative arts therapist and two nursing aides, not usually employed by the home, developed and implemented the programme. On average, 3–6 hours of activities per week were provided for each resident. After a 2-week adjustment to the activity programme, the psychiatrist, who had taken over drug prescription from primary care physicians, re-assessed patients' prescribed medication. Educational rounds consisting of weekly 1-hour meetings between the psychiatrist and the activities staff were held to discuss each person with dementia's behavioural, functional and medical status. The trial lasted 6 months and demonstrated the efficacy of the programme in reducing behaviour disorders, antipsychotic drug use and physical restraints. Patients and carers appeared to enjoy being involved in the activities programme. Most staff valued the programme, although some resented 'experts' being brought in who altered usual care routines.

A brief in-service training programme on the psychosocial management of behaviour that challenges in UK residential care showed that, although the incidence of problematic behaviour did not change 3 months after training, staff reported a significant improvement in their ability to manage such behaviour (Moniz-Cook *et al.*, 1998). The training was based on the person-centred care approach, with each training session following a standardised protocol: a formal talk by a consultant psychiatrist or clinical psychologist, small group work facilitated by a community psychiatric nurse, small group feedback to the whole group and a homework task. The improvements in staff reports of their ability to manage difficult behaviour were not maintained a year later, but the reasons for this were unclear.

Psychosocial, nursing and medical interventions were individually tailored for nursing home residents by a team of a psychiatrist, psychologist and nurses to determine whether this reduced the frequency and severity of behaviour that challenges (Opie *et al.*, 2002). The team met weekly to discuss referrals and formulate individualised care plans, and numbers of interventions per resident ranged from two to seven, with an average of 4.6. The consultancies were effective and well received by staff.

Burgio and colleagues (2002) report results from a programme aimed at teaching and maintaining behaviour-management skills in a nursing home using in-house lectures and workplace training. They found that staff maintained their skills over 6 months when subjected to formal staff management by specially trained senior staff as compared to conventional, less structured staff management.

Testad and colleagues (2005) conducted a study aiming to reduce behaviour that challenges and the use of restraint for people with dementia. Staff were given guidance in groups for 1 hour a month for 6 months. It was found that, although the levels of agitated behaviour remained unchanged or increased, the training programme did lead to a reduction in the use of restraint.

Schindel-Martin and colleagues (2003) aimed to teach staff to respond effectively to cognitively impaired residents who displayed self-protective behaviours. A 7.5-hour educational programme delivered in a single workshop included all professional and non-professional staff in the care homes. Some also attended pre- and post-training focus groups. Six weeks after the training, staff demonstrated increased knowledge and skill in response techniques. Staff thought they would become more confident over time as the programme helped to relieve concerns about handling residents in ways feared to be inappropriate and unsafe.

Fossey and colleagues (2006) conducted a cluster randomised trial assessing the effects of training and support of staff in 12 nursing homes in the UK. Each nursing home had a minimum of 25% of people with dementia who were taking antipsychotic drugs. The aims of the study were to reduce drug use and agitation. The training intervention was conducted over a period of 10 months and consisted of skills training, behaviour management techniques and application of person-centred care. After 12 months, there was a 19.1% reduction in antipsychotic drug use in the intervention homes compared to the control homes. This was not at the cost of increased agitation, as there were no significant differences in levels of agitation after 12 months.

Person-centred/emotion-oriented care
The Staff Training in Assisted-Living Residences (STAR) trial provided two 4-hour workshops, four individualised on-site consultations and three leadership sessions in 15 assisted-living residences in the USA (Teri *et al.*, 2005b). The study aimed to reinforce values of dignity and respect for residents and improve staff responsiveness,

skills and job satisfaction. The workshops covered multiple approaches to learning, including didactic content, case studies, discussion, and group exercises. The individualised sessions allowed on-the-job practice of training skills. Leadership sessions included supervisors and administrators in workshops. STAR was exceptionally well received; after the training, residents showed significantly reduced levels of affective and behavioural distress compared with control residents. STAR residents improved, whereas control residents worsened, and staff with STAR training reported less adverse impact and reaction to residents' problems and more job satisfaction.

Hillman and colleagues (2001) investigated the effect of moderating aggressive problem behaviours in the development of more positive attitudes towards nursing-home residents. Programmes encouraged staff to look at individuals' social histories to ascertain whether these could account for current behavioural issues and to discover whether staff attitudes to individuals became more positive if their social history was known. Hillman and colleagues concluded that the use of a social history intervention alone failed to generate the expected increases in the formation of more positive attitudes towards patients and in greater perceived rewards of care giving among nursing home staff. The social history information did appear to allow staff to maintain more neutral attitudes towards patients, after statistically controlling for the impact of patients' aggressive behaviour.

Three reports from the Netherlands have focused on emotion-oriented care (Schrijnemaekers *et al.*, 2002; Schrijnemaekers *et al.*, 2003; Finnema *et al.*, 2005). Emotion-oriented care in dementia is defined as care aimed at improving emotional and social functioning and the quality of life of people with dementia. Outcomes from the first two reports were not conclusive in relation to effects on care-home residents (Schrijnemaekers *et al.*, 2002) or on care staff, where emotion-oriented care did have a moderate effect on work-related outcomes, but these effects were not maintained over time (Schrijnemaekers *et al.*, 2003). Finnema and colleagues (2005) assessed the effect of integrated emotion-oriented care versus usual care on older persons with dementia in a nursing home and on nursing assistants. Over 9 months, nursing assistants were trained to apply emotion-oriented care combined with a care-planning approach. Five nursing assistants in each care unit were given advanced training and one staff member per unit was trained as an adviser in emotion-oriented care. People with mild to moderate dementia showed less stress and more positive attitudes following the implementation of emotion-oriented care. Such effects were not found for people with severe dementia.

Other training interventions
An interactive computer-based training video on depression and dementia, which staff could use at their own pace, was compared with staff attending lectures or receiving workplace training (Rosen *et al.*, 2002*)*. Certified nursing assistants and other nursing staff from three not-for-profit homes participated in the study as part of their required training. The computer program scheduled staff for 45 minutes each month of individual self-paced training using the interactive video modules. Other participants attended a monthly 45-minute lecture with identical learning objectives delivered by an advanced-degree nurse educator. Knowledge was assessed before

each monthly training session and with a post-training exam at the end of the 6-month study. Individual self-paced interactive video education for nursing-home staff resulted in greater compliance and satisfaction with training and more knowledge of core concepts compared with staff attending lectures or receiving workplace training at the end of the 6-month study. The knowledge of staff using the computer training was significantly higher after 6 months compared with the other training methods.

Nursing-home residents with moderate to severe dementia were included in a study to ascertain whether a nursing-assistant communication skills programme improved residents' well-being, increased staff knowledge and reduced staff turnover (McCallion *et al.*, 1999). The skills programme was delivered as part of normal in-service training. At 3 and 6 months of training, the well-being of nursing-home residents had improved. There was greater knowledge of care-giving responses and reduced turnover of staff but no increase in knowledge about dementia.

In a study by Proctor and colleagues (1999) conducted over a 6-month period, care workers from nursing and residential homes in the UK attended seminars from a hospital outreach team and received weekly visits from a psychiatric nurse to develop care-planning skills. It was found that, with a focused intervention, residents were responsive and that staff could be trained to develop skills in assessment and care planning to implement the programme in everyday care, and to assess the effect of the programme on the way residents functioned. Improvements in mood and cognitive function, but not behaviours that challenge, were identified.

Liaison services

Two trials were identified on liaison services (Baldwin *et al.*, 2004; Ballard *et al.*, 2002a). Baldwin and colleagues assessed whether a nurse-led mental health liaison service for older people reduced psychiatric morbidity in four acute general medical wards in a district general hospital in the UK. The intervention group received a multi-faceted intervention from a registered mental nurse with 3 years' post-qualification experience. Interventions for depression included medication concordance, enhancing self-esteem, managing anxiety, problem solving, addressing role transitions and adjusting to loss. Liaison support comprised encouragement of person-centred care, education about mental disorder, nutrition and safety issues, and signposting to relevant services. Interventions were tailored to the person and lasted for a maximum of 6 weeks. The trial authors concluded that whilst this intervention was unlikely to reduce psychiatric morbidity, services that focus on the prevention of delirium and target specific disorders such as depression are more likely to be effective.

Ballard and colleagues (2002a) examined whether psychiatric liaison helped to reduce antipsychotic drug use and health-service utilisation for people with dementia residing in care facilities in the UK. The service was delivered by a full-time psychiatric nurse with a diploma in cognitive therapy who visited the six participating care facilities each week. Supervision was provided by a consultant old age psychiatrist with two sessions a week dedicated to the service and one session a week from a clinical psychologist. The ethos of the service was to base interventions on a detailed evaluation using antecedent-behaviour-consequence diaries in order to develop individual management plans tailored to the needs of specific residents. The service was provided for 9 months. The trial was partially successful, but the authors suggested that a more intensive intervention is probably required to improve the overall quality of care.

9.4.2 Health economics evidence

No economic evidence on models of training for health and social care staff was identified.

9.4.3 Qualitative review

Evidence included
Eight sources of qualitative evidence on the experiences of people with dementia and their carers that have some relevance to staff training met the eligibility criteria set by the GDG: primary research looking at communication involving 40 staff and 25 people with dementia (Allan, 2001); a consultation exercise on respite services involving professionals and 20 carers (Arksey *et al.*, 2004); a personal account with evidence from a carer (Butterworth, 1995); a case study with evidence from a person with early Alzheimer's disease (Clare *et al.*, 2003); a case study recounting the experiences of a professional in the role of carer for his or her own relative with dementia (Smith, 1991); a descriptive account of carers' roles in professional education with evidence from carers of people with dementia (Soliman & Butterworth, 1998); primary research with evidence from professionals and carers of people with dementia (Walker *et al.*, 1999); and a narrative review with evidence from professionals and people with dementia (Wilkinson & Milne, 2003).

Key findings
One source, a descriptive account of carers' roles in professional education, has direct relevance to the development of professional education and staff training programmes as it reports that input from carers can add value to professional education (Soliman & Butterworth, 1998). No source of qualitative evidence on the involvement of people with dementia in the training of professionals was identified.

Six of the sources of evidence identified by the qualitative review point to particular staff training needs identified by carers and professionals. Two of these sources identify particular areas where staff training might be valuable. A single case study of cognitive rehabilitation points to potential gains for people with dementia from staff training in cognitive rehabilitation techniques (Clare *et al.*, 2003). A study looking at how staff could improve their communication with people with dementia notes that relationships between staff and the people with dementia they care for are important and reports that there are techniques to improve communication, such as using pictures or responding more to non-verbal communication (Allan, 2001). The findings suggest that, while many care staff have high levels of skill and expertise, they need help and support to develop these skills, with communication with people with dementia being a particular area where there is a need for training.

Three sources identified training needs that relate to the relationship between carers and staff and professionals. A study involving professionals and carers that looked at opportunities for greater carer involvement in care planning for people with dementia identified a need for staff training that addresses carer involvement and the different expectations of individual carers (Walker *et al.*, 1999). Two sources – a literature review and a case study – point to the need for professional and staff training to address the gap between the perspectives of staff and people with dementia and carers (Wilkinson & Milne, 2003; Smith, 1991). Particular areas that are identified relate to the disclosure of the diagnosis, and also acknowledging that the perspectives of people with dementia, carers and staff may differ.

One source identified particular training needs in respite services. A consultation on respite care services for people with dementia that involved professionals and carers identified issues around the quality of services, pointing to a need for staff training and continuity to improve the quality of respite services (Arksey *et al.*, 2004).

Finally, a personal account of a carer's experiences identified problems with care services, including care staff often being untrained and high staff turnover (Butterworth, 1995).

9.4.4   Evidence summary

Evaluating the effects of training programmes in dementia care is a challenging task. Typically, cluster randomised trials are required, with the care home, for example, as the unit of randomisation, as training will potentially have an impact on the unit as a whole. Follow-up periods of even 9 months to a year will mean attrition of residents due to high rates of morbidity in severe dementia, and high rates of staff turnover require on-going training input. Major influences, such as a change to the person in charge of a home or other organisational changes, may dilute any effects of training. However, there are a number of positive indications from the evidence reviewed here. Training programmes that teach specific skills (such as the STAR programme) in the workplace, and which build in managerial support, do seem to be associated with positive outcomes. Changes in staff behaviour (for example, avoiding use of restraints and reducing medication use) may be easier to achieve than changes in residents' patterns of behaviour and function but are, arguably, an important part of enhancing quality of care and well-being. Input to care homes from multidisciplinary teams providing training, support and advice on management of residents is associated with favourable outcomes, but it appears that the input may have to be more intensive than has typically been the case in the past and should address the needs of all residents with dementia, not simply those who currently present 'problems'.

Qualitative evidence points to the potential value of input from carers into staff training and identifies particular staff training needs in relation to communicating with people with dementia and understanding their perspective, and also involving and understanding the perspective of carers.

9.5   INTERVENTIONS FOR CARERS OF PEOPLE WITH DEMENTIA

9.5.1   Introduction

When a person is diagnosed with dementia, the effect of the diagnosis on carers is often overlooked and his or her needs not properly met.

Caring for a person with dementia is often compared to bereavement and there may be many losses for carers. These may, for example, include losing the companionship of a spouse or partner, loss of a parent figure, of income and of freedom to live one's own life. Plans for the future may be dramatically altered and consequently carers may need to learn many new skills. For example, a wife may have to take on house maintenance and bill payment, if these were responsibilities that her husband had always undertaken. In contrast to such practicalities, carers may have to provide intimate personal care, which is a difficult role, especially when looking after a parent.

Amongst all groups of carers, those providing care for people with dementia are among the most vulnerable and suffer from high levels of stress, feelings of guilt, depression and other psychological problems (Brodaty *et al.*, 2002; Sorensen *et al.*, 2002). They often ignore their own health needs in favour of those of the person for whom they care. They may become very exhausted and suffer from poorer physical health and feel isolated.

Carers have to make many decisions, important not only to themselves but to the person with dementia and possibly other members of the family, including children, who are affected by the impact of the disease.

To enable them to continue to look after a person with dementia and to make the best possible decisions for all concerned, carers will need information about dementia and the treatments and services available, as well as legal, financial and benefits advice. They also need to be offered emotional support and have their own health needs recognised throughout the duration of the illness and following the death of their loved ones.

The value of the carer's role should always be acknowledged. He or she should at all times be treated with respect, to preserve his or her dignity. When carers are well supported and well informed, people with dementia also benefit as a result and are enabled to live longer in their own communities.

Support for carers in general has been given priority in both England and Wales through carers' strategy documents[80], the Carers (Equal Opportunities) Act 2004, and associated SCIE guidance[81]. Much of the support is provided through voluntary agencies, with some funding from local authorities. Support groups for carers have been developed in most areas of the UK, and training sessions are also offered.

---

[80]Further information can be found on the Department of Health's Caring about Carers website (www.carers.gov.uk/Index.htm) and the National Assembly for Wales' Carers website (www.wales.gov.uk/subicarersnew/index.htm).
[81]Further information can be found on the SCIE website (www.scie.org.uk/publications/practiceguides/carersguidance/index.asp).

Alzheimer's Society support groups and services are widely available, and a specialist nursing service, Admiral Nursing[82], is available in certain areas of England and Wales; this service has as its primary aim the support of family carers of people with dementia.

9.5.2 Databases searched and inclusion/exclusion criteria

Information about the databases searched and the inclusion/exclusion criteria used for this section of the guideline can be found in Table 40.

9.5.3 Studies considered[83]

We conducted a new search for systematic reviews and RCTs that assessed the efficacy and/or safety of interventions for carers (see Table 41).

Two systematic reviews and 25 new trials met eligibility criteria. In addition, 11 studies were excluded from the analysis (further information about both included and excluded studies can be found in Appendix 15j).

For the purposes of the guideline, we categorised all new trials using the same categories as Sorensen and colleagues (2002).

9.5.4 Interventions for carers versus control interventions

For the purposes of the guideline, we used pooled effect sizes adapted from two meta-analyses (BRODATY2003D; SORENSEN2002) (see Table 42) and supplemented this with results from new RCTs that meet the SORENSEN2002 eligibility criteria (see Appendix 15j for the results from each trial).

9.5.5 Health economics evidence

Five non-UK studies were identified by the systematic literature search, which addressed the cost effectiveness of a range of carer interventions compared to standard care. Two studies focused on counselling, one on family counselling (Martikainen *et al.*, 2004) and the other on individual problem-solving counselling (Roberts *et al.*, 1999). The other three studies addressed the cost effectiveness of carer training (Brodaty & Peters, 1991), a multi-component intervention (Drummond *et al.*, 1991) and computer support (McGuire, 1998).

---

[82]Further information can be found on the For Dementia website (www.fordementia.org.uk/index.htm).
[83]Here, and elsewhere in the guideline, each study considered for review is referred to by a study ID in capital letters (primary author and date of study publication, except where a study is in press or only submitted for publication, then a date is not used).

Table 40: Databases searched and inclusion/exclusion criteria

Electronic databases	AMED, BNI, CINAHL, COCHRANE, EMBASE, MEDLINE, PsycINFO, AgeInfo, AgeLine, ASSIA, CareData, HMIC, PAIS International, SIGLE, Social Services Abstracts, Social Work Abstracts, SSCI
Date searched	Database inception to March 2006; table of contents September 2004 to 5 May 2006
Study design	RCT, other quantitative and qualitative research
Patient population	Carers of people with dementia; people with AD/VaD/DLB/PDD/FTD/other dementias (subcortical, mixed dementias)
Interventions	- Psychoeducation - Supportive interventions - Psychotherapy - Training of care recipient - Multicomponent interventions
Outcomes	For the person with dementia: - Psychological well-being - Quality of life - Maintenance of independent living activities - Delayed admission - Neuropsychiatric symptoms For the carer: - Psychological well-being - Carer burden - Social outcomes - Physiological measures - Carer knowledge - Carer equal opportunities (employment, education, leisure)

No firm conclusions on cost effectiveness could be drawn from these studies, due to the inability to generalise results to the UK setting and the sparse evidence for each type of intervention, as well as the lack of statistical power evident in all five studies. Details on characteristics and results of all studies are provided in Appendix 18.

Table 41: Study information table for interventions for carers

	Psychoeducation versus control	Supportive interventions versus control	Psychotherapy versus control
Existing review (no. of studies, total no. of participants)	SORENSEN2002 (K = 21, N = 582)	SORENSEN2002 (K = 5, N = 131)	SORENSEN 2002 (K = 9, N = 271)
Total no. of new trials	16 RCTs	2 RCTs	3 RCTs
New trial study IDs	AKKERMAN2004 BEAUCHAMP2005 COON2003 DAVIS2004 DONE2001 DUCHARME2005A GERDNER2002 GITLIN2003A HEBERT2003 HUANG2003 MARTINCOOK2003 MARTINCOOK2005 NOBILI2004 STOLLEY2002 TERI2005A WRIGHT2001	BRENNAN1995 FUNG2002	BURGIO2003 EISDORFER2003 GARAND2002

Table 41: (*Continued*)

	Training of care recipient versus control	Multicomponent interventions versus control
Existing review (no. of studies, total no. of participants)	SORENSEN2002 (K = 5, N = 79)	SORENSEN2002 (K = 4, N = 366)
Total no. of new trials	–	2 RCTs
New trial study IDs	–	MAHONEY2003 MITTELMAN2004A

Table 42: Summary of results table for meta-analyses of interventions for carers

Intervention	Outcome (pre-post)	No. of effects	No. of participants	ES (95% CI)	Homogeneity of ESs (Q)
Effect sizes adapted from BRODATY2003D					
All	Overall effect on 'any main outcome measure'	30		−0.32 (−0.48 to −0.15)	Not reported
	Carer psychological morbidity	26		−0.31 (−0.50 to 0.13)	Not reported
	Carer burden	20		−0.09 (−0.26 to 0.09)	Not reported
	Changes in the mood of the person with dementia	5		−0.68 (−1.06 to 0.30)	Not reported
	Carer knowledge	8		−0.51 (−0.98 to 0.05)	Not reported
Effect sizes calculated from data reported in BRODATY2003D					
Interventions with support	Psychological morbidity	12	694	−0.29 (−0.45 to −0.13)	34.24***
Interventions with education	Psychological morbidity	8	505	−0.33 (−0.52 to −0.15)	19.09***
Interventions with counselling of carer	Psychological morbidity	7	511	−0.33 (−0.53 to −0.14)	19.09**

Interventions with family counselling, extended family involvement	7	656	−0.20 (−0.37 to −0.03)	10.25
Interventions with stress management	7	329	−0.46 (−0.70 to −0.23)	21.64**
Interventions with involvement of person with dementia	10	425	−0.46 (−0.66 to −0.25)	26.57**
Interventions with training	4	137	−0.81 (−1.2 to −0.42)	6.61
Effect sizes adapted from SORENSEN2002				
Psychoeducation	Carer burden	21	582	−0.12 (−0.24 to −0.01)	26.50
	Carer depression	15	370	−0.23 (20.38 to 20.08)	46.80***
	Carer well-being	3	66	0.25 (−0.14 to 0.63)	3.57
	Carers' ability/knowledge	19	523	−0.37 (−0.51 to −0.24)	26.71
	Care recipients' symptoms	15	508	−0.19 (−0.22 to 0.03)	7.02

Continued

Table 42: *(Continued)*

Intervention	Outcome (pre-post)	No. of effects	No. of participants	ES (95% CI)	Homogeneity of ESs (Q)
Supportive interventions	Carer burden	4	121	−0.35 (−0.50 to −0.10)	5.21
	Carer depression	5	127	−0.09 (−0.33 to 0.16)	10.82
	Carer well-being	2	58	−0.17 (−0.52 to 0.18)	0.02
	Carers' ability/knowledge	5	131	−0.54 (−0.78 to −0.30)	6.04
	Care recipients' symptoms	2	63	−0.17 (−0.52 to 0.18)	0.48
Psychotherapy	Carer burden	8	240	−0.22 (−0.41 to −0.03)	1.96
	Carer depression	9	271	−0.27 (−0.45 to −0.09)	24.89**
	Carer well-being	2	43	−0.52 (−0.96 to −0.08)	0.02
	Carers' ability/knowledge	4	158	−0.38 (−0.61 to −0.14)	0.98
	Care recipients' symptoms	7	228	−0.19 (−0.38 to −0.00)	13.50

Training of care recipient	Carer burden	5	79	−0.13 (−0.46 to 0.20)	4.77
	Carer depression	4	56	−0.27 (−0.67 to 0.13)	8.25*
	Carer well-being	1	21	−0.74 (−1.42 to −0.06)	–
	Carers' ability/ knowledge	2	44	0.16 (−0.27 to 0.59)	5.41*
	Care recipients' symptoms	5	79	−0.51 (−0.84 to −0.18)	
Multi-component	Carer burden	4	366	−0.65 (20.84 to 20.46)	19.00***
	Carer depression	4	190	−0.02 (−0.22 to 0.18)	4.95
	Carer well-being	2	42	−0.78 (−1.29 to −0.27)	4.35
	Carers' ability/knowledge	3	50	−0.86 (−1.31 to −0.42)	5.37
	Care recipients' symptoms	2	81	−0.02 (−0.34 to 0.30)	1.18

Notes: homogeneity: significant effects indicate heterogeneity of the effect sizes; psychotherapy: 9 out of 10 studies included in the Sorensen and colleagues (2002) meta-analysis used a CBT approach.

*p < 0.05; **p < 0.01; ***p < 0.001.

9.5.6 Qualitative review

Evidence included
Twenty sources of qualitative evidence on carers' experiences of interventions for them met the eligibility criteria set by the GDG (no sources provided evidence on the experiences of people with dementia): primary research involving 30 carers of people with dementia (Adamson, 2001); a descriptive account of a carer's experiences (Bailey, 2002); a personal account by a carer (Butterworth, 1995); primary research involving interviews with 37 carers (Davies & Nolan, 2003); primary research involving 16 carers of people with dementia (Fear, 2000); primary research involving 109 carers of people with dementia (Graham *et al.*, 1997a); primary research involving 130 carers of people with dementia (Graham *et al.*, 1997b); a descriptive account involving a carer and a person with dementia (Grant, 1993); a descriptive account involving a carer of a person with dementia (Jones, 1997); a descriptive account involving carers of people with dementia (Mellor & Glover, 2000); case studies with evidence from three carers, two support groups and two professionals (Milne *et al.*, 2004); primary research with evidence from interviews with 20 carers (Murray *et al.*, 1999); primary research involving 205 carers of people with dementia (Paton *et al.*, 2004); a descriptive account with evidence from professionals and carers (Pieroni & Mackenzie, 2001); a descriptive account of one carer's experience (Runciman, 2003); primary research with evidence from ten carers (Ryan & Scullion, 2000); primary research involving 15 carers of people with dementia (Simpson, 1997); primary research involving 176 carers of older people (Smith *et al.*, 2003); primary research involving 19 carers with evidence from professionals and carers (Dementia Plus, 2003); and primary research involving 100 carers of people with dementia (Wald *et al.*, 2003).

Key findings
A number of sources identified in the qualitative review provide evidence that carers may benefit from interventions for them. Findings from primary research involving 109 carers of people with dementia indicate that better informed carers have lower depression but not lower anxiety or better physical health (Graham *et al.*, 1997a). The findings lead Graham and colleagues to suggest that information and knowledge can decrease the risk of depression in carers, and that educational interventions and the provision of information for carers at an early stage are therefore potentially beneficial and important, although it is noted that it is important to watch for carers' raised anxiety.

Three sources identified by the qualitative review point to benefits of attending support groups for carers. A descriptive account with evidence from carers about their experiences provides evidence that support groups are valued and may assist carers, although they do not negate carers' feelings of loneliness and emotional distress (Grant, 1993). Primary research involving carers provides evidence that members of an Alzheimer's support group seemed better informed than other carers, and indicates that carers' needs for information and education could potentially be met by local support groups with support from local services (Graham *et al.*, 1997b). A descriptive account that looked at the experiences of carers attending an Alzheimer's Society training and support programme and focused on the relationship of the carer and the person with dementia found that educational, training and support programmes or groups for carers can help with access to services and may be more accessible if run by the voluntary sector rather than the statutory sector (Mellor & Glover, 2000). This collection of carers' views and examples of action or ideas arising as a result of attendance on a course demonstrates that carers need support and that working with carers can makes services more useful and add value.

Other sources identified by the qualitative review look at specific interventions. A descriptive account by a carer records appreciation of a helpline and professional support at times of crisis when no longer able to cope (Jones, 1997). Evidence from primary research that evaluated the piloting of carer-held records indicates that they are valued by carers and may be a way for them to achieve the better communication with professionals and the acknowledgement of their role that they want (Simpson, 1997). The study suggests that carers and professionals can share information formally with good results. A descriptive account of an intervention in which carers were asked to write a first-person account imagining being a person with dementia proposes that doing so can help carers to empathise more with what dementia means to the person affected and to understand better what is like to have dementia (Pieroni & Mackenzie, 2001). However, this source does not provide information on what carers thought of the exercise and whether it helped in any way.

The qualitative review also identified evidence of carers' needs for education and information about dementia at the time of diagnosis and beyond. Two sources provide evidence that carers' understanding of dementia needs to be developed. Primary research involving 205 carers found that most carers attributed changes in the person with dementia's behaviour to causes other than dementia and many believed that the person with dementia had control of his or her behaviour – furthermore a substantial number of the carers believed that the person with dementia would return to normal (Paton *et al.*, 2004). In addition, needs for culturally sensitive education for black and minority ethnic carers were identified by primary research involving 30 such carers of people with dementia (Adamson, 2001). Culturally sensitive services were also advocated by another source that reported on a review of the first operational year of a service development strategy for dementia care for African-Caribbean and Asian older people in Wolverhampton (Dementia Plus, 2003). The review found that carers were critical of the processes of getting help and information and would like ethnic minority specialist services.

Other evidence identified by the qualitative review indicates that carers want information. Primary research, involving 100 carers, found that carers wanted information at the time of diagnosis in order to be forewarned (Wald *et al.*, 2003). The findings indicated that carers wanted both verbal and written – but not electronic – information from several sources. Primary research exploring carers' attitudes and experiences when managing medication for older relatives found that carers have worries about it that need to be addressed (Smith *et al.*, 2003).

Carers' needs for support are identified by a number of sources. Evidence from 20 spouse carers indicates that they can find caring rewarding but need support from

289

services as they find the loss of companionship very hard, and feelings of burden can be compounded by their workload, isolation and loss of support (Murray *et al.*, 1999). Descriptive accounts of carers' experiences provide evidence that carers find support-ive services inadequate. Bailey (2002) reports that carers have needs for support and respite, and find that there are too few services, that they lack rights of access to serv-ices and have to fight for them; Butterworth (1995) identifies problems with an initial lack of information and with deficiencies of support and suggests that specific support for carers might be beneficial in reducing strain. Runciman (2003) suggests that direct support is more likely to be offered to parents of disabled children than carers of people with dementia and points to a need for staff to be trained to work with carers. Three sources identify particular needs for support, including emotional support, and help for carers at the time, when they may feel guilty, of considering admission of the person with dementia to residential care (Davies & Nolan, 2003; Ryan & Scullion, 2000) and after admission (Milne *et al.*, 2004). Findings suggest that support may help carers to see the move more positively.

Of relevance to the design of interventions for carers is a source reporting on primary research involving 16 carers that looked at whether there are differences in caring styles between men and women and found evidence of gender differences in the approach to caring – men tended to use problem-solving strategies whereas women tended to use emotion-focused strategies (Fear, 2000). These differences suggest that there may be value in developing supportive interventions for carers on gender lines.

9.5.7　　Evidence summary

There is now extensive literature on interventions with family carers of people with dementia. A wide range of interventions has been developed and evaluated using an equally wide range of outcome domains and measures. This makes comparisons between studies difficult at times, both in terms of judging whether two intervention programmes share common features and in relation to the comparability of different outcomes. The most recent meta-analysis (Brodaty *et al.*, 2003d) included 30 controlled trials and concluded that the quality of studies had improved over the period searched (1985–2001). Although outcomes were variable, overall there appeared to be at least a small intervention effect. Interventions involving training or stress management or involving the person with dementia alongside the carer appeared to have the largest effect on the carer's psychological health and well-being. Sorensen and colleagues (2002) report a larger meta-analysis, including studies where carers of people with dementia were not specifically targeted, although in all the stud-ies the care recipients had an average age of 60 or over. The results from this analysis (considering RCTs only), suggested that psychological therapy (typically CBT) and psychoeducation programmes had the best outcome in relation to depres-sion (although effect sizes were still small), whereas multi-component interventions were associated with effects of medium size on carer burden and well-being. It is noteworthy that effect sizes were lower in studies where only carers of people with dementia had been included.

For this review, 25 new studies have been identified, meeting the criteria established for the Sorensen meta-analysis. Again, the results from these studies are mixed, with around a quarter not identifying a significant effect of the intervention being evaluated on relevant outcome variables; others had effects on some measures but not others. Several of the recently reported studies form part of the REACH (Resources for Enhancing Alzheimer's Caregiver Health) initiative in the USA, where six centres collaborated to use common measures and procedures, whilst evaluating interventions developed and implemented independently at each site. At a 6-month evaluation, active interventions, whatever the type, were superior to control conditions in relation to carer burden (Gitlin *et al.*, 2003). Differences in treatment response were identified in relation to gender, ethnicity, education and relationship with the person with dementia. Gitlin and colleagues conclude that interventions should be 'multi-component and tailored'.

It is clear that carer interventions can be effective in relation to psychological health, burden and well-being, although the relatively small effect sizes for some domains and the large variability between studies suggest that there is much to be learned regarding which interventions will be most helpful for which carers. No one approach is sufficient to meet the range of needs, situations and preferences of carers. Multi-component interventions perhaps offer the best chance of success, in combining, say, psychoeducation, skills training and support groups, and there is increasing development of telephone and internet-based systems for provision of information and support, which may be a useful additional component. The relative efficacy of psychological therapy, usually CBT, on symptoms of depression and anxiety is evident and is likely be most helpful when targeted at those care givers whose anxiety and depression levels are within, or close to, the clinical range. The carer literature also gives encouraging indications that interventions with carers will often have a positive effect on the care recipient, in relation to the person's behaviour or function, or the length of time remaining at home.

The qualitative review identified evidence that carers benefit from and/or value educational/information-giving interventions, support groups and helplines, all of which can be provided by voluntary sector organisations. However, evidence suggests that providers of educational interventions for carers of people with dementia at an early stage after diagnosis should be aware of the possibility that education about dementia may sometimes have an adverse effect on a carer's anxiety. The qualitative review also identified evidence of particular needs relating to interventions for carers: interventions providing education and information for carers, including at the time of diagnosis, and addressing medication management; support groups where carers may learn from one another and which can provide education and information with support from local services; and educational and supportive interventions for black and minority ethnic carers that are culturally oriented. Further evidence suggests that when designing educational and training interventions for carers it may be useful to take account of gender differences in approaches to caring.

9.6 RESEARCH RECOMMENDATIONS

9.6.1 Psychological interventions for carers of people with dementia

For carers of people with dementia, is a psychological intervention cost effective when compared with usual care?

Why this is important

Those providing care for people with dementia are one of the most vulnerable groups of carers and often have high levels of stress, feelings of guilt, depression and other psychological problems. They often ignore their own health needs in favour of those of the person for whom they care. They may become exhausted, have poor physical health and feel isolated. Current research suggests that psychological interventions may be effective, but there is insufficient evidence to establish cost effectiveness. The promotion of good mental health in older people (many carers are the spouses of people with dementia) – included in standard 7 of the National Service Framework for older people – is vital, especially because the proportion of people with dementia will rise in line with our aging population. Support for carers in general has been given priority in England and Wales through Carers' Strategy documents. Further research is urgently needed to generate a better evidence base for the update of this guideline.

9.6.2 The effect of staff training on behaviour that challenges

Does training of care staff in dementia-specific person-centred care lead to improvement in behaviour that challenges and reduced prescription of medication to control such behaviour in people with dementia requiring 24-hour care when compared with current practice?

Why this is important

According to prescribing advice published by the Royal College of Psychiatrists, there is a history of inappropriate use of antipsychotic drugs in people with dementia. The proportion of people with dementia with behaviour that challenges tends to rise as the dementia progresses; therefore this issue is of particular importance for people requiring 24-hour care.

9.7 CLINICAL AND SOCIAL CARE RECOMMENDATIONS

9.7.1 Training and development of health and social care staff

9.7.1.1 Health and social care managers should ensure that all staff working with older people in the health, social care and voluntary sectors have access to dementia-care training (skill development) that is consistent with their roles and responsibilities. [For the evidence, see section 9.4]

9.7.1.2   When developing educational programmes for different health and social care staff, trainers should consider the following elements, combined according to the needs of the staff being trained (if staff care for people with learning disabilities, the training package should be adjusted accordingly).

● Early signs and symptoms suggestive of dementia and its major subtypes.

● The natural history of the different types of dementia, the main signs and symptoms, the progression and prognosis, and the consequences for the person with dementia and his or her carers, family and social network.

● The assessment and pharmacological treatment of dementia including the administration of medication and monitoring of side effects.

● Applying the principles of person-centred care when working with people with dementia and their carers; particular attention should be paid to respect, dignity, learning about each person's life story, individualising activities, being sensitive to individuals' religious beliefs and spiritual and cultural identity, and understanding behaviour that challenges as a communication of unmet need.

● The importance of and use of communication skills for working with people with dementia and their carers; particular attention should be paid to pacing of communication, non-verbal communication and the use of language that is non-discriminatory, positive, and tailored to an individual's ability.

● Assertive outreach techniques to support people who may not be engaged with services.

● A clear description of the roles of the different health and social care professionals, staff and agencies involved in the delivery of care to people with dementia and basic advice on how they should work together in order to provide a comprehensive service.

● Basic introduction to local adult protection policy and procedures, including the reporting of concerns or malpractice and, in particular, who to contact.

● The palliative care approach. [For the evidence, see section 9.4]

9.7.1.3   Managers of local mental health and learning disability services should set up consultation and communication channels for care homes and other services for people with dementia and their carers. [For the evidence, see section 9.4]

9.7.1.4   Liaison teams from local mental health and learning disability services should offer regular consultation and training for healthcare professionals in acute hospitals who provide care for people with dementia. This should be planned by the acute hospital trust in conjunction with mental health, social care and learning disability services. [For the evidence, see section 9.4]

9.7.1.5   Evidence-based educational interventions, such as decision-support software and practice-based workshops[84], to improve the diagnosis and management of dementia should be made widely available and implemented in primary care. [For the evidence, see section 6.3.1]

9.7.2   Interventions for the carers of people with dementia

9.7.2.1   Those carrying out carers' assessment should seek to identify any psychological distress and the psychosocial impact on the carer. This should be an ongoing process and should include any period after the person with dementia has entered residential care. [For the evidence, see sections 4.1.4, 4.6.4 and 9.5.1]

9.7.2.2   Care plans for carers of people with dementia should involve a range of tailored interventions. These may consist of multiple components including:
- individual or group psychoeducation
- peer-support groups with other carers, tailored to the needs of individuals depending on the stage of dementia of the person being cared for and other characteristics
- support and information by telephone and through the internet
- training courses about dementia, services and benefits, and communication and problem solving in the care of people with dementia
- involvement of other family members as well as the primary carer in family meetings. [For the evidence, see section 9.5]

9.7.2.3   Consideration should be given to involving people with dementia in psychoeducation, support, and other meetings for carers. [For the evidence, see section 9.5]

9.7.2.4   Health and social care professionals should ensure that support, such as transport or short-break services, is provided for carers to enable them to participate in interventions. [For the evidence, see section 4.6.4]

9.7.2.5   Carers of people with dementia who experience psychological distress and negative psychological impact should be offered psychological therapy, including cognitive behavioural therapy, conducted by a specialist practitioner. [For the evidence, see section 9.5]

---

[84]See, for example, Downs *et al.*, 2006.

10.   APPENDICES

Appendices

Appendix 18: Health economics evidence tables [CD-ROM]   On CD

Appendix 19: Search strategies for the identification of qualitative studies   On CD
[CD-ROM]

Appendix 20: Forest plots from the quantitative reviews [CD-ROM]   On CD

APPENDIX 1:

SCOPE FOR THE DEVELOPMENT OF A CLINICAL GUIDELINE ON DEMENTIA

FINAL VERSION
6th September 2004

GUIDELINE TITLE

Dementia: supporting people with dementia and their carers[84]

Short title

Dementia

BACKGROUND

a) The National Institute for Health and Clinical Excellence (NICE or 'the Institute') has commissioned the National Collaborating Centre for Mental Health (NCCMH) to develop guidance on dementia for use in the NHS in England and Wales. This follows referral of the topic by the Department of Health and Welsh Assembly Government (see Appendix below for scope). The guidance will provide recommendations for good practice that are based on the best available evidence of clinical and cost effectiveness. Cross reference will be made to these and other documents as appropriate. The guideline will also include relevant recommendations from a Technology Appraisal currently being carried out by the Institute, which is due for publication in 2006. This is *Drugs for the Treatment of Alzheimer's Disease* (which will include memantine and incorporate a review of NICE's donepezil, rivastigmine and galantamine appraisal guidance from 2001).

b) The Institute's clinical guidelines will support the implementation of National Service Frameworks (NSFs) in those aspects of care where a Framework has been published. The statements in each NSF reflect the evidence that was used at the time the Framework was prepared. The clinical guidelines and technology appraisals published by the Institute after an NSF has been issued will have the effect of updating the Framework. The guidance will support national initiatives outlined in the NSF for Older People and the NHS plan.

---

[84]The title changed to *Dementia: Supporting People with Dementia and their Carers in Health and Social Care* in the course of development

c) This guideline is being developed jointly by the National Institute for Health and Clinical Excellence and the Social Care Institute for Excellence (SCIE) to reflect the fact that most people with dementia, and their carers, receive care and support from both the health and social care sectors.

Need for the guideline

a) Dementia is a progressive and largely irreversible clinical syndrome characterised by a widespread impairment of mental function, with some or all of the following features: memory loss, language impairment, disorientation, change in personality, difficulties with activities of daily living, self-neglect and behaviour that is out of character (for example, aggression, sleep disturbance or sexual disinhibition).

b) Dementia has many causes, of which the most common are:
   i.   Alzheimer's disease – this causes up to 60% of cases of dementia. It is characterised by short-term memory loss and difficulties with language in its early stages and gradually becomes more severe over several years.
   ii. Vascular dementia – this is the consequence of strokes and/or insufficient blood flow to the brain and causes up to 20% of cases of dementia. It has a varied clinical picture depending on which parts of the brain are most affected. In any individual, Alzheimer's disease and vascular dementia can co-exist.
   iii. Dementia with Lewy bodies – this causes up to 15% of dementia cases and is characterised by symptoms similar to Parkinson's disease as well as hallucinations and a tendency to fall.

c) Dementia is a very common condition, although there is substantial variation in estimates of prevalence, probably because of difficulties of establishing 'caseness' in marginal and mild cases. It is estimated that about 700,000 people in the UK have dementia, with the incidence and prevalence increasing with age. This represents 5% of the total population aged 65 and over, and 20% of the population aged 80 and over.

d) Dementia is associated with complex needs and, especially in the later stages, high levels of dependency and morbidity. These care needs are often beyond the skills and capacity of carers and services. Of the people with dementia, about 154,000 live alone. Those living with carers (a further 250,000) present serious challenges to their carers and wider social networks. About 200,000 patients live in care homes with nursing, of whom about a third receive antipsychotic medication. Recent evidence suggests that some types of antipsychotic may also increase the risk of stroke amongst people with some types of dementia. The annual direct costs in England of caring for people with Alzheimer's disease alone were estimated in 2001 at £7–15 million. Indirect costs are likely to be very much higher than this.

e) As the condition progresses and in the later stages, people with dementia can present carers and social care staff with complex and challenging management and support problems, including aggressive behaviour, restlessness and wandering, eating problems, incontinence, delusions and hallucinations, and mobility difficulties which can lead to falls and fractures. The impact of dementia upon a person may be compounded by personal circumstances such as changes in accommodation or bereavement.

f) People from minority ethnic groups have special considerations. Increased incidence of hypertension and diabetes among African, Caribbean and Asian people increases the risk of developing vascular dementia in older age. Also, impairment of memory can exacerbate communication problems if English is not the person's first language.

g) Current treatment options include the use of the acetylcholinesterase inhibitor family of drugs (donepezil, rivastigmine and galantamine) to improve cognitive functioning, and psychosocial and drug interventions for behavioural problems. The use of antipsychotic drugs for symptomatic and behavioural control has already been referred to. Rehabilitation is often provided and can include promoting and maximising physical mobility and independence in daily activities such as communication, self-care and domestic, social, work and leisure activities. A variety of service-level interventions are in use, including community dementia support teams, day treatment, inpatient admission and long-term institutional care both inside and outside the NHS, and those provided by social services. The families and carers of people with dementia often need support and help, provided both formally and informally through the NHS and social services.

h) A number of guidelines, consensus statements and local protocols exist, including a practice guide for assessing the mental health needs of older people, developed by SCIE in 2002. This guideline will review evidence of clinically effective and cost-effective practice, together with current guidelines, and will offer guidance on best practice.

The guideline

a) The guideline development process is described in detail in two publications, which are available from the NICE website (see 'Further information' below). *The Guideline Development Process – An Overview for Stakeholders, the Public and the NHS (Second Edition)* describes how organisations can become involved in the development of a guideline. *The Guidelines Manual 2006* provides advice on the technical aspects of guideline development. The process for developing a SCIE practice guide is described in SCIE's work plan 2003–2004, which is available on the SCIE website (www.scie.org.uk) or in hard copy. It is intended that this guideline will be developed in accordance with NICE development processes, whilst incorporating important and relevant elements of SCIE methodology. The resulting enhanced development process is outlined in the work plan for this guideline, which can be found on the NICE website.

b) This document is the scope. It defines exactly what this guideline will (and will not) examine and what the guideline developers will consider. The scope is based on the referral from the Department of Health and Welsh Assembly Government (see Appendix below).

c) The areas that will be addressed by the guideline are described in the following sections.

Population

Groups that will be covered

a) Both sexes of all ages.

b) All the major forms of dementia, including Alzheimer's disease, vascular dementia, dementia with Lewy bodies, subcortical dementia, frontotemporal dementias, and mixed cortical and subcortical dementia. Dementia encountered in the course of Parkinson's disease will be addressed. The guideline will, where appropriate, address the differences in treatment and care for people with mild, moderate and severe dementia.

c) The guideline will include special considerations for people with dementia who have learning disabilities.

d) The guideline will be sensitive to:
  - the diverse attitudes and responses to dementia of different ethnic and cultural groups
  - the risk of both internal (to the NHS and social services) and external social exclusion.

e) Dementia usually affects the whole family or household and the guideline will recognise the role of carers in the care and support of people living with dementia.

Health and social care settings

a) Care provided by health and social care staff who have direct contact with people with dementia in hospital, community, home-based, group care, residential or specialist care settings.

b) Health and social care staff operating in the NHS, integrated health and social care services, statutory social services and the voluntary and independent sectors.

c) The guideline will contribute to the management of dementia in the following services:
  - domiciliary support
  - assisted housing
  - care management
  - day centres/day activities
  - residential care

d) The guideline will include effective management of the interface of health and social care services.

e) Housing associations and private organisations contracted by either the NHS or social services to provide care for people with dementia.

Social care and clinical management

Areas that will be covered
The guideline will cover the following areas of practice and will do so in a way that is sensitive to the cultural, ethnic and religious backgrounds of people with dementia and their carers.
a) The full range of care routinely provided for people with dementia by the NHS, councils with social services responsibilities and independent and voluntary sector providers of social services.
b) Early diagnosis and identification of dementia.
c) Risk assessment and its role in preventing harm to people with dementia.
d) Appropriate use of psychosocial and social interventions, which may include:
   ● behavioural and psychosocial interventions for dementia
   ● care management
   ● social support
   ● promotion and maintenance of independent functioning
   ● maintenance of mobility
   ● cognitive behavioural treatments
   ● skills training for carers.
e) Pharmacological treatment (including the use of antipsychotics) for people with dementia, including type, dose and duration.
f) When referring to pharmacological treatments, normally guidelines will recommend use only within the licensed indications. However, where the evidence clearly supports it, recommendations for use outside the licensed indications may be made in exceptional circumstances. It is the responsibility of prescribers to be aware of circumstances where medication is contraindicated. The guideline will assume that prescribers are familiar with the side-effect profile and contraindications of medication they prescribe for patients with dementia.
g) Appropriate use of self-management strategies, for example, self-help methods and interventions to promote medication/treatment adherence.
h) Assessments and referrals required to maintain physical health (for example, continence and dental care).
i) The role of the family and other carers in the treatment and support of people with dementia and the provision of relevant support and information to them.
j) Guidance on supporting people with dementia to exercise choice.
k) Ethical issues that are specific to the care of people with dementia, for example, mental capacity, consent, covert medication, restraint and end-of-life issues.
l) Special considerations for people with dementia who have learning disabilities.

Areas that will not be covered
The following areas will not be addressed by this guideline:
a) The treatment and management of Creutzfeldt-Jakob disease (CJD), Huntington's chorea and human immunodeficiency virus (HIV). However, the guideline will be relevant to the treatment of dementia associated with these conditions.

b) The physical treatments of organic disease sometimes associated with different forms of dementia, such as the treatment of convulsions or motor disorders.
c) The treatment of physical ill health that is commonly encountered amongst elderly people, especially those with dementia, such as cardiovascular and neurological disease/disorders, except where the treatment of such conditions may alter the progress of dementia.

Notes for implementers

a) This guideline will be of relevance for both NHS and social services staff who are involved in the care of people who develop dementia and their carers, including GPs, psychiatrists, other mental healthcare professionals, social workers, care home managers, care staff and community pharmacists.
b) It will also be of relevance to professionals working in the private sector who provide housing, support and care for people with dementia, where they are contracted or commissioned to do so by either the NHS or local social services.

Audit support within the guidance

The guideline will include review criteria for the audit of key recommendations (key priorities for implementation), which will enable objective measurements to be made of the extent and nature of local implementation of this guidance and particularly of its impact upon practice and outcomes for people with dementia.

Status

Scope
This is the scope, which has been through a 4-week period of consultation with stakeholders and reviewed by the Guidelines Review Panel and the Institute's Guidance Executive.

Guideline
The development of the guideline recommendations will begin in September 2004.

FURTHER INFORMATION

Information on the guideline development process is provided in:
- *The Guideline Development Process – An Overview for Stakeholders, the Public and the NHS (Second Edition)*
- *The Guidelines Manual 2006.*

These booklets are available as PDF files from the NICE website (www.nice.org.uk). Information on the progress of the guideline will also be available from the website.

The process for developing a SCIE practice guide is described in:

● *Social Care Institute for Excellence Work Plan 2003–2004* (available from www.scie.org.uk).

APPENDIX – REFERRAL FROM THE DEPARTMENT OF HEALTH AND WELSH ASSEMBLY GOVERNMENT

The Department of Health and Welsh Assembly Government asked the Institute: 'to prepare a clinical guideline for the NHS in England and Wales for the assessment and management of dementia. This will form part of the National Service Framework for Older People giving guidance on the treatments aimed at improving cognitive (memory) impairment and the behavioural and psychological symptoms of dementia. The guideline will cover:

● all forms of dementia
● patients of all ages
● early identification and diagnosis of patients with dementia
● psychological, social, drug based and non-drug approaches to treatment and management; and specifically
● the prescribing of antipsychotic medication for older people with dementia for General Practitioners and other prescribers, including care home managers, care staff and community pharmacists as means of ensuring good practice.

Guidance will also be given on the support to be offered to those caring for persons with dementia'.

APPENDIX 2:
SPECIAL ADVISORS TO THE GUIDELINE
DEVELOPMENT GROUP

The dementia Guideline Development Group and the National Collaborating Centre for Mental Health review team would like to thank the following people who acted as advisors on specialist topics:

Mr Andrew Archibald	Head of Community Care – Older People's Strategy, Dorset County Council
Ms Julie Ayres	Nurse Specialist Liaison, Psychiatry, United Bristol Healthcare Trust
Ms Helen Brown	Manager, Older People's Services, West Gloucestershire Primary Care Trust
Ms Rosalind Macbeth	Carer Support Worker, Alzheimer's Society, Bristol and South Gloucestershire Branch
Dr Niall Moore	Consultant Psychogeriatrician, Avon and Wiltshire Partnership Mental Health Trust and Chair of the Dementia Care Trust, Bristol
Ms Susie Newton	Business Lead, Devon Older People's Mental Health Development Programme
Mr Charlie Sheldrick	Head of Adult Social Care and Well-Being, Borough of Poole
Mr Nick Webber	Lead Community Psychiatric Nurse, Integrated Team for Older Adults, Exeter
Ms Anabel Westall	Team Manager, Team for Older People, Dorset Social Care and Health
Mr Stephen Whitfield	Team Manager, Gloucestershire Partnership NHS Trust

APPENDIX 3:

STAKEHOLDERS WHO RESPONDED TO EARLY REQUESTS FOR EVIDENCE

Alzheimer's Society
Association of British Neurologists
Cambridge Cognition
College of Occupational Therapists
Cornwall Partnership Trust
Down's Syndrome Association
Eisai
GE Health Care
Hampshire County Council
Hampshire Partnership NHS Trust
Janssen-Cilag
Lundbeck Ltd
Methodist Homes for the Aged
National Institute for Mental Health in England
Novartis
Pfizer
Royal College of Nursing
Royal College of Speech and Language Therapists
Royal Pharmaceutical Society of Great Britain
Scottish Intercollegiate Guidelines Network
Shire
South West London and St George's Mental Health NHS Trust
Tavistock and Portman NHS Trust
University of Cambridge

APPENDIX 4:

STAKEHOLDERS AND EXPERTS WHO RESPONDED TO THE CONSULTATION DRAFT OF THE GUIDELINE

STAKEHOLDERS

Age Concern England
Alzheimer's Society
Association for Continence Advice
Association of British Neurologists
Association for Family Therapy and Systemic Practice in the UK
AstraZeneca
Barnsley Primary Care Trust
Birmingham City Council
Bolton, Salford and Trafford Mental Health NHS Trust
British Association for Behavioural and Cognitive Psychotherapies
British Association for Psychopharmacology
British Geriatrics Society
British Nuclear Medicine Society
The British Psychological Society
Cambridgeshire and Peterborough Mental Health Partnership NHS Trust
Clinical Accountability, Service Planning and Evaluation
Chartered Society of Physiotherapy
College of Occupational Therapists
Commission for Social Care Inspection
Continence Foundation
Department of Health
Eisai
English Community Care Association
Federation of Ophthalmic and Dispensing Opticians
Hampshire Partnership NHS Trust
Hertfordshire Partnership NHS Trust
Institute for Ageing and Health
Lewy Body Society
Lundbeck
National Council for Palliative Care
Nottinghamshire Healthcare NHS Trust
Novartis
Nutricia
Oxleas NHS Foundation Trust

Parkinson's Disease Society
Patient and Public Involvement Programme
Primary Care Neurology Society
Royal College of General Practitioners
Royal College of Nursing
Royal College of Psychiatrists
Royal College of Speech and Language Therapists
Social Care Institute for Excellence
Sheffield Care Trust
Sheffield South West Primary Care Trust
Sheffield Teaching Hospitals NHS Foundation Trust
Shire
South West Yorkshire Mental Health NHS Trust
Suffolk Mental Health Partnership NHS Trust
Surrey and Borders Partnership NHS Trust
Sustain: The alliance for better food and farming
Tees, Esk and Wear Valleys NHS Trust
UK Psychiatric Pharmacy Group

EXPERTS

Professor Dawn Brooker
Dr Julian Hughes
Jane Fossey

APPENDIX 5:

RESEARCHERS CONTACTED TO REQUEST

INFORMATION ABOUT UNPUBLISHED OR

SOON-TO-BE-PUBLISHED STUDIES

Dr Timo Erkinjuntti
Professor Martin Orrell
Rachel Denton
Simon Evans
Professor Ian McKeith
Karen Jewitt
Sandra Pickon
Mariamma Thalanany
Alex Mitchell
Dr Daniel Murman
Professor Martin Knapp
Dr Gill Livingston
Dr Zuzana Walker

APPENDIX 6:

KEY QUESTIONS

Areas of good practice

- For people with dementia, what type of information and support is helpful/unhelpful?
- For people with dementia, what are the issues concerning end of life that support the dignity and intrinsic worth of the individual?
- How can it be ensured that people with dementia have a choice about their care environment?
- Are there any circumstances in which acting without/contrary to the consent of a person with dementia is appropriate?
- Are there barriers to people with dementia getting optimal physical healthcare (including acute hospital care)?
- For people with dementia, does an assessment of carer needs compared to no assessment produce benefits/harm in the specified outcomes?

Considerations relevant to the care of all people with dementia and to carers of people with dementia

- For people with dementia, what is the best way of organising and planning services in terms of the coordination of care?
- For people with dementia, what is the best way of organising and planning services in terms of risk taking and empowerment, and the interface with multidisciplinary assessment?
- For people with dementia, what is the best way of organising and planning services in terms of the quality of care (continuity of service provision)?
- What is best practice design of care homes?
- For people with dementia, do interventions for carers when compared to 'standard care'/no support produce benefits/harm in the specified outcomes?

Prevention, early identification, assessment and diagnosis of dementia

- Are there any groups of people who are at increased risk of developing dementia?
- For people at risk of developing dementia, are there any lifestyle or other interventions that can prevent or delay onset of dementia?
- Are there advantages/disadvantages to early identification?

- What should the assessment process to diagnose dementia consist of (for example, MRI, PET, CT and SPECT, blood battery, protocol, informant history, physical examination, EEG and comprehensive cognitive testing)?
- What are the characteristics of the process of assessment and diagnosis associated with a positive or negative experience of the assessment processes?

Pharmacological treatment of dementia

- For people with dementia, do acetylcholinesterase inhibiting drugs/memantine when compared to [an appropriate comparator] produce benefits/harm in the specified outcomes?
- For people with dementia, do drugs (or other medicine) other than acetylcholinesterase inhibitors/memantine (for example, codergocrine mesylate) when compared to [an appropriate comparator] produce benefits/harm in the specified outcomes?
- For people with VaD, do drugs that control risk factors (drugs for hypertension, drugs that control glucose levels for people with diabetes, anti-platelet treatment, statins and other cholesterol-lowering drugs) when compared to placebo/a comparator drug produce benefits/harm in cognitive outcomes?
- For people with dementia and non-cognitive symptoms of dementia, does appropriate drug treatment when compared to placebo/a comparator produce benefits/harm in the specified outcomes?

Non-pharmacological interventions for dementia

- For people with dementia, are there strategies for promoting independence that produce benefits/harm in the specified outcomes?
- For people with dementia, do cognitive rehabilitation and behavioural interventions when compared to [an appropriate comparator] produce benefits/harm in the specified outcomes?
- For people with dementia, do psychosocial/behavioural interventions for the management of behaviour that challenges (including aggression, agitation, disinhibition [sexual], apathy, wandering, disruptive vocalisations, eating disorders, hoarding, psychosis and sleep disturbance) when compared to 'standard care' produce benefits/harm in the specified outcomes?
- For people with dementia and depression/anxiety, do psychological interventions when compared to 'standard care' produce benefits/harm in the specified outcomes?
- For people with dementia, do educational interventions increase knowledge and awareness?
- For people with dementia, does the systematic use of DCM and other systematic approaches to inform care planning, result in positive outcomes when compared with 'standard care'?

- What models of training (liaison) for health and social care staff have positive outcomes for people with dementia?

Drug versus non-drug/combination treatment

- For people with dementia, are there any combination treatments/augmentation strategies for the cognitive symptoms of dementia that produce benefits/harm in the specified outcomes?
- For people with dementia, are there any combination treatments/augmentation strategies for the non-cognitive symptoms of dementia that produce benefits/harm in the specified outcomes?

APPENDIX 7:

DECLARATIONS OF INTERESTS

BY GDG MEMBERS

With a range of practical experience relevant to dementia in the GDG, members were appointed because of their understanding and expertise in health and social care for people with dementia and support for their carers, including: scientific issues; health and social care research; the delivery and receipt of health and social care, along with the work of the healthcare industry; social care; and the role of professional organisations and organisations for people with dementia and carers.

To minimise and manage any potential conflicts of interest, and to avoid any public concern that commercial or other financial interests have affected the work of the GDG and influenced guidance, members of the GDG must declare as a matter of public record any interests held by themselves or their families which fall under specified categories (see below). These categories include any relationships they have with the health and social care industries, professional organisations and organisations for people with dementia and carers.

Individuals invited to join the GDG were asked to declare their interests before being appointed. To allow the management of any potential conflicts of interest that might arise during the development of the guideline, GDG members were also asked to declare their interests at each GDG meeting throughout the guideline development process. The interests of all the members of the GDG are listed below, including interests declared prior to appointment and during the guideline development process.

CATEGORIES OF INTEREST

- **Paid employment**
- **Personal interests related to dementia:** payment and/or funding from the dementia-related healthcare industry, including consultancies, grants, fee-paid work and shareholdings or other beneficial interests.
- **Personal interests not specifically related to dementia:** any other payment and/or funding from the healthcare industry, including consultancies, grants and shareholdings or other beneficial interests.
- **Non-personal interests:** funding from the healthcare industry received by the GDG member's organisation or department, but where the GDG member has not personally received payment, including fellowships and other support provided by the healthcare industry.
- **Other interests relating to dementia:** funding from governmental or non-governmental organisations, charities, and so on, and/or ownership in a company that provides therapy or treatments likely to be covered in the guideline.

Declarations of interest

Dr Andrew Fairbairn

Employment	Consultant in Old Age Psychiatry, Newcastle General Hospital, Northumberland, Tyne and Wear NHS Trust
Personal interests related to dementia	None
Personal interests not specifically related to dementia	None
Non-personal interests	Sponsorship of 'well-being' work in the trust (Eli Lilly, benefit in kind)
Other interests related to dementia	Multi-centre epidemiological survey of the prevalence of dementia in the UK (Department of Health/Medical Research Council, £250,000; Medical Research Council Cognitive Function and Ageing Study extension, £70,000); handbook on services for older adults with mental health problems (Department of Health, £44,000)

Professor Nick Gould

Employment	Professor of Social Work, University of Bath
Personal interests related to dementia	None
Personal interests not specifically related to dementia	Consultancy from Hong Kong Polytechnic University (<£1,000)
Non-personal interests	None
Other interests related to dementia	National Institute for Mental Health in England/SCIE Fellowship in Social Care

Dr Tim Kendall

Employment	Joint Director, NCCMH; Deputy Director, Royal College of Psychiatrists Research and Training Unit; Consultant Psychiatrist and Medical Director, Sheffield Care Trust

Personal interests related to dementia	None
Personal interests not specifically related to dementia	None
Non-personal interests	None
Other interests related to dementia	Annual grant to develop guidelines (NICE, c £1,080,000); funding for attendance at a 2-day symposium on evidence-based medicine in psychiatry at the London School of Economics (Economic and Social Research Council)
Mr Peter Ashley	
Employment	Former non-executive director, Warrington Primary Care Trust
Personal interests related to dementia	Presentations to Alzheimer Europe conference (funded by Pfizer) and Novartis conference (fee)
Personal interests not specifically related to dementia	None
Non-personal interests	None
Other interests related to dementia	Sponsored by the Alzheimer's Society to present a paper at the Alzheimer's Disease International 2006 Berlin conference (paid for directly by the Alzheimer's Society); member of: Department of Health National Diagnostic Group, National Institute for Mental Health in England North West Board (unpaid), Care Services Improvement Partnership North West (unpaid), and Electronic Social Care Records Implementation Board (unpaid)
Mr Ian Bainbridge	
Employment	Deputy Director, Commission for Social Care Inspection, South East Region
Personal interests related to dementia	None

Personal interests not specifically related to dementia	None
Non-personal interests	None
Other interests related to dementia	None
Ms Lizzie Bower	
Employment	Health Economist, NCCMH (2005–2006)
Personal interests related to dementia	None
Personal interests not specifically related to dementia	None
Non-personal interests	None
Other interests related to dementia	None
Professor Stephen Brown	
Employment	Consultant Psychiatrist in Learning Disability, Cornwall Partnership NHS Trust; Honorary Professor of Developmental Neuropsychiatry, Peninsula Medical School Developmental Disabilities Research and Education Group
Personal interests related to dementia	Occasional presentations to meetings on epilepsy or on dementia where there is sponsorship from a pharmaceutical company (in such cases, a donation is made to Cornwall Partnership Trust Research Endowment Fund in lieu of an honorarium)
Personal interests not specifically related to dementia	None
Non-personal interests	None
Other interests related to dementia	Action on Neurology pilot site developing telemedicine clinics for epilepsy and dementia – funding held by Cornwall Partnership NHS Trust (NHS Modernisation Agency, £85,000)

Mr Alan Duncan

Employment	Systematic Reviewer, NCCMH
Personal interests related to dementia	None
Personal interests not specifically related to dementia	None
Non-personal interests	None
Other interests related to dementia	None

Ms Gillian Garner

Employment	Lead Occupational Therapist, Mental Health for Older Adults, South London and Maudsley NHS Trust
Personal interests related to dementia	None
Personal interests not specifically related to dementia	None
Non-personal interests	None
Other interests related to dementia	None

Professor Jane Gilliard

Employment	Change Agent, Care Services Improvement Partnership
Personal interests related to dementia	Funding for workshop on nurse practitioners (Eisai/Pfizer, £500)
Personal interests not specifically related to dementia	None
Non-personal interests	None
Other interests related to dementia	Grant-funded projects: evaluating enabling technology for people with dementia (European Commission 2001–2004, (€99,330); rehabilitation services for people with dementia (Department of Health 2003–2006, £61,200); project panels in dementia care (Department of Health 2004–2007, £112,950); English Dementia Services Development Centre web (Department of Health

	2004–2006, £17,500); At Home with Assistive Technology (Sir Halley Stewart Trust 2002–2004, £69,205)

Ms Karen Harrison

Employment	Senior Nurse, Mental Health Services for Older People, Leicestershire Partnership NHS Trust
Personal interests related to dementia	None
Personal interests not specifically related to dementia	None
Non-personal interests	None
Other interests related to dementia	None

Ms Sarah Hopkins

Employment	Research Assistant, NCCMH
Personal interests related to dementia	None
Personal interests not specifically related to dementia	None
Non-personal interests	None
Other interests related to dementia	None

Dr Steve Iliffe

Employment	Reader in General Practice, University College London
Personal interests relating to dementia	Unrestricted research funding on obstacles to early recognition of dementia in primary care (Eisai 2003–2004, £183,000); consultancy as a member of the Aricept Advisory Board conference on early recognition of dementia (Pfizer/Eisai 2004, <£1,000); presentation on practice-based commissioning and dementia at 100 Years of Alzheimer's Disease conference (Pfizer/Eisai

	2006, <£1,000)
Personal interests not specifically related to dementia	Grant for developmental work on community-oriented primary care (Merck Company Foundation 2003–2005, £140,000)
Non-personal interests	Named Associate Director of the Dementias and Neurodegenerative Diseases Research Network Coordinating Centre
Other interests related to dementia	Funding for a randomised controlled trial of educational interventions in primary care (Alzheimer's Society 1999–2002, £340,000).
Professor Roy Jones	
Employment	Director, The Research Institute for the Care of the Elderly, Bath; Professor of Clinical Gerontology, School for Health, University of Bath; Honorary Consultant Geriatrician, Avon and Wiltshire Mental Health Partnership NHS Trust/Bath and North East Somerset Primary Care Trust
Personal interests related to dementia	Attendance at 25th annual Hong Kong Geriatrics Society conference funded by Lundbeck; received various honoraria for lectures from Eisai (£1,500), Lundbeck (£10,000), Merz (£1,300) and Pfizer (£6,500) and for advisory board attendance from Lundbeck (£5,400), Pfizer/Eisai (£2,750) and Shire
Personal interests not specifically related to dementia	None
Non-personal interests	Research grants (Novartis, Eisai/Pfizer, Lundbeck/Merz, Shire/Janssen-Cilag, Pharmacia, Eli Lilly, Wyeth Research, Elan Pharmaceuticals, Servier Research and Myriad Pharmaceuticals); funding in the past

	to support Research Institute memory clinics (Eisai/Pfizer and Lundbeck); organisation of a conference (Shire, £3,500) (in lieu of departmental lecture fees); capital support (Eisai, Lundbeck and Merz) totalling £200,000 for new research building (total cost £1.95 million) for Research Institute for the Care of the Elderly at the Royal United Hospital, Bath
Other interests related to dementia	Grants to Research Institute from Thomas Pocklington Trust, Economic and Social Research Council, European Community, Alzheimer's Society and Alzheimer's Research Trust
Professor Jill Manthorpe	
Employment	Professor of Social Work, Social Care Workforce Research Unit, King's College London
Personal interests related to dementia	Research Editor, Journal of Dementia Care (Hawker Publications); publication work (Reed Publishing, Royal College of Nursing)
Personal interests not specifically related to dementia	None
Non-personal interests	None
Other interests related to dementia	Grants for work on individual budgets and reimbursement (Department of Health, share of grants totalling £900,000); funding for the Social Care Workforce Research Unit (£375,000 per annum); other Department of Health research programmes (share of £200,000); other funding (Healthcare Commission, £375,000; Joseph Rowntree Foundation, £60,000; SCIE, £50,000; Comic Relief, share of £70,000; Help the Aged, £80,000;

319

	Better Government for Older People, £10,000); non-executive directive, West Hull Primary Care Trust, and member of the Hull and East Riding branch of the Alzheimer's Society
Dr Ifigeneia Mavrazenouli	
Employment	Senior Health Economist, NCCMH
Personal interests related to dementia	None
Personal interests not specifically related to dementia	None
Non-personal interests	None
Other interests related to dementia	None
Dr Nick Meader	
Employment	Systematic Reviewer, NCCMH
Personal interests related to dementia	None
Personal interests not specifically related to dementia	None
Non-personal interests	None
Other interests related to dementia	None
Ms Mary Murrell	
Employment	Alzheimer's Society volunteer, Lewisham and Greenwich
Personal interests related to dementia	None
Personal interests not specifically related to dementia	None
Non-personal interests	None
Other interests related to dementia	Member of the Oxleas Trust User Council representing older people in Greenwich (<£1,000 fee for attending meetings, donated to the Alzheimer's Society)
Professor John O'Brien	
Employment	Professor of Old Age Psychiatry, Newcastle University, Wolfson

	Research Centre, Institute for Ageing and Health
Personal interests related to dementia	Consultant to GE Healthcare regarding PD301 study (2004–2007: 2004, £8,000; 2005, £10,000); lectures (Shire and Eisai/Pfizer 2004, £1,000; Shire 2005, £3,000); member of the Dementia Scientific Steering Committee for Servier (£2,500) and the Novartis advisory board (2006, £1,200); honoraria for talks and/or attending advisory board meetings from Janssen, Novartis, Eli Lilly, Shire, Eisai/Pfizer and Lundbeck within last 5 years (amounts all <£1,000)
Personal interests not specifically related to dementia	None
Non-personal interests	Ad hoc sponsorship from pharmaceutical companies with central nervous system products (including Lundbeck, Novartis, Eisai, Pfizer, Wyeth, Janssen, Eli Lilly and GE Healthcare) for regular NHS and university educational meetings, such as journal clubs, and for attendance by members of the department at educational meetings and national and international conferences, such as meetings of the Royal College of Psychiatrists and British Association for Psychopharmacology
Other interests related to dementia	Grant to investigate nicotinic SPECT changes in dementia (Alzheimer's Society, £197,000)
Dr Catherine Pettinari	
Employment	Centre Manager, NCCMH
Personal interests related to dementia	None
Personal interests not specifically	None

related to dementia	
Non-personal interests	None
Other interests related to dementia	None
Ms Sarah Stockton	
Employment	Information Scientist, NCCMH
Personal interests related to dementia	None
Personal interests not specifically related to dementia	None
Non-personal interests	None
Other interests related to dementia	None
Dr Clare Taylor	
Employment	Editor, NCCMH
Personal interests related to dementia	None
Personal interests not specifically related to dementia	None
Non-personal interests	None
Other interests related to dementia	None
Ms Sophie Weithaler	
Employment	Service Development Manager, Hillingdon Primary Care Trust
Personal interests related to dementia	None
Personal interests not specifically related to dementia	None
Non-personal interests	None
Other interests related to dementia	None
Dr Craig Whittington	
Employment	Senior Systematic Reviewer, NCCMH
Personal interests related to dementia	None
Personal interests not specifically related to dementia	None

Non-personal interests	None
Other interests related to dementia	None
Ms Jacqui Wood	
Employment	Alzheimer's Society volunteer, Enfield branch
Personal interests related to dementia	None
Personal interests not specifically related to dementia	None
Non-personal interests	None
Other interests related to dementia	Voluntary membership of: working party with social services in a tendering process for the management of a residential home for people with dementia; local implementation group for older people; local NSF for Older People Standard 7 group; joint commissioning group for carers; project on assistive technology with the joint commissioner for older people (Primary Care Trust and local authority); working party on day care for people with dementia focusing on the needs of black and minority ethnic communities; capacity planning group on timely hospital discharge, primary care, service coordination and preventing unnecessary inpatient admissions; continuing care group with Barnet, Enfield and Haringey Mental Health Trust
Professor Bob Woods	
Employment	Professor of Clinical Psychology of Older People, University of Wales, Bangor
Personal interests related to dementia	Royalties for publications and ad hoc lecture fees on dementia-related issues

	(each <£1,000)
Personal interests not specifically related to dementia	None
Non-personal interests	Associate Editor, Ageing & Mental Health (£1,000 pa); royalties from a manual on cognitive stimulation in dementia, published by Hawker Publications (2006) and Freiberg Press, USA (2005) (<£1,000); support for a memory clinic liaison worker employed through the Dementia Services Development Centre Wales (12 months' funding by Pfizer/Eisai, £14,000); grant to Dementia Services Development Centre Wales for 'Coping with Forgetting' groups (Shire, <£1,000); commissioned research in relation to nursing home care (Barchester Healthcare, £8,000); consultancy on nursing home design (Fairways Homes, <£1,000)
Other interests related to dementia	Research funding: professional intervention in primary care for older people with dementia and their carers (Department of Health 1997–2000, £233,820); identifying and addressing the needs of older people with dementia in residential care (Wellcome Trust 2001–2004, £265,781); the effects of the Carers' Strategy in Wales (Wales Office of Research and Development for Health and Social Care 2003–2006, £189,941); the effectiveness of the National Strategy for Carers (Department of Health 2003–2006, £331,570); reminiscence groups for people with dementia and their carers (Medical Research Council 2004–2006, £227,056); carers survey

	(£3,500); functional and anatomical mechanisms underlying the effects of cognitive rehabilitation in early-stage Alzheimer's disease (Alzheimer's Society 2005–2008, £140,000).
	Funding for the Wales Dementias and Neurodegenerative Diseases Research Network (Wales Office of Research and Development for Health and Social Care 2005–2008, £260,000). Member of Alzheimer's Society branch committee North West Wales (voluntary).
Dr Claire Young	
Employment	Consultant in Old Age Psychiatry, Older Adult Mental Health Care Group, Sheffield
Personal interests related to dementia	None
Personal interests not specifically related to dementia	None
Non-personal interests	Funding to employ a nurse

11.   REFERENCES

Aarsland, D., Andersen, K., Larsen, J.P., *et al.* (2003) Prevalence and characteristics of dementia in Parkinson disease: an 8-year prospective study. *Archives of Neurology, 60,* 387–392.

Adamson, J. (2001) Awareness and understanding of dementia in African/Caribbean and South Asian families. *Health and Social Care in the Community, 9,* 391–396.

Addington-Hall, J. (1998) *Reaching Out: Specialist Palliative Care for Adults with Non-Malignant Diseases.* Occasional Paper 14. London: National Council for Hospice and Specialist Palliative Care Services.

Adoh, T.O. & Woodhouse, J.M. (1994) The Cardiff acuity test used for measuring visual acuity development in toddlers. *Vision Research, 34,* 555–560.

Aggarwal, N., Vass, A.A., Minardi, H.A., *et al.* (2003) People with dementia and their relatives: personal experiences of Alzheimer's and of the provision of care. *Journal of Psychiatric and Mental Health Nursing, 10,* 187–197.

Agich, G.J. (2003) *Dependence and Autonomy in Old Age: An Ethical Framework for Long-Term Care.* Cambridge: Cambridge University Press.

AGREE Collaboration (2003) Development and validation of an international appraisal instrument for assessing the quality of clinical practice guidelines: the AGREE project. *Quality and Safety in Health Care, 12,* 18–23.

Ahronheim, J.C., Morrison, R.S., Morris, J., *et al.* (2000) Palliative care in advanced dementia: a randomized controlled trial and descriptive analysis. *Journal of Palliative Medicine, 3,* 265–273.

Akhondzadeh, S., Noroozian, M., Mohammadi, M., *et al.* (2003) Salvia officinalis extract in the treatment of patients with mild to moderate Alzheimer's disease: a double blind, randomized and placebo-controlled trial. *Journal of Clinical Pharmacy and Therapeutics, 28,* 53–59.

Akkerman, R.L. & Ostwald, S.K. (2004) Reducing anxiety in Alzheimer's disease family caregivers: the effectiveness of a 9-week cognitive-behavioral intervention. *American Journal of Alzheimer's Disease and Other Dementias, 19,* 117–123.

Albinsson, L. & Strang, P. (2003) Differences in supporting families of dementia patients and cancer patients: a palliative perspective. *Palliative Medicine, 17,* 359–367.

Allan, K. (2001) *Communication and Consultation: Exploring Ways for Staff to Involve People with Dementia in Developing Services.* Bristol: Policy Press.

Alm, N., Astell, A., Ellis, M., *et al.* (2004) A cognitive prosthesis and communication support for people with dementia. *Neuropsychological Rehabilitation, 14,* 117–134.

Altman, D.G. (1998) Confidence intervals for the number needed to treat. *British Medical Journal, 317,* 1309–1312.

Altmann, P., Cunningham, J., Dhanesha, U., *et al.* (1999) Disturbances of cerebral function in people exposed to drinking water contaminated with aluminium sulphate: retrospective study of the Camelford water incident. *British Medical Journal, 319,* 807–811.

Alvarez-Fernández, B., García-Ordoñez, M., Martínez-Manzanares, C., *et al.* (2005) Survival of a cohort of elderly patients with advanced dementia: nasogastric tube feeding as a risk factor for mortality. *International Journal of Geriatric Psychiatry*, *20*, 363–370.

Alzheimer's Society (2000) *Food for Thought*. Alzheimer's Society, London.

Alzheimer's Society (2004) *Drugs for the Treatment of Alzheimer's Disease: Submission to the National Institute for Clinical Excellence (NICE) June 2004*. London: Alzheimer's Society. Available at: www.alzheimers.org.uk/News_and_Campaigns/Campaigning/accesstodrugs.htm

Alzheimer's Society (2005) *Memo to the House of Commons Health Select Committee on Continuing Care*. London: Alzheimer's Society.

American Psychiatric Association (1987) *Diagnostic and Statistical Manual of Mental Disorders (3rd edn, revised) DSM III-R*. Washington, DC: American Psychiatric Association.

American Psychiatric Association (2000) *Diagnostic and Statistical Manual of Mental Disorders (4th edn, text revision) DSM IV-TR*. Washington, DC: American Psychiatric Association.

Aminoff, B.Z. & Adunsky, A. (2004) Dying dementia patients: too much suffering, too little palliation. *American Journal of Alzheimer's Disease and Other Dementias*, *19*, 243–247.

Ancoli-Israel, S., Gehrman, P., Martin, J.L., *et al.* (2003) Increased light exposure consolidates sleep and strengthens circadian rhythms in severe Alzheimer's disease patients. *Behavioural Sleep Medicine*, *1*, 22–36.

Andreasen, N. & Blennow, K. (2005) CSF biomarkers for mild cognitive impairment and early Alzheimer's disease. *Clinical Neurology and Neurosurgery*, *107*, 165–173.

Annerstedt, L. (1993) Development and consequences of group living in Sweden. A new mode of care for the demented elderly. *Social Science and Medicine*, *37*, 1529–1538.

Annerstedt, L. (1994) An attempt to determine the impact of group living care in comparison to traditional long-term care on demented elderly patients. *Aging: Clinical and Experimental Research*, *6*, 372–380.

Annerstedt, L. (1997) Group-living care: an alternative for the demented elderly. *Dementia and Geriatric Cognitive Disorders*, *8*, 136–142.

Anonymous (2002) A Carer's Voice. *Caring*. 18 July 2002.

Arber, A. & Gallagher, A. (2003) Breaking bad news revisited: the push for negotiated disclosure and changing practice implications. *International Journal of Palliative Nursing*, *9*, 166–172.

Areosa Sastre, A. & Grimley Evans, J. (2003) Effect of the treatment of Type II diabetes mellitus on the development of cognitive impairment and dementia. *Cochrane Database of Systematic Reviews*, *1*, CD003804.

Arksey, H., Jackson, K., Croucher, K., *et al.* (2004) *Review of Respite Services and Short-Term Breaks for Carers of People with Dementia*. London: NCCSDO. Available at: www.sdo.lshtm.ac.uk/sdo482003.html

Audit Commission (2000) *Forget Me Not: Mental Health Services for Older People*. London: Audit Commission.

References

Awoke, S., Mouton, C.P. & Parrott, M. (1992) Outcomes of skilled cardiopulmonary resuscitation in a long-term-care facility: futile therapy? *Journal of the American Geriatrics Society*, 40, 593–595.

Aylward, E.H., Burt, D.B., Thorpe, L.U., *et al.* (1997) Diagnosis of dementia in individuals with intellectual disability. *Journal of Intellectual Disability Research*, 41, 152–164.

Bäckman, L., Jones, S., Berger, A.K., *et al.* (2004) Multiple cognitive deficits during the transition to Alzheimer's disease. *Journal of Internal Medicine*, 256, 195–204.

Bailey, E. (2002) Article posted in *Reflections on Community Care* website, 7 February 2002. Available at: www.communitycare.co.uk/articles/2002/02/07/34999/reflections. html?key=REFLECTIONS.

Baines, S., Saxby, P. & Ehlert, K. (1987) Reality orientation and reminiscence therapy. A controlled cross-over study of elderly confused people. *The British Journal of Psychiatry*, 151, 222–231.

Bains, J., Birks, J.S. & Dening, T.D. (2002) Antidepressants for treating depression in dementia. *Cochrane Database of Systematic Reviews*, 4, CD003944.

Baker, R., Dowling, Z., Wareing, L.A., *et al.* (1997) Snoezelen: its long-term and short-term effects on older people with dementia. *British Journal of Occupational Therapy*, 60, 213–218.

Baker, R., Bell, S., Baker, E., *et al.* (2001) A randomized controlled trial of the effects of multi-sensory stimulation (MSS) for people with dementia. *British Journal of Clinical Psychology*, 40, 81–96.

Baker, R., Holloway, J., Holtkamp, C.C., *et al.* (2003) Effects of multi-sensory stimulation for people with dementia. *Journal of Advanced Nursing*, 43, 465–477.

Baldwin, R., Pratt, H., Goring, H., *et al.* (2004) Does a nurse-led mental health liaison service for older people reduce psychiatric morbidity in acute general medical wards? A randomised controlled trial. *Age and Ageing*, 33, 472–478.

Balfour, J.E. & O'Rourke, N. (2003) Older adults with Alzheimer disease, comorbid arthritis and prescription of psychotropic medications. *Pain Research and Management*, 8, 198–204.

Ball, K., Berch, D.B., Helmers, K.F., *et al.* (2002) Effects of cognitive training interventions with older adults: a randomized controlled trial. *The Journal of the American Medical Association*, 288, 2271–2281.

Ball, S.L., Holland, A.J., Huppert, F.A., *et al.* (2004) The modified CAMDEX informant interview is a valid and reliable tool for use in the diagnosis of dementia in adults with Down's syndrome. *Journal of Intellectual Disability Research*, 48, 611–620.

Ballard, C., Bannister, C., Solis, M., *et al.* (1996a) The prevalence, associations and symptoms of depression amongst dementia sufferers. *Journal of Affective Disorders*, 36, 135–144.

Ballard, C., Fossey, J., Chithramohan, R., *et al.* (2001) Quality of care in private sector and NHS facilities for people with dementia: cross-sectional survey. *British Medical Journal*, 323, 426–427.

Ballard, C., Powell, I., James, I., *et al.* (2002a) Can psychiatric liaison reduce neuroleptic use and reduce health service utilization for dementia patients residing in care facilities? *International Journal of Geriatric Psychiatry*, 17, 140–145.

328

Ballard, C., Margallo-Lana, M., Juszczak, E., *et al.* (2005) Quetiapine and rivastigmine and cognitive decline in Alzheimer's disease: randomised double blind placebo controlled trial. *British Medical Journal, 330*, 874.

Ballard, C.G., Patel, A., Solis, M., *et al.* (1996b) A one-year follow-up study of depression in dementia sufferers. *The British Journal of Psychiatry, 168*, 287–291.

Ballard, C.G., O'Brien, J.T., Reichelt, K., *et al.* (2002b) Aromatherapy as a safe and effective treatment for the management of agitation in severe dementia: the results of a double-blind, placebo-controlled trial with Melissa. *Journal of Clinical Psychiatry, 63*, 553–558.

Ballard, E.L. (1995) Attitudes, myths, and realities: helping family and professional caregivers cope with sexuality in the Alzheimer's patient. *Sexuality and Disability, 13*, 255–270.

Bamford, C., Lamont, S., Eccles, M., *et al.* (2004) Disclosing a diagnosis of dementia: a systematic review. *International Journal of Geriatric Psychiatry, 19*, 151–169.

Barber, R., Gholkar, A., Scheltens, P., *et al.* (1999) Medial temporal lobe atrophy on MRI in dementia with Lewy bodies. *Neurology, 52*, 1153–1158.

Barker, S.B. & Dawson, K.S. (1998) The effects of animal-assisted therapy on anxiety ratings of hospitalized psychiatric patients. *Psychiatric Services, 49*, 797–801.

Barnes, C., Mercer, G., Shakespeare, T. (1999) *Exploring Disability: A Sociological Introduction.* Cambridge: Polity Press.

Barrowclough, C. & Fleming, I. (1986) *Goal Planning with Elderly People: How to Make Plans to Meet an Individual's Needs: a Manual of Instruction.* Manchester: Manchester University Press.

Bates, J., Boote, J. & Beverley, C. (2004) Psychosocial interventions for people with a milder dementing illness: a systematic review. *Journal of Advanced Nursing, 45*, 644–658.

Bauld, L., Chesterman, J. & Judge, K. (2000) Measuring satisfaction with social care amongst older service users: issues from the literature. *Health and Social Care in the Community, 8*, 316–324.

Bayer, A. (1994) Carers have different priorities. *The Journal of Dementia Care, 2*, 14–15.

Bayer, A. (2006) Death with dementia – the need for better care. *Age and Ageing, 35*, 101–102.

Beattie, A., Daker-White, G., Gilliard, J., *et al.* (2005) 'They don't quite fit the way we organise our services' – results from a UK field study of marginalised groups and dementia care. *Disability and Society, 20*, 67–80.

Beauchamp, T.L. & Childress, J.F. (2001) *Principles of Biomedical Ethics* (5th edn). Oxford: Oxford University Press.

Beauchamp, N., Irvine, A.B., Seeley, J., *et al.* (2005) Worksite-based internet multimedia program for family caregivers of persons with dementia. *The Gerontologist, 45*, 793–801.

Beck, C., Heacock, P., Mercer, S.O., *et al.* (1997) Improving dressing behaviour in cognitively impaired nursing home residents. *Nursing Research, 46*, 126–132.

References

Beck, C., Cody, M., Souder, E., *et al.* (2000) Dementia diagnostic guidelines: methodologies, results, and implementation costs. *Journal of the American Geriatrics Society*, *48*, 1195–1203.

Beck, C.K., Vogelpohl, T.S., Rasin, J.H., *et al.* (2002) Effects of behavioral interventions on disruptive behavior and affect in demented nursing home residents. *Nursing Research*, *51*, 219–228.

Benamer, T.S., Patterson, J., Grosset, D.G., *et al.* (2000) Accurate differentiation of parkinsonism and essential tremor using visual assessment of [123I]-FP-CIT SPECT imaging: the [123I]-FP-CIT study group. *Movement Disorders*, *15*, 503–510.

Benbow, S.M., Marriott, A., Morley, M., *et al.* (1993) Family therapy and dementia: review and clinical experience. *International Journal of Geriatric Psychiatry*, *8*, 717–725.

Berlin, J.A. (2001) Does blinding of readers affect the results of meta-analyses? *Lancet*, *350*, 185–186.

Bianchetti, A., Scuratti, A., Zanetti, O., *et al.* (1995) Predictors of mortality and institutionalization in Alzheimer disease patients 1 year after discharge from an Alzheimer dementia unit. *Dementia*, *6*, 108–12.

Biessels, G.J., Staekenborg, S., Brunner, E., *et al.* (2006). Risk of dementia in diabetes mellitus: a systematic review. *Lancet Neurology*, *5*, 64–74.

Bird, M., Alexopoulos, P. & Adamowicz, J. (1995) Success and failure in five case studies: use of cued recall to ameliorate behaviour problems in senile dementia. *International Journal of Geriatric Psychiatry*, *10*, 305–311.

Bird, M., Caldwell, T. & Korten, A. (2004) *Alzheimer's Australia Early Stage Dementia Support and Respite ('Living with Memory Loss') Project: First Report on the National Evaluation.* New South Wales: Southern Area Health Service.

Birks, J. & Grimley-Evans, J. (2002) Ginkgo Biloba for cognitive impairment and dementia. *Cochrane Database of Systematic Reviews*, *4*, CD003120.

Bischkopf, J., Busse, A. & Angermeyer, M.C. (2002) Mild cognitive impairment – a review of prevalence, incidence and outcome according to current approaches. *Acta Psychiatrica Scandinavica*, *106*, 403–414.

Black, D.A. (1987) Mental state and presentation of myocardial infarction in the elderly. *Age and Ageing*, *16*, 125–127.

Black, S., Roman, G.C., Geldmacher, D.S., *et al.* (2003) Efficacy and tolerability of donepezil in vascular dementia: positive results of a 24-week, multicenter, international, randomized, placebo-controlled clinical trial. *Stroke*, *34*, 2323–2330.

Bolam v Friern Hospital Management Committee [1957] 1 WLR 582.

Bond, J., Cuddy, R., Dixon, G., *et al.* (1999) The financial abuse of mentally incompetent adults: a Canadian study. *Journal of Elder Abuse and Neglect*, *11*, 23–38.

Bonnie, R.J. & Wallace, R.B. (2003) *Elder Mistreatment: Abuse, Neglect, and Exploitation in an Aging America.* Washington DC: National Academic Press.

Boothby, H., Blizard, R., Livingston, G., *et al.* (1994) The Gospel Oak Study stage III: the incidence of dementia. *Psychological Medicine*, *24*, 89–95.

Boothby, L.A. & Doering, P.L. (2005) Vitamin C and Vitamin E for Alzheimer's disease. *The Annals of Pharmacotherapy*, *39*, 2073–2080.

Bosanquet, N., May, J. & Johnson, N. (1998) *Alzheimer's Disease in the United Kingdom: Burden of Disease and Future Care.* Health Policy Review Paper No. 12. London: University of London, Health Policy Unit.

Bottino, C.M., Carvalho, I.A., Alvarez, A.M., *et al.* (2005) Cognitive rehabilitation combined with drug treatment in Alzheimer's disease patients: a pilot study, *Clinical Rehabilitation, 19,* 861–869.

Bourgeois, M.S., Burgio, L.D., Schulz, R., *et al.* (1997) Modifying repetitive verbalizations of community-dwelling patients with AD. *The Gerontologist, 37,* 30–39.

Bourgeois, M.S., Dijkstra, K., Burgio, L., *et al.* (2001) Memory aids as an augmentative and alternative communication strategy for nursing home residents with dementia. *Augmentative and Alternative Communication, 17,* 196–210.

Bourgeois, M.S., Camp., C., Rose, M., *et al.* (2003) A comparison of training strategies to enhance use of external aids by persons with dementia. *Journal of Communication Disorders, 36,* 361–378.

Boustani, M., Peterson, B., Hanson, L., *et al.* (2003) Screening for dementia in primary care: a summary of the evidence for the US Preventive Services Task Force. *Annals of Internal Medicine, 138,* 927–937.

Bower, H.M. (1967) Sensory stimulation and the treatment of senile dementia. *Medical Journal of Australia, 1,* 1113–1119.

Bowes, A. & Wilkinson, H. (2003) 'We didn't know it would get that bad': South Asian experiences of dementia and the service response. *Health and Social Care in the Community, 11,* 387–396.

Brane, G., Karlsson, I., Kihlgren, M., *et al.* (1989) Integrity-promoting care of demented nursing home patients: psychological and biochemical changes. *International Journal of Geriatric Psychiatry, 4,* 165–172.

Brennan, P.F., Moore, S.M. & Smyth, K.A. (1995) The effects of a special computer network on caregivers of persons with Alzheimer's disease. *Nursing Research, 44,* 166–172.

Breuil, V., De Rotrou, J., Forette, F., *et al.* (1994) Cognitive stimulation of patients with dementia: preliminary results. *International Journal of Geriatric Psychiatry, 9,* 211–217.

British Medical Association & Royal Pharmaceutical Society of Great Britain (2004) *British National Formulary (BNF) 48.* London: British Medical Association & Royal Pharmaceutical Society of Great Britain.

British Medical Association & Royal Pharmaceutical Society of Great Britain (2005) *British National Formulary (BNF) 50.* London: British Medical Association & Royal Pharmaceutical Society of Great Britain.

Brodaty, H. & Gresham, M. (1989) Effect of a training programme to reduce stress in carers of patients with dementia. *British Medical Journal, 299,* 1375–1379.

Brodaty, H. & Peters, K.E. (1991) Cost effectiveness of a training program for dementia carers. *International Psychogeriatrics, 3,* 11–22.

Brodaty, H., Pond, D., Kemp, N.M., *et al.* (2002) The GPCOG: a new screening test for dementia designed for general practice. *Journal of the American Geriatrics Society, 50,* 530–534.

Brodaty, H., Ames, D., Snowdon, J., *et al.* (2003a) A randomized placebo-controlled trial of risperidone for the treatment of aggression, agitation, and psychosis of dementia. *Journal of Clinical Psychiatry*, *64*, 134–143.

Brodaty, H., Draper, B.M., Millar, J., *et al.* (2003b) Randomized controlled trial of different models of care for nursing home residents with dementia complicated by depression or psychosis. *Journal of Clinical Psychiatry*, *64*, 63–72.

Brodaty, H., Draper, B.M. & Low, L.F. (2003c) Behavioural and psychological symptoms of dementia: a seven-tiered model of service delivery. *Medical Journal of Australia*, *178*, 231–234.

Brodaty, H., Green, A. & Koschera, A. (2003d) Meta-analysis of psychosocial interventions for caregivers of people with dementia. *Journal of the American Geriatrics Society*, *51*, 657–664.

Brook, P., Degun, G. & Mather, M. (1975) Reality orientation, a therapy for psychogeriatric patients: a controlled study. *The British Journal of Psychiatry*, *127*, 42–45.

Brooke, P. & Bullock, R. (1999) Validation of a 6-item cognitive impairment test with a view to primary care usage. *International Journal of Geriatric Psychiatry*, *14*, 936–940.

Brooker, D. (2005) Dementia care mapping: a review of the research literature. *The Gerontologist*, *45*, 11–18.

Brooker, D. & Woolley, R. (2006) Enriching opportunities for people living with dementia: the development of a blueprint for a sustainable activity-based model. *Aging and Mental Health*, in press.

Brooker, D., Foster, N., Banner, A., *et al.* (1998) The efficacy of Dementia Care Mapping as an audit tool: report of a 3-year British NHS evaluation. *Aging and Mental Health*, *2*, 60–70.

Brown, L., Tucker, C. & Domokos, T. (2003) Evaluating the impact of integrated health and social care teams on older people living in the community. *Health and Social Care in the Community*, *11*, 85–94.

Buchanan, J.A. & Fisher, J.E. (2002) Functional assessment and non-contingent reinforcement in the treatment of disruptive vocalization in elderly dementia patients. *Journal of Applied Behavior Analysis*, *35*, 99–103.

Buckman, R. (1996). Talking to patients about cancer. *British Medical Journal*, *313*, 699–700.

Bucks, R.S., Ashworth, D.L., Wilcock, G.K., *et al.* (1996) Assessment of activities of daily living in dementia: development of the Bristol Activities of Daily Living Scale. *Age and Ageing*, 25, 113–120.

Burgio, L., Stevens, A., Guy, D., *et al.* (2003) Impact of two psychosocial interventions on white and African American family caregivers of individuals with dementia. *The Gerontologist*, *43*, 568–579.

Burgio, L.D. & Burgio, K.L. (1990) Institutional staff training and management: a review of the literature and a model for geriatric, long-term care facilities. *International Journal of Aging & Human Development*, *30*, 287–302.

Burgio, L.D., Stevens, A., Burgio, K.L., *et al.* (2002) Teaching and maintaining behavior management skills in the nursing home. *The Gerontologist*, *42*, 487–496.

Burns, A., Byrne, J., Ballard, C., *et al.* (2002) Sensory stimulation in dementia. *British Medical Journal, 325,* 1312–1313.

Burt, D.B. & Aylward, E.H. (2000) Test battery for the diagnosis of dementia in individuals with intellectual disability. Working Group for the Establishment of Criteria for the Diagnosis of Dementia in Individuals with Intellectual Disability. *Journal of Intellectual Disability Research, 44,* 175–180.

Butterworth, M. (1995) Dementia: The family giver's perspective. *Journal of Mental Health, 4,* 125–132.

Cahn-Weiner, D.A., Malloy, P.F., Rebok, G.W., *et al.* (2003) Results of a randomized placebo-controlled study of memory training for mildly impaired Alzheimer's disease patients. *Applied Neuropsychology, 10,* 215–223.

Cameron, M., Lonergan, E. & Lee, H. (2003) Transcutaneous electrical nerve stimulation (TENS) for dementia. *Cochrane Database of Systematic Reviews, 3,* CD004032.

Canadian Study of Health and Ageing (1994) Risk factors for Alzheimer's disease in Canada. *Neurology, 44,* 2073–2080.

Cantley, C., Steven, K. & Smith, M. (2003) *'Hear What I Say': Developing Dementia Advocacy Services.* Newcastle upon Tyne: Dementia North/Northumbria University.

Cantley, C., Woodhouse, J. & Smith, M. (2005) *Listen to us: Involving People with Dementia in Planning and Developing Services.* Newcastle upon Tyne: Dementia North/Northumbria University.

Care Services Improvement Partnership & Department of Health (2005) *Moving On: Key Learning from Rowan Ward.* Available at: www.dh.gov.uk/assetRoot/ 04/11/50/23/04115023.pdf.

Cash, M. (2003) Assistive technology and people with dementia. *Reviews in Clinical Gerontology, 13,* 313–319.

Cedazo-Minguez, A. & Cowburn, R.F. (2001) Apolipoprotein E: a major piece in the Alzheimer's disease puzzle. *Journal of Cellular and Molecular Medicine, 5,* 254–266.

Ceravolo, R., Volterrani, D., Gambaccini, G., *et al.* (2004) Presynaptic nigro-striatal function in a group of Alzheimer's disease patients with parkinsonism: evidence from a dopamine transporter imaging study. *Journal of Neural Transmission, 111,* 1065–1073.

Challis, D. & Hughes, J. (2002) Frail old people at the margins of care: some recent research findings. *The British Journal of Psychiatry, 180,* 126–130.

Challis, D., Mozley, C.G., Sutcliffe, C., *et al.* (2000) Dependency in older people recently admitted to care homes. *Age and Ageing, 29,* 255–260.

Challis, D., Von Abendorff, R., Brown, P., *et al.* (2002) Care management, dementia care and specialist mental health services: an evaluation. *International Journal of Geriatric Psychiatry, 17,* 315–325.

Chalmers, J., Todd, A., Chapman, N., *et al.* (2003) International Society of Hypertension (ISH): statement on blood pressure lowering and stroke prevention. *Journal of Hypertension, 21,* 651–663.

Chandler, J.M., Duncan, P.W., Kochersberger, G., *et al.* (1998) Is lower extremity strength gain associated with improvement in physical performance and disability in frail, community-dwelling elders? *Archives of Physical Medicine and Rehabilitation*, *79*, 24–30.

Chang, C.Y. & Silverman, D.H. (2004) Accuracy of early diagnosis and its impact on the management and course of Alzheimer's disease. *Expert Review of Molecular Diagnostics*, *4*, 63–69.

Chapman, S.B., Weiner, M.F., Rackley, A., *et al.* (2004) Effects of cognitive-communication stimulation for Alzheimer's disease patients treated with donepezil. *Journal of Speech, Language and Hearing Research*, *47*, 1149–1163.

Chen, J.H., Lamberg, J.L., Chen, Y.C., *et al.* (2006) Occurrence and treatment of suspected pneumonia in long-term care residents dying with advanced dementia. *Journal of the American Geriatrics Society*, *54*, 290–295.

Cheston, R. (1996) Stories and metaphors: talking about the past in a psychotherapy group for people with dementia. *Ageing and Society*, *16*, 579–602.

Cheston, R. & Jones, K. (2000) A place to work it all out together. *The Journal of Dementia Care*, *8*, 22–24.

Cheston, R., Jones, K. & Gilliard, J. (2003a) Group psychotherapy and people with dementia. *Aging and Mental Health*, *7*, 452–461.

Cheston, R., Jones, K. & Gilliard, J. (2003b) Remembering and forgetting: group work with people who have dementia. In *Dementia Care* (eds. T. Adams & J. Manthorpe). London: Arnold.

Chibnall, J.T., Tait, R.C., Harman, B., *et al.* (2005) Effect of acetaminophen on behavior, well-being, and psychotropic medication use in nursing home residents with moderate-to-severe dementia. *Journal of the American Geriatrics Society*, *53*, 1921–1929.

Chong, M.S. & Sahadevan, S. (2003) An evidence-based clinical approach to the diagnosis of dementia. *Annals of the Academy of Medicine, Singapore*, *32*, 740–748.

Chu, P., Edwards, J., Levin, R., *et al.* (2000) The use of clinical case management for early stage Alzheimer's patients and their families. *American Journal of Alzheimer's Disease and Other Dementias*, *15*, 284–290.

Chui, H. & Zhang, Q. (1997) Evaluation of dementia: a systematic study of the usefulness of the American Academy of Neurology's practice parameters. *Neurology*, *49*, 925–935.

Chui, H.C., Victoroff, J.I., Margolin, D., *et al.* (1992) Criteria for the diagnosis of ischemic vascular dementia proposed by the State of california Alzheimer's disease diagnostic and treatment centers. *Neurology*, *42*, 473–480.

Chung, J.C., Lai, C.K., Chung, P.M., *et al.* (2002) Snoezelen for dementia. *Cochrane Database of Systematic Reviews*, *4*, CD003152.

Churchill, M., Safaoui, J., McCabe, B.W., *et al.* (1999) Using a therapy dog to alleviate the agitation and desocialization of people with Alzheimer's disease. *Journal of Psychosocial Nursing and Mental Health Services*, *37*, 16–22.

Cipher, D.J. & Clifford, P.A. (2004) Dementia, pain, depression, behavioral disturbances, and ADLs: toward a comprehensive conceptualization of quality of life in long-term care. *International Journal of Geriatric Psychiatry*, *19*, 741–748.

Clare, L. (2003) Cognitive training and cognitive rehabilitation for people with early-stage dementia. *Reviews in Clinical Gerontology*, *13*, 75–83.

Clare, L. (2004) Awareness in early-stage Alzheimer's disease: a review of methods and evidence. *British Journal of Clinical Psychology*, *43*, 177–196.

Clare, L. & Woods, R.T. (2004) Cognitive training and cognitive rehabilitation for people with early-stage Alzheimer's disease: a review. *Neuropsychological Rehabilitation*, *14*, 385–401.

Clare, L., Wilson, B.A., Carter, G., *et al.* (2003) Cognitive rehabilitation as a component of early intervention in Alzheimer's disease: a single case study. *Aging and Mental Health*, *7*, 15–21.

Clarfield, A.M. (2003) The decreasing prevalence of reversible dementias: an updated meta-analysis. *Archives of Internal Medicine*, *163*, 2219–2229.

Clarke, C.L. (1999) Family care-giving for people with dementia: some implications for policy and professional practice. *Journal of Advanced Nursing*, *29*, 712–720.

Clayton, J., Fardell, B., Hutton-Potts, J., *et al.* (2003) Parenteral antibiotics in a palliative care unit: prospective analysis of current practice. *Palliative Medicine*, *17*, 44–48.

Closs, S.J., Barr, B., Briggs, M., *et al.* (2002) *Pain assessment in nursing home residents with varying degrees of cognitive impairment*. London: The Mental Health Foundation.

Cohen-Mansfield, J. & Werner, P. (1998) The effects of an enhanced environment on nursing home residents who pace. *The Gerontologist*, *38*, 199–208.

Comas-Herrera, A., Wittenberg, R., Pickard, L., *et al.* (2003) *Cognitive Impairment in Older People: its Implications for Future Demand for Services and Costs*. PSSRU Discussion paper 1728. London: London School of Economics.

Compton, S.A., Flanagan, P. & Gregg, W. (1997) Elder abuse in people with dementia in Northern Ireland: prevalence and predictors in cases referred to a psychiatry of old age service. *International Journal of Geriatric Psychiatry*, *12*, 632–635.

Conroy, S.P., Luxton, T., Dingwall, R., *et al.* (2006) Cardiopulmonary resuscitation in continuing care settings: time for a rethink? *British Medical Journal*, *332*, 479–482.

Cook, A.K.R., Niven, C.A. & Downs, M.G. (1999) Assessing the pain of people with cognitive impairment. *International Journal of Geriatric Psychiatry*, *14*, 421–425.

Coon, D.W., Thompson, L., Steffen, A., *et al.* (2003) Anger and depression management: psychoeducational skill training interventions for women caregivers of a relative with dementia. *The Gerontologist*, *43*, 678–689.

Cooper, B. & Holmes, C. (1998) Previous psychiatric history as a risk factor for late-life dementia: a population-based case control-study. *Age and Ageing*, *27*, 181–188.

Cooper, S.A. (1997) High prevalence of dementia among people with learning disabilities not attributable to Down's syndrome. *Psychological Medicine*, *27*, 609–616.

Copeland, J.R., Davidson, I.A., Dewey, M.E., *et al.* (1992) Alzheimer's disease, other dementias, depression and pseudodementia: prevalence, incidence and three-year outcome in Liverpool. *The British Journal of Psychiatry*, *161*, 230–239.

Corbeil, R.R., Quayhagen, M.P. & Quayhagen, M. (1999) Intervention effects on dementia caregiving interaction: a stress-adaptation modeling approach. *Journal of Aging Health*, *11*, 79–95.

Cornwall County Council (2005) *Dementia Carers Consultation Survey 2005 Report*. Health and Adult Social Care Overview and Scrutiny Committee.

Cosin, L.Z., Mort, M., Post, F., *et al.* (1958) Experimental treatment of persistent senile confusion. *International Journal of Social Psychiatry*, *4*, 24–42.

Council of Europe (2003) *Convention for Protection of Human Rights and Fundamental Freedoms as Amended by Protocol 11*. Strasbourg: Council of Europe. Also available at: www.echr.coe.int/NR/rdonlyres/D5CC24A7-DC13-4318-B457-5C9014916D7A/0/EnglishAnglais.pdf

Cruts, M., van Duijn, C.M., Backhovens, H., *et al.* (1998) Estimation of the genetic contribution of presenilin-1 and -2 mutations in a population-based study of presenile Alzheimer disease. *Human Molecular Genetics*, 7, 43–51.

Cummings, J.L. (2000) Cholinesterase inhibitors: a new class of psychotropic compounds. *The American Journal of Psychiatry*, *157*, 4–15.

Curtis, L. & Netten, A. (2005) *Unit Costs of Health and Social Care 2005*. Canterbury: Personal Social Services Research Unit, University of Kent.

Dalton, A.J. & Fedor, B.L. (1998) Onset of dyspraxia in aging persons with Down syndrome: longitudinal studies. *Journal of Intellectual and Developmental Disability*, *23*, 13–24.

Davey, B., Levin, E., Iliffe, S., *et al.* (2005) Integrating health and social care: implications for joint working and community care outcomes for older people. *Journal of Interprofessional Care*, *19*, 22–34.

Davies, E. (2004) What are the palliative care needs of older people and how might they be met? Copenhagen: WHO Regional Office for Europe (Health Evidence Network report).

Davies, H.D., Zeiss, A. & Tinkenberg, J.R. (1992)'Til death do us part: intimacy and sexuality in the marriages of Alzheimer's patients. *Journal of Psychosocial Nursing and Mental Health Services*, *30*, 5–10.

Davies, H.D., Zeiss, A.M., Shea, E.A., *et al.* (1998) Sexuality and intimacy in Alzheimer's patients and their partners. *Sexuality and Disability*, *16*, 193–203.

Davies, S. & Nolan, M. (2003) 'Making the best of things': relatives' experiences of decisions about care-home entry. *Ageing and Society*, *23*, 429–450.

Davies, S. & Nolan, M. (2004) 'Making the move': relatives' experiences of the transition to a care home. *Health and Social Care in the Community*, *12*, 517–526.

Davis, T. & Davis, S. (2005) Our views on rehabilitation. In *Perspectives on Rehabilitation and Dementia* (ed. M. Marshall), pp. 86–90.

Davis, L.L., Burgio, L.D., Buckwalter, K.C., *et al.* (2004) A comparison of in-home and telephone-based skill training interventions with caregivers of persons with dementia. *Journal of Mental Health and Aging*, *10*, 31–44.

Davis, R.N., Massman, P.J. & Doody, R.S. (2001) Cognitive intervention in Alzheimer disease: a randomized placebo-controlled study. *Alzheimer Disease and Associated Disorders*, *15*, 1–9.

Day, K., Carreon, D. & Stump, C. (2000) The therapeutic design of environments for people with dementia: a review of the empirical research. *The Gerontologist, 40*, 397–416.

De Craen, A.J., Gussekloo, J., Vrijsen, B., *et al.* (2005) Meta-analysis of nonsteroidal antiinflammatory drug use and risk of dementia. *American Journal of Epidemiology, 161*, 114–120.

De Deyn, P.P., Rabheru, K., Rasmussen, A., *et al.* (1999) A randomized trial of risperidone, placebo, and haloperidol for behavioral symptoms of dementia. *Neurology, 53*, 946–955.

De Deyn, P.P., Carrasco, M.M., Deberdt, W., *et al.* (2004) Olanzapine versus placebo in the treatment of psychosis with or without associated behavioral disturbances in patients with Alzheimer's disease. *International Journal of Geriatric Psychiatry, 19*, 115–126.

De Deyn, P.P., Jeste, D.V., Swanink, R., *et al.* (2005) Aripiprazole for the treatment of psychosis in patients with Alzheimer's disease: a randomized, placebo-controlled study. *Journal of Clinical Psychopharmacology, 25*, 463–467.

De Lepeleire, J. & Heyrman, J. (1999) Diagnosis and management of dementia in primary care at an early stage: the need for a new concept and an adapted procedure. *Theoretical Medicine and Bioethics, 20*, 215–228.

De Lepeleire, J., Heyman, J. & Buntinx, F. (1998) The early diagnosis of dementia: triggers, early signs and luxating events. *Family Practice, 15*, 431–436.

De Lepeleire, J., Aertgeerts, B., Umbach, I., *et al.* (2004) The diagnostic value of IADL evaluation in the detection of dementia in general practice. *Aging and Mental Health, 8*, 52–57.

Deb, S., De Silva, P.N., Gemmell, H.G., *et al.* (1992) Alzheimer's disease in adults with Down's syndrome: the relationship between regional cerebral blood flow equivalents and dementia. *Acta Psychiatrica Scandinavica, 86*, 340–345.

Deb, S., Mathews, T., Holt, G. & Bouras, N. (2001) *Practice Guidelines for the Assessment and Diagnosis of Mental Health Problems in Adults with Intellectual Disability*. Brighton: Pavilion Publishing.

Deberdt, W.G., Dysken, M.W., Rappaport, S.A., *et al.* (2005) Comparison of olanzapine and risperidone in the treatment of psychosis and associated behavioral disturbances in patients with dementia. *American Journal of Geriatric Psychiatry, 13*, 722–730.

Deeks, J.J. (2002) Issues in the selection of a summary statistic for meta-analysis of clinical trials with binary outcomes. *Statistics in Medicine, 21*, 1575–1600.

DeKosky, S. (2003) Early intervention is key to successful management of Alzheimer disease. *Alzheimer Disease and Associated Disorders, 17*, S99–S104.

Dementia Plus (2003) *Twice a Child II: Service Development for Dementia Care for African-Caribbean and Asian Older People in Wolverhampton*. Wolverhampton: Dementia Plus.

Department for Constitutional Affairs (DCA) (2005) *Mental Capacity Act 2005: Draft Code of Practice*. Available at: www.dca.gov.uk/consult/codepractise/draftcode 0506b.pdf

Department of Health (2001a) *Valuing People: A New Strategy for Learning Disability for the 21st Century.* London: Department of Health.

Department of Health (2001b) *National Service Framework for Older People.* London: Department of Health.

Department of Health (2001c) *Seeking Consent: Working with Older People.* London: Department of Health. Available at: www.dh.gov.uk/assetRoot/04/06/70/20/04067020.pdf

Department of Health (2001d) *Reference Guide to Consent for Examination or Treatment.* London: Department of Health. Available at: www.dh.gov.uk/assetRoot/04/01/90/79/04019079.pdf

Department of Health (2002) *Care Homes for Older People: National Minimum Standards.* London: The Stationery Office.

Department of Health (2003) *Fair Access to Care Services: Guidance on Eligibility Criteria for Adult Social Care.* London: Department of Health.

Department of Health (2004) *Advice on the Decision of the European Court of Human Rights in the Case of HL v UK (the 'Bournewood' Case).* Gateway Ref 4269. Available at: www.dh.gov.uk/assetRoot/04/09/79/92/04097992.pdf and from the National Assembly for Wales (Welsh Health Circular WHC (2005) 005).

Department of Health (2005a) *Building Telecare in England.* London: Department of Health.

Department of Health (2005b) *Action on Elder Abuse: Report on the Project to Establish a Monitoring and Reporting Process for Adult Protection Referrals Made in Accordance with 'No Secrets'.* London: Department of Health.

Department of Health (2006a) *A New Ambition for Old Age – Next Steps in Implementing the National Service Framework for Older People.* London: Department of Health.

Department of Health (2006b) *NHS Reference Costs 2005.* London: Department of Health.

Department of Health/Care Services Improvement Partnership (2005) *Everybody's Business – Integrated Mental Health Services for Older Adults: a Service Development Guide.* London: Department of Health.

Department of Health/Home Office (2000) *No Secrets: Guidance on Developing and Implementing Multi-Agency Policies and Procedures to Protect Vulnerable Adults from Abuse.* London: Department of Health.

DerSimonian, R. & Laird, N. (1986) Meta-analysis in clinical trials. *Controlled Clinical Trials,* 7, 177–188.

Desmond, D.W., Tatemichi, T.K., Paik, M., *et al.* (1993) Risk factors for cerebrovascular disease as correlates of cognitive function in a stroke-free cohort. *Archives of Neurology,* 50, 162–166.

Detweiler, M.B., Trinkle, D.B. & Anderson, M.S. (2002) Wander gardens: expanding the dementia treatment environment. *Annals of Long-Term Care,* 10, 68–74.

Diwan, S. & Phillips, V.L. (2001) Agitation and dementia-related problem behaviors and case management in long-term care. *International Psychogeriatrics,* 13, 5–21.

Doll, R. (1993) Review: Alzheimer's disease and environmental aluminium. *Age and Ageing*, *22*, 138–153.

Donaldson, C., Tarrier, N. & Burns, A. (1997) The impact of the symptoms of dementia on caregivers. *The British Journal of Psychiatry*, *170*, 62–68.

Donaldson, C., Tarrier, N. & Burns, A. (1998) Determinants of carer stress in Alzheimer's disease. *International Journal of Geriatric Psychiatry*, *13*, 248–256.

Done, D.J. & Thomas, J.A. (2001) Training in communication skills for informal carers of people suffering from dementia: a cluster randomized clinical trial comparing a therapist led workshop and a booklet. *International Journal of Geriatric Psychiatry*, *16*, 816–821.

Dooley, N.R. & Hinojosa, J. (2004) Improving quality of life for persons with Alzheimer's disease and their family caregivers: brief occupational therapy intervention. *The American Journal of Occupational Therapy*, *58*, 561–569.

Dougall, N.J., Bruggink, S. & Ebmeier, K.P. (2004) Systematic review of the diagnostic accuracy of 99mTc-HMPAO-SPECT in dementia. *American Journal of Geriatric Psychiatry*, *12*, 554–570.

Dowling, G.A., Mastick, J., Hubbard, E.M., *et al.* (2005) Effect of timed bright light treatment for rest-activity disruption in institutionalized patients with Alzheimer's disease. *International Journal of Geriatric Psychiatry*, *20*, 738–743.

Downs, M., Turner, S., Bryans, M., *et al.* (2006) Effectiveness of educational interventions in improving detection and management of dementia in primary care: a cluster randomised controlled study. *British Medical Journal*, *332*, 692–696.

Drummond, M.F. & Jefferson, T.O. (1996) Guidelines for authors and peer reviewers of economic submissions to the BMJ. *BMJ*, *313*, 275–283.

Drummond, M.F., Mohide, E.A., Tew, M., *et al.* (1991) Economic evaluation of a support program for caregivers of demented elderly. *International Journal of Technology Assessment in Health Care*, *7*, 209–219.

Ducharme, F., Levesque, L., Lachance, L., *et al.* (2005a) 'Taking care of myself': efficacy of an intervention programme for caregivers of a relative with dementia living in a long-term care setting. *Dementia: The International Journal of Social Research and Practice*, *4*, 23–47.

Ebell, M.H., Becker, L.A., Barry, H.C., *et al.* (1998) Survival after in-hospital cardiopulmonary resuscitation. A meta-analysis. *Journal of General Internal Medicine*, *13*, 805–816.

Eccles, M., Freemantle, N. & Mason, J. (1998) North of England evidence based guideline development project: methods of developing guidelines for efficient drug use in primary care. *British Medical Journal*, *316*, 1232–1235.

Eisdorfer, C., Czaja, S.J., Loewenstein, D.A., *et al.* (2003) The effect of a family therapy and technology-based intervention on caregiver depression. *The Gerontologist*, *43*, 521–531.

Elie, M., Cole, M.G, Primeau, F.J., *et al.* (1998) Delirium risk factors in elderly hospitalized patients. *Journal of General Internal Medicine*, *13*, 204–212.

Ellershaw, J. & Wilkinson, S. (2003) *Care of the Dying. A Pathway to Excellence.* Oxford: Oxford University Press.

References

Elmståhl, S., Annerstedt, L. & Åhlund, O. (1997) How should a group living unit for demented elderly be designed to decrease psychiatric symptoms? *Alzheimer Disease and Associated Disorders*, *11*, 47–52.

Eloniemi-Sulkava, U., Notkola, I.L., Hentinen, M., *et al.* (2001) Effects of supporting community-living demented patients and their caregivers: a randomized trial. *Journal of the American Geriatrics Society*, *49*, 1282–1287.

Erkinjuntti, T. (2002) Broad therapeutic benefits in patients with probable vascular dementia or Alzheimer's disease with cerebrovascular disease after treatment with galantamine. *European Journal of Neurology*, *9*, 545.

Erkinjuntti, T., Inzitari, D., Pantoni, L., *et al.* (2000) Research criteria for subcortical vascular dementia in clinical trials. *Journal of Neural Transmission. Supplementum*, *59*, 23–30.

Erkinjuntti, T., Kurz, A., Gauthier, S., *et al.* (2002) Efficacy of galantamine in probable vascular dementia and Alzheimer's disease combined with cerebrovascular disease: a randomised trial. *The Lancet*, *359*, 1283–1290.

Etminan, M., Gill, S. & Samii, A. (2003a) Effect of non-steroidal anti-inflammatory drugs on risk of Alzheimer's disease: systematic review and meta-analysis of observational studies. *British Medical Journal*, *327*, 128.

Etminan, M., Gill, S. & Samii, A. (2003b) The role of lipid-lowering drugs in cognitive function: a meta-analysis of observational studies. *Pharmacotherapy*, *23*, 726–730.

Evenhuis, H.M. (1996) Further evaluation of the Dementia Questionnaire for Persons with Mental Retardation (DMR). *Journal of Intellectual Disability Research*, *40*, 369–373.

Evenhuis, H.M., Kengen, M.M.F. & Eurlings, H.A.L. (1990) *Dementia Questionnaire for Mentally Retarded Persons.* Zwammerdam, The Netherlands: Hooge Burch Institute for Mentally Retarded Persons.

Evers, M.M., Purohit, D., Perl, D., *et al.* (2002) Palliative and aggressive end-of-life care for patients with dementia. *Psychiatric Services*, *53*, 609–613.

Fabiszewski, K.J., Volicer, B. & Volicer, L. (1990) Effect of antibiotic treatment on outcome of fevers in institutionalized Alzheimer patients. *The Journal of the American Medical Association*, *263*, 3168–3172.

Fahy, M., Wald, C., Walker, Z., *et al.* (2003) Secrets and lies: the dilemma of disclosing the diagnosis to an adult with dementia. *Age and Ageing*, *32*, 439–441.

Fear, T. (2000) Male and female care: a different experience? *The Journal of Dementia Care*, *8*, 28–29.

Feigin, V., Ratnasabapathy, Y. & Anderson, C. (2005) Does blood pressure lowering treatment prevent dementia or cognitive decline in patients with cardiovascular and cerebrovascular disease? *Journal of the Neurological Sciences*, *229–230*, 151–155.

Feinberg, M.J., Ekberg, O., Segall, L., *et al.* (1992) Deglutition in elderly patients with dementia: findings of videoflurographic evaluation and impact on staging and management. *Radiology*, *183*, 811–814.

Feldman, H., Gauthier, S., Hecker, J., *et al.* (2001) A 24-week, randomized, double-blind study of donepezil in moderate to severe Alzheimer's disease. *Neurology*, *57*, 613–620.

Ferrario, E., Cappa, G., Molaschi, M., *et al.* (1991) Reality Orientation Therapy in institutionalized elderly patients: preliminary results. *Archives of Gerontology and Geriatrics, 12*, 139–142.

Ferrell, B.A., Ferrell, B.R. & Osterweil, D. (1990) Pain in the nursing home. *Journal of the American Geriatrics Society, 38*, 409–414.

Ferrell, B.A., Ferrell, B.R. & Rivera, L. (1995) Pain in cognitively impaired nursing home patients. *Journal of Pain and Symptom Management, 10*, 591–598.

Finnema, E., Droes, R.M., Ettema, T., *et al.* (2005) The effect of integrated emotion-oriented care versus usual care on elderly persons with dementia in the nursing home and on nursing assistants: a randomized clinical trial. *International Journal of Geriatric Psychiatry, 20*, 330–343.

Finucane, T.E., Christmas, C. & Travis, K. (1999) Tube feeding in patients with advanced dementia: a review of the evidence. *The Journal of the American Medical Association, 282*, 1365–1370.

Fioravanti, M. & Flicker, L. (2001) Nicergoline for dementia and other age associated forms of cognitive impairment. *Cochrane Database of Systematic Reviews, 4*, CD003159.

Fisher, A.G. (2003) *Assessment of Motor and Process Skills. Vol. 2: User Manual* (5th edn). Fort Collins, CO: Three Star Press.

Fleminger, S., Oliver, D.L., Lovestone, S., *et al.* (2003) Head injury as a risk factor for Alzheimer's disease: the evidence 10 years on; a partial replication. *Journal of Neurology, Neurosurgery and Psychiatry, 74*, 857–862.

Fontana Gasio, P., Krauchi, K., Cajochen, C., *et al.* (2003) Dawn-dusk simulation light therapy of disturbed circadian rest-activity cycles in demented elderly. *Experimental Gerontology, 38*, 207–216.

Forette, F., Seux, M.L., Staessen, J.A., *et al.* (1998) Prevention of dementia in randomised double-blind placebo-controlled Systolic Hypertension in Europe (Syst-Eur) trial. *The Lancet, 352*, 1347–1351.

Fossey, J., Ballard, C., Juszczak, E., *et al.* (2006) Effect of enhanced psychosocial care on antipsychotic use in nursing home residents with severe dementia: cluster randomised trial. *British Medical Journal, 332*, 756–761.

Frampton, M., Harvey, R.J. & Kirchner, V. (2003) Propentofylline for dementia. *Cochrane Database of Systematic Reviews, 2*, CD002853.

Fried, T.R., Gillick, M.R. & Lipsitz, L.A. (1995) Whether to transfer? Factors associated with hospitalization and outcome of elderly long-term care patients with pneumonia. *Journal of General Internal Medicine, 10*, 246–250.

Friel McGowan, D. (1993) *Living in the Labyrinth: a Personal Journey Through the Maze of Alzheimer's.* San Francisco, CA: Elder Books.

Fulford, K.W.M. (2004) Facts/values. Ten principles of values-based medicine. In *The Philosophy of Psychiatry: a Companion* (ed. J. Radden). Oxford: Oxford University Press.

Fung, W.Y. & Chien, W.T. (2002) The effectiveness of a mutual support group for family caregivers of a relative with dementia. *Archives of Psychiatric Nursing, 16*, 134–144.

341

Gangulai, M., Ratcliff, G. & Chandra, V., *et al.* (1995) A Hindi version of the MMSE: the development of a cognitive screening instrument for a largely illiterate rural elderly population in India. *International Journal of Geriatric Psychiatry*, *10*, 367–377.

Garand, L., Buckwalter, K.C., Lubaroff, D., *et al.* (2002) A pilot study of immune and mood outcomes of a community-based intervention for dementia caregivers: the PLST intervention. *Archives of Psychiatric Nursing*, *16*, 156–167.

Gedye, A. (1995) *Dementia Scale for Down Syndrome: Manual.* Vancouver, BC: Gedye Research and Consulting.

Geerlings, M.I., Ruitenberg, A., Witteman, J.C., *et al.* (2001) Reproductive period and risk of dementia in postmenopausal women. *The Journal of the American Medical Association*, *285*, 1475–1481.

Gely-Nargeot, M.C., Derouesne, C., Selmes, J., *et al.* (2003) European survey on current practice and disclosure of the diagnosis of Alzheimer's disease. A study based on caregivers' reports. *Psychologie et Neuropsychiatrie du Vieillissement*, *1*, 45–55.

General Medical Council (GMC) (1998) *Seeking Patients' Consent: the Ethical Considerations.* London: GMC. Also available at: www.gmc-uk.org/guidance/current/library/consent.asp

General Medical Council (GMC) (2002) *Withholding and Withdrawing Life-Prolonging Treatments: Good Practice in Decision-Making.* London: GMC. Available at: www.gmc-uk.org/guidance/current/library/index.asp

General Medical Council (GMC) (2004) *Confidentiality: Protecting and Providing Information.* London: GMC. Also available at: www.gmcuk.org/guidance/current/library/confidentiality.asp

Geppert, C.J. (1998) The long bereavement: ageing from a social point of view. *Age and Ageing*, 27, 5–9.

Gerdner, L.A., Buckwalter, K.C. & Reed, D. (2002) Impact of a psychoeducational intervention on caregiver response to behavioral problems. *Nursing Research*, *51*, 363–374.

Gibson, F. (2004) *The Past in the Present: Using Reminiscence in Health and Social Care.* Baltimore: Health Professions Press.

Gibson, F., Whittington, D., *et al.* (1995) *Day Care in Rural Areas.* York: Joseph Rowntree Foundation.

Gibson, S. (2005) A personal experience of successful doll therapy. *The Journal of Dementia Care*, *13*, 22.

Gifford, D.R., Holloway, R.G. & Vickrey, B.G. (2000) Systematic review of clinical prediction rules for neuroimaging in the evaluation of dementia. *Archives of Internal Medicine*, *160*, 2855–2862.

Gilleard, C. (1984) *Living with Dementia: Community Care of the Elderly Mentally Infirm.* London: Croom Helm.

Gilleard, C.J. (1996) Family therapy with older clients. In *Handbook of the Clinical Psychology of Ageing* (ed. R.T. Woods). Chichester: J. Wiley and Sons.

Gilliard, J., Means, R., Beattie, A., *et al.* (2005) Dementia care in England and the social model of disability: lessons and issues. *Dementia*, *4*, 571–586.

Gillick, M.R. (2000) Rethinking the role of tube feeding in patients with advanced dementia. *The New England Journal of Medicine, 342*, 206–210.

Gillies, B. & Johnston, G. (2004) Identity loss and maintenance: commonality of experience in cancer and dementia. *European Journal of Cancer Care, 13*, 436–442.

Gillies, B.A. (2000) A memory like clockwork: accounts of living through dementia. *Aging and Mental Health, 4*, 366–374.

Gitlin, L.N., Winter, L., Corcoran, M., *et al.* (2003) Effects of the home environmental skill-building program on the caregiver-care recipient dyad: 6-month outcomes from the Philadelphia REACH Initiative. *Gerontologist, 43*, 532–546.

Gitlin, L.N., Hauck, W.W., Dennis, M.P., *et al.* (2005) Maintenance of effects of the home environmental skill-building program for family caregivers and individuals with Alzheimer's disease and related disorders. *The Journals of Gerontology. Series A: Biological Sciences and Medical Sciences, 60*, 368–374.

Gjerdingen, D.K., Neff, J.A., Wang, M., *et al.* (1999) Older persons' opinions about life-sustaining procedures in the face of dementia. *Archives of Family Medicine, 8*, 421–425.

Glasby, J. (2004) Social services and the Single Assessment Process: early warning signs? *Journal of Interprofessional Care, 18*, 129–139.

Gold, G., Bouras, C., Canuto, A., *et al.* (2002) Clinicopathological validation study of four sets of clinical criteria for vascular dementia. *The American Journal of Psychiatry, 159*, 82–87.

Golding, E. (1989) *MEAMS: The Middlesex Elderly Assessment of Mental State.* Titchfield: Thames Valley Test Company.

Goldwasser, A.N., Auerbach, S.M. & Harkins, S.W. (1987) Cognitive, affective, and behavioral effects of reminiscence group therapy on demented elderly. *International Journal of Aging and Human Development, 25*, 209–222.

Gormley, N., Lyons, D. & Howard, R. (2001) Behavioural management of aggression in dementia: a randomized controlled trial. *Age and Ageing, 30*, 141–145.

GRADE Working Group (2004) Grading quality of evidence and strength of recommendations. *British Medical Journal, 328*, 1490–1497.

Graff, M.J.L., Vernooij-Dassen, M.J.F.J, Hoefnagels, W.H., *et al.* (2003) Occupational therapy at home for older individuals with mild to moderate cognitive impairments and their primary caregivers: a pilot study. *Occupational Therapy Journal of Research: Occupation, Participation, and Health, 23*, 155–164.

Graham, C., Ballard, C. & Sham, P. (1997a) Carers' knowledge of dementia, their coping strategies and morbidity. *International Journal of Geriatric Psychiatry, 12*, 931–936.

Graham, C., Ballard, C. & Sham, P. (1997b) Carers' knowledge of dementia and their expressed concerns. *International Journal of Geriatric Psychiatry, 12*, 470–473.

Grant, B. (1993) Does Alzheimer's have Chris? *Intouch*, May 1993.

Green, R.C., Cupples, L.A., Kurz, A., *et al.* (2003) Depression as a risk factor for Alzheimer disease: the MIRAGE Study. *Archives of Neurology, 60*, 753–759.

Groene, R.W. (1993) Effectiveness of music therapy 1:1 intervention with individuals having Senile Dementia of the Alzheimer's Type. *Journal of Music Therapy, 30*, 138–157.

Guo, Z., Cupples, L.A., Kurz, A., *et al.* (2000) Head injury and the risk of AD in the MIRAGE study. *Neurology, 54*, 1316–1323.

Gustafson, D., Rothenberg, E., Blennow, K., *et al.* (2003) An 18-year follow-up of overweight and risk of Alzheimer disease. *Archives of Internal Medicine, 163*, 1524–1528.

Hachinski, V.C., Iliff, L.D., Zilhka, E., *et al.* (1975) Cerebral blood flow in dementia. *Archives of Neurology, 32*, 632–637.

Hanks, N. (1992) The effects of Alzheimer's disease on the sexual attitudes and behaviors of married caregivers and their spouses. *Sexuality and Disability, 10*, 137–151.

Hardy, J. (1996) New insights into the genetics of Alzheimer's disease. *Annals of Medicine, 28*, 255–258.

Harris, L., Weir, M. (1998) Inappropriate sexual behaviour in dementia: a review of the treatment literature. *Sexuality and Disability, 16*, 205–216.

Harvey, R.J., Skelton-Robinson, M. & Rossor, M.N. (2003) The prevalence and causes of dementia in people under the age of 65 years. *Journal of Neurology, Neurosurgery, and Psychiatry, 74*, 1206–1209.

Heart Protection Study Collaborative Group (HPSCG) (2002) MRC/BHF Heart Protection Study of cholesterol lowering with simvastatin in 20,536 high-risk individuals: a randomised placebo-controlled trial. *The Lancet, 360*, 7–22.

Hebert, R., Lindsay, J., Verreault, R., *et al.* (2000) Vascular dementia: incidence and risk factors in the Canadian study of health and aging. *Stroke, 31*, 1487–1493.

Hebert, R., Levesque, L., Vezina, J., *et al.* (2003) Efficacy of a psychoeducative group program for caregivers of demented persons living at home: a randomized controlled trial. *The Journals of Gerontology. Series B: Psychological Sciences and Social Sciences, 58*, S58–S67.

Heiser, S. (2002) People with dementia reveal their views of homecare. *The Journal of Dementia Care, 10*, 22–24.

Heiss, W.D., Kessler, J., Mielke, R., *et al.* (1994) Long-term effects of phosphatidylserine, pyritinol, and cognitive training in Alzheimer's disease. A neuropsychological, EEG, and PET investigation. *Dementia, 5*, 88–98.

Hentschel, F., Kreis, M., Damian, M., *et al.* (2005) The clinical utility of structural neuroimaging with MRI for diagnosis and differential diagnosis of dementia: a memory clinic study. *International Journal of Geriatric Psychiatry, 20*, 645–650.

Herrmann, N., Mamdani, M. & Lanctot, K. L. (2004) Atypical antipsychotics and risk of cerebrovascular accidents. *American Journal of Psychiatry, 161*, 1113–1115.

Higgins, J.P.T. & Thompson, S.G. (2002) Quantifying heterogeneity in a meta-analysis. *Statistics in Medicine, 21 (11)*, 1539–1558.

Hillman, J., Skoloda, T.E., Angelini, F., *et al.* (2001) The moderating effect of aggressive problem behaviors in the generation of more positive attitudes toward nursing home residents. *Aging and Mental Health, 5*, 282–288.

HMSO (1983) *Mental Health Act 1983*. London: Her Majesty's Stationery Office.

Hofman, A., Rocca, W.A., Brayne, C., *et al.* (1991) The prevalence of dementia in Europe: a collaborative study of 1980–1990 findings. Eurodem Prevalence Research Group. *International Journal of Epidemiology*, *20*, 736–748.

Hofman, A., Ott, A., Breteler, M.M., *et al.* (1997) Atherosclerosis, apolipoprotein E and prevalence of dementia and Alzheimer's disease in the Rotterdam Study. *The Lancet*, *349*, 151–154.

Hogervorst, E., Yaffe, K., Richards, M., *et al.* (2002) Hormone replacement therapy for cognitive function in postmenopausal women. *Cochrane Database of Systematic Reviews*, *2*, CD003122.

Hoglund, K., Wiklund, O., Vanderstichele, H., *et al.* (2004) Plasma levels of beta-amyloid(1–40), beta-amyloid(1–42), and total beta-amyloid remain unaffected in adult patients with hypercholesterolemia after treatment with statins. *Archives of Neurology*, *61*, 333–337.

Holden, U.P. & Woods, R.T. (1995) *Positive approaches to dementia care* (3rd edn). Edinburgh: Churchill Livingstone.

Holland, A.J., Hon, J., Huppert, F.A., *et al.* (1998) Population-based study of the prevalence and presentation of dementia in adults with Down's syndrome. *The British Journal of Psychiatry*, *172*, 493–498.

Holmes, C., Fortenza, O., Powell, J., *et al.* (1997) Do neuroleptic drugs hasten cognitive decline in dementia? Carriers of apolipoprotein E epsilon 4 allele seem particularly susceptible to their effects. *British Medical Journal*, 314, 1411; author reply 1412.

Holmes, C., Wilkinson, D., Dean, C., *et al.* (2004) The efficacy of donepezil in the treatment of neuropsychiatric symptoms in Alzheimer disease. *Neurology*, *63*, 214–219.

Holmes, J. & House, A. (2000) Psychiatric illness predicts poor outcome after surgery for hip fracture: a prospective cohort study. *Psychological Medicine*, *30*, 921–929.

Holmes, J., Pugner, K., Phillips, R., *et al.* (1998) Managing Alzheimer's disease: the cost of care per patient. *British Journal of Health Care Management*, *4*, 332–337.

Holtkamp, C.C., Kragt, K., Van Dongen, M.C., *et al.* (1997) Effect of snoezelen on the behaviour of demented elderly. *Tijdschrift voor Gerontologie en Geriatrie*, *28*, 124–128.

Hon, J., Huppert, F.A., Holland, A.J., *et al.* (1999) Neuropsychological assessment of older adults with Down's syndrome: an epidemiological study using the Cambridge Cognitive Examination (CAMCOG). *British Journal of Clinical Psychology*, *38*, 155–165.

Hope, R.A. & Fairburn, C.G. (1990) The nature of wandering in dementia: a community based study. *International Journal of Geriatric Psychiatry*, *5*, 239–245.

Horgas, A.L. & Tsai, P.F. (1998) Analgesic drug prescription and use in cognitively impaired nursing home residents. *Nursing Research*, *47*, 235–242.

House of Commons Health Committee (2004a) *Elder Abuse: Second Report of Session 2003–2004*. London: The Stationery Office.

House of Commons Health Committee (2004b) *Palliative Care: Fourth Report of Session 2003–2004*. Available at: www.publications.parliament.uk/

Howard, R., Ballard, C., O'Brien, J., *et al.* (2001) Guidelines for the management of agitation in dementia. *International Journal of Geriatric Psychiatry, 16*, 714–717.

Hsich, G., Kenney, K., Gibbs, C.J, *et al.* (1996) The 14-3-3 brain protein in cerebrospinal fluid as a marker for transmissible spongiform encephalopathies. *New England Journal of Medicine, 335*, 924–930.

Huang, H.L., Shyu, Y.I., Chen, M.C., *et al.* (2003) A pilot study on a home-based caregiver training program for improving caregiver self-efficacy and decreasing the behavioral problems of elders with dementia in Taiwan. *International Journal of Geriatric Psychiatry, 18*, 337–345.

Hubbard, G., Downs, M.G. & Tester, S. (2003) Including older people with dementia in research: challenges and strategies. *Aging and Mental Health, 7*, 351–362.

Hughes, J.C. & Louw, S.J. (2002) Confidentiality and cognitive impairment: professional and philosophical ethics. *Age and Ageing, 31*, 147–150.

Hughes, J.C. & Robinson, L. (2005) General practice perspectives: co-ordinating end-of-life care. In: *Palliative Care in Severe Dementia* (ed. J.C. Hughes). Dinton: Quay Books.

Hughes, J.C., Hedley, K. & Harris, D. (2005a) The practice and philosophy of palliative care in dementia. In *Palliative Care in Severe Dementia* (ed. J.C. Hughes). Dinton: Quay Books.

Hughes, J.C., Robinson, L. & Volicer, L. (2005b) Specialist palliative care in dementia. *British Medical Journal, 330*, 57–58.

Hurley, A.C., Volicer, B.J. & Volicer, L. (1996) Effect of fever-management strategy on the progression of dementia of the Alzheimer type. *Alzheimer Disease and Associated Disorders, 10*, 5–10.

Husband, H.J. (1999) The psychological consequences of learning a diagnosis of dementia: three case examples. *Aging and Mental Health, 3*, 179–183.

Husband, H.J. (2000) Diagnostic disclosure in dementia: an opportunity for intervention? *International Journal of Geriatric Psychiatry, 15*, 544–547.

Iliffe, S., Wilcock, J., Austin, T., *et al.* (2002) Dementia diagnosis and management in primary care: developing and testing educational models. *Dementia, 1*, 11–23.

Iliffe, S., Wilcock, J. & Haworth, D. (2006) Obstacles to shared care for patients with dementia: a qualitative study. *Family Practice, 23*, 353–362.

Innes, A., Blackstock, K., Mason, A., *et al.* (2005) Dementia care provision in rural Scotland: service users' and carers' experiences. *Health and Social Care in the Community, 13*, 354–365.

Jack, C.R. Jr., Petersen, R.C., Xu, Y.C., *et al.* (1999) Prediction of AD with MRI-based hippocampal volume in mild cognitive impairment. *Neurology, 52*, 1397–1403.

Jacobson, S. & Jerrier, H. (2000) EEG in delirium. *Seminars in Clinical Neuropsychiatry, 5*, 86–92.

Jadad, A.R., Moore, R.A., Carroll, D., *et al.* (1996) Assessing the quality of reports of randomised clinical trials: is blinding necessary? *Controlled Clinical Trials, 17*, 1–12.

Jagust, W., Thisted, R., Devous, M.D. Sr., *et al.* (2001) SPECT perfusion imaging in the diagnosis of Alzheimer's disease: a clinical-pathologic study. *Neurology, 56*, 950–956.

Jeffrey, D. (2001) Collusion in doctor-patient communication. Specialist palliative care staff could act as treatment brokers. *British Medical Journal, 322,* 1063.

Jellinger, K.A. (2004) Head injury and dementia. *Current Opinion in Neurology, 17,* 719–723.

Jick, H., Zornberg, G.L., Jick, S.S., Seshadri, S., *et al.* (2000) Statins and the risk of dementia. *The Lancet, 356,* 1627–1631.

Johansen, A., White, S. & Waraisch, P. (2003) Screening for visual impairment in older people: validation of the Cardiff Acuity Test. *Archives of Gerontology and Geriatrics, 36,* 289–293.

Jones, J. (1997) 'Thank God for Careline'. *Signpost, 2,* 11–13.

Jones, R.W. (2000) *Drug Treatment in Dementia.* Oxford: Blackwell Science Ltd.

Jonkman, E.J. (1997) The role of the electroencephalogram in the diagnosis of dementia of the Alzheimer type: an attempt at technology assessment. *Neurophysiologie Clinique, 27,* 211–219.

Jönsson, L., Eriksdotter Jönhagen, M., Kilander, L., *et al.* (2006) Determinants of costs of care for patients with Alzheimer's disease. *International Journal of Geriatric Psychiatry, 21,* 449–459.

Jorm, A.F. (2000) Is depression a risk factor for dementia or cognitive decline? A review. *Gerontology, 46,* 219–227.

Jorm, A.F. & Jacomb, P.A. (1989) The Informant Questionnaire on Cognitive Decline in the Elderly (IQCODE): socio-demographic correlates, reliability, validity and some norms. *Psychological Medicine, 19,* 1015–1022.

Jorm, A.F. & Jolley, D. (1998) The incidence of dementia: a meta-analysis. *Neurology, 51,* 728–733.

Jorm, A.F., Korten, A.E. & Henderson, A.S. (1987) The prevalence of dementia: a quantitative integration of the literature. *Acta Psychiatrica Scandinavica, 76,* 465–479.

Judd, S., Marshall, M., Phippen, P. (eds.) (1997) *Design for Dementia.* London: Hawker.

Kabir, Z.N. & Herlitz, A. (2000) The Bangla adaptation of Mini Mental State Examination (BAMSE): an instrument to assess cognitive function in illiterate and literate individuals. *International Journal of Geriatric Psychiatry, 15,* 441–450.

Kao, C.H., Wang, P.Y., Wang, S.J., *et al.* (1993) Regional cerebral blood flow of Alzheimer's disease-like pattern in young patients with Down's syndrome detected by 99Tcm-HMPAO brain SPECT. *Nuclear Medicine Communications, 14,* 47–51.

Katz, I.R., Jeste, D.V., Mintzer, J.E., *et al.* (1999) Comparison of risperidone and placebo for psychosis and behavioral disturbances associated with dementia: a randomized, double-blind trial. Risperidone Study Group. *Journal of Clinical Psychiatry, 60,* 107–115.

Kay, D.W., Forster, D.P. & Newens, A.J. (2000) Long-term survival, place of death, and death certification in clinically diagnosed pre-senile dementia in northern England. Follow-up after 8–12 years. *The British Journal of Psychiatry, 177,* 156–162.

Keady, J. & Gilliard, J. (2002) Testing times: the experience of neuro-psychological assessment for people with suspected Alzheimer's disease. In *The Person with*

Alzheimer's Disease: Pathways to Understanding the Experience (ed. P.B. Harris). Baltimore: The Johns Hopkins University Press.

Keady, J., Nolan, M.R. & Gilliard, J. (1995) Listen to the voices of experience. *Journal of Dementia Care*, *3*, 15–17.

Keady, J., Woods, B., Hahn, S., *et al.* (2004) Community mental health nursing and early intervention in dementia: developing practice through a single case history. *International Journal of Older People Nursing* in association with *Journal of Clinical Nursing*, *13*, 57–67.

Kerr, D. & Wilkinson, H. (2005) *In the Know: Implementing Good Practice, Information and Tools for Anyone Supporting People with a Learning Disability and Dementia*. York: Pavilion Publishing/Joseph Rowntree Foundation.

Kertesz, A. (2002) Efficacy of galantamine in probable vascular dementia and Alzheimer's disease combined with cerebrovascular disease: a randomized trial. *Current Neurology and Neuroscience Reports*, *2*, 503–504.

Kihlgren, M., Bråne, G., Karlsson, I., *et al.* (1992) Long-term influences on demented patients in different caring milieus, a collective living unit and a nursing home: a descriptive study. *Dementia*, *3*, 342–349.

Kipling, T., Bailey, M. & Charlesworth, G. (1999) The feasibility of a cognitive behavioural therapy group for men with mild/moderate cognitive impairment. *Behavioural and Cognitive Psychotherapy*, *27*, 189–193.

Kirchner, V., Elloy, M.D., Silver, L.E., *et al.* (2000) Dementia: The cost of care for behaviourally disturbed patients living in the community. *International Journal of Geriatric Psychiatry*, *15*, 1000–1004.

Kitwood, T. & Benson, S. (1995) *The New Culture of Dementia Care*. London: Hawker Publications.

Kitwood, T. & Bredin, K. (1992) Towards a theory of dementia care: personhood and well-being. *Ageing and Society*, *12*, 269–287.

Kitwood, T.M. (1997) *Dementia Reconsidered: the Person Comes First*. Buckingham: Open University Press.

Kivipelto, M., Ngandu, T., Fratiglioni, L., *et al.* (2005) Obesity and vascular risk factors at midlife and the risk of dementia and Alzheimer disease. *Archives of Neurology*, *62*, 1556–1560.

Klunk, W.E., Engler, H., Nordberg, A., *et al.* (2004) Imaging brain amyloid in Alzheimer's disease with Pittsburgh Compound-B. *Annals of Neurology*, *55*, 306–319.

Knapp, M., Thorgrimsen, L., Patel, A., *et al.* (2006). Cognitive stimulation therapy for people with dementia: cost-effective analysis. *The British Journal of Psychiatry*, *188*, 574–580.

Knopman, D.S., DeKosky, S.T., Cummings, J.L., *et al.* (2001) Practice parameter: diagnosis of dementia (an evidence-based review). Report of the Quality Standards Subcommittee of the American Academy of Neurology. *Neurology*, *56*, 1143–1153.

Kolanowski, A.M., Litaker, M. & Buettner, L. (2005). Efficacy of theory-based activities for behavioral symptoms of dementia. *Nursing Research*, *54*, 219–228.

Koltai, D.C., Welsh-Bohmer, K.A. & Smechel, D.E. (2001) Influence of anosognosia on treatment outcome among dementia patients. *Neuropsychological Rehabilitation*, *11*, 455–475.

Koppel, R. (2002) *Alzheimer's Disease: The Cost to U.S. Businesses in 2002.* Pennsylvania: Social Research Corporation and Department of Sociology, University of Pennsylvania.

Kuhn, D.R. (1994) The changing face of sexual intimacy in Alzheimer's disease. *The American Journal of Alzheimer's Care and Related Disorders and other Dementias, 9,* 7–14.

Kuhn, D., Kasayka, R.E. & Lechner, C. (2002) Behavioral observations and quality life among persons with dementia in 10 assisted living facilities. *American Journal of Alzheimer's Disease and Other Dementias, 17,* 291–298.

Kuusisto, J., Koivisto, K., Kervinen, K., *et al.* (1994) Association of apolipoprotein E phenotypes with late onset Alzheimer's disease: population based study. *British Medical Journal, 309,* 636–638.

LaFrance, N.D., Parker, J.R., Smith, M.D., *et al.* (1998) Dynamic susceptibility contrast MR imaging for the evaluation of probable Alzheimer disease: a cost-effectiveness analysis. *Academic Radiology, 5,* S231–S233.

Lai, C.K., Chi, I. & Kayser-Jones, J. (2004) A randomized controlled trial of a specific reminiscence approach to promote the well-being of nursing home residents with dementia. *International Psychogeriatrics, 16,* 33–49.

Larson, E.B., Reifler, B.V., Sumi, S.M., *et al.* (1986) Diagnostic tests in the evaluation of dementia. A prospective study of 200 elderly outpatients. *Archives of Internal Medicine, 146,* 1917–1922.

Launer, L.J., Andersen, K., Dewey, M.E., *et al.* (1999) Rates and risk factors for dementia and Alzheimer's disease: results from EURODEM pooled analyses. EURODEM Incidence Research Group and Work Groups. European Studies of Dementia. *Neurology, 52,* 78–84.

Lawton, M.P., Liebowitz, B. & Charon, H. (1970) Physical structure and the behavior of senile patients following ward remodeling. *Aging and Human Development, 1,* 231–239.

Leibson, C.L., Rocca, W.A., Hanson,V.A., *et al.* (1997) Risk of dementia among persons with diabetes mellitus: a population-based cohort study. *American Journal of Epidemiology, 145,* 301–308.

Letenneur, L. (2004) Risk of dementia and alcohol and wine consumption: a review of recent results. *Biological Research, 37,* 189–193.

Li, G., Higdun, R., Kukull, W.A., *et al.* (2004) Statin therapy and risk of dementia in the elderly: a community-based prospective cohort study. *Neurology, 63,* 1624–1628.

Lichtenberg, P.A., Kemp-Havican, J., MacNeill, S.E., *et al.* (2005) Pilot study of behavioral treatment in dementia care units. *The Gerontologist, 45,* 406–410.

Liddel, J., Williamson, M. & Irwig, L. (1996) *Method for Evaluating Research and Guideline Evidence.* Sydney: New South Wales Health Department.

Lindesay, J., Jagger, K., Mlynik-Szmid, A., *et al.* (1997) The Mini Mental State Examination (MMSE) in an elderly immigrant Gujarati population in the United Kingdom. *International Journal of Geriatric Psychiatry, 12,* 1155–1167.

Lindsay, J., Herbert, R. & Rockwood, K. (1997) The Canadian Study of Health and Aging: risk factors for vascular dementia. *Stroke, 28,* 526–530.

Lintern, T., Woods, R.T. & Phair, L. (2002) Before and after training: a case study of intervention. In *Dementia Topics for the Millennium and Beyond* (ed. S. Benson). London: Hawker Publications.

Lippa, C.F., Swearer, J.M., Kane, K.J., *et al.* (2000) Familial Alzheimer's disease: site of mutation influences clinical phenotype. *Annals of Neurology, 48,* 376–379.

Litvan, I., Bhatia, K.P., Burn, D.J., *et al.* (2003) Movement Disorders Society Scientific Issues Committee report: SIC Task Force appraisal of clinical diagnostic criteria for Parkinsonian disorders. *Movement Disorders, 18,* 467–486.

Livingston, G., Johnston, K., Katona, C., *et al.* (2005) Systematic review of psychological approaches to the management of neuropsychiatric symptoms of dementia. *The American Journal of Psychiatry, 162,* 1996–2021.

Lloyd-Williams, M. (1996) An audit of palliative care in dementia. *European Journal of Cancer Care, 5,* 53–55.

Lobo, A., Launer, L.J., Fratiglioni, L., *et al.* (2000) Prevalence of dementia and major subtypes in Europe: a collaborative study of population-based cohorts. Neurologic Diseases in the Elderly Research Group. *Neurology, 54,* S4–S9.

Loewenstein, D.A., Acevedo, A., Czaja, S.J., *et al.* (2004) Cognitive rehabilitation of mildly impaired Alzheimer disease patients on cholinesterase inhibitors. *The American Journal of Geriatric Psychiatry, 12,* 395–402.

Lonergan, E., Luxenberg, J. & Colford, J. (2002) Haloperidol for agitation in dementia. *Cochrane Database of Systematic Reviews, 2,* CD002852.

Lonn, E., Bosch, J., Yusuf, S., *et al.* (2005) The HOPE and HOPE-TOO Trial Investigators. Effects of long-term vitamin E supplementation on cardiovascular events and cancer: a randomized controlled trial. *The Journal of the American Medical Association, 293,* 1338–1347.

López-Arrieta, J.M. & Birks, J. (2002) Nimodipine for primary degenerative, mixed and vascular dementia. *Cochrane Database of Systematic Reviews, 3,* CD000147.

Low, L.F. & Anstey, K.J. (2006) Hormone replacement therapy and cognitive performance in postmenopausal women – a review by cognitive domain. *Neuroscience and Biobehavioral Reviews, 30,* 66–84.

Lowin, A., Knapp, M. & McCrone, P. (2001) Alzheimer's disease in the UK: comparative evidence on cost of illness and volume of health services research funding. *International Journal of Geriatric Psychiatry, 16,* 1143–1148.

Luchins, D.J. & Hanrahan, P. (1993) What is appropriate health care for end-stage dementia? *Journal of the American Geriatrics Society, 41,* 25–30.

Luchsinger, J.A., Tang, M.X., Shea, S., *et al.* (2003) Antioxidant vitamin intake and risk of Alzheimer disease. *Archives of Neurology, 60,* 203–208.

Lyketsos, C.G., Lindell Veiel, L., Baker, A., *et al.* (1999) A randomized, controlled trial of bright light therapy for agitated behaviors in dementia patients residing in long-term care. *International Journal of Geriatric Psychiatry, 14,* 520–525.

Lyketsos, C.G., Del Campo, L., Steinberg, M., *et al.* (2003) Treating depression in Alzheimer disease: efficacy and safety of sertraline therapy, and the benefits of depression reduction: the DIADS. *Archives of General Psychiatry, 60,* 737–746.

McAllister, C.L. & Silverman, M.A. (1999) Community formation and community roles among persons with Alzheimer's disease: a comparative study of experiences in a residential Alzheimer's facility and a traditional nursing home. *Qualitative Health Research*, 9, 65–85.

McCallion, P., Toseland, R.W., Lacey, D., *et al.* (1999) Educating nursing assistants to communicate more effectively with nursing home residents with dementia. *The Gerontologist*, *39*, 546–558.

McCarthy, M., Addington-Hall, J. & Altmann, D. (1997) The experience of dying with dementia: a retrospective study. *International Journal of Geriatric Psychiatry*, *12*, 404–409.

McCracken, A.L. & Fitzwater, E. (1989) The right environment for Alzheimer's: which is better – open versus closed units? Here's how to tailor the answer to the patient. *Geriatric Nursing*, *10*, 293–294.

McCurry, S.M., Gibbons, L.E., Logsdon, R.G., *et al.* (2005) Nighttime insomnia treatment and education for Alzheimer's disease: a randomized, controlled trial. *Journal of the American Geriatrics Society*, *53*, 793–802.

McGeer, E.G. & McGeer, P.L. (1999) Brain inflammation in Alzheimer disease and the therapeutic implications. *Current Pharmaceutical Design*, *5*, 821–836.

McGilton, K.S., Rivera, T.M. & Dawson, P. (2003) Can we help persons with dementia find their way in a new environment? *Aging and Mental Health*, *7*, 363–371.

McGuire, R.C. (1998) A case study in cost-effectiveness analysis for computer technology used in support of caregivers with Alzheimer's disease patients. In *Information Systems Innovations for Nursing: New Visions and Ventures* (eds. S. Moorhead & C. Delaney). Thousand Oaks, CA: Sage Publications.

Maciejewski, C. (1999) A focus group for carers of people with young onset dementia. *Signpost*, *4*, 13–15.

McKeith, I., Del Sur, T., Spano, P., *et al.* (2000a) Efficacy of rivastigmine in dementia with Lewy bodies: a randomised, double-blind, placebo-controlled international study. *The Lancet*, *356*, 2031–2036.

McKeith, I., Mintzer, J., Aarsland, D., Burn, D., *et al.* (2004) Dementia with Lewy Bodies. *Lancet Neurology*, *3*, 19–28.

McKeith, I.G., Galasko, D., Kosaka, K., *et al.* (1996) Consensus guidelines for the clinical and pathologic diagnosis of dementia with Lewy bodies (DLB): report of the consortium on DLB international workshop. *Neurology*, *47*, 1113–1124.

McKeith, I.G., Ballard, C.G., Perry, R.H., *et al.* (2000b) Prospective validation of consensus criteria for the diagnosis of dementia with Lewy bodies. *Neurology*, *54*, 1050–1058.

McKeith, I.G., Dickson, D.W., Lowe, J., *et al.* (2005) Diagnosis and management of dementia with Lewy bodies: third report of the DLB Consortium. *Neurology*, *65*, 1863–1872.

McKhann, G., Drachman, D., Folstein, M., *et al.* (1984) Clinical diagnosis of Alzheimer's disease: report of the NINCDS-ADRDA Work Group under the auspices of Department of Health and Human Services Task Force on Alzheimer's Disease. *Neurology*, *34*, 939–944.

McKhann, G.M., Albert, M.S., Grossman, M., *et al.* (2001) Clinical and pathological diagnosis of frontotemporal dementia: report of the Work Group on Frontotemporal Dementia and Pick's Disease. *Archives of Neurology*, *58*, 1803–1809.

References

McKillop, J. & Wilkinson, H. (2004) Make it easy on yourself! Advice to researchers from someone with dementia on being interviewed. *Dementia, 3,* 117–125.

McMahon, P.M., Araki, S.S., Neumann, P.J., *et al.* (2000) Cost-effectiveness of functional imaging tests in the diagnosis of Alzheimer disease. *Radiology, 217,* 58–68.

McMahon, P.M., Araki, S.S., Sandberg, E.A., *et al.* (2003) Cost-effectiveness of PET in the diagnosis of Alzheimer disease. *Radiology, 228,* 515–522.

McNamee, P., Bond, J. & Buck, D. (2001) Costs of dementia in England and Wales in the 21st century. *The British Journal of Psychiatry, 179,* 261–266.

McShane, R., Keene, J., Gedling, K., *et al.* (1997) Do neuroleptic drugs hasten cognitive decline in dementia? Prospective study with necropsy follow up. *British Medical Journal, 314,* 266–270.

Magnusson, L., Hanson, E. & Borg, M. (2004) A literature review study of information and communication technology as a support for frail older people living at home and their family carers. *Technology and Disability, 16,* 223–235.

Mahoney, D.F., Tarlow, B.J. & Jones, R.N. (2003) Effects of an automated telephone support system on caregiver burden and anxiety: findings from the REACH for TLC intervention study. *The Gerontologist, 43,* 556–567.

Malouf, R. & Areosa Sastre, A. (2003) Vitamin B_{12} for cognition. *Cochrane Database of Systematic Reviews, 3,* CD004394.

Malouf, R., Grimley Evans, J. & Areosa Sastre, A. (2003) Folic acid with or without vitamin B_{12} for cognition and dementia. *Cochrane Database of Systematic Reviews, 4,* CD004514.

Manfredi, P.L., Breuer, B., Wallenstein, S., *et al.* (2003) Opioid treatment for agitation in patients with advanced dementia. *International Journal of Geriatric Psychiatry, 18,* 700–705.

Mann, T. (1996) *Clinical Guidelines: Using Clinical Guidelines to Improve Patient Care within the NHS.* London: Department of Health.

Mann, D.M., Iwatsubo, T., Ihara,Y., *et al.* (1996) Predominant deposition of amyloid-beta 42(43) in plaques in cases of Alzheimer's disease and hereditary cerebral hemorrhage associated with mutations in the amyloid precursor protein gene. *The American Journal of Pathology, 148,* 1257–1266.

Manthorpe, J. & Iliffe, S. (2005) Timely responses to dementia: exploring the social work role. *Journal of Social Work, 5,* 191–203.

Manthorpe, J., Iliffe, S. & Eden, A. (2003) The implications of the early recognition of dementia for multiprofessional teamworking: conflicts and contradictions in practitioner perspectives. *Dementia, 2,* 163–179.

Manthorpe, J., Penhale, B., Pinkney, L., *et al.* (2004) A Systematic Literature Review in Response to Key Themes Identified in the Report of the House of Commons Select Committee on Elder Abuse (2004). Available at: www.prap.group.shef.ac.uk/hoc.pdf

Manthorpe, J., Perkins, N., Penhale, B., *et al.* (2005) Select questions: considering the issues raised by a Parliamentary Select Committee Inquiry into elder abuse. *Journal of Adult Protection, 7,* 19–32.

Marcusson, J., Rother, M., Kittner, B., *et al.* (1997) A 12-month, randomized, placebo-controlled trial of propentofylline (HWA 285) in patients with dementia according to DSM III-R. The European Propentofylline Study Group. *Dementia and Geriatric Cognitive Disorders*, 8, 320–328.

Marriott, A., Donaldson, C., Tarrier, N., *et al.* (2000) Effectiveness of cognitive-behavioural family intervention in reducing the burden of care in carers of patients with Alzheimer's disease. *The British Journal of Psychiatry*, *176*, 557–562.

Marshall, M. (2000) *Astrid: A Social and Technological Response to Meeting the Needs of Individuals with Dementia and their Carers.* London: Hawker Publications.

Marshall, M. (2001) Care settings and the care environment. In *A Handbook of Dementia Care* (ed. C. Cantley). Buckingham: Open University Press.

Marshall, M. (2004) *Perspectives on Rehabilitation and Dementia.* London: Jessica Kingsley Publishers.

Martikainen, J., Valtonen, H. & Pirttila, T. (2004) Potential cost-effectiveness of a family-based program in mild Alzheimer's disease patients. *The European Journal of Health Economics*, 5, 136–142.

Martin-Cook, K., Remakel-Davis, B., Svetlik, D., *et al.* (2003) Caregiver attribution and resentment in dementia care. *American Journal of Alzheimer's Disease and Other Dementias*, *18*, 366–374.

Martin-Cook, K., Davis, B.A., Hynan, L.S., *et al.* (2005) A randomized, controlled study of an Alzheimer's caregiver skills training program. *American Journal of Alzheimer's Disease and Other Dementias*, *20*, 204–210.

Marzinski, L.R. (1991) The tragedy of dementia: clinically assessing pain in the confused nonverbal elderly. *Journal of Gerontological Nursing*, *17*, 25–28.

Mather, J.A., Nemecek, D. & Oliver, K. (1997) The effect of a walled garden on behavior of individuals with Alzheimer's. *American Journal of Alzheimer's Disease and Other Dementias*, *12*, 252–257.

Mathuranath, P.S., Nestor, P.J., Berrios, G.E., *et al.* (2000) A brief cognitive test battery to differentiate Alzheimer's disease and frontotemporal dementia. *Neurology*, *55*, 1613–1620.

Mayeux, R., Ottman, R., Tang, M.X., *et al.* (1993) Genetic susceptibility and head injury as risk factors for Alzheimer's disease among community-dwelling elderly persons and their first-degree relatives. *Annals of Neurology*, *33*, 494–501.

Means, R. (2000) Residential and institutional provision for older people. In *The Blackwell Encyclopaedia of Social Work* (ed. M. Davies). Oxford: Blackwell Publishers.

Medicines and Healthcare products Regulatory Agency (2004) Summary of clinical trial data on cerebrovascular adverse events (CVAEs) in randomised clinical trials of risperidone conducted in patients with dementia. Available at www.mhra.gov.uk.

Meehan, K.M., Wang, H., David, S.R., *et al.* (2002) Comparison of rapidly acting intra- muscular olanzapine, lorazepam, and placebo: a double-blind, randomized study in acutely agitated patients with dementia. *Neuropsychopharmacology*, *26*, 494–504.

Melin, L. & Gotestam, K.G. (1981) The effects of rearranging ward routines on communication and eating behaviours of psychogeriatric patients. *Journal of Applied Behavior Analysis*, *14*, 47–51.

Mellor, C. & Glover, S. (2000) In partnership with carers. *Journal of Dementia Care*, *8*, 14.

Mental Health Foundation (2006) *Feeding Minds: the Impact of Food on Mental Health*. London: Mental Health Foundation.

Meulen, E.F., Schmand, B., Van Campen, J.P., *et al.* (2004) The seven minute screen: a neurocognitive screening test highly sensitive to various types of dementia. *Journal of Neurology, Neurosurgery and Psychiatry*, *75*, 700–705.

Mielke, R. & Heiss, W.D. (1998) Positron emission tomography for diagnosis of Alzheimer's disease and vascular dementia. *Journal of Neural Transmission. Supplementum*, *53*, 237–250.

Miller, E.R. 3rd, Pastor-Barriuso, R., Dalal, D., *et al.* (2005) Meta-analysis: high-dosage vitamin E supplementation may increase all-cause mortality. *Annals of Internal Medicine*, *142*, 37–46.

Milne, A., Hatzidimitriadou, E. & Chryssanthopoulou, C. (2004) Carers of older relatives in long term care: support needs and services. *Generations Review*, *14*, 4–9.

Mintzer, J., Greenspan, A., Caers, I., *et al.* (2006). Risperidone in the treatment of psychosis of Alzheimer disease: results from a prospective clinical trial. *The American Journal of Geriatric Psychiatry*, *14*, 280–291.

Mishima, K., Hishikawa, Y. & Okawa, M. (1998) Randomized, dim light controlled, crossover test of morning bright light therapy for rest-activity rhythm disorders in patients with vascular dementia and dementia of Alzheimer's type. *Chronobiology International*, *15*, 647–654.

Mitchell, S.L., Kiely, D.K. & Hamel, M.B. (2004a) Dying with advanced dementia in the nursing home. *Archives of Internal Medicine*, *164*, 321–326.

Mitchell, S.L., Morris, J.N., Park, P.S., *et al.* (2004b) Terminal care for persons with advanced dementia in the nursing home and home care settings. *Journal of Palliative Medicine*, *7*, 808–816.

Mittelman, M.S., Roth, D.L., Coon, D.W., *et al.* (2004a) Sustained benefit of supportive intervention for depressive symptoms in caregivers of patients with Alzheimer's disease. *The American Journal of Psychiatry*, *161*, 850–856.

Mittelman, M.S., Roth, D.L., Haley, W.E., *et al.* (2004b) Effects of a caregiver intervention on negative caregiver appraisals of behavior problems in patients with Alzheimer's disease: results of a randomized trial. *The Journals of Gerontology. Series B: Psychological Sciences and Social Sciences*, *59*, 27–34.

Moniz-Cook, E., Agar, S., Silver, M., *et al.* (1998) Can staff training reduce behavioural problems in residential care for the elderly mentally ill? *International Journal of Geriatric Psychiatry*, *13*, 149–158.

Moniz-Cook, E., Stokes, G. & Agar, S. (2003) Difficult behaviour and dementia in nursing homes: five cases of psychosocial intervention. *Clinical Psychology & Psychotherapy, 10*, 197–208.

Moniz-Cook, E., Woods, R.T. & Richards, K. (2001) Functional analysis of challenging behaviour in dementia: the role of superstition. *International Journal of Geriatric Psychiatry, 16*, 45–56.

Monteleoni, C. & Clark, E. (2004) Using rapid-cycle quality improvement methodology to reduce feeding tubes in patients with advanced dementia: before and after study. *British Medical Journal, 329*, 491–494.

Moore, K.D. (1999). Dissonance in the dining room: a study of social interaction in a special care unit. *Qualitative Health Research, 9*, 133–155.

Moore, M.J., Zhu, C.W. & Clipp, E.C. (2001) Informal costs of dementia care: estimates from the National Longitudinal Caregiver Study. *The Journals of Gerontology. Series B: Psychological Sciences and Social Sciences, 56*, S219–S228.

Morgan, D.G. & Stewart, N.J. (1998) High versus low density special care units: impact on the behavior of elderly residents with dementia. *Canadian Journal on Aging, 17*, 143–165.

Morgan, S. (2000) *The Impact of a Structured Life Review Process on People with Memory Problems Living in Care Homes.* Unpublished DClinPsy thesis, University of Wales, Bangor.

Moroney, J.T., Tang, M.X., Berglund, L., *et al.* (1999a) Low-density lipoprotein cholesterol and the risk of dementia with stroke. *The Journal of the American Medical Association, 282*, 254–260.

Moroney, J.T., Tseng, C.L., Paik, M.C., *et al.* (1999b) Treatment for the secondary prevention of stroke in older patients; the influence of dementia status. *Journal of the American Geriatrics Society, 47*, 824–829.

Morris, J.C. (2005) Dementia update 2005. *Alzheimer Disease and Associated Disorders, 19*, 100–117.

Morrison, R.S. & Siu, A.L. (2000) Survival in end-stage dementia following acute illness. *The Journal of the American Medical Association, 284*, 47–52.

Mortimer, J.A., French, L.R., Hutton, J.T., *et al.* (1985) Head injury as a risk factor for Alzheimer's disease. *Neurology, 35*, 264–267.

Mosconi, L. (2005) Brain glucose metabolism in the early and specific diagnosis of Alzheimer's disease. FDG-PET studies in MCI and AD. *European Journal of Nuclear Medicine and Molecular Imaging, 32*, 486–510.

Moulin-Romsee, G., Maes, A., Silverman, D., *et al.* (2005) Cost-effectiveness of 18F-fluorodeoxyglucose positron emission tomography in the assessment of early dementia from a Belgian and European perspective. *European Journal of Neurology, 12*, 254–263.

Mozley, C.G., Huxley, P., Sutcliffe, C., *et al.* (1999) 'Not knowing where I am doesn't mean I don't know what I like': cognitive impairment and quality of life responses in elderly people. *International Journal of Geriatric Psychiatry, 14*, 776–783.

MRC/CFAS (1998) Cognitive function and dementia in six areas of England and Wales: the distribution of MMSE and prevalence of GMS organicity level in the

MRC CFA Study. The Medical Research Council Cognitive Function and Ageing Study (MRC CFAS). *Psychological Medicine, 28,* 319–335.

MRC/CFAS (2001) Pathological correlates of late-onset dementia in a multicentre, community-based population in England and Wales. Neuropathology Group of the Medical Research Council Cognitive Function and Ageing Study (MRC CFAS). *The Lancet, 357,* 169–175.

Murman, D.L., Chen, Q., Powell, M.C., *et al.* (2002) The incremental direct costs associated with behavioral symptoms in AD. *Neurology, 59,* 1721–1729.

Murman, D.L., Kuo, S.B., Powell, M.C., *et al.* (2003) The impact of parkinsonism on costs of care in patients with AD and dementia with Lewy bodies. *Neurology, 61,* 944–949.

Murray, J., Schneider, J., Banerjee, S., *et al.* (1999) EUROCARE: a cross-national study of co-resident spouse carers for people with Alzheimer's disease: II – a qualitative analysis of the experience of caregiving. *International Journal of Geriatric Psychiatry, 14,* 662–667.

Namazi, K.H. & DiNatale Johnson, B. (1992) Dressing independently: a closet modification model for Alzheimer's disease patients. *American Journal of Alzheimer's Disease and Other Dementias, 7,* 22–28.

National Council for Palliative Care (2006) *Exploring Palliative Care for People with Dementia: a Dicussion Document.* London: National Council for Palliative Care.

National Institute for Health and Clinical Excellence (NICE) (2004a) *Guidance on Cancer Services. Improving Supportive and Palliative Care for Adults with Cancer.* London: National Institute for Clinical Health and Excellence. Available at: www.nice.org.uk

National Institute for Health and Clinical Excellence (NICE) (2004b) *Falls: the Assessment and Prevention of Falls in Older People.* London: National Institute for Health and Clinical Excellence. Available at: www.nice.org.uk/guidance/CG21.

National Institute for Health and Clinical Excellence (NICE) (2006). *Statins for the Prevention of Cardiovascular Events. Technology Appraisal 94.* Available at: www.nice.org.uk/TA094.

Neal, M. & Barton Wright, P. (2003) Validation therapy for dementia (review). *Cochrane Database of Systematic Reviews, 3,* CD001394.

Neary, D., Snowden, J.S., Gustafson, L., *et al.* (1998) Frontotemporal lobar degeneration: a consensus on clinical diagnostic criteria. *Neurology, 51,* 1546–1554.

Nestor, P.J., Scheltens, P. & Hodges, J.R. (2004) Advances in the early detection of Alzheimer's disease. *Nature Reviews. Neuroscience,* 5, S34–S41.

Netten, A. (1993) *A Positive Environment? Physical and Social Influences on People with Senile Dementia in Residential Care.* Aldershot: Ashgate.

Newcastle, North Tyneside and Northumberland Mental Health NHS Trust Drugs and Therapeutics Committee (2006) *Guidance on Physical Health Monitoring of Patients on Psychotropic Drugs.*

Newcastle upon Tyne Hospitals NHS Trust (2006) *Diagnostic Services Tariff 2005.* Personal communication.

Nightingale, S., Holmes, J., Mason, J., *et al.* (2001) Psychiatric illness and mortality after hip fracture. *The Lancet, 357,* 1264–1265.

Nobili, A., Riva, E., Tettamanti, M., *et al.* (2004) The effect of a structured intervention on caregivers of patients with dementia and problem behaviors: a randomized controlled pilot study. *Alzheimer Disease and Associated Disorders, 18*, 75–82.

Nolan, B.A. & Mathews, R.M. (2004) Facilitating resident information seeking regarding meals in a special care unit: an environmental design intervention. *Journal of Gerontological Nursing, 30*, 12–16.

Nolan, B.A., Mathews, R.M. & Harrison, M. (2001) Using external memory aids to increase room finding by older adults with dementia. *American Journal of Alzheimer's Disease and Other Dementias, 16*, 251–254.

Nunez, M., Hasselbalch, S., Heun, R., *et al.* (2003) Donepezil-treated Alzheimer's disease patients with apparent initial cognitive decline demonstrate significant benefits when therapy is continued: results from a randomised, placebo-controlled trial. *Poster presented at the Second Annual Dementia Congress, September 12–14, 2003*. Washington, DC.

Nygaard, H.A. & Jarland, M. (2005) Are nursing home patients with dementia diagnosis at increased risk for inadequate pain treatment? *International Journal of Geriatric Psychiatry, 20*, 730–737.

O'Brien, J.T., Erkinjuntti, T., Reisberg, B., *et al.* (2003) Vascular cognitive impairment. *The Lancet Neurology, 2*, 89–98.

O'Brien, J.T., Colloby, S., Fenwick, J., *et al.* (2004) Dopamine transporter loss visualized with FP-CIT SPECT in the differential diagnosis of dementia with Lewy bodies. *Archives of Neurology, 61*, 919–925.

Oborne, C.A., Hooper, R., Li, K.C., *et al.* (2002) An indicator of appropriate neuroleptic prescribing in nursing homes. *Age and Ageing, 31*, 435–439.

Oddy, R. (2003). *Promoting Mobility for People with Dementia: a Problem Solving Approach.* London: Age Concern England.

Olin, J., Schneider, L., Novit, A., *et al.* (2000) Hydergine for dementia. *Cochrane Database of Systematic Reviews, 3*, CD000359.

Olin, J.T., Fox, L.S., Pawluczyk, S., *et al.* (2001) A pilot randomized trial of carbamazepine for behavioral symptoms in treatment-resistant outpatients with Alzheimer disease. *The American Journal of Geriatric Psychiatry, 9*, 400–405.

Olsson, A., Csajbok, L., Ost, M., *et al.* (2004) Marked increase of beta-amyloid (1–42) and amyloid precursor protein in ventricular cerebrospinal fluid after severe traumatic brain injury. *Journal of Neurology, 251*, 870–876.

Onder, G., Zanetti, O., Giacobini, E., *et al.* (2005) Reality orientation therapy combined with cholinesterase inhibitors in Alzheimer's disease: randomised controlled trial. *The British Journal of Psychiatry, 187*, 450–455.

Opie, J., Doyle, C. & O'Connor, D.W. (2002) Challenging behaviours in nursing home residents with dementia: a randomized controlled trial of multidisciplinary interventions. *International Journal of Geriatric Psychiatry, 17*, 6–13.

Orgogozo, J.M., Rigaud, A.S., Stoffler, A., *et al.* (2002) Efficacy and safety of memantine in patients with mild to moderate vascular dementia: a randomized, placebo-controlled trial (MMM 300). *Stroke, 33*, 1834–1839.

References

Orrell, M., Howard, R., Payne, A., *et al.* (1992) Differentiation between organic and functional psychiatric illness in the elderly: an evaluation of four cognitive tests. *International Journal of Geriatric Psychiatry, 7,* 263–275.

Ott, A., Breteler, M.M., Van Harskamp, F., *et al.* (1995) Prevalence of Alzheimer's disease and vascular dementia: association with education. The Rotterdam Study. *British Medical Journal, 310,* 970–973.

Ott, A., Breteler, M.M., De Bruyne, M.C., *et al.* (1997) Atrial fibrillation and dementia in a population-based study. The Rotterdam Study. *Stroke, 28,* 316–321.

Ott, A., Slooter, A.J., Hofman, A., *et al.* (1998) Smoking and risk of dementia and Alzheimer's disease in a population-based cohort study: The Rotterdam Study. *The Lancet, 351,* 1840–1843.

Ott, A., Stolk, R.P., Van Harskamp, F., *et al.* (1999) Diabetes mellitus and the risk of dementia: The Rotterdam Study. *Neurology, 53,* 1937–1942.

Parsons, M. (2001) Living at home. In *A Handbook of Dementia Care* (ed. C. Cantley). Buckingham: Open University Press.

Passini, R., Pigot, H., Rainville, C., *et al.* (2000) Wayfinding in a nursing home for advanced dementia of the Alzheimer's type. *Environment and Behavior, 32,* 684–710.

Patel, N., Mirza, N., Linblad, P., *et al.* (1998) *Dementia and Minority Ethnic Older People: Managing Care in the UK, Denmark and France.* Lyme Regis: Russell House Publishing.

Patel, P., Goldberg, D. & Moss, S. (1993) Psychiatric morbidity in older people with moderate and severe learning disability. II: The prevalence study. *British Journal of Psychiatry, 163,* 481–491.

Paton, J., Johnston, K., Katona, C., *et al.* (2004) What causes problems in Alzheimer's disease: attributions by caregivers. A qualitative study. *International Journal of Geriatric Psychiatry, 19,* 527–532.

Patwardhan, M.B., McCrory, D.C., *et al.* (2004) Alzheimer's disease: operating characteristics of PET – a meta-analysis. *Radiology, 231,* 73–80.

Pearce v United Bristol Healthcare NHS Trust [1998] 48 BMLR 118.

Pedersen, N.L., Gatz, M., Berg, S., *et al.* (2004) How heritable is Alzheimer's disease late in life? Findings from Swedish twins. *Annals of Neurology, 55,* 180–185.

Petersen, R.C., Smith, G.E., Waring, S.C., *et al.* (1999) Mild cognitive impairment: clinical characterization and outcome. *Archives of Neurology, 56,* 303–308.

Petersen, R.C., Thomas, R.G., Grundman, M., *et al.* (2005) Vitamin E and donepezil for the treatment of mild cognitive impairment. *The New England Journal of Medicine, 352,* 2379–2388.

Petrovitch, H., White, L.R., Izmirilian, G., *et al.* (2000) Midlife blood pressure and neuritic plaques, neurofibrillary tangles, and brain weight at death: the HAAS. Honolulu-Asia Aging Study. *Neurobiology of Aging, 21,* 57–62.

Petracca, G., Teson, A., Chemerinski, E., *et al.* (1996) A double-blind placebo-controlled study of clomipramine in depressed patients with Alzheimer's disease. *The Journal of Neuropsychiatry and Clinical Neurosciences, 8,* 270–275.

Petracca, G.M., Chemerinski, E. & Starkstein, S.E. (2001) A double-blind, placebo-controlled study of fluoxetine in depressed patients with Alzheimer's disease. *International Psychogeriatrics, 13,* 233–240.

Phillips, C.D., Sloane, P.D., Hawes, C., *et al.* (1997) Effects of residence in Alzheimer disease special care units on functional outcomes. *The Journal of the American Medical Association, 278,* 1340–1344.

Pieroni, K. & Mackenzie, L. (2001) How can we know what it's like? *The Journal of Dementia Care, 9,* 12.

Pinfold, V., Farmer, P., Rapaport, J., *et al.* (2004) *Positive and Inclusive? Effective Ways for Professionals to Involve Carers in Information Sharing. Report to the National Co-ordinating Centre for NHS Service Delivery and Organisation R & D (NCCSDO).* NCCSDO.

Pinner, G. & Bouman, W.P. (2003) What should we tell people about dementia? *Advances in Psychiatric Treatment, 9,* 335–341.

Pinkney, L., Manthorpe, J., Perkins, N., *et al.* (2005) The many guises of elder abuse. *Community Care,* 10–16 March, 36–37.

Plassman, B.L., Havlik, R.J., Steffens, D.C., *et al.* (2000) Documented head injury in early adulthood and risk of Alzheimer's disease and other dementias. *Neurology, 55,* 1158–1166.

Poirier, J., Davignon, J., Bouthillier, D., *et al.* (1993) Apolipoprotein E polymorphism and Alzheimer's disease. *The Lancet, 342,* 697–699.

Pool, J. (2002) *The Pool Activity Level Instrument for Occupational Profiling of People with Cognitive Impairment.* London: Jessica Kingsley Publishers.

Porsteinsson, A.P., Tariot, P.N., Erb, R., *et al.* (2001) Placebo-controlled study of divalproex sodium for agitation in dementia. *The American Journal of Geriatric Psychiatry, 9,* 58–66.

Poser, S., Zerr, I., Schroeter, A., *et al.* (2000) Clinical and differential diagnosis of Creutzfeldt-Jakob disease. *Archives of Virology. Supplementum, 16,* 153–159.

Potkins, D., Bradley, S., Shrimanker, J., *et al.* (2000) End of life treatment decisions in people with dementia: carers' views and the factors which influence them. *International Journal of Geriatric Psychiatry, 15,* 1005–1008.

Pratt, R. & Wilkinson, H. (2003) A psychosocial model of understanding the experience of receiving a diagnosis of dementia. *Dementia, 2,* 181–199.

Prince, M., Cullen, M. & Mann, A. (1994) Risk factors for Alzheimer's disease and dementia: a case-control study based on the MRC elderly hypertension trial. *Neurology, 44,* 97–104.

Proctor, G. (2001) Listening to older women with dementia: relationships, voices and power. *Disability and Society, 16,* 361–376.

Proctor, R., Burns, A., Stratton-Powell, H., *et al.* (1999) Behavioural management in nursing and residential homes: a randomised controlled trial. *The Lancet, 354,* 26–29.

Pulsford, D., Rushforth, D. & Connor, I. (2000) Woodlands therapy: an ethnographic analysis of a small-group therapeutic activity for people with moderate or severe dementia. *Journal of Advanced Nursing, 32,* 650–657.

Purtilo, R.B. & Ten Have, H.A.M.J. (2004) *Ethical Foundations of Palliative Care for Alzheimer Disease.* Baltimore: Johns Hopkins University Press.

Pusey, H. & Richards, D. (2001) A systematic review of the effectiveness of psychosocial interventions for carers of people with dementia. *Aging and Mental Health, 5,* 107–119.

References

Qazi, A., Shankar, K. & Orrell, M. (2003) Managing anxiety in people with dementia. A case series. *Journal of Affective Disorders, 76,* 261–265.

Quayhagen, M.P., Quayhagen, M., Corbeil, R.R., *et al.* (2000) Coping with dementia: evaluation of four nonpharmacologic interventions. *International Psychogeriatrics, 12,* 249–265.

Rabe, A., Wisniewski, K.E., Schupf, N., *et al.* (1990) Relationship of Down's syndrome to Alzheimer's disease. In *Application of Basic Neuroscience to Child Psychiatry* (eds. S.I. Deutsch, A. Weizman & R. Weizman). New York: Plenum Press.

Raina, P., Waltner-Toews, D., Bonnett, B., *et al.* (1999) Influence of companion animals on the physical and psychological health of older people: an analysis of a one-year longitudinal study. *Journal of the American Geriatrics Society, 47,* 323–329.

Rait, G., Morley, M., Lambat, I., *et al.* (1997) Modification of brief cognitive assessments for use with elderly people from the South Asian sub-continent. *Aging & Mental Health, 1,* 356–363.

Rait, G., Burns, A., Baldwin, R., *et al.* (2000) Validating screening instruments for cognitive impairment in older South Asians in the United Kingdom. *International Journal of Geriatric Psychiatry, 15,* 54–62.

Randolph, C. (1998) *The Repeatable Battery for the Assessment of Neuropsychological Status (RBANS).* London: Harcourt Assessment.

Rands, G., Orrel, M. & Spector, A. (2000) Aspirin for vascular dementia. *Cochrane Database of Systematic Reviews, 4,* CD001296.

Rea, T.D., Breitner, J.C., Psaty, B.M., *et al.* (2005) Statin use and the risk of incident dementia: the cardiovascular health study. *Archives of Neurology, 62,* 1047–1051.

Reed, P.S., Zimmerman, S., Sloane, P.D., *et al.* (2005) Characteristics associated with low food and fluid intake in long-term care residents with dementia. *The Gerontologist, 45,* 74–80.

Regnard, C. & Huntley, M.E. (2005) Managing the physical symptoms of dying. In *Palliative Care in Severe Dementia* (ed. J.C. Hughes). Dinton: Quay Books.

Reifler, B.V., Teri, L., Raskind, M., *et al.* (1989) Double-blind trial of imipramine in Alzheimer's disease patients with and without depression. *The American Journal of Psychiatry, 146,* 45–49.

Reisberg, B., Doody, R., Stoffler, A., *et al.* (2003) Memantine in moderate-to-severe Alzheimer's disease. *The New England Journal of Medicine, 348,* 1333–1341.

Resuscitation Council (UK) (2001). Decisions Relating to Cardiopulmonary Resuscitation: A Joint Statement from the British Medical Association, the Resuscitation Council (UK) and the Royal College of Nursing. Available from www.resus.org.uk/pages/dnar.htm

Retz, W., Gsell, W., Munch, G., *et al.* (1998) Free radicals in Alzheimer's disease. *Journal of Neural Transmission. Supplementum, 54,* 221–236.

Reynolds, T., Thornicroft, G., Abas, M., *et al.* (2000) Camberwell Assessment of Need for the Elderly (CANE). Development, validity and reliability. *The British Journal of Psychiatry, 176*, 444–452.

Richardson, B., Kitchen, G. & Livingston, G. (2002) The effect of education on knowledge and management of elder abuse: a randomized controlled trial. *Age and Ageing, 31*, 335–341.

Robb, S.S., Stegman, C.E. & Wolanin, M.O. (1986) No research versus research with compromised results: a study of validation therapy. *Nursing Research, 35*, 113–118.

Robert, P.H., Verhey, F.R., Byrne, E.J., *et al.* (2005) Grouping for behavioral and psychological symptoms in dementia: clinical and biological aspects. Consensus paper of the European Alzheimer disease consortium. *European Psychiatry, 20*, 490–496.

Roberts, J., Browne, G., Milne, C., *et al.* (1999) Problem-solving counseling for caregivers of the cognitively impaired: effective for whom? *Nursing Research, 48*, 162–172.

Robinson, L., Hughes, J., Daley, S., *et al.* (in press) End-of-life care and dementia. *Reviews in Clinical Gerontology.*

Rocca, W.A., Hofman, A., Brayne, C., *et al.* (1991) Frequency and distribution of Alzheimer's disease in Europe: a collaborative study of 1980–1990 prevalence findings. The EURODEM-Prevalence Research Group. *Annals of Neurology, 30*, 381–390.

Rockwood, K., Mintzer, J., Truyen, L., *et al.* (2001) Effects of a flexible galantamine dose in Alzheimer's disease: a randomised, controlled trial. *Journal of Neurology, Neurosurgery and Psychiatry, 71*, 589–595.

Rogers, J.C., Holm, M.B., Burgio, L.D., *et al.* (1999) Improving morning care routines of nursing home residents with dementia. *Journal of the American Geriatrics Society, 47*, 1049–1057.

Roman, G.C., Tatemichi, T.K., Erkinjuntti, T., *et al.* (1993) Vascular dementia: diagnostic criteria for research studies. Report of the NINDS-AIREN international Workshop. *Neurology, 43*, 250–260.

Rosen, A. & Proctor, E.K. (eds.) (2003) *Developing Practice Guidelines for Social Work Interventions: Issues, Methods, and Research Agenda.* New York: Columbia University Press.

Rosen, J., Mulsant, B.H., Kollar, M., *et al.* (2002) Mental health training for nursing home staff using computer-based interactive video: a 6-month randomized trial. *Journal of the American Medical Directors Association, 3*, 291–296.

Rosen, W.G., Terry, R.D., Fuld, P.A., *et al.* (1980) Pathological verification of ischemic score in differentiation of dementias. *Annals of Neurology, 7*, 486–488.

Rosen, W.G., Mohs, R.C. & Davis, K.L. (1984) A new rating scale for Alzheimer's disease. *The American Journal of Psychiatry, 141*, 1356–1364.

Roth, M., Huppert, F.A., Mountjoy, C.Q., *et al.* (1998) *CAMDEX–R: The Cambridge Examination for Mental Disorders of the Elderly.* Cambridge: Cambridge University Press.

References

Rovio, S., Kareholt, I., Helkala, E.L., *et al.* (2005) Leisure-time physical activity at midlife and the risk of dementia and Alzheimer's disease. *The Lancet Neurology*, *4*, 705–711.

Rovner, B.W., Steele, C.D., Shmuely, Y., *et al.* (1996) A randomized trial of dementia care in nursing homes. *Journal of the American Geriatrics Society*, *44*, 7–13.

Rowland, J.T., Basic, D., Storey, J.E., *et al.* (2006) Rowland Universal Dementia Assessment Scale (RUDAS) and the Folstein mini mental state examination (MMSE) for diagnosis of dementia in a multicultural cohort of elderly persons. *International Psychogeriatrics*, *18*, 111–120.

Royal College of Psychiatrists (2001) DC-LD (Diagnostic Criteria for Psychiatric Disorders for Use with Adults with Learning Disabilities/Mental Retardation). Occasional Paper OP 48. London: Gaskell Press.

Royal College of Psychiatrists (2005a) *Who Cares Wins – Improving the Outcome for Older People Admitted to the General Hospital: Guideline for the Development of Liaison Mental Health Services for Older People*. London: Royal College of Psychiatrists.

Royal College of Psychiatrists (2005b) *Forgetful but not Forgotten: Assessment and Aspects of Treatment of People with Dementia by a Specialist Old Age Psychiatry Service*. London: Royal College of Psychiatrists.

Royal College of Psychiatrists (2006a): Good Psychiatric Practice: Confidentiality and Information Sharing (CR133). London: Royal College of Psychiatrists. Also available at: www.rcpsych.ac.uk/publications/collegereports/cr/cr133.aspx

Royal College of Psychiatrists (2006b) *Atypical Antipsychotics and Behaviourial and Psychiatric Symptoms of Dementia: Prescribing Update for Old Age Psychiatrists*. Available at: www.rcpsych.ac.uk/PDF/BPSD.pdf

Runciman, P. (2003) Family carers' experiences: reflections on partnership. *Nursing Older People*, *15*, 14–16.

Ryan, A.A. & Scullion, H.F. (2000) Nursing home placement: an exploration of the experiences of family carers. *Journal of Advanced Nursing*, *32*, 1187–1195.

Sabat, S.R. (2001) *The Experience of Alzheimer's Disease: Life Through a Tangled Veil*. Oxford: Blackwell.

Sacco, R.L., Adams, R., Albers, G., *et al.* (2006) Guidelines for prevention of stroke in patients with ischemic stroke or transient ischemic attack: a statement for healthcare professionals from the American Heart Association/American Stroke Association Council on Stroke: co-sponsored by the Council on Cardiovascular Radiology and Intervention: the American Academy of Neurology affirms the value of this guideline. *Stroke*, *37*, 577–617.

Salloway, S., Ferris, S., Kluger, A., *et al.* (2004) Efficacy of donepezil in mild cognitive impairment: a randomized placebo-controlled trial. *Neurology*, *63*, 651–657.

Sampson, E.L., Ritchie, C.W., Lai, R., *et al.* (2005) A systematic review of the scientific evidence for the efficacy of a palliative care approach in advanced dementia. *International Psychogeriatrics*, *17*, 31–40.

Sampson, E.L., Gould, V., Lee, D., *et al.* (2006) Differences in care received by patients with and without dementia who died during acute hospital admission: a retrospective case note study. *Age and Ageing*, *35*, 187–189.

Samus, Q.M., Rosenblatt, A., Steele, C., *et al.* (2005) The association of neuropsychiatric symptoms and environment with quality of life in assisted living residents with dementia. *The Gerontologist, 45*, 19–26.

Sanders, D.S. (2004) Quality improvements in percutaneous endoscopic gastrostomy feeding, in patients with dementia: is there an effective strategy for the United Kingdom? Rapid Responses, *British Medical Journal.* At: http://bmj.bmjjournals.com/cgi/eletters/329/7464/491

Sanders, D.S., Anderson, A.J. & Bardhan, K.D. (2004) Percutaneous endoscopic gastrostomy: an effective strategy for gastrostomy feeding in patients with dementia. *Clinical Medicine, 4*, 235–241.

Saunders, P.A., Copeland, J.R., Dewey, M.E., *et al.* (1991) Heavy drinking as a risk factor for depression and dementia in elderly men. Findings from the Liverpool longitudinal community study. *The British Journal of Psychiatry, 159*, 213–216.

Scahill, R.I., Schott, J.M., Stevens, J.M., *et al.* (2002) Mapping the evolution of regional atrophy in Alzheimer's disease: unbiased analysis of fluid-registered serial MRI. *Proceedings of the National Academy of Sciences of the United States of America, 99*, 4703–4707.

Schellenberg, G.D., Anderson, L., O'dahl, S., *et al.* (1991) APP717, APP693 and PRIP gene mutations are rare in Alzheimer's disease. *American Journal of Human Genetics, 49*, 511–517.

Scherder, E., Oosterman, J., Swaab, D., *et al.* (2005) Recent developments in pain in dementia. *British Medical Journal, 330*, 461–464.

Schindel-Martin, L., Morden, P., Cetinski, G., *et al.* (2003) Teaching staff to respond effectively to cognitively impaired residents who display self-protective behaviors. *American Journal of Alzheimer's Disease and Other Dementias, 18*, 273–281.

Schmand, B., Smit, J.H., Geerlings, M.I., *et al.* (1997) The effects of intelligence and education on the development of dementia. A test of the brain reserve hypothesis. *Psychological Medicine, 27*, 1337–1344.

Schneider, J., Murray, J., Banerjee, S., *et al.* (1999) EUROCARE: a cross-national study of co-resident spouse carers for people with Alzheimer's disease: I – Factors associated with carer burden. *International Journal of Geriatric Psychiatry, 14*, 651–661.

Schneider, J., Hallam, A., Murray, J., *et al.* (2002) Formal and informal care for people with dementia: factors associated with service receipt. *Aging & Mental Health 6*, 255–265.

Schneider, J., Hallam, A., Kamrul Islam, M., *et al.* (2003) Formal and informal care for people with dementia: variations in costs over time. *Ageing and Society, 23*, 303–326.

Schneider, L.S., Pollock, V.E. & Lyness, S.A. (1990) A meta-analysis of controlled trials of neuroleptic treatment in dementia. *Journal of the American Geriatrics Society, 38*, 553–563.

Schneider, L.S., Dagerman, K.S. & Insel, P. (2005) Risk of death with atypical antipsychotic drug treatment for dementia: meta-analysis of randomized placebo-controlled trials. The *Journal of the American Medical Association*, *294*, 1934–1943.

Schnelle, J.F., Alessi, C.A., Simmons, S.F., *et al.* (2002) Translating clinical research into practice: a randomized controlled trial of exercise and incontinence care with nursing home residents. *Journal of American Geriatrics Society*, *50*, 1476–1483.

Scholey, K.A. & Woods, B.T. (2003) A series of brief cognitive therapy interventions with people experiencing both dementia and depression: a description of techniques and common themes. *Clinical Psychology and Psychotherapy*, *10*, 175–185.

Schrijnemaekers, V.J., Van Rossum, E., Candel, M.J., *et al.* (2002) Effects of emotion-oriented care on elderly people with cognitive impairment and behavioral problems. *International Journal of Geriatric Psychiatry*, *17*, 926–937.

Schrijnemaekers, V.J., Van Rossum, R., Candel, M.J., *et al.* (2003) Effects of emotion-oriented care on work-related outcomes of professional caregivers in homes for elderly persons. The *Journals of Gerontology. Series B: Psychological Sciences and Social Sciences*, *58*, S50–S57.

Schulz, R. & Beach, S.R. (1999) Caregiving as a risk factor for mortality: the Caregiver Health Effects Study. *The Journal of the American Medical Association*, *282*, 2215–2219.

Scott, H.D., Laake, K. (2001) Statins for the prevention of Alzheimer's disease. *Cochrane Database of Systematic Reviews*, *3*, CD003160.

Scottish Intercollegiate Guidelines Network (SIGN) (2001) *SIGN 50: A Guideline Developer's Handbook*. Edinburgh: SIGN.

Scottish Intercollegiate Guidelines Network (SIGN) (2006) *Management of Patients with Dementia: a National Clinical Guideline*. Edinburgh: SIGN.

Seddon, D. & Robinson, C.A. (2001) Carers of older people with dementia: assessment and the Carers Act. *Health and Social Care in the Community*, *9*, 151–158.

Seltzer, M.M., Litchfield, L.C., Kapust, L.R., *et al.* (1992) Professional and family collaboration in case management: a hospital-based replication of a community-based study. *Social Work in Health Care*, *17*, 1–22.

Sengstaken, E.A. & King, S.A. (1993) The problems of pain and its detection among geriatric nursing home residents. *Journal of the American Geriatrics Society*, *41*, 541–544.

Seshadri, S., Beiser, A., Selhub, J., *et al.* (2002) Plasma homocysteine as a risk factor for dementia and Alzheimer's disease. *The New England Journal of Medicine*, *346*, 476–483.

Shega, J.W., Levin, A., Hougham, G.W., *et al.* (2003) Palliative Excellence in Alzheimer Care Efforts (PEACE): a program description. *Journal of Palliative Medicine*, *6*, 315–320.

Shelton, P., Schraeder, C., Dworak, D., *et al.* (2001) Caregivers' utilization of health services: results from the Medicare Alzheimer's Disease demonstration, Illinois site. *Journal of the American Geriatrics Society*, *49*, 1600–1605.

Shepherd, J., Blauw, G.J., Murphy, M.B., *et al.* (2002) Pravastatin in elderly individuals at risk of vascular disease (PROSPER): a randomised controlled trial. *The Lancet, 360,* 1623–1630.

Shimada, H., Uchiyama, Y. & Kakurai, S. (2003) Specific effects of balance and gait exercises on physical function among the frail elderly. *Clinical Rehabilitation, 17,* 472–479.

Shumaker, S.A., Legault, C., Kuller, L., *et al.* (2004) Conjugated equine estrogens and incidence of probable dementia and mild cognitive impairment in postmenopausal women: women's health initiative memory study. *The Journal of the American Medical Association, 291,* 2947–2958.

Sidaway v Board of Governors of the Bethlem Royal Hospital and the Maudsley Hospital [1984] 1 All ER 1018, CA; [1985] 1 All ER 643, HL.

Silverman, D.H., Gambhir, S.S., Huang, H.W., *et al.* (2002) Evaluating early dementia with and without assessment of regional cerebral metabolism by PET: a comparison of predicted costs and benefits. *Journal of Nuclear Medicine, 43,* 253–266.

Simpson, R.G. (1997) Carers as equal partners in care planning. *Journal of Psychiatric and Mental Health Nursing, 4,* 345–354.

Singleton, A.B., Wharton, A., O'Brien, K.K., *et al.* (2002) Clinical and neuropathological correlates of apolipoprotein E genotype in dementia with Lewy bodies. *Dementia and Geriatric Cognitive Disorders, 14,* 167–175.

Sink, K.M., Holden, K.F. & Yaffe, K. (2005) Pharmacological treatment of neuropsychiatric symptoms of dementia: a review of the evidence. The *Journal of the American Medical Association, 293,* 596–608.

Sival, R.C., Haffmans, P.M., Jansen, P.A., *et al.* (2002) Sodium valproate in the treatment of aggressive behavior in patients with dementia: a randomized placebo controlled clinical trial. *International Journal of Geriatric Psychiatry, 17,* 579–585.

Skea, D. & Lindesay, J. (1996) An evaluation of two models of long-term residential care for elderly people with dementia. *International Journal of Geriatric Psychiatry, 11,* 233–241.

Skoog, I., Lernfelt, B., Landahl, S., *et al.* (1996) 15-year longitudinal study of blood pressure and dementia. *The Lancet, 347,* 1141–1145.

Skoog, I., Hesse, C., Aevarsson, O., *et al.* (1998) A population study of apoE genotype at the age of 85: relation to dementia, cerebrovascular disease and mortality. *Journal of Neurology, Neurosurgery and Psychiatry, 64,* 37–43.

Sloane, P.D., Mitchell, C.M., Preisser, J.S., *et al.* (1998) Environmental correlates of resident agitation in Alzheimer's disease special care units. *Journal of the American Geriatrics Society, 46,* 862–869.

Small, B.J., Mobly, J.L., Laukka, E.J., *et al.* (2003) Cognitive deficits in preclinical Alzheimer's disease. *Acta Neurologica Scandinavica. Supplementum,* 179, 29–33.

Smallwood, J., Brown, R., Coulter, F., *et al.* (2001) Aromatherapy and behaviour disturbances in dementia: a randomized controlled trial. *International Journal of Geriatric Psychiatry, 16,* 1010–1013.

Smith, A.P. & Beattie, B.L. (2001) Disclosing a diagnosis of Alzheimer's disease: patient and family experiences. *The Canadian Journal of Neurological Sciences*, 28, S67–S71.

Smith, F., Francis, S.A., Gray, N., *et al.* (2003) A multi-centre survey among informal carers who manage medication for older care recipients: problems experienced and development of services. *Health and Social Care in the Community*, 11, 138–145.

Smith, K. (1991) Advocacy. Home truths. *Nursing the Elderly*, 3, 10–12.

Snowdon, D.A., Kemper, S.J., Mortimer, J.A., *et al.* (1996) Linguistic ability in early life and cognitive function and Alzheimer's disease in late life. Findings from the Nun Study. *The Journal of the American Medical Association*, 275, 528–532.

Snowdon, D.A., Greiner, L.H., Mortimer, J.A., *et al.* (1997) Brain infarction and the clinical expression of Alzheimer disease. The Nun Study. *JAMA*, 277, 813–7.

Social Care Institute for Excellence (2005) *Practice Guide 5: Implementing the Carers (Equal Opportunities) Act 2004*. London: Social Care Institute for Excellence. Available at: www.scie.org.uk/publications/practiceguides/carers-guidance/files/pg5.pdf

Social Care Institute for Excellence (2006) *Practice Guide 2: Assessing the Mental Health Needs of Older People*. London: Social Care Institute for Excellence. Available at: www.scie.org.uk/publications/practiceguides/practiceguide02/index.asp

Social Policy on Ageing Information Network (2001) *The Underfunding of Social Care and its Consequences for Older People*. London: Help the Aged.

Soliman, A. & Butterworth, M. (1998) Why carers need to educate professionals. *The Journal of Dementia Care*, 6, 26–27.

Sorensen, S., Pinquart, M. & Duberstein, P. (2002) How effective are interventions with caregivers? An updated meta-analysis. *The Gerontologist*, 42, 356–372.

Souetre, E., Thwaites, R.M. & Yeardley, H.L. (1999) Economic impact of Alzheimer's disease in the United Kingdom. Cost of care and disease severity for non-institutionalised patients with Alzheimer's disease. *The British Journal of Psychiatry*, 174, 51–55.

Spaan, P.E., Raaijmakers, J.G. & Jonker, C. (2003) Alzheimer's disease versus normal ageing: a review of the efficiency of clinical and experimental memory measures. *Journal of Clinical and Experimental Neuropsychology*, 25, 216–233.

Sparks, D.L., Sabbagh, M.N., Connor, D.J., *et al.* (2005) Atorvastatin for the treatment of mild to moderate Alzheimer disease: preliminary results. *Archives of Neurology*, 62, 753–757.

Spector, A., Orrell, M., Davies, S., *et al.* (1999) Developing an evidence based therapy programme. *The Journal of Dementia Care*, 7, 28–32.

Spector, A., Thorgrimsen, L., Woods, B., *et al.* (2003) Efficacy of an evidence-based cognitive stimulation therapy programme for people with dementia: randomised controlled trial. *The British Journal of Psychiatry*, 183, 248–254.

Spencer, L., Ritchie, J., Lewis, J., *et al.* (2003) *Quality in Qualitative Evaluation: a Framework for Assessing Research Evidence.* London: Government Chief Social Researcher's Office. Available at: www.policyhub.gov.uk/docs/qqe_rep.pdf

Sperlinger, D. & Furst, M. (1994) The service experiences of people with presenile dementia: a study of carers in one London borough. *International Journal of Geriatric Psychiatry, 9,* 47–50.

Sperlinger, L. & McAuslane, D. (1994) *I Don't Want You to Think I'm Ungrateful... But it Doesn't Satisfy What I Want.* Monograph from the Department of Psychology, St. Helier NHS Trust, Sutton Hospital, Surrey.

Spillantini, M.G., Bird, T.D. & Ghetti, B. (1998) Frontotemporal dementia and Parkinsonism linked to chromosome 17: a new group of tauopathies. *Brain Pathology 8,* 387–402.

Spruyt, O. & Kausae, A. (1998) Antibiotic use for infective terminal respiratory secretions. *Journal of Pain and Symptom Management, 15,* 263–264.

Stalker, K., Duckett, P. & Downs, M. (1999) *Going with the Flow: Choice, Dementia and People with Learning Difficulties.* Brighton: Pavilion Publishing/Joseph Rowntree Foundation.

Standridge, J.B. (2005) Current status and future promise of pharmacotherapeutic strategies for Alzheimer's disease. *Journal of the American Medical Directors Association, 6,* 194–199.

Stanley, D. & Cantley, C. (2001) Assessment, care planning and care management. In *A Handbook of Dementia Care* (ed. C. Cantley). Buckingham: Open University Press.

Stevens, T., Livingston, G., Kitchen, G., *et al.* (2002) Islington study of dementia subtypes in the community. *The British Journal of Psychiatry, 180,* 270–276.

Stewart, R., Prince, M. & Mann, A. (1999) Vascular risk factors and Alzheimer's disease. *The Australian and New Zealand Journal of Psychiatry, 33,* 809–813.

Stokes, G. (2004) 'What have I done to deserve this?': understanding 'aggressive resistance'. *The Journal of Dementia Care, 12,* 30–31.

Stolley, J.M., Reed, D. & Buckwalter, K.C. (2002) Caregiving appraisal and interventions based on the progressively lowered stress threshold model. *American Journal of Alzheimer's Disease and Other Dementias, 17,* 110–120.

Stoub, T.R., Bulgakova, M., Leurgans, S., *et al.* (2005) MRI predictors of risk of incident Alzheimer disease: a longitudinal study. *Neurology, 64,* 1520–1524.

Street, J.S., Clark, W.S., Gannon, K.S., *et al.* (2000) Olanzapine treatment of psychotic and behavioral symptoms in patients with Alzheimer disease in nursing care facilities: a double-blind, randomized, placebo-controlled trial. The HGEU Study Group. *Archives of General Psychiatry, 57,* 968–976.

Strittmatter, W.J., Saunders, A.M., Schmechel, D., *et al.* (1993) Apolipoprotein E: high-avidity binding to beta-amyloid and increased frequency of type 4 allele in late-onset familial Alzheimer disease. *Proceedings of the National Academy of Sciences of the United States of America, 90,* 1977–1981.

Summersall, J. & Wight, S. (2005) When it's difficult to swallow: the role of the speech therapist. In *Palliative Care in Severe Dementia* (ed. J.C. Hughes). Dinton: Quay Books.

Sunderland, T., Hill, J.L., Mellow, A.M., *et al.* (1989) Clock drawing in Alzheimer's disease. A novel measure of dementia severity. *Journal of the American Geriatrics Society*, *37*, 725–729.

Sutherland, S. (1999) *Report of the Royal Commission on Long Term Care for the Elderly.* London: HMSO.

Sutton, L.J. (1994) *What it is to Lose One's Mind.* Paper presented at 10th International Conference of Alzheimer's Disease International, University of Edinburgh.

Szekely, C.A., Thorne, J.E., Zandi, P.P., *et al.* (2004) Nonsteroidal anti-inflammatory drugs for the prevention of Alzheimer's disease: a systematic review. *Neuroepidemiology*, *23*, 159–169.

Tabet, N. & Feldman, H. (2002) Indomethacin for Alzheimer's disease. *Cochrane Database of Systematic Reviews*, Issue 2.

Tabet, N., Birks, J., Grimley-Evans, J., *et al.* (2000) Vitamin E for Alzheimer's disease. *Cochrane Database of Systematic Reviews*, *4*, CD002854.

Tang, M.X., Maestre, G., Tsai, W.Y., *et al.* (1996) Relative risk of Alzheimer disease and age-at-onset distributions, based on ApoE genotypes among elderly African Americans, Caucasians, and Hispanics in New York City. *American Journal of Human Genetics*, *58*, 574–584.

Tappen, R.M. (1994) The effect of skill training on functional abilities of nursing home residents with dementia. *Research in Nursing and Health*, *17*, 159–165.

Tappen, R.M., Roach, K.E., Applegate, E.B., *et al.* (2000) Effect of a combined walking and conversation intervention on functional mobility of nursing home residents with Alzheimer disease. *Alzheimer Disease and Associated Disorders*, *14*, 196–201.

Tariot, P.N., Erb, R., Podgorski, C.A., *et al.* (1998) Efficacy and tolerability of carbamazepine for agitation and aggression in dementia. *The American Journal of Psychiatry*, *155*, 54–61.

Tariot, P.N., Solomon, P.R., Morris, J.C., *et al.* (2000) A 5-month, randomized, placebo-controlled trial of galantamine in AD. *Neurology*, *54*, 2269–2276.

Tariot, P.N., Cummings, J.L., Katz, I.R., *et al.* (2001a) A randomized, double-blind, placebo-controlled study of the efficacy and safety of donepezil in patients with Alzheimer's disease in the nursing home setting. *Journal of the American Geriatrics Society*, *49*, 1590–1599.

Tariot, P.N., Schneider, L.S., Mintzer, J.E., *et al.* (2001b) Safety and tolerability of divalproex sodium in the treatment of signs and symptoms of mania in elderly patients with dementia: results of a double-blind, placebo-controlled trial. *Current Therapeutic Research*, *62*, 51–67.

Tariot, P.N., Schneider, L., Katz, I.R., *et al.* (2006) Quetiapine treatment of psychosis associated with dementia: a double-blind, randomized, placebo-controlled clinical trial. *The American Journal of Geriatric Psychiatry*, *14*, 767–776.

Tatemichi, T.K., Desmond, D.W., Mayeux, R., *et al.* (1992) Dementia after stroke: baseline frequency, risks, and clinical features in a hospitalized cohort. *Neurology*, *42*, 1185–1193.

Tatemichi, T.K., Desmond, D.W., Paik, M., *et al.* (1993) Clinical determinants of dementia related to stroke. *Annals of Neurology*, *33*, 568–575.

Taulbee, L.R. & Folsom, J.C. (1966) Reality orientation for geriatric patients. *Hospital and Community Psychiatry*, *17*, 133–135.

Teri, L. (1994) Behavioral treatment of depression in patients with dementia. *Alzheimer Disease and Associated Disorders*, *8*, 66–74.

Teri, L., Logsdon, R.G., Uomoto, J., *et al.* (1997) Behavioral treatment of depression in dementia patients: a controlled clinical trial. *The Journals of Gerontology. Series B: Psychological Sciences and Social Sciences*, *52*, 159–166.

Teri, L., Logsdon, R.G., Peskind, E., *et al.* (2000) Treatment of agitation in AD: a randomized, placebo-controlled clinical trial. *Neurology*, *55*, 1271–1278.

Teri, L., Gibbons, L.E., McCurry, S.M., *et al.* (2003) Exercise plus behavioral management in patients with Alzheimer disease: a randomized controlled trial. *Journal of the American Medical Association*, *290*, 2015–2022.

Teri, L., McCurry, S.M., Logsdon, R., *et al.* (2005a) Training community consultants to help family members improve dementia care: a randomized controlled trial. *The Gerontologist*, *45*, 802–811.

Teri, L., Huda, P., Gibbons, L., *et al.* (2005b) STAR: a dementia-specific training program for staff in assisted living residences. *The Gerontologist*, *45*, 686–693.

Testad, I., Aasland, A.M. & Aarsland, D. (2005) The effect of staff training on the use of restraint in dementia: a single-blind randomised controlled trial. *International Journal of Geriatric Psychiatry*, *20*, 587–590.

The Nuffield Institute for Health (2002) *Exclusivity or Exclusion? Meeting Mental Health Needs in Intermediate Care*. Leeds: The Nuffield Institute for Health.

The PROP Group (2005) Some views of people with dementia. In *Perspectives on Rehabilitation and Dementia* (ed. M. Marshall), pp. 82–85. London: Jessica Kingsley Publishers.

The Stationery Office (TSO) (2005) *Mental Capacity Act 2005*. Norwich: The Stationery Office.

Thomas, K. (2003) *Caring for the Dying at Home. Companions on the Journey*. Abingdon: Radcliffe Medical Press.

Thompson, R.S., Hall, N.K., Szpiech, M., *et al.* (1997) Treatments and outcomes of nursing-home-acquired pneumonia. *The Journal of the American Board of Family Practice*, *10*, 82–87.

Thorgrimsen, L., Schweitzer, P. & Orrell, M. (2002) Evaluating reminiscence for people with dementia: a pilot study. *The Arts in Psychotherapy*, *29*, 93–97.

Thorgrimsen, L., Spector, A., Wiles, A., *et al.* (2003) Aroma therapy for dementia. *Cochrane Database of Systematic Reviews*, *3*, CD003150.

Timlin, A., Gibson, G., Curran, S., *et al.* (2005) *Memory Matters: a Report Exploring Issues Around the Delivery of Anti-Dementia Medication*. Huddersfield: The University of Huddersfield.

Tinker, A. (2000) Eldercare. In *The Blackwell Encyclopaedia of Social Work* (ed. M. Davies). Oxford: Blackwell Publishers.

Torrington, J. (2006) What has architecture got to do with dementia care? Explorations of the relationship between quality of life and building design in two EQUAL projects. *Quality in Ageing*, *7*, 38–48.

References

Toseland, R.W., Diehl, M., Freeman, K., *et al.* (1997) The impact of validation group therapy on nursing home residents with dementia. *Journal of Applied Gerontology*, *16*, 31–50.

Tracy, C.S., Drummond, N., Ferris, L.E., *et al.* (2004) To tell or not to tell? Professional and lay perspectives on the disclosure of personal health information in community-based dementia care. *Canadian Journal on Aging*, *23*, 203–215.

Tyrell, J., Cosgrave, M., McCarron, M., *et al.* (2001) Dementia in people with Down's syndrome. *International Journal of Geriatric Psychiatry*, *16*, 1168–1174.

Tzourio, C., Anderson, C., Chapman, N., *et al.* (2003). Effects of blood pressure lowering with perindopril and indapamide therapy on dementia and cognitive decline in patients with cerebrovascular disease. *Archives of Internal Medicine*, *163*, 1069–1075.

Valenzuela, M.J. & Sachdev, P. (2005) Brain reserve and dementia: a systematic review. *Psychological Medicine*, *35*, 1–14.

Van Der Steen, J.T., Ooms, M.E., Van Der Wal, G., *et al.* (2002) Pneumonia: the demented patient's best friend? Discomfort after starting or withholding antibiotic treatment. *Journal of the American Geriatrics Society*, *50*, 1681–1688.

Van Dongen, M., Van Rossum, E., Kessels, A., *et al.* (2003) Ginkgo for elderly people with dementia and age-associated memory impairment: a randomized clinical trial. *Journal of Clinical Epidemiology*, *56*, 367–376.

Van Hout, H., Vernooij-Dassen, M., Bakker, K., *et al.* (2000) General practitioners on dementia: tasks, practices and obstacles. *Patient Education and Counseling*, *39*, 219–225.

Verghese, J., Lipton, R.B., Katz, M.J., *et al.* (2003) Leisure activities and the risk of dementia in the elderly. *The New England Journal of Medicine*, *348*, 2508–2516.

Visser, F.E., Aldenkamp, A.P., Van Huffelen, A.C., *et al.* (1997) Prospective study of the prevalence of Alzheimer-type dementia in institutionalized individuals with Down syndrome. *American Journal of Mental Retardation*, *101*, 400–412.

Volicer, L., Rheaume, Y. & Brown, J. (1986) Hospice approach to the treatment of patients with advanced dementia of the Alzheimer type. *The Journal of the American Medical Association*, *256*, 2210–2213.

Volicer, L., Collard, A., Hurley, A., *et al.* (1994) Impact of special care unit for patients with advanced Alzheimer's disease on patients' discomfort and costs. *Journal of the American Geriatrics Society*, *42*, 597–603.

Waite, J. (2002) Keep taking the medicine? *Age and Ageing*, *31*, 423–425.

Wald, C., Fahy, M., Walker, Z., *et al.* (2003) What to tell dementia caregivers – the rule of threes. *International Journal of Geriatric Psychiatry*, *18*, 313–317.

Walker, A.E., Livingston, G., Cooper, C.A., *et al.* (2006) Caregivers' experience of risk in dementia: The LASER-AD Study. *Aging and Mental Health*, 10, 532–538.

Walker, E., Dewar, B., Ridell, H. (1999) *Guidelines to Facilitate the Involvement of Lay Carers in the Care Planning of the Person with Dementia in Hospital.* Edinburgh: The Royal Bank of Scotland Centre for the Older Person's Agenda. Queen Margaret University College.

Walker, M.P., Ayre, G.A., Cummings, J.L., *et al.* (2000) Quantifying fluctuation in dementia with Lewy bodies, Alzheimer's disease, and vascular dementia. *Neurology*, *54*, 1616–1625.

Walker, Z., Costa, D.C., Walker, R.W., *et al.* (2002) Differentiation of dementia with Lewy bodies from Alzheimer's disease using a dopaminergic presynaptic ligand. *Journal of Neurology, Neurosurgery and Psychiatry*, 73, 134–140.

Wallis, G.G., Baldwin, M. & Higginbotham, P. (1983) Reality orientation therapy – a controlled trial. *The British Journal of Medical Psychology*, *56*, 271–277.

Wancata, J., Musalek, M., Alexandrowicz, R., *et al.* (2003) Number of dementia sufferers in Europe between the years 2000 and 2050. *European Psychiatry*, *18*, 306–313.

Wang, H.X., Fratiglioni, L., Frisoni, G.B., *et al.* (1999) Smoking and the occurrence of Alzheimer's disease: cross-sectional and longitudinal data in a population-based study. *American Journal of Epidemiology*, *149*, 640–644.

Ware, C.J., Fairburn, C.G. & Hope, A.H. (1990) A community-based study of aggressive behaviour in dementia. *International Journal of Geriatric Psychiatry*, *5*, 337–342.

Warren, J.D., Schott, J.M., Fox, N.C., *et al.* (2005) Brain biopsy in dementia. *Brain*, 128, 2016–2025.

Watkins, R., Cheston, R., Jones, K., *et al.* (2006) 'Coming out' with Alzheimer's disease: changes in awareness during a psychotherapy group for people with dementia. *Aging and Mental Health*, *10*, 166–176.

Watson, R., Manthorpe, J., Stimpson, A. (2002) *More Food for Thought*. A report submitted to the Alzheimer's Society. Available at: www.qrd.alzheimers.org.uk/pdf_files/FFTreport.pdf

Wentzel, C., Rockwood, K., MacKnight, C., *et al.* (2001) Progression of impairment in patients with vascular cognitive impairment without dementia. *Neurology*, *57*, 714–716.

Whalley, L.J., Thomas, B.M., McGonigal, G., *et al.* (1995) Epidemiology of presenile Alzheimer's disease in Scotland (1974–1988) I: non-random geographical variation. *The British Journal of Psychiatry*, *167*, 728–731.

White, N., Scott, A., Woods, R.T., *et al.* (2002) The limited utility of the mini mental state examination in screening people over the age of 75 years for dementia in primary care. *The British Journal of General Practice*, *52*, 1002–1003.

Wilcock, G., Mobius, H.J., Stoffler, A., *et al.* (2002) A double-blind, placebo-controlled multicentre study of memantine in mild to moderate vascular dementia (MMM500). *International Clinical Psychopharmacology*, *17*, 297–305.

Wilkinson, D., Doody, R., Helme, R., *et al.* (2003) Donepezil in vascular dementia: a randomized, placebo-controlled study. *Neurology*, *61*, 479–486.

Wilkinson, H. & Milne, A.J. (2003) Sharing a diagnosis of dementia – learning from the patient perspective. *Aging and Mental Health*, *7*, 300–307.

Wilkinson, H., Kerr, D., Cunningham, C., *et al.* (2004) *Home for Good?: Preparing to Support People with Learning Difficulties in Residential Settings When They Develop Dementia*. Brighton: Pavilion Publishing.

Williams, M.A., Fleg, J.L., Ades, P.A., *et al.* (2002) Secondary prevention of coronary heart disease in the elderly (with emphasis on patients > or =75 years of age): an

American Heart Association scientific statement from the Council on Clinical Cardiology Subcommittee on Exercise, Cardiac Rehabilitation, and Prevention. *Circulation*, *105*, 1735–1743.

Williams, J.G., Huppert, F.A., Matthews, F.E., *et al.* (2003) Performance and normative values of a concise neuropsychological test (CAMCOG) in an e lderly population sample. *International Journal of Geriatric Psychiatry*, *18*, 631–644.

Wilson, R.S., Mendes De Leon, C.F., Barnes, L.L., *et al.* (2002) Participation in cognitively stimulating activities and risk of incident Alzheimer disease. *The Journal of the American Medical Association*, *287*, 742–748.

Wiltfang, J., Lewczuk, P., Riederer, P., *et al.* (2005) Consensus paper of the WFSBP Task Force on Biological Markers of Dementia: the role of CSF and blood analysis in the early and differential diagnosis of dementia. *The World Journal of Biological Psychiatry*, *6*, 69–84.

Wimo, A., Nelvig, A., Nelvig, J., *et al.* (1993) Can changes in ward routines affect the severity of dementia? A controlled prospective study. *International Psychogeriatrics*, *5*, 169–180.

Winblad, B., Bonura, M.L., Rossini, B.M., *et al.* (2001a) Nicergoline in the treatment of mild-to-moderate Alzheimer's disease: a European multicentre trial. *Clinical Drug Investigation*, *21*, 621–632.

Winblad, B., Engedal, K., Soininen, H., *et al.* (2001b) A 1-year, randomized, placebo-controlled study of donepezil in patients with mild to moderate AD. *Neurology*, *57*, 489–495.

Woodbridge, K. & Fulford, K.W.M. (2004) *Whose Values? A Workbook for Values-Based Practice in Mental Health Care.* London: Sainsbury Centre for Mental Health.

Woods, R.T. (1979) Reality orientation and staff attention: a controlled study. *The British Journal of Psychiatry*, *134*, 502–507.

Woods, R.T. (1999) Promoting well-being and independence for people with dementia. *International Journal of Geriatric Psychiatry*, *14*, 97–105.

Woods, R.T. (2001). Discovering the person with Alzheimer's disease: cognitive, emotional and behavioural aspects. *Aging and Mental Health*, *5*, S7–S16.

Woods, R.T. (2003) Evidence-based practice in psychosocial intervention in early dementia: how can it be achieved? *Aging & Mental Health*, *7*, 5–6.

Woods, R.T., Portnoy, S., Head, D., *et al.* (1992) Reminiscence and life review with persons with dementia: which way forward? In *Care Giving in Dementia: Research and Applications* (eds. G. Jones & B. Miesen), pp. 137–161. London: Tavistock/Routledge.

Woolham, J. & Frisby, B. (2002) How technology can help people feel safe at home. *The Journal of Dementia Care*, *10*, 27–28.

Working Group for the Faculty of the Psychiatry of Old Age of the Royal College of Psychiatrists, Royal College of General Practitioners, British Geriatric Society & Alzheimer's Society (2004) *Summary Guidance for the Management of Behavioural and Psychiatric Symptoms in Dementia and the Treatment of Psychosis in People with History of Stroke/TIA.*

World Health Organization (1990) *Cancer Pain Relief and Palliative Care. Technical Report Series 804*. Geneva: World Health Organization.

World Health Organization (1992) *The ICD-10 Classification of Mental and Behavioural Disorders: Clinical Descriptions and Diagnostic Guidelines.* Geneva: WHO.

World Health Organization (2004) *Better Palliative Care for Older People* (eds. E. Davies & I. J. Higginson). Copenhagen: WHO.

World Health Organization (2006) WHO's Pain Ladder. At: www.who.int/cancer/palliative/painladder/en/print.html

Worm, C., Vad, E., Puggaard, L., *et al.* (2001) Effects of a multicomponent exercise program on functional ability in community-dwelling, frail older adults. *Journal of Aging and Physical Activity*, 9, 414–424.

Wright, F. (2003) Discrimination against self-funding residents in long-term residential care in England. *Ageing and Society*, 23, 603–624.

Wright, L.K., Litaker, M., Laraia, M.T., *et al.* (2001) Continuum of care for Alzheimer's disease: a nurse education and counseling program. *Issues in Mental Health Nursing*, 22, 231–252.

Yale, R. (1995) *Developing Support Groups for Individuals with Early Stage Alzheimer's Disease: Planning, Implementation and Evaluation*. London: Health Professions Press.

Yip, A.G., Green, R.C., Huyck, M., *et al.* (2005) Nonsteroidal anti-inflammatory drug use and Alzheimer's disease risk: the MIRAGE Study. *BMC Geriatrics*, 5, 2.

Zakzanis, K.K., Graham, S.J. & Campbell, Z. (2003) A meta-analysis of structural and functional brain imaging in dementia of the Alzheimer's type: a neuroimaging profile. *Neuropsychology Review*, 13, 1–18.

Zandi, P.P., Anthony, J.C., Khachaturian, A.S., *et al.* (2004) Reduced risk of Alzheimer disease in users of antioxidant vitamin supplements: the Cache County Study. *Archives of Neurology*, 61, 82–88.

Zarit, S.H., Femia, E.E., Watson, J., *et al.* (2004) Memory Club: a group intervention for people with early-stage dementia and their care partners. *The Gerontologist*, 44, 262–269.

Zhang, M.Y., Katzman, R., Salmon, D., *et al.* (1990) The prevalence of dementia and Alzheimer's disease in Shanghai, China: impact of age, gender and education. *Annals of Neurology*, 27, 428–437.

Zigman, W.B., Schupf, N., Devenny, D.A., *et al.* (2004) Incidence and prevalence of dementia in elderly adults with mental retardation without down syndrome. *American Journal of Mental Retardation*, 109, 126–141.

Zwakhalen, S.M.G., Hamers, J.P.H., Abu-Saad, H.H., *et al.* (2006) Pain in elderly people with severe dementia: a systematic review of behavioural pain assessment tools. *BMC Geriatrics*, 6. Available at: www.biomedcentral.com/1471-2318/6/3

Zweig, S.C. (1997) Cardiopulmonary resuscitation and do-not-resuscitate orders in the nursing home. *Archives of Family Medicine*, 6, 424–429.

12. GLOSSARY

Acetylcholinesterase inhibitors: Drugs that prevent the breakdown of acetylcholine, a neurotransmitter thought to be important in the chemical basis of a number of cognitive processes, including memory, thought and judgement. Acetylcholinesterase inhibitors used in clinical practice include rivastigmine, donepezil and galantamine.

Activities of daily living (ADL): Everyday parts of normal life, for example, shopping, maintaining a home and personal care, mobility, toileting and language skills.

Adverse event: Any undesirable experience that results from the administration of a pharmacologically active agent, and regarded to be a serious adverse event if it results in any of the following outcomes: death, a life-threatening experience, inpatient hospitalisation or prolongation of existing hospitalisation, a persistent or significant disability/incapacity, or a congenital anomaly/birth defect.

Alzheimer's disease (AD): A disease usually characterised by loss of memory, especially for learning new information, reflecting deterioration in the functioning of the medial temporal lobe and hippocampus areas of the brain. Later in the illness, other higher functions of the cerebral cortex become affected: these include language, praxis (putting theoretical knowledge into practice) and executive function (involved in processes such as planning, abstract thinking, rule acquisition, initiating appropriate actions and inhibiting inappropriate actions, and selecting relevant sensory information). Behavioural and psychiatric disturbances are also seen, which include depression, apathy, agitation, disinhibition, psychosis (delusions and hallucinations), wandering, aggression, incontinence and altered eating habits.

Alzheimer's Disease and Related Disorders Association (ADRDA): The former title of the Alzheimer's Association, a US voluntary health organisation dedicated to finding prevention methods, treatments and an eventual cure for Alzheimer's disease. Its aim is the advancement of research to provide and enhance care and support for those affected and to reduce the risk of dementia through the promotion of brain health.

Animal-assisted therapy: The use of trained animals in facilitating patients' progress toward therapeutic goals (Barker & Dawson, 1998).

Anxiolytics: Drugs used to alleviate anxiety states.

Antipsychotics: This group of medicines acts on a brain chemical, dopamine. Their main use is in psychotic illness, but their dopamine-blocking properties can help, when used together with other medicines, in some people with OCD, especially those who do not respond to standard treatments.

Asthenia: Lack or loss of strength; weakness.

Behavioural and psychological symptoms of dementia (BPSD): A term used to describe the behavioural and psychiatric disturbances often seen in later stages of dementia. Symptoms commonly include depression, apathy, agitation, disinhibition, psychosis (delusions and hallucinations), wandering, aggression, incontinence and altered eating habits.

Cardiopulmonary resuscitation (CPR): An emergency first-aid procedure administered to a person who has suffered a cardiac arrest (that is, an unconscious person in whom neither breathing nor pulse can be detected). It consists of giving rescue breaths (mouth-to-mouth breathing) and chest compressions. In some cases, this can restart the heart and breathing, but more commonly it allows sufficient blood to circulate to lengthen the time before organ damage occurs.

Care management: An alternative term for the **care programme approach**.

Case management: A term referring to the application of the **care programme approach** to the management of chronic diseases.

Care programme approach (CPA): Introduced in 1991, this approach was designed to ensure that different community services are coordinated and work together towards an individual's care. It requires that professionals from the health authority and local authority arrange care collaboratively, and it applies to all patients accepted for care by the specialist mental health services.

Case series: A study of the treatment of a number of people that is normally evaluated with standardised instruments at different times, such as before treatment, after treatment and at follow-up some time after treatment. Unlike controlled trials or cohort studies, there is usually no control or comparison group. Although useful in early studies of new treatments, case series are not considered to be a rigorous test of a treatment.

Case study: A detailed description of the treatment of a single individual. Such studies may have an important role in the development of new treatments but do not generally allow strong conclusions to be made about effectiveness.

Cerebrospinal fluid (CSF): A nutrient-rich fluid, continuously being produced and absorbed, which flows in the ventricles (cavities) within the brain and around the surface of the brain and spinal cord.

Committee on Safety of Medicines (CSM): One of the independent advisory committees established under the Medicines Act (Section 4) that advises the UK Licensing Authority on the quality, efficacy and safety of medicines in order to ensure that appropriate public health standards are met and maintained. On 30 October 2005, the Commission on Human Medicines was established, which combines the functions of the Committee on Safety of Medicines and the Medicines Commission.

Consortium to Establish a Registry for Alzheimer's Disease (CERAD): A US group established in 1986 by a grant from the National Institute on Aging to standardise procedures for the evaluation and diagnosis of patients with Alzheimer's disease.

Cognitive behavioural therapies (CBT): A range of behavioural and cognitive behavioural therapies, in part derived from the cognitive behavioural model of affective disorders, in which the patient works collaboratively with a therapist using a shared formulation to achieve specific treatment goals. Such goals may include recognising the impact of behavioural and/or thinking patterns on feeling states and encouraging alternative cognitive and/or behavioural coping skills to reduce the severity of target symptoms and problems.

Cognitive rehabilitation: Individually tailored intervention, working on personal goals, often using external cognitive aids and some use of learning strategies.

Cognitive stimulation (reality orientation): Exposure to and engagement with activities and materials involving some degree of cognitive processing, usually within a social context. The intervention is often group-based, with the emphasis on enjoyment of activities.

Cognitive stimulation therapy (CST): A brief group-based treatment for people with mild to moderate dementia, which involves 14 sessions of themed activities (physical games, sound, childhood, food, current affairs, faces/scenes, word association, being creative, categorising objects, orientation, using money, number games, word games and a team quiz), running over a 7-week period. Sessions aim to actively stimulate and engage people with dementia, whilst providing an optimal learning environment and the social benefits of a group therapy.

Cognitive training: Involves training exercises geared to specific cognitive functions, and practice and repetition of these exercises. It may be computer assisted, and individual or group based.

Cohort study (also known as **follow-up, incidence, longitudinal** or **prospective** study)**:** An observational study in which a defined group of people (the cohort) is followed over time. Outcomes are compared in subsets of the cohort who were exposed or not exposed (or exposed at different levels) to an intervention or other factor of interest.

Comorbidity: Two or more diseases or conditions occurring at the same time, such as depression and anxiety.

Computed tomography (CT): A medical imaging method (that is, evaluation of an area of the patient's body that is not externally visible) employing tomography (imaging by sections). A three-dimensional image of the area is generated from a large series of two-dimensional x-ray images taken around a single axis of rotation.

Confidence interval (CI): The range within which the 'true' values (for example, size of effect of an intervention) are expected to lie with a given degree of certainty (for example, 95% or 99%). (Note: confidence intervals represent the probability of random errors, but not systematic errors or bias.)

Cost-effectiveness analysis: A type of full economic evaluation that compares competing alternatives of which the costs and consequences vary. The outcomes are measured in the same non-monetary (natural) unit. It expresses the result in the form of an incremental (or average or marginal) cost-effectiveness ratio.

Costs (direct): The costs of all the goods, services and other resources that are consumed in the provision of a health intervention. They can be medical or non-medical.

Costs (indirect): The lost productivity suffered by the national economy as a result of an employee's absence from the workplace through illness, decreased efficiency or premature death.

Counselling: In its broadest sense, refers to a psychological therapy that allows people to explore their symptoms and problems with a trained individual. The emphasis is on enabling the subject to help him/herself and does not involve giving advice or directing him/her to take specific actions. It is usually delivered on an individual basis, although it can also be delivered in groups. The term counselling is sometimes used interchangeably with a number of specific psychological therapies.

Creative arts therapy: Intentional usage of the creative arts as a form of therapy (for example, dance therapy, music therapy and drama therapy).

Creutzfeldt-Jakob disease (CJD): A rapidly progressing disease of the nervous system, which causes deterioration of brain tissue. There are several forms of the disease, the most common of which is sporadic CJD, which currently has no identifiable cause and which affects mostly middle-aged or elderly people.

Dementia care mapping (DCM): An observation tool designed to examine quality of care from the perspective of the person with dementia, it is part of a process of bringing about improvements to care and is designed to be used only in formal care settings. It is grounded in the philosophy of person-centred care, which promotes the personhood of people with dementia and a holistic approach to their care. The dementia care mapping process involves briefing staff who work in the area to be 'mapped' about the method, observation of participants with dementia within the setting for at least 6 hours, processing the analysed data, feeding back this information to staff and using it to create an action plan for change in the setting. Therefore, it is a means for bringing about change and improvements based on direct observations of the care being delivered (www.bradford.ac.uk/acad/health/bdg/dcm/index.php).

Dementia with Lewy bodies (DLB): One of the most common types of progressive dementia and shares characteristics with both Alzheimer's and Parkinson's diseases. Its central feature is progressive cognitive decline, combined with three additional defining features: pronounced fluctuations in alertness and attention, such as frequent drowsiness, lethargy, lengthy periods of time spent staring into space or disorganised speech; recurrent visual hallucinations; and parkinsonian motor symptoms, such as rigidity and the loss of spontaneous movement. The symptoms of DLB are caused by the build-up of Lewy bodies (protein deposits found in nerve cells) in areas of the brain that control particular aspects of memory and motor control.

Detection bias: Systematic differences between the comparison groups in outcome assessment.

Double blind (also termed **double masked**): A trial in which neither the participants nor the investigators (outcome assessors) are aware of which intervention the participants are given. The purpose of blinding the participants (recipients and providers of care) is to prevent **performance bias**. The purpose of blinding the investigators (outcome assessors) is to protect against **detection bias**.

Economic evaluation: Technique developed to assess both costs and consequences of alternative health strategies and to provide a decision-making framework.

Effect size (ES): An estimate of the size of the effect that a given treatment has compared with a control treatment (for example, another active treatment, no treatment or 'treatment as usual'). Examples of effect sizes are the **relative risk** statistic (used for dichotomous outcomes), and the **weighted mean difference** and **standardised mean difference** statistics (both used for continuous outcomes).

Effectiveness: The extent to which a specific intervention, when used under ordinary circumstances, does what it is intended to do. Clinical trials that assess effectiveness are sometimes called management trials.

Efficacy: The extent to which an intervention produces a beneficial result under ideal conditions. Clinical trials that assess efficacy are sometimes called explanatory trials and are restricted to participants who fully cooperate. The randomised controlled trial is the accepted 'gold standard' for evaluating the efficacy of an intervention.

Electroencephalogram (EEG): A non-invasive, diagnostic technique that records the electrical impulses produced by brain-cell activity via electrodes attached to the scalp. An EEG reveals characteristic brain-wave patterns that may assist in the diagnosis of neurological conditions, such as seizure disorders, impaired consciousness, and brain lesions or tumours.

Emotion-oriented care: Care aimed at improving emotional and social functioning and the quality of life of people with dementia.

Fluoro-2-deoxy-D-glucose (FDG): A compound used in **positron emission tomography (PET)** that binds to a radioactive tracer isotope (the agent detected by the imaging scanner) and which, upon injection into the body, facilitates the tracer's passage through the blood flow into the tissues of interest in the body.

Frontotemporal dementia (FTD): A type of dementia associated with shrinking of the frontal and temporal anterior lobes of the brain. The symptoms of FTD fall into two clinical patterns that involve either changes in behaviour or problems with language. Spatial skills and memory remain intact. There is a strong genetic component to the disease and it often runs in families.

Forest plot: A graphical display of results from individual studies on a common scale, allowing visual comparison of trial results and examination of the degree of heterogeneity between studies.

General Medical Council (GMC): A body that registers doctors to practise medicine in the UK. Its purpose is to protect, promote and maintain the health and safety of the public by ensuring proper standards in the practice of medicine.

Genetic counselling: Providing an assessment of heritable risk factors and information to individuals and their relatives concerning the consequences of a disorder, the chance of developing or transmitting it, how to cope with it, and ways in which it can be prevented, treated and managed.

Guideline development group (GDG): The group of academic experts, clinicians and patients responsible for developing the guideline.

Guideline implementation: Any intervention designed to support the implementation of guideline recommendations.

Guideline recommendation: A systematically developed statement that is derived from the best available research evidence, using predetermined and systematic methods to identify and evaluate evidence relating to the specific condition in question.

Guideline Review Panel (GRP): A panel that contributes to the guideline development process by providing external validation for the guidelines, mainly by ensuring stakeholders' comments on the drafts of the scope and guideline are addressed and that the final recommendations can be implemented.

Health Technology Appraisal: The process of determining the clinical and cost effectiveness of a health technology in order to develop recommendations on the use of new and existing medicines and other treatments within the NHS in England and Wales.

Healthcare professional: A generic term used in this guideline to cover all health professionals such as GPs, psychologists, psychotherapists, psychiatrists, paediatricians, nurses, health visitors, counsellors, art therapists, music therapists, drama therapists, occupational therapists.

Heterogeneity: A term used to illustrate the variability or differences between studies in the estimates of effects.

Hexamethylpropyleneamine oxime (HMPAO): A compound used in **single-photon emission computed tomography (SPECT)** brain scanning that binds to a gamma-emitting tracer (the agent detected by the nuclear gamma camera in the scanning process) and which, upon injection into the body, facilitates the tracer's passage through the blood flow into the brain.

Homogeneity: A term used to illustrate when there are no, or minor, variations in the directions and degrees of results between individual studies that are included in the systematic review.

Incremental cost-effectiveness ratio (ICER): The difference in the mean costs in the population of interest divided by the differences in the main outcomes in the population of interest.

Iodine I 123-radiolabeled 2beta-carbomethoxy-3beta-(4-iodophenyl)-N-(3_fluoropropyl) nortropane (FP-CIT):A form of **single-photon emission computed tomography (SPECT),** FP-CIT is licensed for the investigation of suspected parkinsonism and shows high sensitivity and specificity in separating cases of Parkinson's disease from disorders such as essential tremor.

Key questions: Questions posed by the Guideline Development Group, which are used to guide the identification and interrogation of the evidence base relevant to the topic of the guideline.

Life review: A naturally occurring process where the person looks back on their life and reflects on past experiences, including unresolved difficulties and conflicts. This concept was incorporated in a psychotherapy for older people, which emphasises that life review can be helpful in promoting a sense of integrity and adjustment. Life--review therapy has its roots in psychotherapy, involving evaluation of personal (sometimes painful) memories with a therapeutic listener, usually in a one-to-one setting. (Woods *et al.*, in press).

Magnetic resonance imaging (MRI): A form of medical imaging used to visualise and evaluate an area of the patient's body that is not externally visible. It uses radio frequency signals and a magnet to acquire its images and is best suited to soft tissue examinations. In clinical practice, MRI is used to distinguish pathological tissue (such as a brain tumour) from normal tissue.

Medical Research Council (MRC): A national organisation funded by the UK taxpayer. It promotes research into all areas of medical and related science with the aim of improving the health and quality of life of the public.

Medicines and Healthcare products Regulatory Agency (MHRA): The UK licensing authority (a government agency) that is responsible for ensuring that medicines and medical devices work and are acceptably safe.

Memantine hydrochloride: a moderate-affinity uncompetitive **NMDA**-receptor antagonist licensed in the UK for treating moderate to severe Alzheimer's disease. It works by regulating glutamate, a chemical involved in information processing, storage and retrieval.

Meta-analysis: The use of statistical techniques in a systematic review to integrate the results of several independent studies.

Mild cognitive impairment (MCI): An isolated cognitive impairment(s) (a reduction in the ability to think, concentrate, formulate ideas, reason and remember) identified as abnormal by a statistical rule and representing a decline from previous level of function. The cognitive impairment should not be so severe as to affect social or occupational functioning (at which point the diagnosis of dementia would be more appropriate).

Multidisciplinary: For the purposes of this guideline, this term refers to professionals who are involved in the care of people with dementia working in partnership across disciplines or fields of expertise.

National Collaborating Centre for Mental Health (NCCMH): One of seven centres established by the **National Institute for Health and Clinical Excellence (NICE)** to develop guidance on the appropriate treatment and care of people with specific diseases and conditions within the NHS in England and Wales. Established in 2001, the NCCMH is responsible for developing mental health guidelines, and is a partnership between the Royal College of Psychiatrists and the British Psychological Society.

National Institute for Health and Clinical Excellence (NICE): An independent organisation responsible for providing national guidance on the promotion of good health and the prevention and treatment of ill health. It provides guidance on three areas of health: public health, health technologies and clinical practice.

National Institute of Neurological Disorders and Stroke (NINDS): An organisation affiliated to the National Institutes of Health (an agency of the Public Health Service within the US) that supports and conducts biomedical research on disorders of the brain and nervous system.

National Institute of Neurological Disorders and Stroke and the Association Internationale pour la Recherche et l'Enseignement en Neurosciences (NINDS-AIREN): An international workshop convened by the neuroepidemiology branch of the **National Institute of Neurological Disorders and Stroke** and supported by the Association Internationale pour la Recherche et l'Enseignement en Neurosciences with the aim of drawing up criteria for the diagnosis of vascular dementia.

N-methyl-D-aspartate (NMDA): A water-soluble synthetic substance that mimics the action of the neurotransmitter glutamate on the NMDA receptor. In contrast to glutamate, NMDA binds to and opens the NMDA receptor only, and not other glutamate receptors.

Non-cognitive symptoms: Symptoms often experienced by people with dementia that are sometimes described as neuropsychiatric symptoms or 'behavioural and psychological symptoms of dementia' (BPSD), which include delusions, hallucinations, depression, anxiety, apathy and a range of behaviours, such as aggression, wandering, disinhibition and agitation.

Non-steroidal anti-inflammatory drugs (NSAIDs): Drugs with analgesic, antipyretic and anti-inflammatory effects (that is, they reduce pain, fever and inflammation). The term 'non-steroidal' is used to distinguish them from glucocortoids (a type of steroid also used to reduce inflammatory conditions).

Number needed to treat for benefit (NNTB): In a trial comparing a new treatment with a standard one, the number needed to treat for benefit is the estimated number of participants who need to be treated with the new treatment rather than the standard treatment for one additional participant to benefit. The lower the number needed to benefit, the higher the likelihood of benefit.

Number needed to treat for harm (NNTH): In a trial comparing a new treatment with a standard one, the number needed to treat for harm is the estimated number of participants who need to be treated with the new treatment rather than the standard treatment for one additional participant to be harmed. The lower the number needed to harm, the higher the likelihood of harm.

Performance bias: Systematic differences in the care provided to the participants in the comparison groups other than the intervention under investigation.

Peripheral oedema: An observable swelling in the feet and legs resulting from the accumulation of excess fluid in interstitial spaces (spaces within the tissues that are outside of the blood vessels) under the skin.

Placebo: A non-drug, or physically inactive substance (sugar, distilled water or saline solution), which is given as part of a clinical research trial. It has no specific pharmacological activity against illness.

Positron emission tomography (PET): Positron emission tomography is a nuclear medicine (medicine in which radioactive substances are administered to the patient) medical imaging technique which produces a three-dimensional image or map of functional processes in the body. It is commonly used in the diagnosis of dementias.

Psychoeducation: Programmes for individuals or groups of people that involve an explicitly described educational interaction between the intervention provider and the recipient as the prime focus of the study.

Psychological therapies: A group of treatment methods that involve psychosocial rather than physical intervention. They include cognitive behavioural therapy, family therapy, systemic family therapy, non-directive supportive therapy, psychodynamic psychotherapy, group psychotherapy, counselling, art therapy, interpersonal psychotherapy, guided self-help and any other form of therapy that aims to be helpful through the communication of thoughts and feelings in the presence of a therapist, who works with the material using a systematic framework for understanding and responding to it.

Psychosis: A condition in which an individual is not in contact with reality. This can include sensing things that are not really there (hallucinations), having beliefs that are not based on reality (delusions), problems in thinking clearly and not realising that there is anything wrong (called 'lack of insight').

Psychosocial: Involving aspects of social and psychological behaviour.

Quality adjusted life year (QALY): A form of utility measure calculated by estimating the total life years gained from a treatment and weighting each year with a quality-of-life score in that year.

Quality of life (QoL): Used in some treatment studies to show improvement in a person's condition beyond reduction in symptoms, measures of QoL can be defined broadly and include satisfaction, especially within important areas of one's life, the level of functioning in different areas and the objective circumstances in which one lives. In many studies, however, QoL is defined narrowly as the level of functioning or degree of handicap, which is one important aspect but limited as a marker of quality.

Randomisation: A method used to generate a random allocation sequence, such as using tables of random numbers or computer-generated random sequences. The method of randomisation should be distinguished from concealment of allocation, because if the latter is inadequate, selection bias may occur despite the use of randomisation. For instance, a list of random numbers may be used to randomise participants, but if the list were open to the individuals responsible for recruiting and allocating participants, those individuals could influence the allocation process, either knowingly or unknowingly.

Randomised controlled trial (RCT) (also termed **randomised clinical trial**): An experiment in which investigators randomly allocate eligible people into groups to receive or not to receive one or more interventions that are being compared. The results are assessed by comparing outcomes in the different groups. Through randomisation, the groups should be similar in all aspects, apart from the treatment they receive during the study.

Relative risk (RR) (also known as **risk ratio**): The ratio of risk in the intervention group to the risk in the control group. The risk (proportion, probability or rate) is the ratio of people with an event in a group to the total in the group. An RR of 1 indicates no difference between comparison groups. For undesirable outcomes, an RR that is less than 1 indicates that the intervention was effective in reducing the risk of that outcome.

Relaxation therapy: Relaxation therapy uses a variety of physical and mental techniques (for example, tensing and relaxing different muscle groups in turn, imagining peaceful scenes, and so on) to help people to reduce bodily and psychological tension in a systematic way, which they can practice at home and use when under stress. It can be used as a component of a treatment package (for example, behaviour therapy) or as a therapy in its own right.

Reminiscence: Involves the discussion of past activities, events and experiences, usually with the aid of tangible prompts (for example, photographs, household and other familiar items from the past, music and archive sound recordings). Reminiscence therapy in a group context has the aim of enhancing interaction in an enjoyable, engaging fashion. (Woods *et al.*, 1992).

Resources for Enhancing Alzheimer's Caregiver Health (REACH): An initiative of the US National Institute on Aging in which six centres collaborated to use common measures and procedures to evaluate interventions for family carers of people with Alzheimer's disease. Interventions were developed and implemented independently at each site.

Scottish Intercollegiate Guidelines Network (SIGN): A network formed in 1993 to improve the quality of healthcare for patients in Scotland by reducing variation in practice and outcome. This is achieved through the development and dissemination of national clinical guidelines containing recommendations for effective practice based on current evidence.

Selective serotonin reuptake inhibitors (SSRIs): A class of antidepressant medications that increase the level of serotonin (a neurotransmitter believed to influence mood) in the brain.

Sensitivity: Refers to the proportion of people with disease who have a positive test result.

Sensitivity analysis: Sensitivity analysis is a technique used in economic analysis or decision making to allow for uncertainty by testing whether plausible changes in the values of the main variables affect the results of the analysis.

Single-photon emission computed tomography (SPECT): A nuclear medicine (medicine in which radioactive substances are administered to the patient) imaging technique using gamma rays, which provides three-dimensional information. This information is typically presented as cross-sectional slices through the patient, but can be reformatted or manipulated as required.

Snoezelen: Provides sensory stimuli to stimulate the primary senses of sight, hearing, touch, taste and smell through the use of lighting effects, tactile surfaces, massage, meditative music and the odour of relaxing essential oils. (Chung *et al.*, 2002).

Social Care Institute for Excellence (SCIE): An independent registered charity, launched in 2001 as part of a government drive to improve social care, governed by a board of trustees, whose role is to develop and promote knowledge about good practice in social care.

Specificity: Refers to the proportion of people without disease who have a negative test result.

Standard care: The usual care given to those suffering from acute psychiatric episodes in the area concerned.

Standard deviation (SD): A statistical measure of variability in a population of individuals or in a set of data. Whilst the average measures the expected middle position of a group of numbers, the standard deviation is a way of expressing how different the numbers are from the average. The standard deviation is (approximately) the amount by which the average person's score differs from the average of all scores.

Standard error (SE): A statistical estimate of the population standard deviation based on the mean and standard deviation of one sample. Standard error is calculated by dividing the standard deviation of the sample by the square root of the number of subjects in the sample.

Standardised mean difference (SMD): In a **meta-analysis**, an SMD is a way of combining the results of studies that may have measured the same outcome in different ways, using different scales. Statistically, it is calculated by dividing the weighted average effect size by the pooled standard deviation. The SMD is expressed as a standard value with no units.

Statistical significance: A result is significant if it is unlikely to have occurred by chance, given that, in reality, the independent variable (the test condition being examined) has no effect. In practice, an **effect size** that is statistically significant is

385

one where the probability of achieving the result by chance is less than 5% (that is, a p-value less than 0.05).

Systematic review (SR): Research that summarises the evidence on a clearly formulated question according to a predefined protocol using systematic and explicit methods to identify, select and appraise relevant studies, and to extract, collate and report their findings. It may or may not use statistical **meta-analysis**.

Validation therapy: Based on the general principle of validation, the acceptance of the reality and personal truth of another's experience, validation therapy incorporates a range of specific techniques. Validation, in this general sense, can be considered as a kind of philosophy of care. It is identified as providing a high degree of empathy and an attempt to understand a person's entire frame of reference, however disturbed that might be. Important features of validation therapy are said to include: a means of classifying behaviours; provision of simple, practical techniques that help restore dignity; prevention of deterioration into a vegetative state; provision of an emphatic listener; respect and empathy for older adults with Alzheimer's-type dementia, who are struggling to resolve unfinished business before they die; and acceptance of the person's reality. These features are not, however, unique to validation. (Neal & Barton Wright, 2003).

Vascular dementia (VaD): A common form of dementia that results from narrowing and blockage of the arteries that supply blood to the brain.

Values-based medicine (VBM): An extension of evidence-based medicine, which demands that the appropriateness of clinical interventions be justified by the existence of high-quality evidence for their effectiveness. The value of the intervention is defined as the improvement the intervention confers in length and/or quality of life, taking into consideration the patient's perception of the value of the intervention. The perceived value of the intervention is combined with the associated cost of the intervention to give a final cost utility.

Waitlist control: A term used in controlled trials when participants are allocated to a 'waitlist' condition. Outcome measures are taken from these participants at the end of the waiting period and compared with those from participants who received the treatment. The waitlist participants then receive the treatment.

Weighted mean difference (WMD): A method of **meta-analysis** used to combine measures on continuous scales (such as the ADAS-cog), where the mean, standard deviation and sample size in each group are known. The weight given to each study (for example, how much influence each study has on the overall results of the meta-analysis) is determined by the precision of its estimate of effect and, in the statistical software used by the NCCMH, is equal to the inverse of the variance. This method assumes that all of the trials have measured the outcome on the same scale.

13. ABBREVIATIONS

AD	Alzheimer's disease
ADAS-Cog	Alzheimer's Disease Assessment Scale for Cognition
ADCS	Alzheimer's Disease Cooperative Study
ADFACS	Alzheimer's Disease Functional Assessment and Change Scale
ADL	activities of daily living
ADRDA	Alzheimer's Disease and Related Disorders Association
AgeInfo	Information service about old age and ageing provided by the Library and Information Service of the Centre for Policy on Ageing
AgeLine	An abstract (not full text) database of social gerontology literature
AGREE	Appraisal of Guidelines for Research and Evaluation Instrument
AMED	A bibliographic database produced by the Health Care Information Service of the British Library
AMPS	Assessment of Motor and Process Skills
ASSIA	Applied Social Sciences Index and Abstracts
BEHAVE-AD	Behavioural Pathology in Alzheimer's Disease Scale
BGP	Behaviour Rating Scale for Geriatric Patients
BLT	bright light therapy
BMD	Behaviour and Mood Disturbance Scale
BNF	British National Formulary
BNI	British Nursing Index
BPSD	behavioural and psychological symptoms of dementia
BPT	Brief Praxis Test
CADASIL	cerebral autosomal dominant arteriopathy with subcortical infarcts and leukoencephalopathy
CAMCOG	Cambridge Cognitive Examination (R: revised)
CAMDEX	Cambridge Examination for Mental Disorders of the Elderly
CAPE	Clifton Assessment Procedure for the Elderly
CareData	Community, care and health information database relating to services provided in north-east Scotland
CBS	Carer Burden Scale
CBT	cognitive behavioural therapy
CDR	Clinical Dementia Rating (SB: Sum of the Boxes)
CENTRAL	Cochrane Central Register of Controlled Trials
CERAD	Consortium to Establish a Registry for Alzheimer's Disease
CFAS	Cognitive Function and Ageing Study
CGC	Clinical Global Change Scale
CGI	Clinical Global Improvement
CGIC	Clinical Global Impression of Change
CI	confidence interval

Abbreviations

CIBC	Clinician's Interview-Based Impression of Change
CINAHL	Cumulative Index to Nursing and Allied Health Literature
6-CIT	6-Item Cognitive Impairment Test
CJD	Creutzfeldt-Jakob disease
CMA	cost-minimisation analysis
CMAI	Cohen-Mansfield Agitation Inventory
CPR	cardiopulmonary resuscitation
CSF	cerebrospinal fluid
CSM	Committee on Safety of Medicines
CST	cognitive stimulation therapy
CT	computed tomography
DARE	Database of Abstracts of Reviews of Effects
DC-LD	diagnostic criteria for psychiatric disorders for use with adults with learning disabilities/mental retardation
DCM	dementia care mapping
DLB	dementia with Lewy bodies
DMR	Dementia Questionnaire for Mentally Retarded Persons
DSCU	dementia special care units
DSDS	Dementia Scale for Down Syndrome
DSM	Diagnostic and Statistical Manual of Mental Disorders (versions III-R and IV-TR)
DVLA	Driver and Vehicle Licensing Agency
EEG	electroencephalogram
EMBASE	Excerpta Medica database
EMEA	European Medicines Agency
EPSG	European Propentofylline Study Group
ES	effect size
ESRS	Extrapyramidal Symptoms Rating Scale
FDG	fluoro-2-deoxy-D-glucose
FP-CIT	iodine I 123-radiolabeled 2beta-carbomethoxy-3beta-(4-iodophenyl)-N-(3-fluoropropyl)nortropane
FTD	frontotemporal dementia
GDG	Guideline Development Group
GDS	Geriatric Depression Scale
GeroLit	German-language database of social gerontology literature
GMC	General Medical Council
GP	general practitioner
GPCOG	General Practitioner Assessment of Cognition
GRADE	Grading of Recommendations: Assessment, Development and Evaluation (Working Group)
GRP	Guideline Review Panel

HIS	Hachinski Ischemic Score
HIV	human immunodeficiency virus
HMIC	Health management and policy database from the Healthcare Management Information Consortium
HMPAO	hexamethylpropyleneamine oxime
HMSO	Her Majesty's Stationery Office
HRSD	Hamilton Rating Scale for Depression
HRQoL	health-related quality of life
HRT	hormone replacement therapy
HTA	Health Technology Assessment (Database)
IADL	instrumental activities of daily living
IBSS	International Bibliography of the Social Sciences
ICD	International Classification of Diseases (10th edition)
ICER	incremental cost-effectiveness ratio
IQCODE	Informant Questionnaire on Cognitive Decline in the Elderly
IM	Intramuscular
LOCF	last observation carried forward
MCI	mild cognitive impairment
MDS-ADL	Minimum Data Set – Activities of Daily Living
MEAMS	Middlesex Elderly Assessment of Mental State
MEDLINE	Compiled by the US National Library of Medicine and published on the web by Community of Science, MEDLINE is a source of life sciences and biomedical bibliographic information
MHRA	Medicines and Healthcare products Regulatory Agency
M-ID	multi-infarct dementia
MIS	Memory Impairment Screen
MMSE	Mini Mental State Examination
MOSES	Multidimensional Observation Scale for Elderly Subjects
MR	magnetic resonance
MRC	Medical Research Council
MRI	magnetic resonance imaging
MSQ	Mental Status Questionnaire
NAB	Nurberger-Alters-Beobachtungs-Skala
NCCMH	National Collaborating Centre for Mental Health
NHS	National Health Service
NHS EED	National Health Service Economic Evaluation Database
NICE	National Institute for Health and Clinical Excellence
NINCDS	National Institute of Neurological and Communicative Disorders and Stroke (renamed National Institute of Neurological Disorders and Stroke [NINDS] in 1988)

NINDS-AIREN	National Institute of Neurological Disorders and Stroke and the Association Internationale pour la Recherche et l'Enseignement en Neurosciences
NMDA	N-methyl-D-aspartate
NNT	number needed to treat (B: benefit; H: harm)
NOSGER	Nurses' Observation Scale for Geriatric Patients
NPI	Neuropsychiatric Inventory (NH: Nursing Home version)
NSAID	non-steroidal anti-inflammatory drug
NSF	National Service Framework
OHE HEED	Office of Health Economics, Health Economics Evaluation Database
PAIS International	Database containing references to a wide range of indexed research material from over 120 countries
PANSS (-EC)	Positive and Negative Symptom Scale (—Excited Component)
PDD	Parkinson's disease dementia
PEACE	Palliative Excellence in Alzheimer Care Efforts (Programme)
PET	positron emission tomography
PGCMS	Philadelphia Geriatric Center Morale Scale
PICO	patient, intervention, comparison and outcome
PLB	placebo
PsycINFO	An abstract (not full text) database of psychological literature from the 1800s to the present
QALY	quality adjusted life years
QoL	quality of life
QoL-AD	quality of life in Alzheimer's disease
RAID	Rating Anxiety in Dementia Scale
RBANS	Repeatable Battery for the Assessment of Neuropsychological Status
RCT	randomised controlled trial
REACH	Resources for Enhancing Alzheimer's Caregiver Health
RR	relative risk
SADS	Schedule for Affective Disorders and Schizophrenia
SCAG	Sandoz Clinical Assessment of Geriatric Scale
SCIE	Social Care Institute for Excellence
SD	standard deviation
SE	standard error
SIGLE	System for Information on Grey Literature in Europe database
SIGN	Scottish Intercollegiate Guidelines Network
SKT	Short Cognitive Performance Test

SMD	standardised mean difference
SPECT	single-photon emission computed tomography (q: quantitative; c: conventional)
SR	systematic review
SSCI	Social Sciences Citation Index
SSRI	selective serotonin reuptake inhibitor
STAR	Staff Training in Assisted-Living Residences
TENS	transcutaneous electrical nerve stimulation
TESS	Treatment Emergent Symptom Scale
TSO	The Stationery Office
VaD	vascular dementia
VBM	values-based medicine
WHO	World Health Organization
WIB	Well-being/Ill-being Scale
WMD	weighted mean difference